PRAISE FOR ELYSSA MAXX GOODMAN

"*Glitter and Concrete* is precise and comprehensive and beautifully written. It brings to life the whole long tragic-comic history of drag in New York. As a gay New Yorker I learned as much as I relived. It is indispensable!"

—Edmund White

"Elyssa Goodman has achieved the near impossible; a history of drag that is as entertaining as it is comprehensive. From Eltinge to RuPaul, all of the great personalities with their triumphs and tragedies are woven into a vivid and vibrant tapestry of the city of New York."

—Charles Busch, award-winning playwright and author of *Leading Lady: A Memoir of a Most Unusual Boy*

"Fascinating and delightful. Elyssa Maxx Goodman has written a comprehensive, thoughtful, yet thoroughly entertaining history of drag as experienced in New York from the Gilded Age to today."

—Paulina Bren, bestselling author of *The Barbizon*

"What a gift downtown historian Elyssa Maxx Goodman has given us with her rigorously researched ode to drag through the ages! A love letter to New York City past and present, *Glitter and Concrete* documents drag's shimmering potential for community, self-expression, and pure joy."

—Ada Calhoun, *New York Times* bestselling author of *St. Marks Is Dead*

"As drag is absurdly under attack by the right wing, along comes this well researched book that celebrates its glittery renown. Elyssa Maxx Goodman lovingly explores drag's trajectory in NYC from 1865 to the present, spanning activism, oppression, flamboyance and Emmy Awards. Brava!"

—Michael Musto, author and journalist for *The Village Voice*

"As drag's enemies attempt to eradicate it from public life, we'd do well to learn from its underground roots. Now more than ever, we need the stories of the artform's ancestresses. *Glitter and Concrete* provides a thorough and accessible introduction to this ancient tradition of resilience, resistance and divine shapeshifting."

—Devin Antheus, coauthor of *Legends of Drag*

"Glamor. Survival. Performance. Community—That's drag...and that's New York. And that's why this remarkable book is so important. Elyssa Goodman takes us all the way to the 19th century and back to explore and explain the special role drag has played in making New York the place where the world comes to truly be itself. Deeply researched and featuring a cast of characters who can truly be described as fabulous, *Glitter and Concrete* is urban history on fire."

—**Thomas Dyja, author of**
New York, New York, New York: Four Decades of Success, Excess, and Transformation

"*Glitter and Concrete* is so much more than a simple deep dive into the glamorously complex world of drag in New York City; it stands as a testament to the art form's roots of revolution and protest. Combining exhaustive research and razor-sharp prose, Elyssa Maxx Goodman pays homage to drag's vitally important, necessary role in the larger American consciousness and of its refusal to be culturally exorcised. I loved every minute of this dazzling book."

—**Alex Espinoza, author of** *Cruising: An Intimate History of a Radical Pastime*

"Hey babes, take a read on the wild sides, past and present, of NYC's prismatic drag scenes."

—**Joe E. Jeffreys, Drag Historian**

"A thorough, riveting, and timely tribute that proves gender-benders have always existed, survived and thrived in beauty and creativity and rebellion no matter what the world throws at us. Goodman is not only beyond an expert, she's a true lover of the artform which sings from the pages of this book."

—**Gabriel Shane Dunn,** *New York Times* **bestselling coauthor of**
I Hate Everyone But You

"This sparkling history of drag in New York City is a timely reminder that playing publicly with gender norms has always been political. It's also great fun to read this story of the art form!"

—**Jonathan Ned Katz, author of** *The Invention of Heterosexuality*

"Elyssa Goodman's timely and important history of New York City's drag culture, is beautifully written, deeply researched, and as wonderfully riotous as her subject matter. Goodman has made a fantastic debut as a historian and storyteller."

—**Abbott Kahler,** *New York Times* **bestselling author**

ELYSSA MAXX GOODMAN

GLITTER AND CONCRETE

A CULTURAL HISTORY OF DRAG
IN NEW YORK CITY

HANOVER
SQUARE
PRESS

HANOVER
SQUARE
PRESS™

Recycling programs
for this product may
not exist in your area.

ISBN-13: 978-1-335-44936-8

Glitter and Concrete

Hanover Square Press
22 Adelaide St. West, 41st Floor
Toronto, Ontario M5H 4E3, Canada
HanoverSqPress.com
BookClubbish.com

Printed in U.S.A.

For Rani and Jeff, who brought me to my first drag show.

GLITTER AND CONCRETE

"Drag is a fucking plinth, you know?"

—Charlene Incarnate

TABLE OF CONTENTS

PROLOGUE

"Ready or not, here comes mama."

I watched in silence as Patrick Swayze purred into a mirror, hands perched elegantly by his head, eyes sparkling. Then, snapping shut a tape player, he presses Play, and a deep, electric growl begins Salt-N-Pepa's "I Am the Body Beautiful."

"And wheeeeeere issssss the bodyyyyyy…

"Move ovah mothaaaa because I'm going fasssstaaaa than youuuuuu can driiiiiiive."

Slowly he and then Wesley Snipes begin to paint, to put on their makeup, brushing and drawing eyebrows, lips, cheeks into submission. I couldn't look away.

It was 1995, I was about seven years old, and I was looking at the opening scene of the film *To Wong Foo, Thanks for Everything! Julie Newmar*. The film follows the journey of three drag queens—Miss Vida Boheme, Noxeema Jackson, and Chi-Chi Rodriguez, played by Patrick Swayze, Wesley Snipes, and John Leguizamo, respectively—as they attempt to drive cross-country from New York to Los Angeles.

To that point my mother had raised me on movie musicals from the 1950s, the same films my grandmother had shared with her. They were bright, Technicolor explosions of song, dance, and costume. The last in particular always interested me, women's dresses swirling in perfect circles, a crayon box of colors. Their makeup was flawless, cherry-red lips and eyelashes batting from miles away, and hands were lithe, floating to rhythms from the classic American songbook. These musicals transported me as no other films had.

That is, until I watched *To Wong Foo*. I'm not quite sure how I came upon the film for the first time, but as soon as it was in front of my eyes, everything changed. It didn't hurt that my mother learned how to do her makeup from a man named Frank Hill. Frank was an artist, a talented painter, sculptor, and designer, but he also painted his face as an impersonator of Ann-Margret, redhead siren of stage and screen, in bars and clubs across Fort Lauderdale. My mother met him working in the interior design industry in the 1980s, and with a few properly placed brushstrokes, he showed her the best ways of doing her makeup, the importance of highlighting just under the brow bone, darkening the crease, and the magic of mascara. It was a magic she never forgot, and one she never forgot to attribute to Frank. It was no surprise, then, that her apple would fall not too far from the tree.

The connection so many little girls felt to Belle from *Beauty and the Beast* or Ariel from *The Little Mermaid*, dressing up in their Disney-branded outfits for Halloween and eating off of plates bearing their likenesses at birthday parties, was suddenly something I myself felt for Vida, Noxeema, and Chi-Chi in *To Wong Foo*. They were *my* princesses, twirling curves of color like those from movie musicals, but they were *now*. They were alive, they were not in the 1950s, and they were not animated. They were happening at the same time I was happening. The idea that such glamour could exist here, now, in 1995, was miraculous to me, especially when I saw teenagers at the mall wearing giant JNCO jeans that frayed and sloshed against the sidewalk, flannel shirts falling open over skateboarding T-shirts.

I wanted to absorb every eyelash; every wig, every hat and dress and skirt and heel and luscious quip delivered with an acid tongue; every nail on thick, strong hands that clapped in joy; every token of positive wisdom spoken in spite of adversity, bullying, and judgment. They were magical, their outlooks effervescent and exploding with power that's only available to those who've culled it by overcoming years of anguish. They were multidimensional—they felt sad, they felt angry, they hurt, but they never let that stop them from being absolutely fabulous. While we know now *To Wong Foo* has aspects to celebrate, question, and criticize, which are discussed later in this book, the film—amid the '90s drag boom I'll also discuss—helped acquaint a generation with drag, myself of course included.

After seeing *To Wong Foo*, I consumed drag every way I could. At nineteen, I went to my first drag show with my parents at Cinema Paradiso in Fort Lauderdale, where drag magician Cashetta, may she rest in peace, disappeared a balloon down her throat.

I also went with my family to Lips, a drag restaurant and bar on Oakland Park Boulevard in Fort Lauderdale—I didn't know at the time of the original location in New York. There, Diva, who looked a little like 1960s–1970s actress Juliet Mills, hosted a show of ferocious, gorgeous gals including the inimitable Twat LaRouge, who performed in a wig and body formed entirely from painted Styrofoam swirls. I watched the movies—*The Adventures of Priscilla, Queen of the Desert*; *Paris Is Burning*; *The Birdcage*; *Victor/Victoria*; *Connie and Carla*—anything I could get my hands on. Eventually, the inimitable *RuPaul's Drag Race* became the first way I, along with so many others, could see drag on a regular basis at home.

Starting with *To Wong Foo*, the outlook of drag, the triumph of glamour over negativity, would become a driving force of my own life as I navigated through the trials and tribulations of self-doubt, self-acceptance, and self-love. Drag is the thing, the art form, that taught me to love myself, and for this reason, I have always carried for it such great reverence, respect and, well, love. In some ways, I think I have been writing this book for more than twenty-eight years.

In college, my fascination with drag evolved into a deep appreciation for the effects of drag and gender performance, perhaps most famously described by Judith Butler in the 2007 edition of their foundational text *Gender Trouble: Feminism and the Subversion of Identity*: "Drag is an example that is meant to establish that 'reality' is not as fixed as we generally assume it to be. The purpose of the example is to expose the tenuousness of gender 'reality' in order to counter the violence performed by gender norms." Drag shows us that gender is merely a constructed notion, a highly mutable costume a person can put on or take off. "Call it subversive or call it something else," Butler writes. "Although this insight does not itself constitute a political revolution, no political revolution is possible without a radical shift in one's notion of the possible and the real." Whether or not you think drag is subversive, in other words, the fact that it alters our thinking about the limits of gender and its related presentations is undeniable. The magic is truly in the makeup.

From there my love of drag grew to new heights I never expected. Drag performers were not just ferocious entertainers, costume designers, and makeup artists. They were gender punks and outlaws. It seemed they acted however they wanted despite society repeatedly telling them there were rules for how men, women, people acted and anyone who crossed those boundaries was deviant; that they were unnatural, wrong, not good enough, or obscene. Yet performers continued in spite of these messages. Their strength of character became the new backbone for my love of drag. I developed a passion for people who were unapologetically themselves in ways I had hoped to be, artists who created work that (sometimes purposely) upset people and challenged them to think differently about the constructs of society, gender in particular.

I sought to learn as much about drag as I possibly could, and the more I learned, the more I realized there's so much of its history that features New York City as a backdrop and thereby affected the drag we have today. My desire to write this book came from wanting to read a book that didn't exist, wanting to remind lovers of modern drag how the art form got to the place it currently occupies, and wanting to share the role New York City played in that phenomenon. The idea came to me in the month after the legendary New York drag queen Flawless Sabrina passed away in 2017. I wanted to make sure these stories didn't get lost, from turn-of-the-century impersonation on Broadway and Coney Island stages to Harlem drag balls of the 1920s; from drag king strippers in the 1930s West Village to the use of female impersonation as a morale booster in World War II; from downtown drag clubs in the 1950s to the drag queens who helped initiate the Stonewall Uprising in the 1960s; from the rise of ball culture in the Bronx and Harlem in the 1970s to the avant-garde and punk-inspired drag in the 1980s East Village and drag on the runway at New York Fashion Week in the 1990s; from the global rise of drag as a commercial possibility in the 2000s to the revival of drag's genderfucking, punk sensibility in the 2010s; and so much more.

While drag also has deep roots in cities like Atlanta, Los Angeles, Houston, Chicago, and Seattle, among others, New York's role as a global, urban epicenter of culture meant it drew all manner of people looking for a place to work and live authentically. While much of our current interest in drag comes from the success of *RuPaul's Drag Race*, drag history runs even deeper. I often quote *RuPaul's Drag Race All-Stars* Season 3 winner Trixie Mattel, who once said, "Saying you love drag but you only watch *Drag Race* [is] like saying you love music but you only watch *American Idol*." There's more to know than what's on the surface.

The history of drag in New York City is filled with the glory, struggle, and impact of the renegades and rebels who fought against discrimination for their right to self-expression and freedom. But as time passes, so too do the performers who built New York drag. With their passing, their stories also depart, and along with it a part of queer history, too much of which has already gone missing, left undocumented or underreported.

For the purposes of this book, drag will mean the performance of the gender spectrum on or offstage. It may involve lush feathers floating through elegant theaters or sequins sparkling under tiny barroom stage lights; a smartly applied moustache and dashing chapeau; fabulous, sky-high heels; sculptural wigs piled high with a glistening sheen of hairspray or dramatic eyelashes curling flirtatiously. It may also be none (or all) of the above at once. As an art form, drag's interpretations vary greatly, not unlike those in other performative or visual media. There's no one way to do it right, though an intention of creating drag is key.

Throughout the book, the language used to describe those in drag will reflect the word choice of the subjects themselves at the time they lived: female illusionist, female impersonator, male impersonator, drag queen, drag king, drag artist, drag performer, and gender illusionist among them. It's important to note, too, that meanings change over time: for example, while today we would think of a drag queen as a person who performs femininity, at some points in history, "drag queen" meant a transgender woman or a person who only put on drag for Halloween, parties, or special occasions. Subjects' identifications, as well as their own definitions of performance and related context, will be noted throughout. I will also often use the word "queer" to describe people we now understand to be part of the LGBTQIA2S+ community, not wanting to assume someone's identity or attribute an identity that did not yet exist in the time in which they lived. Additionally, there is material throughout the book that reflects the language and experiences of its speakers at the time; some of it is challenging to read now from our current cultural advantage, but it's important to understand these thoughts and ideas in the context of their time, to understand the lives before us.

Our journey begins in the mid-nineteenth century and moves forward to today, with chapters organized by decades. Voices of New York's drag history past and present will join us for the ride, their own trails of glitter never far behind. There is great power in having access to one's history, which should be a right and not a privilege. The people in these pages allow and have allowed drag and queer aesthetics to live beyond the page, to not just exist but thrive and create space for those who came before and will come after them. It has been a privilege to become a student of these people's lives. It is my hope that the book provides a survey and serves as an introduction to these dynamic individuals and compels people to learn even more.

There's a certain way the light hits a New York City sidewalk, a streak of glitter in the daytime, a mystical shine in the darkness at night, that seems to transcend time. Suddenly, when that glitter appears on the concrete, there's a jolt of memory: every pair of heels that's twinkled across its gleaming surface, every tattered Oxford, every chunky combat boot, every life that's come before. We're taught to believe glitter, like drag, is artificial. But when light hits the concrete just the right way and so clearly sends sparkles flying, there's nothing more real.

1

1865–1920

Ella Wesner is smoking. She sits in photographer Napoleon Sarony's studio at 37 Union Square in New York City, white light catching the distant gaze of her dark eyes as spirals of smoke rise from her mouth. She wears a velvet jacket, a necktie, and a fez tilted on her short dark hair.

The photo shoot with Sarony, the most famous celebrity portraitist of his day, would produce images for Little Beauties Cigarettes. While in the late nineteenth century it was considered shocking for a woman to smoke in public, it would be a different situation if that woman was a male impersonator.

Wesner performed as a male impersonator for the first time in 1870 and quickly became a sensation. A ballerina by training, Wesner also served as a dresser to male impersonator Annie Hindle, who had come to New York from England in 1867. Hindle, in her sleek gentleman's suit and curly mop top, became part of American male impersonation's origin story, one of the first people to ever call herself a male impersonator. In her deep alto voice, she played a variety of male characters, at one point actually shaving to grow facial hair, mostly for audiences of men. Hindle toured across the country and became known as "The Great Hindle." She also called herself a "protean" artist, where protean in the theatrical sense means a performer who took on all roles in a story, one right after the other. "Protean" was also a word many gender impersonation performers used to describe themselves in the early days of the form.

Ella Wesner was deeply inspired by Hindle, and developed the same realist impersonation style when she later took to the stage herself. It's possible Hindle even gave Wesner some of her first songs to sing. Wesner would later become Hindle's only competition.

From the mid-1800s to 1900, gender impersonation was a beloved genre of theater. But as industrialization and suffrage advocacy advanced in the US, attitudes changed as women and immigrants entered the workplace and new classes emerged—because of xenophobia, Irish, Italians, Jews, Eastern Europeans, and others were not considered "purely white" then, though these groups are typically recognized this way today. Many non-ethnic white men felt their roles in the workplace would be challenged by their new coworkers and became uncomfortable seeing such performances, feeling their masculinity threatened. As time went on, the gender boundaries that impersonation crossed had become distressing to audiences dominated by men.

Gender impersonators in the early twentieth century had to constantly confirm to their audiences, often via publicity or an end-of-performance gender reveal, that there was nothing about them offstage that subverted traditional gender norms, whether or not this was actually true. Later, drag performers would find themselves constantly navigating the line between art and "respectability."

Attired in a formfitting suit and tie, a waistcoat jauntily dangling a chain, Wesner, like Hindle, performed a variety of male characters drawn from all corners of society. Dominant among them was a well-to-do gentleman who led a life of luxury. This kind of man could have been seen as both a secret aspiration and an open joke by the middle-class male audiences who attended variety shows, a character that was simultaneously easy for them to access and keep at a distance. This caricature endeared Hindle and Wesner to an audience of working-class men. While not considered fully equal to men, male impersonators were often afforded some of their privileges. They could travel freely and unescorted if they desired, they could wear men's clothes in public, and, it seems, they could hold "companionate" relationships with other women in the public sphere.

Hindle's first marriage to a man ended in divorce, but she would be married twice more, both times to women. Interestingly, the marriages were performed by clergymen without issue, though after her first marriage in June 1886, Hindle was so heavily nagged by the press that she told journalists she was actually a man named Charles Hindle just to be left alone. A minister covered for her, Laurence Senelick shares in his book *The Changing Room: Sex, Drag and Theatre*, saying, "The groom gave me her—I mean his—name as Charles Hindle and he assured me that he was a man... I believe they love each other and that they will be happy." On September 27, 1887, shares historian Gillian M. Rodger in her book *Just One of the Boys: Female to Male Cross-Dressing on the American Variety Stage*, the *Buffalo Evening News* casually referred to Hindle as "the only living woman who has a living wife."

Wesner was never married, but she did briefly run away to France with actress Helen "Josie" Mansfield. Interestingly, the scandal that ensued wasn't about two women having an affair, but about Wesner abandoning her stage work in the middle of a theatrical run. That Hindle and Wesner could live with this level of freedom in the nineteenth century, when in a few decades' time neither would be possible, is profound.

As men found their roles challenged by the economic dip of

what would come to be known as "The Long Depression" between 1873 and 1879, they began to seek more escapist forms of entertainment. This meant that if they were going to see women perform, they wanted to feel "like a man" while doing so. For the next generation of male impersonators, performances became more about portraying a dainty boy than a dapper man; it became escapism, not commentary. And no one embodied this "boyish" aesthetic better than Kitty Doner.

Born in Chicago in 1895, Kitty Doner started performing early in her family's act. "My dad was very, very disappointed that I wasn't a boy, and as I grew I turned out sort of gawky," she said later. "I wasn't considered a pretty girl. I was very boyish, and because my dad taught me dancing, my dancing was manish [sic]..." Her father, Joe Doner, was known for his "manly" style of dancing, and his daughter picked up his movements accordingly. "He said, 'She might as well...she's not pretty enough to compete with the beautiful girls in showbusiness.'"

As a solo act, Kitty Doner was heralded for her convincing "masculine" movements and the artistry of her male impersonation, as well as for her talents in comedy and song. By age ten, Kitty Doner was already treading major stages in New York like the Hippodrome. She made her first Broadway appearance the following year in the Shuberts' prestigious revue *The Passing Show of 1913*—their answer to Florenz Ziegfeld's celebrated annual *Follies*. Her performance in *Passing Show* went well, and the Shuberts invited the young actress to perform male roles in more shows opposite celebrated performer Al Jolson.

The Shuberts were not the only ones who saw Doner's talents. The December 1914 issue of *Munsey's Magazine*, a leading monthly cultural publication of the time, referred to her as "a wonder of a dancer in men's clothes" and "a live wire in animation." Backstage, Doner noted how her male costars moved the coarse bristles of a brush through their hair or stroked their mustaches with idle fingers—and absorbed these gestures into her performances. The following year, *The Green Book Magazine*, a women's culture publication, featured her on a full page donning a suit and tie and spats, hair slicked back, a cigarette dangling from her smile. "If the police weren't so sharp-sighted," she told the magazine, "I'd abandon skirts altogether, even for the street, and wear boys' duds," though she's also reported to have said, like many other performers of the day, that she wished she didn't have to wear them at all.

Doner's work took her primarily to higher-end vaudeville circuits, where she was an ever-increasing sensation. She quickly became known as "The Best Dressed Man on the American Stage," though in her solo work she'd play women, too, sometimes to further the illusion of her masculine characters. Historian Anthony Slide describes a 1926 performance thusly in his *Encyclopedia of Vaudeville*:

> With Jack Carroll at the piano, she appeared first in [men's] evening dress, followed by a song as a French dandy. Next came an appearance in skirts to perform some high kicking. Then, onstage, she stripped down to a pair of briefs and a bra for a fast change to a Scotsman. Doner recalled that a pink floodlight was used for her strip change, which gave the audience the distinct impression that she was naked...

Given what we know about the public perception of sexuality at the time, such an act could have been deemed scandalous, but situationally it was understood as merely part of an act. Like the other performers before her, drawing attention to the fact that she was putting on another gender cemented the idea that she was *just a performer* and not what was then thought of as "abnormal" or "indecent." Doner would make between $1,000 and $1,500 a week on the road and in vaudeville revues on Broadway, a significant salary for the 1920s. She'd briefly take to the screen as well.

As vaudeville faded, male impersonation waxed and waned in popularity. And as the art of drag progressed into the early twentieth century, so too did the forces that came to oppress it.

Dressed in multicolored gowns and painted masks festooned with ribbons and cascading horsehair, weapons at the ready, the "Indians" were a collection of young white male tenant farmers living in Upstate New York. They were "Calico Indians," inspired by the "Calico Indian" protesters during the Boston Tea Party who were also not Indigenous. They donned over-the-top costumes to torment rent collectors and challenge outdated land management processes during the Catskills' Anti-Rent War, which had begun in 1839. In response, New York State passed "an act to prevent persons appearing disguised and armed" in 1845. The act read as follows:

> Every person who, having his face painted, discolored, covered, or concealed, or being otherwise disguised, in a manner calculated to prevent him from being identified, shall appear in any road or public highway, or in any field, lot, wood or enclosure, may be pursued and arrested...

In 1846, the land rent system was reconstructed, rendering the masquerade law all but irrelevant. What lawmakers didn't anticipate at the time was how the law would be used against the queer community. Performers now had to be careful about how they moved through the streets: if they wore gender nonconforming clothing offstage, they risked jail.

Despite its historic unpopularity (a *New York Times* article dating back to 1876 calls it "obnoxious") the masquerade law was on the books for almost 200 years. In 2011, law enforcement attempted to leverage it against protesters in masks during the Occupy Wall Street movement, and again in 2012 when supporters of the activist band Pussy Riot donned balaclavas and gathered outside the Russian consulate to raise awareness about their imprisonment in Moscow for ginned-up charges of "hooliganism." In 2020, however, it was repealed, especially as New Yorkers wore masks to protect themselves during the coronavirus pandemic.

What's more, Anthony Comstock founded the Society for the Suppression of Vice in 1872 "for the suppression of the trade in, and circulation of, obscene literature and illustrations, advertisements, and articles of indecent and immoral use, as may be forbidden by the laws of the State of New York, or of the United States." But by 1915, the organization's new leader, John Sumner, began a fervent anti-gay crusade, with raids and arrests in any bars, clubs, and later theaters even rumored to have queer clientele.

"Degenerate resorts," bars south of 14th Street, especially on and near the Bowery, bore the brunt of these reforms. There, a man could not just get a drink but could also solicit a male sex worker, though the area provided dens of vice for any interested party, regardless of sexual orientation. Among these resorts was Columbia Hall—nicknamed Paresis Hall after the medical term for insanity brought on by syphilis. Located at 32 Cooper Square, it closed around 1899. Another, The Slide, was once called "The Wickedest Place in New York." It's noteworthy, too, that a "slide" was slang for "an establishment where male homosexuals dress as women and solicit men," as George Chauncey notes in his masterful history *Gay New York*. Despite pressure from reform societies, halls like this continued to exist because owners paid off police.

Resorts were also populated by "fairies," effeminate, flamboyant, well-dressed young men who might also be sex workers, though not all were. Fairies, and the effeminate man in general, faced social marginalization and violence from both law enforcement and civilians. To outsiders, and those living double lives—in the "straight" world during the week and the "degenerate" world on the weekend, for example—fairies came to represent sexual deviancy. Yet in the downtown scene, fairies were ubiquitous and could find reprieve in working-class social circles where they weren't considered a threat. Related, they were also known as female impersonators.

For the longest time, some men took partners of every sex without having to classify themselves as "gay" or "straight." But as the fairy stereotype emerged, it became the most public representation of male queerness, a stereotype many working-class men sought to defy. At the time, either you were "normal"— wearing traditionally masculine attire and topping your partner— or you were a fairy, an object of scorn. There was no in-between.

Julian Eltinge was not immune to such messaging. Backstage at Broadway's Liberty Theatre in 1911, he prepared for his role in *The Fascinating Widow*, squeezing his five-foot-eight-and-a-half-inch, 185-pound frame into a corset. Jokingly referred to as "Old Ironsides," the corset would condense the actor's thirty-eight-inch midsection down to a mere twenty-six inches, creating the iconic "Gibson Girl" silhouette popular at the time: petite waist, curvaceous bustle, broad chest. Eltinge designed many of his own garments and had a personal dresser who was known to carry a knife in case a corseting situation went awry.

It took an hour and a half for Eltinge to shave and powder his skin pale, darken his lips, and contour his hands with pencil so they'd appear dainty. He pulled hairpins from his dressing table to secure a wig of dark curls, accenting it with refined blooms, ruffled hats, feathers, and lace. He would transform himself into a figure so graceful, so convincing, so charming and elegant, most audiences never knew he was a man until he removed his wig at the end of the show.

As Julian Eltinge became more successful, it became paramount to his reputation that he not only present in public as a man's man, but that he decry the donning of women's garb offstage. He had to make it clear that he looked down on "fairies" whose presentations of femininity were considered "perverse." After his performance, he'd change out of his costume, light a cigar and welcome reporters backstage so they could see how "masculine" he really was. His feats of transformation were so popular the actor would not only have a New York theater named after him in 1912, but would become one of the most famous and highest paid performers in the world, joining the ranks of Mary Pickford, Douglas Fairbanks, and Charlie Chaplin.

Eltinge's career first took root when he was a child. Born William Julian Dalton, he showed an early interest in drama, which his mother accommodated. When he started dressing as a woman and performing in local saloons, however, his father found out and became enraged, so his mother sent him from their Montana home to the Boston area to live with her sister.

While there, Dalton—who would soon change his name to Julian Eltinge, in honor of a boyhood friend named William Eltinge—took a job as a dry goods clerk and studied dance on the side. He performed with the Boston Bank Officers' Association, which every year put on fundraising theatricals in the tradition of Harvard's Hasty Pudding Club, where men would dress in drag.

Eltinge received enthusiastic reviews from *The Boston Globe* for his work in female attire and soon made his Broadway debut in *Mr. Wix of Wickham*. Eltinge plays a young collegiate gentleman who, through twists in the show's plot, must disguise himself as a young woman. The compulsory element was essential because it made cross-dressing a point of comedy rather than a transgression. According to the October 1, 1904, edition of newspaper *The Tammany Times*, Eltinge succeeded as "a very pretty girl and sings 'Not Like Other Girls' to the entire satisfaction of every one concerned." The show flopped anyway. But Eltinge would take this element of compulsion with him throughout his career. He played characters who *had* to dress as women to achieve their goals, whether those goals were marrying the women they loved or claiming a massive inheritance—actively seeking to lend a higher-class status to female impersonators, whose performances were often otherwise confined to dive bars and looked down upon.

Eltinge sought to differentiate himself from "fairies" by cultivating an especially masculine public image. Even a hint of homosexuality, of "abnormality," "degeneracy," or "perversion" (the terms of the time), would have destroyed his career. Instead, Eltinge participated in staged boxing matches and was said (advertised, possibly) to be so tough he was stabbed by a marlin and survived. His agents knew how to manipulate the press, and rumors of his sexuality were mostly averted, though Eltinge remained a lifelong bachelor. Interestingly, this was considered a sign of virility at the time rather than the euphemism it would become. Even so, it is rumored that a long-running relationship with a male sports writer threatened to ruin Eltinge's reputation.

Eltinge became so popular, in fact, in 1907 he was asked to perform for King Edward VII at Windsor Castle. Eltinge's audiences were primarily women who adored him. His characters were often dressed in the finest, most opulent fashions of the day, and women turned to him for inspiration. He also had his own publication, the *Julian Eltinge Magazine*, in which he advised women about makeup and promoted his cosmetics line, which was highly regarded for its cold cream. He even had a line of cigars. The aforementioned Eltinge Theatre was built in his honor at 236 West 42nd Street in 1912. The theater features a mural of three muses, who are allegedly all Eltinge in drag. It still stands today as an AMC Theatre, absorbed into an adjacent building. Eltinge left the stage in 1917, moving to Los Angeles to take on the burgeoning silver screen. He starred in a number of films, yet returned to vaudeville in 1918, and enjoyed regular success until the 1930s.

Julian Eltinge's role in American culture at the peak of his career is arguably equivalent to an actor like Tom Cruise or Will

Smith, two of the highest-paid actors in Hollywood in 2022. His "compulsory" drag storyline became a comedic trope that reverberated for decades to come, from 1959's *Some Like It Hot* to the 1980s television show *Bosom Buddies* and films such as 1982's *Tootsie*, 1993's *Mrs. Doubtfire*, and 2000's *Big Momma's House*, among countless others. While the compulsion aspect of switching between male and female roles might today be considered troublesome, at the time it was one of the ways drag became a more active part of the cultural experience.

Eltinge's career is not without controversy. Like many performers of the time, he also made a name for himself traveling the vaudeville circuit and with the (George M.) Cohan and (Sam H.) Harris Minstrels, performing in drag and in blackface, which unfortunately still drew large, enthusiastic crowds at the time.

While the drag that came to New York had roots in thousands of years of performance that preceded it across cultures, when many women weren't allowed onstage, it also has roots in minstrelsy. Today minstrelsy is a deeply troubling and painful relic of America's past, but in the nineteenth century, it was among the most popular forms of theater. The shows were degrading and, in an equally degrading paradox, also created some of the first outlets for Black Americans to perform onstage.

The minstrel show began with white actors like Eltinge donning blackface and portraying Black Americans as stereotypes we now know to be horrifyingly insulting, like the buffoon, the Jezebel, and the Mammy. Black minstrel troupes developed a few years before the Civil War, the first one coming together in 1855. In them, Black actors often performed in blackface as well and even ran the companies. Since female minstrel troupes did not develop until the mid-nineteenth century, female roles were performed by men for decades: they would become known in particular for characters like the "wench" or "yaller girl" (another phrase for what was then known as a "mulatto" woman, a woman with a Black parent and a white parent). Many minstrel troupes were headquartered in New York.

At the turn of the century, however, Black theater practitioners began to create their own musicals to elevate the Black performer. Many of the most famous female impersonators of the time, Black and white, came from the minstrel world, though most would ultimately leave it behind. One of them was Andrew Tribble, a Black man born in Kentucky in 1879. Tribble would go on to have a respected career as a comedic female impersonator for over four decades by the time he passed in 1935.

Tribble was performing as a singer and a dancer in Chicago when he was discovered by Black theater owner and producer Robert T. Motts in 1904. Motts opened The Pekin Theatre in Chicago the following year. It was the first Black-owned-and-operated theater in the country, and he booked Tribble to perform. In a finale performance one night, Tribble, just five-foot-four, wore a dress for an act and tripped while wearing it, leading to uproarious laughter from the audience. He began to perform in drag for comedic effect regularly at the theater after that.

While visiting the Pekin, the Black theatrical team of Bob Cole and brothers James Weldon Johnson and J. Rosamond Johnson saw Tribble in drag and cast him in their show *The Shoo-Fly Regiment* as the character Ophelia Snow. Snow was, as Errol Hill and James V. Hatch wrote in *A History of African American Theatre*, "a single-minded woman, careless, kindly, tough, and above all desirous for an affair of the heart just the same as her sisters blessed with more beauty." A burlesque of the Spanish-American War, the show would become the first operetta by Black artists. Tribble would later take Ophelia Snow on the road in the 1920s as a starring solo act called *Ophelia Snow from Baltimo'* and would also tour across Europe.

Tribble drew high praise from critics for his comedy stylings, which led to more roles in drag, even on Broadway. Even Sylvester Russell, the notoriously tough "dean of Black entertainment critics," was charmed by Tribble's performances, calling him "the greatest protean artist his race has ever produced." Tribble also performed out of drag, including in the 1931 short film *The Darktown Revue*, a deliberately provocative on-screen caricature of minstrel shows directed by pioneering Black film director Oscar Micheaux. But Tribble's work in drag was always for comedic purposes and influenced generations to come.

As minstrelsy's popularity changed, new opportunities emerged for Black performers. Between 1890 and 1897, *The Creole Show*, which exclusively featured Black performers and was created in part by Black artists, toured the country, including Brooklyn and Manhattan. The finale featured the cakewalk, an intricate dance first performed by enslaved people that mocked their plantation owners, whether the owners knew it or not. The cakewalk in itself was a kind of drag, a parody of one race performed by another. The dance took on more complex, ironic layers when white people began performing it as well, the original parody going over their heads. The dance became nationally popular—though it was also employed to troubling effect by white minstrel performers—and inspired the development of what became ragtime, one of the precursors to American jazz.

While it would be remiss to ignore the othering and objectifying nature of *The Creole Show*, its active avoidance of blackface made it one of the first shows with a racial backdrop to do so. Instead, it gave each of its sixteen female performers a time to showcase their own talent, though they were presented in a form also left over from minstrelsy: elegantly attired, they'd be seated in a semicircle and were introduced by their emcee, or interlocutor. For seven seasons, this interlocutor was male impersonator Florence Hines.

Hines was not just among the first famous Black male impersonators. She was among the first successful Black women onstage at all in the US, beloved by audiences and the press. On September 20, 1890, newspaper *The Indianapolis Freeman* referred to her as "the greatest living female song and dance artist." Historians argue whether or not male impersonation was something Hines truly wanted to do or arrived at by happenstance. She performed in "dandy" attire, the spiffy wardrobe of well-dressed, upper-class men, and would do so for a significant amount of her career. This was something Black Americans had done for decades by the time Hines took the stage, stemming from a time when enslaved people used to don finery at parades and dances as a way to both escape from and mock the forces that oppressed them, not unlike the cakewalk.

In *The Creole Show*'s setting, which already sought to differentiate itself from traditional minstrel shows, Hines's performance encapsulated an ideological move forward in Black presentation onstage; it was not simply a reproduction of the work done by white male impersonators, a degradation or stereotype of Black Americans. She had reinvented the form, making her an essential part of both drag and theater history.

Even with her successes and the progressive nature of her work at the time, Hines at first had to make a living within white men's ideas of what a Black person was. Indeed, many Black performers had to follow a similar path as they began to make their way into spaces that had previously been denied them. From that entry point, though, performers like Hines and Tribble began to make changes from the inside. Theirs would become stories not just of representation, but of evolution, whereby they rebuilt a theatrical foundation with their own values, their own lives in mind. That drag played a role in this transformation cements its status as a powerful vehicle for change.

The women's suffrage movement began in the nineteenth century, and by the start of the twentieth century in the US, (mostly white) women finally started gaining the right to vote in western parts of the United States. By 1920, the Nineteenth Amendment was ratified, though only white women and Black women of western and northern residence were granted the right to vote at the time (many would have to wait until 1965's Voting Rights Act and even 1975's language minority amendments, among other regulations). But in the suffrage movement's early days, gender norms were questioned across all facets of society, and gender impersonation fell under a microscope.

In addition to the Society for the Suppression of Vice, the Committee of Fourteen, mostly made up of well-to-do or high-ranking individuals, also policed gender. "It is stated that there are 122 blocks in New York where the density of population is 750 people to the acre," the Committee wrote in their 1910 treatise, *The Social Evil in New York City: A Study of Law Enforcement*. "This concentration of people, together with the strenuous industrial pace, absence of adequate facilities for recreation, creates a situation calling for every safeguard, moral, educational and legal, which can be erected." The Committee of Fourteen, leveraging its power with the police, sought to regulate public spaces where people acted against traditional gender norms, from bars to cabarets and more. Relying on informants, they'd help orchestrate police raids (though the police, Hugh Ryan writes in his book *When Brooklyn Was Queer*, thought the committee fell "somewhere between helpful informants and moralizing zealots") and shut down the venue in question.

This was especially relevant to drag as it appeared off the stage. Masquerade balls had long been a tradition in "straight" society, and gay men began throwing their own at the end of the nineteenth century. They called these balls "drags," and many dressed in women's clothing. Popular drag balls were held all over downtown, and annually on Thanksgiving beginning in the 1910s. There had already been a tradition of masquerade in New York that day, where children dressed in costume for "ragamuffin parades." But the gay men who reimagined the custom had to be careful. If they did not obtain the proper permits for a masquerade ball, which allowed costume attire to be worn only in that context, that same 1846 law could be used against them. And it often was. Without a permit, an event would almost certainly end with police throwing attendees in jail. But with a permit, the events drew so many people in costume, queer and not, that they became wildly popular affairs in the city for all walks of life.

The Black fraternal organization Grand United Order of Odd Fellows, Hamilton Lodge #710, was at the forefront. In 1869, the organization began hosting their Masquerade and Civic Ball—later the annual Hamilton Lodge Ball—for the Black community, which always drew a wealth of Black female impersonators and later, white patrons. "At an early hour, masqueraders began to arrive in carriages that blocked the street for fully one and a half hours," described local Black newspaper *The New York Freeman*. "The costumes," it went on, "eclipsed any previous effort and many white receptions of a similar kind this season... No doubt this masquerade is the event of the season."

The Hamilton Lodge typically hosted its annual ball at the Manhattan Casino on West 155th Street in Harlem, which had a capacity of 6,000 people. ("Casino" in this context meant "a building or place used for social amusements," not necessarily a gambling establishment.) The venue became a neighborhood staple, renamed The Rockland Palace in 1928.

Harlem, which had been a predominantly white neighborhood, quickly became a nexus of Black life by the early twentieth century. Real estate entrepreneur Philip A. Payton Jr. urged residents who were denied housing elsewhere and forced into Midtown slums to instead fill apartments in the neighborhood. The construction of Penn Station had displaced Black people in sections of the West 30s, many of whom resettled in the neighborhood. The Great Migration also contributed to an influx of Black residents in Harlem, who were looking for a fresh start in New York. In turn, Harlem also became the city's beating heart of Black queer life, drag included.

Harlem's most famous male impersonator for a time was Lillyn Brown. Possibly influenced by Florence Hines, Brown appeared dapper onstage in a luxurious, shiny black top hat and long black tails, a long overcoat with a white scarf and gloves, a cane dangling from her elbow. While comparatively little is known of Brown today, she would have a career of some seventy years in show business—as a male impersonator, a blues singer, a writer, a director, and an acting instructor among many other achievements.

Of Black and Iroquois descent, Brown was born Lillian Thomas in Atlanta, Georgia. Her life in drag began almost by accident at age eleven. After joining the performance troupe Queen City Minstrels, the company's emcee fell ill, and Brown donned breeches and a bow tie and stepped in—she already knew the part by heart. She was an instant hit, later billed as the "Youngest Interlocutor in the World," and when she asked for a raise, the company obliged.

As Brown grew up, male impersonation got easier for her. By age fourteen, in 1899, she had a contralto singing voice, the lowest range for a woman, which allowed her to sing both male and female parts. In trousers and black patent leather shoes, a cigarette dangling from her fingers, she became a vaudeville success. And like some other gender impersonators at the time, Brown accentuated her femininity offstage. The contrast only heightened her perceived talent onstage. In 1913, she married William DeMont Evans, who also became her performance partner. Brown and DeMont, like many Black performers of the time, slyly calibrated their presentation for both Black and white audiences. They subverted stereotypical characters with a generous wink—Brown herself imitated blackface impersonator Al Jolson. This made for the layered, satirical complexity of a Black person imitating a white person imitating a Black person, a kind of drag in itself, bending and growing the idea of who gets to imitate who and how.

Further downtown from Harlem, Webster Hall also hosted all-night masquerade balls filled with costumed revelers, queer and not. From its opening in 1886, Webster Hall was a rendezvous for the Greenwich Village neighborhood, a downtown hotbed of artistic, bohemian, political, and queer life. The Village—previously known as the Ninth Ward and the Fifteenth Ward—had been a locus of freethinking life in New York since the mid-nineteenth century. An influx of factories led to a decrease in property value and an increase in residential space at the beginning of the twentieth century, which attracted immigrants as well as artistic types who brought with them a liberal, nonconformist spirit that created room for queer life. By 1918, Webster Hall became known as the "Devil's Playground" for holding two balls a week.

Queerness at these balls became a draw. While some came from uptown to gawk, others came simply to exist. Drag was important there, too. As George Chauncey shares in *Gay New York*, a police investigator on the Webster Hall premises in 1918 discovered what he called "phenomenal men" who would "wear expensive gowns," "employ rouge," "use wigs," "and in short make up an appearance which looks for everything like a young lady."

Yet as beloved as they were, the balls uptown and downtown would soon be in danger. As the United States entered World War I in 1917, every man between the ages of twenty-one and thirty had to register for the draft; a year later, this grew to men between the ages of eighteen and forty-five. Of the 4.8 million who ultimately served, several hundred thousand traveled to and from New York. Pop culture cast military men as innocent boys, and New York as a salacious vixen bent on their destruction. In order to shield these sweet boys from corruption, groups like the Society for the Suppression of Vice and Committee of Fourteen, who often worked in conjunction with police, helped enforce crackdowns on what they called "disorderly conduct" and "perversion," including, in particular, homosexuality.

Though it wasn't yet illegal to serve queer people or for queer people to congregate publicly, social reform organizations found ways to shut down venues where they believed homosexuality ran rampant, leveraging laws against masquerade, "disorderly conduct," "keeping a disorderly house," and sodomy, which was illegal in New York until 1980. Interracial mixing in public spaces was also prohibited. Surveillance was heavy, and raids were frequent. Bowery "degenerate resorts" known for their fairies were shuttered, as were many bars and clubs where patrons rejected traditionally gendered presentation.

But in a curious paradox, drag was still an important part of the war effort, where it served to raise morale for soldiers in theatrical presentations. For a long time, only men were available to play roles written into wartime shows, female and not. One show, *Yip Yip Yaphank*, was written by a thirty-year-old army corporal named Irving Berlin. By that point, Berlin had a massively successful career on Broadway and a host of hits to his name as a songwriter—news of his army conscription, *Time* magazine notes, "was bigger than Elvis," with one newspaper blaring "Army Takes Berlin!" as its headline in 1918. Berlin was sent to serve on Long Island at Camp Upton, located in a hamlet called Yaphank, where he then produced a musical revue about military life performed entirely by soldiers to raise money for a community center on the base.

The female impersonator roles were incredibly popular with enlisted men. Drag performer Bert Savoy was brought in to guide soldiers on the craft of drag. *Yip Yip Yaphank* would become the most famous of these soldier shows, eventually making its way to Broadway (with Berlin by then promoted to sergeant). It was an instant hit. The *New York Times* noted that drag in the show was an "immeasurable advantage" over other Broadway shows, especially in the chorus numbers. "Assuredly, no one can forget that these chorus maidens are soldiers," the paper shared. "Whoever picked its members was nothing less than inspired."

The show was successful enough to spawn songs still considered classics, like "Oh! How I Hate to Get Up in the Morning." It also led to a stream of successful military shows featuring female impersonation.

Off the military base, however, female impersonation still drew the ire of moral reform organizations. Margot Canaday's book *The Straight State* notes a July 31, 1918, Committee of Fourteen report on a cabaret in Hempstead, Long Island, near the Camp Mills army base, where an informant wrote "alleged females," or female impersonators, performed. "I believe this place should be out of bounds and no soldiers permitted," the informant continued, "as the entire atmosphere is degrading... To my mind the male performers are actually a far greater menace than the female performers." This was just one of many ways the committee attempted to impose its ideas of moral order on New York for years to come.

As the new decade dawned, Prohibition opened a cultural rift that allowed drag performers to live more freely onstage and off. In 1919, the Eighteenth Amendment passed, banning alcohol across the United States beginning January 1920. This led to the birth of speakeasies, illegal establishments where liquor and entertainment flowed heavily and without censorship. In those untamed spaces, the queer community, previously threatened by discriminatory interpretations of vague laws, would be able to thrive, and another, more liberated form of drag would bloom and become beloved.

2

1920–1929

"You mussssst come over!" Bert Savoy purred, reducing his audience to a heaving pile of laughter.

As a female impersonator, Savoy was never without enormous feathers towering out of a hat atop a garish red wig. His high camp stylings edged in fringe or pearls alongside Jay Brennan, the straight man—in the comedic sense, as he and Savoy were also lovers—made them the toast of any town they visited. Where Julian Eltinge's demure characters diverted audiences' attention from sex altogether, Bert Savoy's sexuality drew them in…whether they knew it or not.

Savoy had begun his life as Everett McKenzie in Boston, but by the time he was a teenager, he claimed, he worked as both a "cooch dancer," what we might call a go-go dancer today, and a taxi dancer, a person people paid to be their dance partner. However, in a streetcar chugging along the New York City streets, he'd soon meet a chorus boy named Jay Brennan. As a team, Savoy & Brennan realized quickly how successful their jokes were, as did the Shuberts, who cast them in the *Passing*

Show of 1915. Shortly thereafter, Savoy & Brennan appeared in a string of Broadway shows, but in 1920, full-fledged stardom arrived with the second iteration of the *Greenwich Village Follies*.

By that time, Savoy & Brennan's act was fully formed. Savoy would be in full drag, that bold red wig atop his head with towering hat, drenched in jewels, not to mention a cigarette holder, and brightly colored (and oft-written-about) garters. He found his inspiration in a woman at Rector's, an upscale restaurant on Broadway, filled with people trying to be "seen." This particular woman "waved her fat hands all covered with diamonds, and dished the dirt," he said. Savoy was a wild, uproarious parody, bursting with luscious quips in a high-pitched, flamboyant voice up from his usual baritone, while Brennan, his suit and tie smart, offered a more sedate delivery. For example, a 1921 recording called "You Must Come Over" distributed by Vocalion Records of the Aeolian Piano Company shares:

Brennan: Would you like to go for an automobile ride?
Savoy: No! I'm just walking home from one.

The act was also peppered with Savoy's catchphrases that later infiltrated the larger culture. His "You don't know the half of it, Dearie!," "I'm glad you asked me," and aforementioned "You musssssst come over!" were the "You're a virgin who can't drive" or "I'm not a regular mom, I'm a cool mom" of their time, even making an appearance in the song "The Half of It Dearie Blues" from George and Ira Gershwin's 1924 musical *Lady, Be Good!*, also starring the young sibling dance duo of Fred and Adele Astaire. It's rumored that legendary actress Mae West, no stranger to Greenwich Village and known for her slinky, scintillating repartee, was actually inspired by Savoy's performances. Her famous catchphrase "Why don't you come up sometime and see me?" was not far from "You musssssst come over!" after all. Because of Savoy's high camp onstage and off, he's often considered among the first real drag queens, as we know the phrase now.

Greenwich Village Follies director John Murray Anderson wrote that "a greater comedian and female impersonator never strutted the stage." Out of costume, Anderson writes, Savoy was "bald, paunchy, middle-aged, and blind in one eye," but on the stage he was a revelation. "After an hour in his dressing room, when he had been made up, trussed into a corset by Agnes, his perspiring maid, adjusted his flaming wig and put on his formfitting dress and spreading, feathered hat—he emerged a dashing, if slightly bawdy, fashion plate... The moment he stepped onstage, he held the audience in the palm of his hand." Savoy was a sensation, and appeared in *Vanity Fair*, *Variety*, and countless other publications.

Savoy was among the few female impersonators known to be gay in his time. His mannerisms were blatantly campy offstage, and he referred to himself and his friends as "she" or "her." It was behavior he could get away with and keep his career intact, Laurence Senelick writes in *The Changing Room: Sex, Drag, and Theatre*, because it served as a signal to others, especially straight men, that he wasn't a threat.

Tragically, Savoy died in a freak accident in June 1923, at the peak of his career. A thunderstorm swept in when Savoy and friends were walking on Long Beach, Long Island. Famously Savoy was said to have quipped, "Mercy, ain't Miss God cuttin' up somethin' awful!" just before lightning struck a key suspended on his wet bathing suit, killing him instantly. His death made national news, and the *New York Times* described him in their obituary as "incontestably one of the greatest comedians the American stage has ever known." Jay Brennan attempted to relaunch his career with a new partner, but Savoy's satiny, pointy-toed heels were far too big to fill. Nonetheless, Savoy had created a model that would be an inspiration for many performers to come.

It's significant that the peak of Savoy's fame arrived during Prohibition. Many Americans were already disillusioned with the government and the reform societies that claimed to protect them. In New York, a broader wave of wartime conservatism created an energetic backlash. Throughout the decade and into the 1930s, drag and other forms of queer performance were embraced at clubs and speakeasies run by organized crime syndicates. But its popularity wouldn't last forever.

In New York at least, the new Prohibition legislation was of little, if any, use. "[N]o locale, not even Chicago, flouted Prohibition with quite the elbow-bending, nose-thumbing vivacity of New York City," historian John Strausbaugh wrote in his 2013 history *The Village*. Prohibition ran between 1920 and 1933, and in New York at that time, there were some 32,000 speakeasies. Gangsters ran nightclubs that featured the most popular entertainment trends, "pansy" and drag performances included. Organized crime would continue to play a role in queer nightlife for the next thirty to forty years: as Prohibition ended in 1933, crime syndicates needed new ways to make money. That included owning gay bars and drag clubs.

Even New York's Mayor Jimmy Walker, who presided over the city from 1925 to 1932, openly flouted Prohibition. A former composer of popular music, he was a nightclub and speakeasy regular himself, and he didn't support the Volstead Act, as the National Prohibition Act was known, or the city's dedication to upholding it. As the city emerged from World War I and lifestyle restrictions imposed by the Spanish Flu epidemic, it entered into an era known as the Roaring Twenties: a time of economic boom and shameless decadence, a dismissal of sanctimonious impulses that had started Prohibition in the first place. New York City became known as a national epicenter of the Jazz Age, regaled or reviled, depending on who you asked, for its hedonism and heterodoxy.

The saloon before Prohibition was a man's space. But speak-easies were for everyone, operating outside of society's constrictive laws and ideals regarding sex, gender, class, ethnicity, and propriety. They were frequented by gay and straight, rich and poor, men and women, and—in some places but not all—Black and white. Unchaperoned single men and women had not interacted in public together before, and "dating" as we know it today first took place, leaving behind courtship rituals of the past. Everybody just wanted a drink. But the illegal nature of getting one, and the rollicking evenings that followed, also led people to develop a taste for the verboten in their entertainments and a larger (though by no means total) acceptance of people once considered outsiders, be it in terms of race, gender, sexuality, or social standing.

This was something Francis Renault knew even as he attended Bert Savoy's funeral.

Inspired by Julian Eltinge, Renault, who was known as "The Parisian Fashion Plate," was a signature performer of the Jazz Age. His opulent costumes reflected the era's taste for grandeur. On October 16, 1921, *The New-York Tribune* wrote, "Shubert vaudeville boasts Francis Renault, of the candelabra headdress of paradise, a female impersonator, who took first prize at the recent Hotel Astor and Pennsylvania Fashion Shows as the most beautiful woman on the ballroom floor." Renault's costumes of note included a 100-pound dress covered in "diamonds," and one bedecked in "solid gold sequins" worn with a headdress of "1500 paradise plumes." Yet Renault, like Eltinge, also felt the need to assert his own masculinity in the press. A headline in the December 28, 1921, edition of *The Brooklyn Citizen*, for example, reads, "Francis Renault, Stage Star, Is Clever Boxer."

"To see Renault's act one would hardly imagine that he was much of a scrapper," the paper wrote, "but it is his belief that the manly art is the greatest thing for keeping oneself in proper condition..."

Whereas Eltinge had many Broadway successes in "legitimate" theater, Renault, though wildly successful, mostly appeared in variety performances on the Great White Way. In the 1930s, he was famous enough to have a giant billboard of himself in drag in Times Square.

Karyl Norman was heavily influenced by Francis Renault and even adopted a similar moniker: "The Creole Fashion Plate." "Creole" is most notably defined as "a person of mixed French or Spanish and Black descent speaking a dialect of French or Spanish." Norman would use makeup to cross this racial boundary and take on a race not his own, a troubling prospect today then seen as exotic.

Norman was very close with his mother—she traveled with him throughout most of his career as his dresser. He broke a 1922 engagement with acrobat Ruth Budd, who performed traditionally male acrobatic work, because Budd wanted to bring her mother on their honeymoon but wouldn't let him bring his. But the mother situation is likely not the only reason their engagement was broken, as it was rumored to be a marriage of convenience. When Norman was touring the country with an early incarnation of the Marx Brothers, for example, Groucho introduced him as "The Queer Old Fashion Plate" by accident in Fargo, North Dakota, and was promptly fired.

Norman regularly appeared in drag on the covers of sheet music. In those images, his fine ensembles—splashed with pearls, furs, feathers, sequins, and beads—lived up to his "Fashion Plate" moniker. But his costumes were only one reason he became a star. Norman had been a soprano since he was a boy, but by age fourteen had also developed a baritone. He used this as a part of his act, switching from high to low much to the delight of his audience, and was also among the few female impersonators of his time who wrote his own song lyrics. By 1920, he was already playing New York's Orpheum Theatre, part of the renowned vaudeville Orpheum Circuit, at 126 2nd Avenue.

Norman would start onstage in female attire, his signature dark wig perched atop his head, and sing in that soprano, only to change out of that costume onstage, don overalls, and present his baritone. In 1925, *Variety* even called it a "reverse Kitty Doner." For *Lady Do*, his 1927 Broadway debut, he played four roles in the two-act musical comedy, two male and two female, and also designed the costumes. The role, the *New York Times*'s Brooks Atkinson pointed out, by then followed an established trope: "the prime requisite is always that the hero shall be hustled into feminine garb at some critical moment, and by his machinations bring about the desired end."

Karyl Norman ultimately had more success in vaudeville and nightclubs than in "legitimate theatre." Still, he was famous enough that, when picked up on a morality charge in Detroit, none other than Eleanor Roosevelt intervened. Norman had done a charity event for the first lady and, apparently, according to a once-upon-a-time FBI agent, "she owed him one."

Jean Malin did not have time for your bullshit.

At six feet tall and 200 pounds, he would slice hecklers in half with a celebrated sharpness of tongue and swish of wrist, his peroxide-blond hair in perfect finger waves across his forehead. He would become the king of the "Pansy Craze," a yearslong mainstream taste for queer life that would soon enrapture New York and the rest of the country. "Give them an inch and they'll want a yard and I don't mean lace," as Malin would say.

The Pansy Craze developed alongside the freewheeling spirit of the 1920s that accompanied Prohibition. Despite a growing appetite for queer performance, however, it was not safe or common to be "out." Just the same, queer entertainers—some openly queer, like the aforementioned Bert Savoy—began to populate not just the queer clubs to which they had previously been relegated, but mainstream nightclub spaces where mostly straight audiences gathered. The phenomenon also spawned a rash of performers in "queerface," actors pretending to be gay as pansy performers for the sake of entertainment. Openly queer performers became seen as valid artists and entertainers by mainstream culture.

The Williamsburg-born Malin won city drag balls, floating in ethereal ensembles of velvet, lace, and feathers. He was fierce and unapologetic: when a group of bullies threw a pitcher of hot water at him after a drag ball, he promptly took them into the street and beat them into oblivion. Recounting the story to a newspaper well after he had become famous, Malin was only upset at having ruined his gown in the process. By then, Malin was accustomed to fighting for space. He joined the chorus of Broadway shows, but his overt queerness kept him from any kind of steady work. Leaning into what made him different, however, Malin decided to become a female impersonator and did so with great success.

He first became the toast of Greenwich Village's queer nightlife, making the rounds in the neighborhood's top spots like the Rubaiyat and Paul and Joe's, a former Italian restaurant turned gay cabaret after World War I. The Rubaiyat was one of the first queer clubs to solicit straight audiences as well. The phenomenon of "slumming," where straight (mostly white) patrons went to other neighborhoods to see "how the other half lived," emerged during this era. In Harlem, "slumming" also included a racial element.

At the Rubaiyat, Malin ditched drag for the aforementioned pansy performance, beguiling audiences with what was then a taboo effeminacy through wit and song, wearing a tuxedo with those perfect finger waves in his hair. He succeeded in this regard as well, written about across town. Whether or not he knew it, he created valuable space not just for himself but for many queer performers who would follow him. The Rubaiyat closed in the early 1930s after a police raid, but Malin found a new home for his act as a nightly headliner at the luxurious Club Abbey, 203 West 54th Street between 7th and Broadway.

Malin's performances included witty double entendres and innuendos, to the delight of a mostly straight audience. "I'll lay you out in ten dozen shades of lavender!" he'd say, sauntering through the club's fresco-lined walls in an elegant black tuxedo and white tie while making conversation with the crowd. "We have never watched Jean Malin work without thinking how much brainier he is than are the people who pay their money to see him," wrote one reporter for *The Brooklyn Daily Eagle*. It was certainly a statement with merit—many "sophisticates" who went to see him and similar performers didn't always know what he was talking about, though it was seen as socially important to look like they did.

Malin had been married to a woman (Lucille Malin, later one of New York's most infamous madams), albeit briefly. This was in a world when being openly gay could still prevent you from getting a job, and could get you killed if you turned the wrong corner—and there Malin was, a star largely understood to be queer, who would eventually earn enough money to open his own club.

Malin became famous for songs like "I'd Rather Be Spanish than Mannish," where Spanish became slang for gay, and "That's What's the Matter with Me," both of which he'd record for Columbia Records in 1931 with his Night Club Orchestra. The songs addressed Malin's queerness with a laugh and a wink. Malin was so successful that a wake of pansy performers and female impersonators slowly began to take over uptown clubs, even inspiring a dedicated space, The Pansy Club on West 48th Street and Broadway. On its opening night, the headlining performer and emcee was Karyl Norman, by then one of the most recognizable in his field. Invitations inked with lavender were sent out to New York's chic, nightclub-going elite, a nod to the slang of "lavender" referencing homosexuality. The evening also promised a smattering of "pansies on parade," an experience possibly appropriated from the "parade of the fairies," a ceremony popular at Harlem drag balls. Gender impersonation to that point had not necessarily equated to queerness the way it does today. But the Pansy Craze drew a more direct line between the two.

Despite Mayor Jimmy Walker's penchant for Jazz Age indulgences, government forces fought to suppress that spirit as it sizzled up to the street level, stifling expressions of sexuality on and off the stage. In 1923, the Schackno Bill made it legal for gay men to be arrested for not just solicitation but "attempting" solicitation—so if a police officer felt someone looked suspicious standing on a corner, for example, they could be arrested. Arrests for solicitation did indeed skyrocket, and it became more and more unsafe for gay men to gather in public.

Additionally, the 1927 Wales Padlock Bill barred plays "depicting or dealing with the subject of sex degeneracy, or sex perversion." Under the law, actors and producers could also be arrested for participating in a show that featured these topics or themes. The bill stemmed, in part, from none other than Mae West. While West is now known as a larger-than-life buxom blonde wit on-screen, she was also a playwright in the earlier part of her career and had even been a male impersonator.

West's first play, *Sex*, caused a stir when it opened at Daly's 63rd Street Theatre on April 26, 1926. Despite critical condemnation and police arresting the full cast (West posted bail for twenty-two people and herself, a total of $14,000), it ran to packed houses for almost a year. But the play, following the life of a sex worker, would be one of several Broadway plays that drew the ire of social reform societies and police.

West's next play, *The Drag*, was the story of a closeted gay man in a marriage of convenience. However, as his sexuality is revealed because of a murder, his family decides to hide it. Since *The Drag* would feature roles for gay men, West sought out gay actors—a counter to the "queerface" performances put on by straight entertainers in nightclubs as the rage for pansy and drag performance grew—and had help from gay men when writing the play. The slang she uses writing it, for example, is not far from Bert Savoy's own in the years before he died. It's also worth noting that *Sex*'s lead character is named Margy, the name of another Savoy creation. To assemble the show, she posted a handwritten ad for auditions in a Village gay bar. Those who arrived made her cast.

"*The Drag* had no star; it was meant to be a spectacle," scholar Lillian Schlissel writes in the introduction to her book *Three Plays by Mae West*. As its name would suggest, *The Drag*, which West called a "homosexual comedy-drama," featured a twenty-minute-long scene at a drag ball meant to mimic those West and her actors might have attended. It was significant that West did not use female impersonators as mere scenery, but instead cared about their stories and their ability to tell them. Queer actors and drag artists still fight for such meaningful representation today. West had long kept the company of gay men and female impersonators from as far back as the 1910s, when she performed at venues like Diamond Tony's on Coney Island, which featured queer artists. At one point, she had even been accused by police of being a drag queen herself, and this remained part of her mythos for the rest of her life.

Diamond Tony's was located on 15th Street near Surf Avenue on Coney Island in a section called "The Gut," a hotbed of queer life and illicit activity, and an epicenter of sex work, "just off Ocean Parkway, between West First Street and West Third, off Coney Island Creek," according to *The Brooklyn Daily Eagle*. Nearby were situated "shanties or slum houses among the boarding houses, gambling dens and dance halls," as well as a collection of saloons and cabarets like Diamond Tony's. In 1910, a seventeen-year-old musician named Jimmy Durante played ragtime piano there. Diamond Tony's was a cabaret "where song-pluggers included female impersonators and singing waiters added to their earnings by working as pimps," Michael Immerso writes in his book *Coney Island: The People's Playground*, though the venue was meant for straight clientele. Durante also played piano at a venue called Jack's, which he described in his 1931 book *Night Clubs*, written with Jack Kofoed:

...the entertainers were all boys who danced together and lisped. They called themselves Edna May and Leslie Carter and Big Tess and things like that. You know... When they had sung their numbers, they sat at the tables the way hostesses do today, "spinning their web," as they called it. Some of them were six feet tall and built like Dempsey, so it was never very healthy to make nasty cracks.

Mae West began developing her onstage sensibilities after seeing female impersonators at places like these. *The Drag* was sympathetic to the lives they led, a highly unusual idea at the time. Not only was *The Drag*'s main character a gay man (albeit a closeted one), female impersonators also played by gay men moved the story forward. The unprecedented nature of the show was not lost on theater owners, many of whom canceled its performance or refused to mount it altogether. Those that did dare run it were sometimes raided by police. And before the play even set foot in New York, reform societies like the New York Society for the Suppression of Vice were ready to not only rail against it, but to call for the formal censorship of all work on the Great White Way.

Times Square in that era was a far cry from the Disney-fied ode to consumerism we know today. Rather, what people saw in Times Square directly reflected the values of New York, and could (and did) also influence the values of the entire country.

The popularity of pansy and drag performances there, as well as the trend toward queer-centric performances on Broadway, set a highly visible trend that would in turn inform Hollywood films.

The Drag never ultimately opened on Broadway, but its mere existence inspired calls for censorship, including the Wales Padlock Bill. "Essentially, the bill treated theater as an offshoot of the underworld," writes scholar Rachel Shteir. Overtly gay men and female impersonators, considered part of its "sex degeneracy, or sex perversion" category, would no longer be allowed on the "legitimate" stage by the 1930s, or in clubs and cabarets. The Wales Padlock Bill would remain in effect until 1967, though adherence abated after World War II.

Mae West remained undeterred. She rewrote *The Drag* as *The Pleasure Man*, altering its plot and setting, but keeping the drag ball. A straight man would now be at the center of the story, but drag performers remained significant characters. Its previews in the Bronx and Queens were mostly uncontroversial. This was not the case when it opened on Broadway, where police infiltrated the performance two days in a row. During one raid, cast member Jay Holly shouted amidst the hubbub, decrying the illegality of the raid and the mistreatment of performers in what would become a stunning moment of historical foreshadowing. The entire cast, some in full drag, were arrested. West paid their bail and hired a lawyer to defend the obscenity charges, a proposition that would put her out $60,000. The case was ultimately dropped.

But these experiences never dissuaded West from working with drag performers or gay men. West has been criticized for opportunistically capitalizing on queer stories. But it's also worth noting that she regularly made space for them in her work during a time when openly gay or effeminate men were rarely centered. She was so beloved by the queer community that she frequently became a subject of impersonation herself—Jean Malin even played a Mae West impersonator on-screen in 1933—and still is today. As Schlissel shares, acclaimed (and openly gay) literary editor George Davis wrote, "I love you, Miss West, because YOU are the greatest female impersonator of all time."

On January 24, 1931, at approximately 5:50 a.m., a shower of bullets reduced Club Abbey to wreckage. Furniture splintered, bullets lodged in walls, and blood stained the floor. It was well past closing, but the club was teeming with well-to-do clientele. According to the *New York Daily News*, "stampeding for their ermine wraps and capes, the ultra-fashionables in the place charged into the hotel lobby, elbow to elbow, with racketeering rats running for cover." The venue closed for good, and the incident signaled the beginning of the end for the Pansy Craze. The Pansy Club itself got raided at 1:00 a.m. on January 29, 1931, mere days after the shooting at Club Abbey. Detectives seized a single bottle of unlicensed booze and arrested an employee, though they left the performers alone. Following the "raid," a police officer was stationed at the door of the venue and clubs like it in the area. Needless to say, the popularity of such establishments in Midtown, the partying grounds of many mainstream sophisticates, quickly petered out, as did the pansy and drag performance trend.

As if the forces working against queer performance weren't enough, beginning in 1933, newly elected mayor Fiorello La Guardia prohibited drag of any kind—be it in a performance or appearance—in New York between 14th Street and 72nd Street. Many of La Guardia's new laws, meant to "clean up" the city in the wake of Prohibition's hedonism and prepare the city for the 1939 World's Fair, were deeply homophobic, making it illegal for queer people to gather in public spaces, to be served alcohol, or to be employed in nightlife venues. These rulings and those of the Wales Padlock Bill loosened after 1945 when La Guardia left office, but drag for the most part would remain relegated to venues run by the mob, who would pay off police for protection.

★ ★ ★

Despite the regulations placed on queer life downtown, the popularity of drag balls continued soaring in Harlem. Queer voices were integral to the Harlem Renaissance, especially during the Pansy Craze, even while the neighborhood's churches preached against homosexuality. One of the most famous performers during the Harlem Renaissance was Gladys Bentley. Though Bentley was often called a male impersonator by the press, it was never part of her repertoire to play a man. She had a preference for men's clothes, which she wore onstage and off, but her use of cross-dressing as part of her onstage persona informed much of the drag that came after her.

Bentley arrived in Harlem from Philadelphia in 1923, at age sixteen. She knew her sexuality was different from an early age, and her parents had hoped to "fix" her attraction to women with medical intervention, but the young woman decided to leave home instead. By the time she arrived in Harlem, the Renaissance and its related queer life awaited her. Originally, she performed at "buffet flats," rented apartments that became like nightclubs or speakeasies. They could be risqué venues, full of illegal liquor, gambling, and performances featuring drag, live sex shows, and music. Bentley quickly became known for her piano playing and her unique, jazzy voice. She recorded her first songs not long after arriving in the city.

Bentley soon found work at a venue called The Mad House on West 133rd Street—they were looking for a male pianist, but she quickly convinced them a female pianist was a better choice. It was there that she adopted what would become her signature look, in "immaculate white full dress shirts with stiff collars, small bow ties and skirts, oxfords, short Eton jackets and hair cut straight back," as she wrote in the August 1952 issue of *Ebony* magazine. Performing as Barbara "Bobbie" Minton, she was so popular the venue changed its name to match her stage persona and became Barbara's Exclusive Club.

With her bawdy parodies of popular songs and original music, Bentley quickly assumed the mantle of Harlem royalty. She headlined across the country, always in her signature attire. At Harry Hansberry's Clam House, a noted lesbian and bisexual hangout, she "plays and sings until you'd think she'd drop from exhaustion," the *New York Daily News* wrote. "And just when you believe she has tired she gets up and dances all over the place." Langston Hughes was similarly impressed, describing her in his 1940 autobiography *The Big Sea* as "an amazing exhibition of musical energy—a large, dark, masculine lady, whose feet pounded the floor while her fingers pounded the keyboard—a perfect piece of African sculpture, animated by her own rhythm."

Bentley and her astronomical popularity serve as a reminder of the rich culture of gender nonconformity at the time, when a woman in male attire—a "bulldagger," as queer women would say at the time—could be celebrated. Gladys Bentley was openly gay—notably more so than many of her queer peers—and in 1931 said she married a white woman in a civil ceremony.

But as the 1930s drew to a close, Bentley's career dwindled as the vogue for queerness in popular culture fell out of fashion. By the 1950s, Bentley's career had a resurgence, and she even appeared on a 1958 episode of Groucho Marx's successful television show "You Bet Your Life" (where, delightfully, she very visibly has no time for his nonsense). But to do so, she had to conform to the era's gender presentation, leaving her masculine attire behind; on the show, she wears a curvaceous dress and adorns herself with baubles, her hands still dancing across the keys in her signature style. For her, a reimagining of her gender presentation also involved marrying a man and writing that aforementioned article for *Ebony*, entitled "I Am a Woman Again," where, according to Dwandalyn Reece, curator of Music and Performing Arts at the National Museum of African American History and Culture, it might appear as though she's apologizing for her past, but in actuality she's mourning the opportunity to continue living it fully. While Bentley managed to reinvent herself, not everyone who played with gender onstage had the chance.

At the time, "the life," as a queer lifestyle was known, was still frowned upon, but Harlem was consistently the neighborhood where people felt most comfortable appearing in drag on the sidewalk. It was still risky to wear such attire publicly because of masquerade laws and possible violence from police or vicious passersby, but many braved the streets just the same, popping into one of the many queer clubs in an area like "The Jungle," as a stretch of West 133rd Street was known; or attending a drag ball at the famed Savoy Ballroom at 596 Lenox Avenue, or visiting club Lulu Belle at 341 Lenox Avenue.

Lulu Belle in particular was known for hosting patrons in drag. The club was named for a sexually liberated character in a 1926 David Belasco musical of the same name. While troublingly Lulu Belle was played by a white actress in blackface named Lenore Ulric, the character herself, with her brazenness, gumption, and libertinism, was beloved by many queer Black Harlemites. Though the play was rooted in the stereotyping of Black women as sexually promiscuous and featured fifteen actors in blackface, the rest of the 115-person cast were all Black, which was previously unheard of. The show was both derided and praised by Black critics and thinkers, with W. E. B. DuBois among its positive reviewers.

The popularity of the show led to a white fascination with Harlem. Like Greenwich Village, Harlem was not immune to "slumming," in which wealthy white patrons sought to "explore" neighborhoods populated by marginalized individuals in pursuit of an "authentic" experience of the "other" or, worse, sought to openly condescend. Some nightclubs in Harlem, owned and operated by white people, catered to this kind of individual, like the oft-remembered Cotton Club, which featured Black entertainers, drag performers included, but did not allow Black patrons. Many queer white patrons from the

Village also sought out queer spaces in Harlem, some of which their Black counterparts could not even attend.

While drag balls continued to find a wide audience, the Hamilton Lodge Ball was often the biggest drag event of the year. A typical evening would feature live music by a twenty-piece orchestra, and a costume contest where entrants paraded for a panel of local celebrity judges like renowned singer Ethel Waters and boxer Jack Johnson, the first Black world champion heavyweight. Local papers and national Black newspapers covered the ball every year, some commending the event and others deriding it.

Box seats were purchased by New York royalty like the Astor and Vanderbilt families, not to mention "gay icons" of theater like Tallulah Bankhead and Beatrice Lillie, while more working-class patrons occupied the dance floor. "From the boxes these men look for all the world like very pretty chorus girls parading across the raised platform in the center of the floor," Langston Hughes wrote in *The Big Sea*. "But up close, most of them look as if they need a shave, and some of their evening gowns, cut too low, show hair on the chest." He attended the Hamilton Lodge Ball as a guest of luminary socialite A'Lelia Walker, daughter of renowned entrepreneur Madame C.J. Walker, noting it was and remained "the strangest and gaudiest of all Harlem spectacles in the '20s." The best costumes took home cash prizes. Balls like these would become a precursor to the uptown ballroom scene that emerged at the end of the 1970s, the same subculture that would later spawn voguing.

It was a hot ticket across the five boroughs. "Apparently, for a novitiate to the gay and lesbian subculture of 1920s New York, exclusion from the Rockland drag was the equivalent of social homicide," scholar James F. Wilson notes. In ten years' time, the balls were popular enough to draw up to 8,000 attendees, a spectacle that impressed New Yorkers of all stripes.

The balls, however, were not without their issues. Along with other pansy and drag performances in Midtown, the balls were chased out of venues like Madison Square Garden and the Hotel Astor in the early 1930s, but attempts to shutter them uptown remained futile. Additionally, while the majority of patrons were Black—an infrequent occurrence in the city—wealthy white contestants not infrequently won prizes, inciting one attendee, drag artist Bonnie Clark, to call out the events for racism. Clark had won the Hamilton Lodge balls in 1931 and 1932. But when white contestants won first and second place in 1933, and Clark took third place, she called bullshit in the March 1, 1933, issue of *Amsterdam News*. "You may quote Bonnie Clark as saying there ain't no justice. And no decency either... There is a conspiracy afoot. I participated in seven of these masquerades last year, and except for the one here, they always arranged for the white girls to win."

Harlem's drag scene would continue to thrive into the mid-1930s, when changing social attitudes toward homosexuality and "degeneracy" brought on by the end of Prohibition and the dawn of the Great Depression would alter the presence of queer life in the city for the next three decades.

On October 29, 1929, the New York Stock Exchange crashed on a day that would become known as Black Tuesday. In New York alone, one third of city dwellers would eventually lose their jobs.

The fear and instability of the Great Depression reverberated through American culture. If the previous decade embraced the brash and audacious, now anything upending traditional lifestyles was deemed a threat. A rise in homophobia impacted attitudes toward drag. In Hollywood, the Hays Code banned the depiction of homosexuality in cinema.

In New York, pansy and female impersonator venues were shuttered, and related performers were forbidden from vaudeville, nightclubs, cabarets, and similar theaters. As the February 14, 1931, edition of *The Brooklyn Daily Eagle* cracked, "the [nightclub] Chateau Madrid and Club Abbey are darker than a female impersonator's future." Drag began to entertain in a more underground capacity, on the smaller stages of cabarets and nightclubs queer and not, and at Harlem and Greenwich Village drag balls.

The fascination with female impersonation that grew during the Pansy Craze faded. With the end of Prohibition in 1933, crackdowns emerged that would alter the course of queer life in New York, shuttering drag from the public sphere. Though legal restrictions on homosexuality in theater eased after 1945, a closeted culture persisted.

Drag survived, of course. It always does. But it would be decades before it was aboveground again.

3

1930 – 1939

Jackie Maye's coiffed brows perched in perfect arches accented by long lashes and chiseled cheekbones. With a pinched nose and curled lips, his face would become synonymous with drag through the length of his nationally renowned, forty-year career.

Born John Rushmore Crandall and raised in New York, the young Maye sang in the boys' choir at the Metropolitan Opera, only to be kicked out when his voice changed. Trying to adapt, Maye auditioned for male roles to no avail until, at a party one night, a guest asked him to hit the soprano notes of his youth, which he did with aplomb. A nightclub owner attending the party offered Maye a gig as a female impersonator. The money was good enough that Maye didn't mind squeezing his broad shoulders into elegant, sparkling evening gowns and cocktail dresses, his own hair under a brunette wig.

When Maye made his debut at Club Calais in 1930 during the height of the Pansy Craze, heads immediately began to turn. "The main novelty here," the New York Daily News wrote, "is a lad named Jackie Maye, who is dressed in girl's clothing and looks better than many a lass." At Club Calais, Maye became known for singing "I Must Have That Man," later popularized by Billie Holiday and Ella Fitzgerald. But, like other female impersonators in the 1930s, his career took a turn with the passing of New York's "cabaret laws," which required licensing for "any room, place, or space in the city in which any musical entertainment, singing, dancing, or other similar amusement is permitted in connection with the restaurant business or the business of directly or indirectly selling the public food or drink."

The cabaret laws were instituted on January 1, 1927. They initially applied to the venues themselves, but by 1940, performers were required to obtain a cabaret license, for which they were fingerprinted and photographed. The laws were considered deeply racist, particularly for the way they targeted Harlem jazz clubs. Artists couldn't get a cabaret card if they had been convicted of prior criminal activity. Lenny Bruce, Thelonious Monk, and Billie Holiday would all have their cards revoked or denied. The general idea was that anyone who performed in a cabaret was from "an odd class of people" and their behavior needed to be overseen, according to historian Joe E. Jeffreys.

Merely existing in public as a queer person, as a queer man especially, during this time could result in arrest for "degeneracy" or "homosexual solicitation." Such a situation was made even worse by the prospect of entrapment, in which plainclothes police officers loitered in cruising areas, arresting anyone who tried to woo them. Over 50,000 men would be arrested for cruising between 1923 and 1966.

The cabaret card bureau also denied anyone who was openly gay from receiving a card. Queer people who hoped to perform in drag at nightclubs had to repress their own existence, for fear of not just being arrested, but being outed and losing their livelihood. Often "the boys" who ran the clubs, as the Mafia were known, would help gender impersonators obtain the necessary paperwork to perform. Organized by club management, performers put on their best straight drag and went to the police station together, usually one that had already been paid off, to get their cards en masse.

On December 5, 1933, President Franklin Delano Roosevelt instituted the Twenty-First Amendment, which ended Prohibition by allowing states to regulate their own alcohol sales. The following year, the newly established New York State Liquor Authority began to push queer culture back to the fringes of society. Laws "forbade the employment in a bar of anyone convicted of a felony or certain other offenses," according to the 2005 edition of historian Paul Chevigny's book *Gigs: Jazz and the Cabaret Laws in New York City.* The "felony and certain other offenses" category included the aforementioned degeneracy and disorderly conduct, for which queer people were arrested at disproportionately higher rates, often by entrapment.

The State Liquor Authority also required bars to maintain orderly conduct on their premises, which was coded language meant to prohibit queer patrons. Bars became strict in their own policing of clientele for fear of losing their liquor licenses: should an undercover agent of the SLA find queer people in their midst while visiting a bar, there would be a zero-tolerance policy. Gay bars shuttered, and their clientele searched for new spots by word of mouth until they'd invariably close, too.

The situation only got worse after the announcement that the 1939 World's Fair would be held in New York. Planning began in 1935, construction the following year. New York had not hosted a World's Fair since 1853, and this one would take place across the 1,200 acres of what's now Flushing Meadows Corona Park in Queens, but had previously been a city dump. When the fair opened on April 30, 1939, it featured approximately sixty countries, thirty-three states, and more than 1,000 exhibitions. Over $150 million would ultimately go into the project, nearly $3 billion in today's currency.

Meant to commemorate the 150th anniversary of George Washington's inauguration, the fair welcomed over 44 million people, including the king and queen of England, who made their way through international pavilions showcasing "The World of Tomorrow."

Ahead of the fair, Mayor La Guardia initiated a cleanup of the entire city. Entrapment continued, and gay men in particular became stereotyped by the State Liquor Authority to be easily "discovered" if on a bar's premises, whether due to "campy behavior [or, as the agents called it, their 'effeminacy'], their use of rouge or lipstick, their practice of calling each other by camp or women's names, the way they talked or the fact that they talked about the opera or other suspect topics, or other aspects of their dress and carriage," as George Chauncey writes.

This engendered in some gay men who "passed" a spirit of contempt for high camp presentation and aesthetics, drag included, an ire that persisted for generations. Yet the cultural backlash didn't stop drag from existing. La Guardia's designation that gender impersonation should appear only below 14th Street or above 72nd Street incubated drag epicenters across New York. The mob continued to pay off police officers in Greenwich Village, and in Harlem, cops, morality societies, and SLA agents were less intrusive, their racism deflecting their gaze toward white neighborhoods instead. With the removal of drag and queer culture from Times Square, New York's showplace to the world, drag was also effectively removed from the mainstream narratives of American culture it had occupied throughout the 1920s and early 1930s.

The turn against queerness was not unique to New York City. Acts specifically designated as "pansy" or "fairy" would no longer be allowed on the vaudeville circuit, and drag became illegal in other parts of the country. Detroit and Cleveland were among the Midwest cities where female impersonation, though highly regulated, was still allowed, but performers weren't allowed to cavort with guests offstage and had to wear male attire outside. Because of the Hays Code, generations of people would not see an openly queer character or a gender impersonator on-screen in the US until at least 1964. A spate of crimes against children in the 1930s, in Washington, New Hampshire, and Florida, among others, incorrectly yet knowingly scapegoated homosexuals in the national media, amplifying a culture of queer panic. And America's apprehension toward queer life would only accelerate during World War II.

By 1932, Phil Black had become the most famous female impersonator Pittsburgh had ever seen, but it was time to think bigger. Phil moved to New York City that year and proceeded to take the Big Apple by storm.

Like many gender impersonators, Phil printed a performance card with a photo of himself in a suit and fedora accompanied by two images of himself in drag, one in white furs and metallic T-strap heels, and another in a gleaming metallic halter top dress, a bangle sparkling on his wrist. In both he wore a wig of black finger waves.

Phil began performing in Greenwich Village and at the Elk's Rendezvous in Harlem. The chic nightclub on West 133rd Street was "host to celebrities and many members of ultra smart Cafe Society," according to Black newspaper *The New York Age*. At the underground club, Phil would sing, dance, and crack jokes, while patrons drank and smoked cigarettes at small tables. Phil performed there for two years, but his greatest legacy was the Funmakers' Ball.

An accomplished seamstress who also studied fashion design, Phil would for a time appear at various balls in costumes of his

own design—that is, unless they were lent to him by stars like
Josephine Baker. Interestingly, he also worked as a part-time
tour guide on the Hudson River and for a private investigator in Harlem. The latter hired him to dress in drag and follow
husbands being investigated for divorce cases. But Phil Black
will forever be synonymous with Funmakers' Ball, an event he
first hosted at the Rockland Palace in Harlem, on Thanksgiving night of 1947. It drew thousands annually from across the
city. The venue would be "packed to the rafters as the youthful
things wore their gowns, furs, and jewels into the hall trying to
cop that first prize," *The New York Age* wrote in 1948. Phil had
strict rules for his balls: when contestants were competing for a
$500 grand prize, for example, they couldn't "weigh over 150
pounds or wear falsies that measure more than 42 inches around
the bust," according to an issue of *Jet* magazine from 1957.

Despite the rules, the ball remained wildly popular and endured for decades, at one time attracting visitors from four con-
tinents. A December 7, 1957, article in *The New York Age* by a
"fellow traveler" (slang for fellow queer person) writing as "Lucius Limpwrist" cited it as "too, too marvellous." With some
3,200 attendees and hundreds more clamoring to get inside, it
was, Lucius wrote, perhaps one of the "best-attended affairs
held in the city." Given the state of gay bars at the time—run
by the Mafia, subject to constant raids, overcharging for drinks,
and generally unsafe—it's no wonder a legally sanctioned queer
event became so popular.

As with balls past, these events also transcended race. Limpwrist writes:

When I say the barriers are down, I mean all the barriers, honey... With all the noise the White Citizens Coun-
cils have been making, they haven't been able to destroy
the integration policies of the gay world. There are always

many of our white "sisters" who attend this ball and some of the most ravishing white men arrive with black, beige, and brown gay boys on their arms and vice versa. It's all most democratic.

Like the Hamilton Lodge Ball, the Funmakers' Ball made space for queer Black attendees when mainstream culture was consistently hostile to them. It was important, Limpwrist notes, for the ball to end before midnight so revelers in drag would not be arrested. While white-dominated law enforcement remained a constant threat, sometimes such hostility came from within the Black community itself: in 1963, for example, a reform group called the Committee for Racial Pride protested the event, citing that drag and homosexuality were blights on the Black community, the latter wrought by white people. That year, Black nationalists would picket the event as well, their signs posted with the slogan "Rear Admirals Stay downtown" and some attendees were "molested by local hoodlums," leading Phil Black to cancel the 1964 event. He'd have to cancel in 1965 as well: due to diabetes, he'd suffer gangrene in his left leg, requiring it to be amputated at the knee. But he'd be fitted with a plastic leg and run the event for another eight years.

Phil Black's Funmakers' Ball, with its combination of drag competition, performance, and pageantry, was another inspiration for the ballroom culture of following decades.

Sepia Gloria Swanson, as she called herself, made her mark in New York after arriving from her native Chicago. She was referred to in the press as a female impersonator, but the glamazon used pronouns "she" and "her" and exclusively wore women's garb, offstage and on. In fact, few ever saw her in male dress until Mayor La Guardia took office and began reinforcing gendered attire. Openly queer Harlem Renaissance writer Richard

Bruce Nugent detailed the performer in his essay "On 'Gloria Swanson' (Real Name: Mr. Winston)." It was not then typical practice to refer to people by their updated names and pronouns, so Nugent refers to Swanson as "he/him/his" throughout the piece. Swanson was a denizen of the night—"his public life was lived in evening gowns, his private life in boa-trimmed negligees," Nugent wrote—and she resided in an apartment fringed with lace.

Swanson arrived in New York as the Pansy Craze was ending, but by 1934, she was appearing at the famed Apollo Theatre and the Harlem Opera House. Her reception there is indicative of the push-and-pull of Harlem's morality at the time, where as many residents favored the seductive nightlife as condemned it. After one performance with legendary musician Fletcher Henderson—where she sang the salacious "I'm a Big Fat Mama with Meat Shaking on My Bones" with the delicious lyric "And every time I shake, some skinny gal loses her home"—the writer Augustus Austin claimed in *The New York Age* that her act made him sick to his stomach. But it didn't seem to affect Swanson's career: she continued to shine as a regular at Harlem's most beloved entertainment venues and drag balls.

By 1935, her movements made the gossip columns when she took on new boyfriends and headlined at Harlem's Theatrical Grill. She offered bawdy parodies of popular songs and an occasional dance, all the while "lifting modestly to just above the knee [her] perennial net and sequins or [her] velvet-trimmed evening-gown skirts, displaying with professional coyness a length of silk-clad limb," as Nugent wrote. Though drag was still allowed above 72nd Street, Swanson was hit hard by the city's crackdown. Now required to don male attire and use "he/him" pronouns offstage while traversing the city, this was more of a "masquerade" for her, as Nugent said, than her furs and gowns. Nugent posited that this forced masculinity had something to do with a recurring cardiac illness that led to her death in 1940, at just thirty-three years old.

Her obituary in *The Chicago Defender* quotes Swanson's mother, Mrs. Sarah Winston Myers, who praised and defended her child: "Regardless to what people have or will say, I'm more than grateful to the profession and those friends…who rallied with their support to give me great consolation," she said. Similarly, the reverend at Gloria's funeral reminded some 200 mourners that "'folks who live in glass houses' must refrain from gossip and scorn." Both statements were somewhat radical for their time, coming from voices who could have easily dismissed Swanson. In the *Defender* obituary, writer Maurice Dancer refers to her as "one of the entertainment world's most picturesque and 'glamorous' characters," a description she certainly would have loved. Her memory also serves as a recognition of the longstanding role of Black transgender and gender nonconforming individuals in drag.

Downtown, nestled on West 3rd Street in Greenwich Village, stood The Howdy Club, "where the Village begins and ends."

A canopy bearing the words "Howdy Revue" covered the entrance, from which female impersonators in glittering gowns beckoned passersby. The club was owned and operated by Anthony "Tony Bender" Strollo, a member of the notorious and long-running Genovese crime family headed by Vito Genovese, with longtime Mafia partner Stephen Franse. It opened in 1935 and quickly became a popular lesbian hangout when spots for queer women were few and far between. The club also catered to other queer and straight crowds, including soldiers during World War II. For a $2 cover, patrons crowded at short, round tables covered in white tablecloths. At three different shows— 10:00 p.m., 12:00 a.m., and 2:30 a.m.—they might see a swing orchestra, a singer, strippers, a comedian, or dance teams, but there were almost always gender impersonators.

On a 1940 postcard, the female waitstaff appeared in drag, donning sporty, collegiate-style football jerseys for each letter in the club's name, which itself has an interesting history. "Generally, [at the time] you did not give pictures of people who were not dead because they might be identified as gay, which was not something that you would do to a friend of yours if they weren't, shall we say, *out* in society," says historian Lisa E. Davis, who met and befriended some of the former Howdy male impersonators in the mid-1960s. Decades later, when it was safer to be out, "[male impersonator] Buddy [Kent] gave us the picture of the wait staff at the Howdy Club, and the Lesbian Herstory Archives used that for years as a postcard for the archives."

Waitresses and waiters at the Howdy Club made good money. "The girls served the drinks and got big tips, so they didn't mind," Davis said. "The tips were fabulous. This is back in the time when an apartment in the Village was $60, so you could make, as they told me, $200 a weekend in tips."

On their nights off, male impersonators would still go out attired as men to high-end nightclubs like the Latin Quarter or the Copacabana. "The girls there all knew who we were because they would come to our club, cruising us," Kent said. "It was quite the thing [to] be seen around town with a lesbian." Male impersonators were occasionally recruited by mafiosos as well. The mobsters would hang out at many of the bars downtown, and when girls came in wearing pants and jackets—or would arrive in skirts and change into pants—the men would approach them, asking if they'd like to audition for a show at a new venue. Those who said yes sometimes ended up performing at a variety of drag venues across the West Village, if not across the world.

While drag was, by Mayor La Guardia's standards, allowed

below 14th Street, the words "female impersonation" or "female impersonator" weren't typically used in advertising. The genre had become the victim of homophobic lawmaking and negative media coverage. Instead, papers like *The Brooklyn Daily Eagle* and Brooklyn's *Times-Union* would often list the name of the act or its producer as a shorthand for what audiences could expect: if you knew, you knew, or you'd soon find out.

Though the Howdy Club was famously considered a shady Mafia-owned joint, Brooklyn's *Times-Union* wrote that it had "long been a favorite haunt of the microphone and stage celebrities." This included renowned burlesque artist Gypsy Rose Lee, though in 1936 she said "the entertainment was kind of rough." A telling example occurred on April 12, 1938, when three robbers attempted to hold up the club and escaped with $400 at 4:00 in the morning. They got into a shootout that left one police officer dead and almost all involved wounded. Despite such dark doings, the Howdy raged on until the end of 1944, when it was ultimately shuttered on a morality charge. Today the Howdy exists only as a memory, razed to create what would eventually become academic buildings for NYU.

Before its extinction, however, the Howdy also became known for male impersonators like Blackie Dennis, a toe-curling crooner in a sharp tux, grinning under a sleek swirl of dark hair. Born Michelina Lombino to an Italian family in East Harlem, she began doing drag in the Village. Dennis became the Howdy's emcee and would begin every evening singing Hoagy Carmichael's "Stardust." She also performed as a stripper in downtown clubs like Jimmy Kelly's, "the Montmartre of New York" at 181 Sullivan Street. Dennis would be joined at Jimmy Kelly's by male impersonator Buddy Kent. Kent performed striptease as Bubbles Kent "because I wanted to get in on some of the big money," she told historian Lisa Davis in 2006. The club's manager initially balked. Why would he hire a lesbian? But the Wall Street types who frequented Kelly's loved her and her lithe dancer's figure. She performed there for more than a year.

Kent started life as Malvina Schwartz in Manhattan, but also lived in the Brownsville/East New York area of Brooklyn. Knowing of her queerness from adolescence, she found sanctuary in Greenwich Village. "Greenwich Village was my territory—like what Israel means to the Jews today! You didn't have to conform because in the Thirties and Forties, there were so many theatrical and aesthetic people around, and they dressed real weird," she'd tell Joan Nestle of the Lesbian Herstory Archives in 1983. "It was really the only place in the city where you were accepted without being looked upon as strange."

Kent abandoned her last name because she found its Eastern European Jewish origin made getting a job more difficult. She had served in the military and played trumpet with the Women's Army Corps band, so she was no stranger to a stage. Kent got her first job in drag as a bartender at Ernie's Restaurant/Three Ring Circus on 3rd Street, run by Ernie Sgroi, Sr., also of the Genovese crime family. Ernie's drew a majority straight crowd, but also attracted working-class queer women.

"When Ernie interviewed me, he said, 'What do you do?' And I said 'Everything, everything,'" Kent told Nestle. Behind the bar with her short brown hair, shirt and tie, she looked like a young man. One night when the club was short an act, Kent took the stage. "I was a hoofer," she told Davis in 2006. "I took classes uptown with [dancer and choreographer] Pearl Primus who'd just started her own dance company. I saw all the Broadway musicals, and borrowed steps for my routines." Kent was successful enough that the club's management helped her put together an actual performance. At twenty-one, Kent became a "chorus boy" at the Genovese-owned Club 181. There, she performed a solo act and stripped, "out of top hat and tails, a Fred Astaire dance and then—with one flip of the hand—my pants flew out from under me," she said. "Then I went into a girl strip. When I finished, people didn't know if I was a boy or a girl because I was quite slim and very flat."

By 1954, however, Kent would leave the stage and become a partner at her own venue with two other queer nightlife entrepreneurs, and of course a mob connection. Called The Page 3, the nightclub was located at 140 7th Avenue South and is today a Mexican restaurant called Agave. The Page 3 had been open already and wasn't doing well, but the new group turned it around. They'd sit in suits and ties at round tables topped with white cloth, surrounded by friends, cocktails never too far away.

Prohibition ended in 1933, allowing states to regulate their own liquor laws. But the establishment of the New York State Liquor Authority brought corruption. If same-sex partners were spotted in a bar, it could be closed for "keeping a disorderly house." Seeing this, the mob began to capitalize on the public's desire for queer gathering places and pay off police to stay away.

The Genovese family came to control much of Greenwich Village, especially its gay bars. Interestingly, there were quite possibly many queer men in the Genovese ranks, among them Charles Gagliodotto, who dressed in drag while assassinating marks. Anna Genovese, wife of mob boss Vito Genovese, would herself be involved in long-term relationships with women. Perhaps driven by a desire for queer spaces of her own, she would also become a foundational figure in the development of New York City drag culture.

Queer people and gender impersonators found homes at Mafia-run venues, but their off-the-books dealings meant performers could be exploited: many had no other place to turn for jobs and were at the mercy of the venues, which the Mafia knew well. Yet with regular pay from the Mafia, gender impersonators could also have a safer life. A bartender from a gay

club was quoted in the *New York Post* in 2014 saying, "If anybody ever threatened me or intimidated me, I had recourse. I
had been stopped by the police and...all I had to do was give
them the name of my employer and they let me go, because we
were both working for the same people." With this protection,
they could worry less about run-ins with the law.

In September 1939, war broke out in Europe. After the December 7, 1941, attack on Pearl Harbor, many people who later
became gender impersonators would serve their country and encounter a different relationship to drag within the armed forces.
While post-Depression attitudes toward drag and queerness persisted, the art form remained a popular escapist pleasure during
and after the war. And how better to get away for a while than
by slipping into something a little more glamorous than fatigues?

4

1940 – 1959

"'Ladies of the Chorus,' curtain."

Soon they emerge for their eponymous number, wigs blond and frothy like cotton candy, shoulders bare, chest hair exposed. Garters holding up black socks tuck into clunky, shiny black shoes. Released in 1943, the soldiers of the smash Broadway musical *This Is the Army* artfully transitioned to the screen under the direction of Michael Curtiz, who directed *Casablanca* the year prior.

The proposition of drag during and after the war was a challenging one. As attitudes toward queerness moved from interest in the Pansy Craze and Prohibition to fear and disdain during the Great Depression and after, spaces for drag would have to be artfully crafted. In government-sanctioned arenas, drag's background as a dignified aspect of theater history was thrust to the forefront, while in underground venues run by the Mafia, for example, it would remain a lure of the forbidden subject to obscenity charges. And then there were the spaces in between, those created by queer individuals in hopes of providing legal, aboveground entertainment in order to make a living for themselves and the drag artists they employed. These people had to work the narrative of drag in both directions: indulging audiences' desire for the taboo while also rooting themselves in theatrical tradition to remain legal. As the decade wore on, drag would be affected by New York's changing shape as soldiers came back from war. Highways expanded, meaning drag troupes could more easily tour. Suburbs emerged, separating audiences. And even though queer soldiers who had found camaraderie during the war flooded New York—some of whom performed in drag while enlisted and would go on to perform in the city—queerness continued to be criminalized in a multitude of forms, affecting how performers (and everyone else) maneuvered through their lives.

Drag's verboten nature meant it was consumed more as a novelty than an art form, a withering glare cast upon it by straight and queer communities alike. But while traversing these stages, difficult though it may have been, drag performers still maintained a hold in New York's cultural lexicon. Underground and aboveground, drag would prove resilient, forming a foundation upon which future artists would continue to build.

While World War II began on September 1, 1939, upon Hitler's invasion of Poland, the United States didn't enter the war until after the Japanese bombing of Pearl Harbor in Hawaii on December 7, 1941. More American people than ever before—eventually over 16 million men and women—were dispatched to fight for the Allied Forces all over the globe. Entertainment and morale-boosting were considered central to the fight. Soldiers were recruited from within the army to participate in revues and join the Special Services Division of the War Department, created in 1940 to function as the entertainment wing of the military. The Special Services Division would also be responsible for *This Is the Army*.

This Is the Army began as a benefit for the Army Emergency Relief Fund, a sequel to Irving Berlin's *Yip Yip Yaphank*, for which Berlin would again cast soldiers and write a few new songs. In military shows, men often dressed in drag since women were not initially allowed to join their productions. *This Is the Army* arrived on the Great White Way on July 4, 1942. On its opening night alone, it made $45,000, making it wildly successful for the time, and Irving Berlin received a standing ovation. Between Broadway and touring, the show raised some $10 million.

The film, with many of the same cast members, made its world premiere in New York on July 28, 1943 and the rest of the country on August 14, 1943. Like *Yip Yip Yaphank*, *This Is the Army* would also feature an all-male cast, this time of 300 soldiers. Some participated in drag numbers, of which there were several in the show, like the ballet for "A Soldier's Dream" with long, flowing gowns or that aforementioned "Ladies of the Chorus" number. Black soldiers' performances, which also featured drag in numbers like "What the Well-Dressed Man in Harlem Will Wear," were segregated throughout most of the show. In "Stage Door Canteen," a number named after a venue near Times Square where military members could enjoy performances, dance, and food, bewigged soldiers donned Americana regalia, all bows, ruffles and stripes. Other soldiers appeared in drag as famous stage actresses like Jane Cowl and Lynne Fontanne. It was all seen as celebratory, morale-boosting fun. But if there were any queer performers in the company, they had to remain hidden.

Among them was Corporal Nelson Barclift, also known as Edgar Nelson Barclift, an Indigenous performer who had an established career in dance before the war. Barclift cochoreographed *This Is the Army* and appeared in drag throughout the show. At one point, likely during the war, Barclift became the lover of renowned composer Cole Porter. According to Barclift, Porter's tune "You'd Be So Nice to Come Home To," from the 1943 musical film *Something to Shout About*, was their song. Barclift also inspired the classic "Night and Day."

This Is the Army, officially sanctioned by the military, had to use press savvy to work around drag's associations with homosexuality. The show's 1942 souvenir program calls back to *Yip Yip Yaphank*, reminding audiences of the revue's morale-boosting properties during the war some twenty-five years earlier with another show that featured drag. *This Is the Army*'s program also includes portraits of the army's commanders, with Commander-in-Chief President Franklin Delano Roosevelt, Secretary of War Henry L. Stimson, Chief of Staff General George C. Marshall, and more expressing their appreciation for the show. An introduction waxes poetic about the importance of morale-boosting during war dating back to the times of the Romans: "Morale is fuel for the fighting machine! Soldier entertainment contributes to this conviction, and 'This Is the Army' is the distillation of the best in soldier entertainment." The press played along, too. There was nary a negative review of the show when it opened on Broadway or when it toured.

World War II, unlike wars in which the United States participated afterward, drew high levels of support from the entire country: by the time Pearl Harbor was bombed, for example, 91% of Americans surveyed by Gallup believed President Roosevelt should have declared war on Germany as well as Japan. With enthusiasm for the war effort at a high, it would have been unlikely for anyone to speak out against *This Is the Army*. Soldiers' drag performances, writes historian Allan Bérubé in his remarkable 1991 book *Coming Out Under Fire: The History of Gay Men and Women in World War II*, were defended by the press as "wholesome, patriotic, and masculine." In *This Is the Army* in particular, drag was intended as a joke. It had to be, given the steely structures of masculinity and gender presentation that arose before and during the war. Drag in the military could not be associated at all with queerness. When drag was funny and parodied female presentation with beards and chest hair in full view, as opposed to, say, embodying it in a glamorous way or creating a feminine illusion, it was relatable and comfortable to the hordes of civilian audiences that would see the show and (straight) soldiers who would see it and participate in it.

This Is the Army's success led to regular revues at military bases around the world, drag included. You can see this phenomenon depicted in Rodgers and Hammerstein's famous musical *South Pacific*, which took to the Broadway stage in 1949 and to the screen in 1958. During the song "Honey Bun" in the film version, the character Nellie Forbush, played by Mitzi Gaynor, entertains naval officers while dressed in a men's sailor uniform. She is joined by dance partner Luther Billis, played by Ray Walston, in a coconut bra, hula skirt, and straw hair bedecked with flowers. "A hundred and one pounds of fun/ That's my little honey bun!/Get a load of honey bun tonight," she sings of Billis's femme presentation. It's high comedic drag, in the tradition of Andrew Tribble and those like him, especially since Billis has a giant ship tattooed on his stomach and has by no means sheared his chest hair. His appearance is met by roars from his crew.

Drag became not just an acceptable form of entertainment in the army during World War II, but a revered one, even though national attitudes toward homosexuality remained oppressive. In the war's other morale-boosting shows, soldiers in drag would impersonate the likes of swing-singing group The Andrews Sisters, famed burlesque artist Gypsy Rose Lee, and Brazilian actress Carmen Miranda, she of the elaborate befruited headpieces. In fact, Ms. Miranda was so frequently impersonated that some soldiers considered her depiction trite.

Dwight D. Eisenhower, who during the war would be the Allied Forces' commanding general in Europe, even offered his praise to an Algerian army base revue in which there were several drag performers. Eisenhower's words were recounted by Sergeant Sterling Holloway, an actor stationed there who'd later voice Winnie-the-Pooh among many other characters, when he wrote a letter to his mother that was partly reprinted in Camden, New Jersey's *Morning Post* on December 3, 1943:

> It's a great show... You are entertaining soldiers; you are not fighting with machine guns, but your job is just as important. All officers admire men who do their jobs well. As long as you are doing your job well—and you are doing it extremely well—you will be rendering a service, and a great one, to your fellow soldiers and your country.

Gay soldiers found in officially sanctioned drag a haven to express parts of themselves that could otherwise get them kicked out of the armed services. But they did so precariously, for open homosexuality in any branch of the American military was grounds for dishonorable discharge. A dishonorable discharge meant they wouldn't qualify for the GI Bill, a generous government endowment that allowed free college education and mortgage assistance for veterans. A blue ticket discharge was considered neither honorable or dishonorable, but still disqualified the receiver from gaining said endowments. The military later eased up on these discharges, but many men released on these counts would not receive the support their counterparts did.

By the end of 1941, homosexuality was considered a mental illness. The government had decided to "test" for homosexuality to remove its apparent threat. At each military examination, clinicians examined the body shapes of potential soldiers to root out effeminacy, inquiring about how they dressed, their dating habits, if they were employed in "feminine" industries like dancing or interior design, and more. Not only were these screenings rooted in offensive stereotypes, they also didn't work. Plenty of gay men became members of the armed forces and had the opportunity to meet other "fellow travelers." They continued to nurture those bonds after the war in urban centers like New York.

Yet while those communities flourished, the pathologizing of homosexuality persisted long after the war. In 1952, homosexuality was listed as a mental illness in the American Psychiatric Association's first Diagnostic and Statistical Manual (DSM) and remained there until 1973. For some straight audiences, drag became an oddity—similar to the era's circus freak shows: taboo, frightful, and verboten. Some queer audiences would cast their own aspersions, considering drag offensive for its outward display of flamboyance in a time when such flamboyance could get you killed. But as ever, others—queer and not—would revel in the form without apology.

By finessing the language around gender impersonation, stage producers helped revive the form near the end of the 1930s. The evolution continued in Miami in 1939 with Danny Brown and Doc Benner, native New Yorkers and veteran emcees of female impersonator shows. They dreamed up a way to "bring back the glories of a neglected field of entertainment, to bring back female impersonation as a true art," as they wrote in a program for what would ultimately become the Jewel Box Revue.

"Divorcing the profession of female impersonation from queer identity was very important to many in the impersonation community," writes scholar Mara Dauphin. "Many of these men had worked hard to get female impersonation to the new, lofty position it enjoyed in the nightclub entertainment circuit, and any association of extra-theatrical homosexuality or transvestitism could permanently damage the impersonators' ability to be taken seriously as artists or even to draw straight audiences."

It's important to note, too, that for the length of the Jewel Box Revue's existence, from 1939 to 1975, many cities, New York among them, had laws that forbade queer people from gathering publicly. It was imperative that the Jewel Box underscore the long-held theatrical tradition of female impersonation and position it as an elevated experience for straight crowds. As the next decade began, Brown and Benner would put their ideas to the test and reclaim a space for drag in performance culture.

The Jewel Box Revue managed its reputation so carefully that once it gained momentum, it toured the country for nearly four decades. The way for drag to regain cultural acceptance, it seemed, was to make the performances an elegant affair, with only the most sophisticated humor and the most stylish gowns, absent of lewdness and double entendres of drag acts past.

If Brown and Benner could cater to the values of mainstream audiences, they could successfully tour the country as reputable, upscale nightclub programming, revising the reputation of drag as a true form of theater. "We hope to reach in the nightclub field what Julian Eltinge reached in the theatre—artistry and showmanship combining for a thrilling evening's entertainment," the Jewel Box program said. It would have been essential to evoke someone like Eltinge, highly regarded as an artist and not universally perceived as queer. Eltinge's self-presentation out of drag was again one of high masculinity, one that made his transformation into feminine garb seem all the more an act of capital *T* Talent and capital *S* Skill rather than the "natural" propensity of "some mincing queen." In doing so, the Jewel Box Revue succeeded in reframing drag, allowing it to occupy an active space in mainstream culture while employing a large, rotating cast of queer performers.

In fact, several drag touring companies emerged in its wake. This was in part due to the Genovese family's monopoly on gender impersonation venues in Manhattan, where any other venue attempting to capitalize on the form was suddenly, mysteriously shut down, and in part because road travel was more accessible thanks to the expansion of the American highway system. Shaped by the Federal-Aid Highway Act of 1944, nearly 40,000 miles of highway were completed by 1955. This meant gender impersonators could expand their reach and income by traveling to small towns otherwise difficult to reach. Sometimes those small towns bit back, as female impersonation in particular would become outlawed in many of them. But a show like the Jewel Box angled itself around such restrictions. It was always done with an outward laugh: high style and high comedy. "You were making fun of yourself, so to speak, so society could accept you," former Jewel Box performer Jerry Ross told authors Don Paulson and Roger Simpson for their 1996 book *An Evening at the Garden of Allah.* "If you were serious, the public would be offended, so you kept it light, a novelty."

The Jewel Box Revue would be a variety show of sorts, not unlike a drag version of the Shuberts' *Passing Show* or Ziegfeld's *Follies*, with singers, dancers, burlesque performers, comedians, and magicians all in drag, always with glamorous pageantry and a live orchestra. These were the days long before lip-synching became de rigueur. "We were very famous. It was a big, live show. There was no pantomime," said Bernie Brandall, who later made a career as a drag magician and performed with the Jewel Box Revue in the 1960s. "It was a beautiful show."

Early on, the Jewel Box Revue became known for its "25 Men and 1 Girl," the latter of whom was a male impersonator named Mickey Mercer. Mickey, with his slicked-back hair curling in the front, was an emcee and singer in the show, billed as "one miss that's a hit." Mercer performed with the Jewel Box Revue until 1955, when he was replaced by Stormé DeLarverie, who remained at the helm for the next fourteen years, until 1969. It became a game of sorts amongst the Jewel Box's mostly straight audiences to try and discover the male impersonator amongst the queens. Admittedly, finding the female impersonators was much easier, their shimmering gowns and crisply-drawn lips giving them away, but that "one girl" remained elusive. At least until the end of every show, that is. At that point, a besuited and mustachioed DeLarverie began to sing in her famed baritone "A Surprise with a Song," disclosing it was her the audience had been looking for the whole time.

"Men's jackets were loose, but the pants were skintight. And if I ever took my jacket off onstage, the dirt was out," Stormé said in the 1987 Michelle Parkerson documentary *Stormé: The Lady of the Jewel Box.* "But you know the strange thing is, I never moved any different than I had when I was wearing women's clothes. [The audience] only saw what they wanted to see and they believed what they wanted to believe."

When Stormé was first considering joining the Jewel Box, many tried to dissuade her, that the reputation she had built previously as a jazz singer would be destroyed. But she had no time for their notions. "It was very easy. All I had to do was just be me and let people use their imaginations," she said in Parkerson's documentary. "It never changed me. I was still a woman."

The Jewel Box was so famous that DeLarverie's own fame followed suit, immortalized in a photograph by Diane Arbus, circulating amongst glitterati like Billie Holiday and Dinah Washington. She became a legendary male impersonator—her preferred terminology—and as the decades passed, her inspiration to others wouldn't stop there.

Yet as exciting as it was, the Jewel Box Revue was still fighting for its legitimacy some twelve years after it began. In an article from the December 5, 1951, edition of *The Miami Herald*, for example, writer George Bourke discusses Danny Brown's desire for a name other than "female impersonator" for his performers, or Jewel Boxers, as they were known, saying that the revue "isn't just an excuse to allow a man who gets a biological kick out of strutting around in women's clothing," and that while the paper doesn't know the performers personally and "cannot vouch for the absence or presence of any possible psychological reason for their masquerading," the paper is optimistic about the performers' "definite talent for the dancing, singing, or comedy which he offers as his forte."

There's much to glean from these statements. First, we see that "female impersonation" outside of the Jewel Box is still regarded as déclassé, lewd, or unsavory. Otherwise, Brown might take no issue with the title. Second, there's a presumption that this unsavory version of "female impersonation" is believed to involve a fetish or psychological issue. Third, this typical "female impersonation" stereotype that Brown hopes to distance himself from isn't thought to include real talent. The Jewel Box Revue, Brown and the writer believe, serves to counter such an idea. By knowing how the Jewel Box hoped to be regarded, in other words, we also get an understanding of how "female impersonation" was typically perceived.

The Jewel Box Revue would actually feature some of the greatest drag performers of its day, including Jackie Maye, T.C. Jones, Lynne Carter, and many others. They would become staples of New York drag for the next several decades. By the 1960s, a young performer named Ronnie Morales had joined their ranks. Conrado Morales, son of Puerto Rican émigrés to New York City, would become known by stage name Nicholas Dante, cowriter of the wildly successful musical *A Chorus Line*. The show features the character Paul, based on Dante himself, whose monologue includes a story of time spent in the Jewel Box Revue:

"Somebody told me they were looking for male dancers for the Jewel Box Revue… And they said to me: 'You're too short to be a boy, would you like to be a pony?' And I said: 'What's that?' And they said: 'A girl.'"

The experience Paul has at the Jewel Box—later in the monologue, he says "It was really tacky," refers to it as "the asshole of show business," and says the performers had no dignity—has been contested by other former Jewel Boxers. Everything about a Jewel Box performance had to be extremely professional with a high production value because of the tenuous way female impersonation was perceived. Nevertheless, it's noteworthy that the drag troupe is mentioned in one of the most successful musicals of all time.

Significantly, the Jewel Boxers encompassed many ethnicities—Black, white, Native American, and Latine individuals among them—which for at least the first twenty-five years of the troupe's existence would have been highly unusual, as few shows were so integrated at the time. For many years, this also affected where in the country they could perform. Former Jewel Boxer Kurt Mann told Queer Music Heritage in 2010 that he remembered Benner and Brown hiring more Black performers for the troupe's runs at New York's famed Apollo Theatre in Harlem at 253 West 125th Street as well. Beginning in 1959, this was often the revue's biggest, most elaborate show of their touring season.

Prior to that, however, the show enjoyed a run that began December 3, 1958, at the Loew's State Theatre, a movie theater on Broadway. Working there wasn't easy: with three shows every day separated by a film, the cast would be inside sixteen hours at a time, lest they depart made up and get thrown in jail.

The Jewel Box's Apollo runs were also notable, because they were one of the few bookings at the famed theater to run more than two weeks. In between shows at the Apollo, the Jewel Boxers could leave only if they took off their lipstick and wore sunglasses to shield the makeup on their eyes. "Locals knew who we were, I mean, how could they not. We were a bunch of boys, some of us white, in makeup and lashes walking 125th Street," Mann said. "There was a bar on Amsterdam Avenue we would frequent, careful not to get shitfaced before the next show."

The Jewel Box's presence at the Apollo continued until the early 1970s. Protests against it started as the Civil Rights Movement swung into full gear by 1964, but the revue continued to give performances there until 1973, when, according to filmmaker and scholar Michelle Parkerson, as quoted by scholar Elizabeth Drorbaugh, the revue was met with "violent homophobic boycotts staged by black nationalist groups which claimed the Jewel Box undermined the black male and the black family, and promoted homosexuality in the black community."

The end of the Jewel Box was in some ways a decade in the making. "During the 1960s, Doc and Danny tried to shift perception of the troupe by rejecting the term 'female impersonator' for 'feminine impressionists' in their press releases and interviews," writes scholar Bud Coleman. "But the prejudice against gender illusionists was too strong to counter," even as the 1960s ushered in a new wave of liberalism. That and the long-running trend for nightclub revues began to go the way of the wind as television became more and more popular. In 1975, one last Jewel Box show ran in New York. The revue disbanded not long after.

When World War II ended on August 14, 1945, some two million people rushed to Times Square to celebrate, ticker tape streaming, confetti floating through the air. The war's end brought with it an economic boom that allowed New York to displace London (still rebuilding from air raids) as a global epicenter of art, industry, and economy.

Longing for a return to pre-war normalcy, many Americans embraced more traditional gender norms. Interestingly, postwar conservatism also extended into parts of the queer community.

Some gay men believed dressing in women's clothes was a vulgar affront, while others suppressed jealousy. "You've got to figure that we were doing things that these people were not capable of doing or could not do," said drag striptease performer Vickie Lynn, who regularly performed at top New York drag venues, in an interview with drag historian Joe E. Jeffreys. "They could not come out and scream that they were gay. We're talking the 50s and the 40s. I was blatant enough to say what I was doing for a living." Lynn recalled in particular going to a party hosted by two gay men where the mere mention of drag venue the 82 Club made her a pariah. "When we walked in there was like an orgy... The minute you said 82 Club they all dropped dead on you. 'How dare you invite that kind of person here.'" And in the midst of an orgy, no less.

After discovering the joys of community in the war, queer veterans sought more permanent connections in America's cities. The influx of vets, both queer and straight, accelerated an already massive shortage of affordable housing in New York because few new residences were built during the Depression. Some 850,000 New Yorkers served during the war. Coming back, many would sign up for public housing in apartments awaiting construction. But instead of waiting for these new apartments to be built, some relocated to the suburbs. With no money down, a soldier could now purchase a home on Long Island for a mere $58 a month, as opposed to city rents in desirable areas like the East 50s for between $75–$125 a month. These suburban communities, like Levittown, were often for whites only, though the policies slowly changed later; but others were "open housing," which allowed everyone. With the home loan assistance offered by the GI Bill, many white soldiers took the opportunity to purchase more private space; Black veterans received the same opportunity with significantly less frequency. The suburbs became largely whitewashed.

★ ★ ★

To make the city more accessible to commuters, urban planner Robert Moses designed new bridges and expressways. Moses troublingly saw New York as a place to be accessed by cars and people who could afford them rather than by public transportation. His creations ended up offering (mostly white) middle-class New Yorkers, many with families, a way out of the city and into neighboring counties. Between 1940 and 1950, some 340,000 white middle- and working-class residents relocated to the suburbs.

As scholar Chad Heap writes in his book *Slumming: Sexual and Racial Encounters in American Nightlife, 1885-1940*, as white middle- and upper-class suburban communities grew more entrenched, the divide between "straight culture" and "queer culture" grew deeper. What's more, suburban communities were often hostile to Jewish, Italian, Black, and queer people, among others. While some members of these communities established their own suburbs, many also remained in cities. Postwar economic opportunity in New York also inspired a Second Great Migration of Black Americans to the city.

Separate social spheres emerged in New York's nightlife in the 1940s and 1950s. "Uptown meant money, power, breeding, class, chic, high society," John Strausbaugh wrote in *The Village*. "Downtown was hip, arty, scruffy, bohemian." Clubs specializing in gender impersonation were mostly located in what we now call the East and West Villages.

Given all of this, the successful 1945 opening of Stephen Franse and Anna Genovese's Club 181, a gender impersonation club in New York's downtown, might have seemed groundbreaking. But the fact that it was backed by the Mafia didn't hurt. Like the other mob-run Greenwich Village venues that preceded it, straight couples "on safari" at Club 181 made up the majority of its audience. Located at 181 2nd Avenue in the

East Village, the 181 boasted a luxurious spiral staircase that descended to the theater. The walls were painted blue and white, and a plush red carpet lay underfoot. Venues like Club 181 often avoided explicit description of what one might encounter in the evening's floor shows: an advertisement for the club in the May 21, 1946, edition of the *New York Daily News*, for example, mentions nothing at all about the performance content, simply stating that there's "never a dull moment," and "It's Smart to be seen at Club 181." The language in the latter statement hearkens back to the Pansy Craze when gender impersonation was sought out by straight audiences seeking sophistication.

Gender impersonation thrived at the 181 with butch queer women in sparkling tuxedos and their male counterparts in glamorous gowns. Female impersonators, or "female illusionists" as they were known at the time, also stripped, sang, danced, and told bawdy jokes. "Drag queen" was considered either an epithet, derisive slang for a transgender woman, or a designation of amateurishness. "Welcome to the 181," the emcee would offer, "where boy meets girl and no one knows the difference." The club thrived, making over $500,000 annually. "It was illegal and forbidden," historian Lisa Davis said. "And people lined up all around the corner and paid big money to see it." The Mafia, the Genovese family in particular, certainly liked that and kept clubs like these in their repertoire for years.

The luxe venue drew stylish celebrities like Elizabeth Taylor, who, as legend would have it, visited one night with Debbie Reynolds, Eddie Fisher, and her then-husband Mike Todd. Talent was allowed to mingle with the audience, and the performer Titanic, nearly seven feet tall when wearing heels with perfectly arching brows and lushly drawn-on lips, waltzed drunkenly over to the famed Ms. Taylor and asked the actress in her throaty voice if it was indeed her. "Fuck no," Taylor replied. "I'm Natalie Wood."

In the 1940s, the Genovese family opened another club heavily featuring gender impersonators called the Moroccan Village. Inside the windowless venue at 23 West 8th Street, a wooden bar accented with a palm tree mural led the way to round tables cloaked in white cloth, all pointing toward a stage with a piano and a bandstand. An early newspaper listing for the club in 1947, a doubtlessly self-aware advertisement for the venue, touts it as "the Village's Gayest Nightspot."

Historian Lisa Davis lists the crowd as mostly straight—"Wall Street brokers, racketeers, the rich and famous"—but the venue also drew a sizable queer crowd and of course employed a wealth of queer performers. Where the 181 was a top-tier venue, the Moroccan Village was the next level down, but still offered a splashy, professional show every night with upward of thirty performers, a chorus, and of course, a collection of gender impersonators.

The clubs in the Village were always at least slightly dangerous and lawless. For example, on February 25, 1950, when Blackie Dennis was performing at the Moroccan Village, robbers forced him from the stage and wounded several performers. These were the days of all-cash businesses, after all, and it was no secret that the Mafia-run clubs were making bank. But the robbers were caught, and Dennis arrived in drag at the Mercer Street Police Station to give testimony, posing with a smile for photographers, dark hair in boyish curls, wearing an oversized suit and floppy bow tie, rings glinting on fingers.

At any gay bar run by the Mafia, the cops were paid off until the center could no longer hold. "In 1949, [the State Liquor Authority] raided the 181 because the neighbors had been complaining about seeing us go in to work in drag," Buddy Kent remembered in 2006. "An unhealthy atmosphere for their kids, they said." By 1951, Club 181, having been "branded a hangout for perverts of both sexes," according to the *New York Daily*

News, would have its liquor license revoked. In their searches, plainclothes police detectives discovered the following:

Male performers wore gals' clothing and makeup, acted effeminately and gave indecent performances.
Female performers wore men's attire, acted like men—and gave indecent performances.
Waitresses wore tuxedos, had mannish hair-dos and mingled with patrons.
Said the SLA [State Liquor Authority]:
Performers of both sexes did strip-tease dances, punctuated with suggestive bumps and grinds and body contortions, used offensive language and sang degrading songs. In between shows the performers sat at tables with patrons and on occasion made dalliances with persons of their own sex.

The 181 would close in 1952, but Franse and Genovese would soon open another club that would become their most successful to date. They set their sights on a new venue at 82 East 4th Street, which they'd call Club 82.

Opened in 1953, it quickly became a hotspot for a predominantly straight audience either "slumming" or seeking what would then be considered a wild night out. The venue's late-night showtimes—10:30 p.m., 12:30 a.m., and 2:30 a.m.—might seem tame by today's standards, but standing on the corner of East 4th Street and 2nd Avenue at those hours was absolutely unheard of at the time. Lines at the 82 began an hour and a half before showtime, winding around the block and across an entire avenue.

People lining up for these shows would have been well aware of transgender pioneer Christine Jorgensen. Her gender-affirmation surgery dominated international headlines throughout the 1950s. After serving in the army, Jorgensen had transitioned, the most well-known American to do so at that point in history. While Jorgensen was transgender and not a drag performer, audiences were still new to the nuances of gender. In their minds, drag may have fallen into the same category. Drag became a draw for crowds curious about gender bending, posits drag historian Joe E. Jeffreys, though that could bring with it a desire to gawk, heckle, or fetishize.

"You name the age, they came," said former 82 waiter Tommye in a 1993 interview with Jeffreys. Tommye remembered people coming from their high school proms. "The audience would come with their prom dates and then send them home in a cab and come home with us," laughed photographer James Bidgood in 2012, who performed at the 82 as Terry Howe; though, notably, performers could not mingle with the crowd…or at least get caught mingling with the crowd while in full drag on a night when the cops came around (and they did come around, but given their payoffs, usually with ample notice).

The club advertised in hotel and travel pamphlets, attracting tourists as well. "That crowd, they've never seen anything like this," said Jeffreys. "Even on television, all they're seeing is Milton Berle, which is not any type of convincing illusion…the type of drag that was being done in a place like the 82 Club was a complete illusion with a talent connected to it that they had not seen." Still, a majority of queer audiences were few and far between. "I think eventually every gay person living in New York City came to the 82 at one time or another and they would see a show once," Tommye said. "But I mean, a gay person, they want to go to a gay bar and mingle. You couldn't mingle at the 82 Club." Incidentally, a gay bar would have been no place for a female impersonator. The performance style was, as in the 1940s, still frowned upon by many in the queer community, though you could sometimes also see gender impersonators performing at private parties or occasionally at dive bars if you ran with an especially progressive, fearless, or curious crowd.

★ ★ ★

Driven by nascent Cold War anxiety and the related threat of Communism, Americans embraced a culture of conformity, and with it, sexual repression. Homosexuality, like Communism, was considered a threat to the American way of life. By 1948, such rhetoric was regularly used in the public sphere. Guy Gabrielson, the Republican Party's national chairman, sent a newsletter to 7,000 members of his party, stating in no uncertain terms that "Sexual perverts...have infiltrated our Government in recent years," and were "perhaps as dangerous as the actual Communists," according to John D'Emilio's vital 1983 history *Sexual Politics, Sexual Communities: The Making of a Homosexual Minority in the United States, 1940-1970.*

In February 1950, Senator Joseph McCarthy declared 205 Communists had permeated the US State Department. In an era where homosexuality was equated with subversion, a "homosexual panic" emerged in the government. Between January 1, 1951, and March 25, 1952, 126 "perverts," as an article in the *New York Times* shared, lost their jobs in the State Department alone. The article quotes Assistant Secretary of State for Administration Carlisle H. Humelsine, who said, "There is no doubt in our minds that homosexuals are security risks." The number of people fired for being homosexual would more than double to 381 in less than a year, with nearly 300 more firings in the next year and a half. This period in which queer people—either suspected or proven—were released from their jobs in the government became known as the "Lavender Scare."

In 1953, President Dwight D. Eisenhower—who a decade earlier had praised troupes with drag performing in World War II—instituted an executive order that legally gave the government the right to fire individuals accused or found guilty of "sexual perversion." Queer people became national scapegoats in the war against Communism and "un-American activity." Raids on venues even remotely associated with queerness were common. Associating with other queer people in public and in private became a high-risk activity that could end in jail.

In 1953, a mayoral election year, crackdowns increased at gay bars and cruising spots around the city. This would continue throughout the decade, despite New York's 1950 reduction of sodomy from a felony to a misdemeanor, though it could still cost one up to six months in prison. An August 1, 1954, article in the *New York Times* acknowledged the crackdowns, sharing that "High police officials expressed themselves as satisfied that a start had been made toward ridding New York of 'undesirables,' organized bands of youthful hoodlums and perverts." It went on to quote Deputy Chief Inspector James B. Leggett, who said these groups of young people and homosexuals in particular "brought a wave of rape, muggings and other crimes of violence often culminating in murder." Because queer people were considered societal threats, they bore an unrestrained brunt of police violence and injustice that almost always went unchecked. As a result, many queer people often lived double lives. As they had after the war, queer enclaves in big cities like New York continued to draw new inhabitants seeking both solace and access amid rampant restriction. Still, negative cultural narratives around homosexuality reinforced internalized homophobia within the queer community.

In 1951, one of the first gay rights organizations, the Mattachine Society, was founded in Los Angeles. Their message at the time was radical: homosexuals were not inferior or deficient; rather, they were "an oppressed minority," D'Emilio writes, and "they affirmed the uniqueness of gay identity, projected a vision of a homosexual culture with its own positive values, and attempted to transform the shame of being gay into a pride in belonging with its own contribution to the human community." The Mattachines would crusade against homophobia through collective action. But many of the organization's early ideals were rooted in Marxism, which—given the nation's paralyzing fear of Communism at the time—upset many members of the community. The conservative Mattachines would ultimately take control of the society in 1953 and bend its radical viewpoints toward respectability politics.

The new leaders of the Mattachine Society promoted a narrative of assimilation, a "pattern of behavior that is acceptable to society in general and compatible with [the] recognized institutions...of home, church, and state." The Mattachines made it clear in their new mission that they were "not seeking to overthrow or destroy any of society's existing institutions, laws or mores, but to be assimilated as constructive, valuable, and responsible citizens," as if the two were mutually exclusive. Such a viewpoint was not unique to new Mattachine members. Internalized homophobia and occasionally jealousy led some gay people to look down on those who presented flamboyantly. When businessman and World War II veteran Hal Call became the president of the Mattachine Society in 1953, for example, he too called for assimilation.

"We hear from so many homosexuals who urge us to please preach that the flamboyant individual should not show off and shouldn't be obvious so that he receives the ridicule and scorn of his fellow man. Well, that would be a good thing if we could teach all of the homosexuals and eliminate these particular mannerisms which are not regarded as very pleasant," Call said on the 1958 radio program "The Homosexual in Our Society." Call would go on to say, however, that the organization "feel[s] like there is a more basic problem to get at... And that is to educate the public so that its attitude toward these people who are displaying these mannerisms—if this attitude can be changed then the mannerisms will no longer be of any significance, and whether they're recognized or not it won't amount to anything." While Call's message is ultimately one of acceptance, his aversion to flamboyant behavior was reflective of many Mattachine members at the time.

On September 11, 1961, Call appeared in the first ever documentary about homosexuality, which aired on San Francisco's educational television network KQED. In *The Rejected*, a panel grapples with the trials and tribulations of the homosexual in America. "We think the swish, or the queen, represents actually a small minority within the whole, homosexual grouping," Call said on the program. "But to the public, this is a stereotyped view or picture by which all homosexuals are judged, it seems. These people, actually, in most cases are not even liked by the rest of their homosexual brethren because they have perhaps rejected themselves and they feel that society has rejected them."

Within this cultural context, there were comparatively few places to seek ideological or physical refuge as a queer person in 1950s New York. Even in Greenwich Village, describes poet Edward Field, "we were a pitifully small band in exile—homosexuals, blacks, sluts, psychotics, drag queens, radicals of all varieties, artists, ne'er-do-wells."

That was when Club 82 opened. And if you did want to see drag, you could go there. As you walked down the stairs of the glamorous nightspot, you'd see white cloth tables filled with cocktails, steak, and shrimp. Proprietress Anna Genovese would be standing at a podium in a cocktail gown, her dark hair in a tightly wound updo that would earn her the moniker "The Bun." Celebrities like Judy Garland, Sophia Loren, Greta Garbo, Salvador Dalí, and Errol Flynn—who was rumored to have whipped out his penis at the club and played the piano with it—graced the space night after night. Scads of tour buses delivered patrons from out of town.

The nightly shows were elaborate productions put on by at least twenty-five female impersonators. Patrons were dutifully attended to by a mostly female waitstaff attired in male drag, usually black tuxedos. The venue was decorated with fake palm trees, white cloth on its tables. Matchbooks decorated with different performers declared "That was no Lady."

Kitt Russell began as a headliner at Club 82, a veteran of both the Jewel Box Revue and the navy. A trained dancer and singer, he had already performed on Broadway in the cast of the Gertrude Lawrence vehicle *Lady in the Dark*, but his friends urged him to try female impersonation instead. At least that's what he told pinup magazine *Hit!*, which featured him in a September 1948 issue declaring him the next Julian Eltinge.

In actuality, Russell's agent in Cleveland told him to consider becoming a female impersonator. But the evocation of Eltinge's name, in a magazine geared toward men, situated the twenty-two-year-old as a talented artist and not a "sissy." Accordingly, a headshot of a smartly coiffed Russell out of drag accompanies the piece with the caption, "Offstage, Russell is a good-looking, athletic American youth."

Russell would ultimately make New York his home, finding regular work in drag at Stephen Franse and Anna Genovese's Club 181. He was considered "high on the list of talented 'femme mimics'" by Walter Winchell and had become noteworthy enough that juicy tidbits about his life would appear in the newspaper, like this gem from the June 21, 1951, edition of *The Brooklyn Daily Eagle*:

When Kit Russell [sic] walked into a Manhattan restaurant at 4 a.m. today, he was leading a three-foot-long leopard.

Manager Kenneth MacSarin told him to leave, but Russell protested he was "a steady customer. I'm not doing anything wrong."

Police ejected Russell and gave him a summons for not having a leopard license.

★ ★ ★

Almost overnight, Club 82 was wildly successful. Thanks to the Genovese crime family, rival downtown clubs often shuttered quickly, under not-so-mysterious circumstances. The 82 cornered and forcefully held on to the market for gender impersonation in New York, paying off cops and fire inspectors as needed. Anna Genovese, estranged wife of mob boss Vito Genovese, and business partner Stephen Franse made sure of that. Franse had been hired by Vito Genovese, who was at the time residing in Italy, to make sure Anna didn't stray...in her business or in her personal life. Anna would make multiple trips to Italy each year to bring her husband a cut of her profits, sometimes up to $750,000 in cash.

While it would have been deeply unusual if not totally unheard of for a woman to get involved in any kind of mob business, the clubs became a part of Anna's repertoire. She was seeking a community of her own in the Village, living there and working there, because she was queer herself. As documentarian Michael Seligman discusses on *Mob Queens*, his fantastic podcast with screenwriter Jessica Bendinger on the life of Anna Genovese, "If she's bisexual [her relationship to men] kind of makes sense, but if she's a lesbian, maybe, like many gay people then and now, she was simply doing what she had to do to fit in: passing for straight because, in a lot of ways, it was easier." But in doing so, she created space and a job for herself at these Village clubs, as well as for her fellow queers. This included her girlfriend, Jackie, who worked in drag as a waiter named Duke at Club 82. Anna and Duke were together from 1957 until Anna's death in 1982.

Anna was strict, and the club was a well-oiled machine. Performers would get $40 a week, half on Friday, and half on Sunday night, partially so performers didn't spend it all on alcohol over the course of the weekend. They'd also get about $20 per night in tips after mingling and chatting with patrons in the audience. Sometimes they'd pose with guests for souvenir photos that could be purchased from the venue's photographer. Certain performers would also take on sex work or engage clients who wanted to "model," or be dressed up in drag themselves. And if Anna had her favorite performers, she might tip them a little extra cash as well.

Anna required female impersonators to enter in male garb, paint and attire themselves backstage, and take it all off before leaving. If they didn't, not only could they be fired, they could be arrested or murdered in the street. That same 1846 masquerade law was still in effect, but police had begun arresting people if they were not publicly wearing at least three items of the clothing corresponding to their gender assigned at birth. What's interesting is that this was never a formal law. Rather, both the police and the queer community used it as a shorthand: the former for arrests and the latter for understanding how they needed to leave the house safely. If encountering a person in gender nonconforming attire, police would often, in an act of humiliation and violence, check their underwear. Those without three articles of the "correct" attire would be arrested and sent to jail; this later became known as the "three-piece" rule. The same went for men who wore makeup or nail polish in public. For safety, some drag performers rented storage spaces for their costumes and makeup.

Anna may have ruled Club 82 with an iron fist, but she wasn't entirely without a heart. In fact, she helped Club 82 performer Terry Noel obtain a gender affirmation surgery in 1965 and paid for all the necessary medical expenses. Another time, when a Club 82 performer attempted suicide, Anna arrived with her own doctor to fix the wound, and neither reported the incident to medical or legal authorities, thus helping the performer avoid the psych ward—or worse, if discovered to be queer—jail.

Yet Anna was still very much being "watched" by Vito's associate Stephen Franse. After she and Vito grew estranged, Anna attempted to sue for spousal maintenance, and was subpoenaed to testify against Vito in court in March 1953. She obliged, citing Vito's involvement in several nefarious activities. Vito blamed Franse for not maintaining his charge, and in June 1953, at fifty-five years old, Franse was found murdered in his blue DeSoto sedan, strangled and beaten, his key still in the car's ignition. With the placement of the car on the high-traffic corner of East 37th Street and 3rd Avenue, he was meant to be found. As Vito told Anna, "I won't kill you, but I'll make your life so bad you'll want to kill yourself."

The last laugh, however, would be Anna's. In 1959, Vito was convicted of drug trafficking and ultimately died in prison. Club 82 remained Anna's, and stayed open as a gender impersonation venue until 1973, when it became an iconic concert venue for the New York punk scene, and later, in the '90s, the Bijou Cinema, a notorious cruising spot where you might take in a movie, among other things.

Many performers who passed through the 82 would leave their mark on American culture. Among them was the previously mentioned James Bidgood, who performed in drag at the 82 as Terry Howe and also designed costumes, sets, and lighting. Away from work, he photographed muscular, often nude men for physique magazines. These experiences informed his art film *Pink Narcissus*. The film, made in his apartment between 1963 and 1970, features the fantasies of a young male sex worker set against candy-colored scenery and became a foundational work of queer cinema. "*Pink Narcissus* came about because he was a narcissist...who was very...pink," Bidgood quipped in 2006.

Another influential performer from Club 82 was Angie Stardust, who also performed as Mel Michaels. Stardust, a Jewel Box Revue alum, was dubbed "the best Pearl Bailey imitation in town" by Walter Winchell and became the club's first Black drag performer. The number of Black drag performers working at clubs like the 82 in New York was far more limited than that of their white or white-presenting counterparts. Stardust's ascendance in the 1960s in the face of such adversity makes her a powerful icon of drag history. Stardust always knew she was a woman, but when she began to transition, she was fired, despite the club's more liberal stances in the past. But Stardust was not to be deterred—in 1974, she made her way to Europe and continued her path to stardom.

Robin Tyler arrived at Club 82 in the early 1960s. She was arrested at a drag ball in 1962 with forty-four drag queens, despite telling police she was a girl. Without a dime for an attorney, Tyler instead called the *New York Post*. The next day, the headline "Cops Grab 44 in Dresses—And a Real Girl in Slacks" appeared in the paper. "I thought, 'Okay, if I could fool the police, this would be a great way to break into show business. So I will try to get a job at the 82 Club,'" she said. Tyler auditioned successfully for Kitt Russell, but she wanted to impersonate a woman, not a man. "He said, 'Well that's never been done...' I said, 'Well, we'll be the first!'" And so Robin Tyler became a *female* female impersonator at Club 82, singing as Judy Garland. She left after two years and went on to become a successful stand-up comedian and activist: she was the first openly gay woman to have a comedy album and to appear on national television, in a Showtime revue hosted by Phyllis Diller. Tyler and former partner Diane Olson also became the first lesbian plaintiffs to challenge California's gay marriage ban in 2008 and became among the first legally married same-sex couples.

1956 was the year of T.C. Jones.

That year, Jones appeared as femme-cee in the revue *New Faces of 1956* at the Ethel Barrymore Theatre on West 47th Street, impersonating female icons like Katharine Hepburn,

Bette Davis, and Tallulah Bankhead. According to the *New York Daily News*, his performance was "astonishingly skillful" and rife with "sharp wit." Jones's name was never absent from papers for long after that. He would appear on *The Ed Sullivan Show* and *The Steve Allen Plymouth Show* later that year.

Jones was drafted into the navy in 1942 and survived a bout of malaria, which left him bald—a perfect hairline for wigs. Though he'd made a name for himself through the Jewel Box Revue, Jones was a tough pitch for *New Faces*. The show's producer Leonard Sillman was advised against it by his colleagues.

"This would be a suicidal act, they told me," Sillman wrote in his 1959 autobiography *Here Lies Leonard Sillman, Straightened Out at Last*. "I had persisted because I never thought of T.C. as a female impersonator, as a man imitating a woman. T.C. on a stage is simply an extraordinarily talented woman."

For Jones to thrive in this era, he needed to position himself as a high-caliber actor. He would refer to himself as a "male actress" because "female impersonator" didn't feel quite right.

It helped, too, that Jones was married, and had been since 1952, to a woman named Connie Dickson. Dickson owned a chain of beauty parlors in San Francisco, and curated Jones's collection of human hair wigs. She and Jones both designed and altered his clothes and sometimes made garments for each other. They never had children, but when they were living in San Francisco, they did parent nineteen Siamese cats.

Interestingly, Jones was also embraced by the Mattachine Society. A 1956 Christmas issue of the *Mattachine Review* praises his artistry. "The rest of us in America are fortunate that he was chosen as a trailblazer, so to speak, in further breaking down barriers of prejudice which exist for no good reason except that some of us hold the notion that [it] is out of order for a man to play a woman's role on the stage except in situations of absolute burlesque," the author writes. Though Hal Call, a Mattachine Society leader who also wrote for the *Review* under multiple pen names, would speak out against the "swish" and the "queen," the Mattachines found acceptability in female impersonation as long as it was relayed as "artistry"…or as long as it was done by someone who appeared "acceptable" in the public eye…or both.

Jones's ascendance continued. "He's the only female impersonator I ever saw—and I guess it's been 25 years since I saw the last one—who isn't somehow slightly offensive," wrote John Chapman in the *New York Daily News*. In the *New York Times*, writer and curator of the Theatre Collection at the New York Public Library George Freedley offered that "Women smile knowingly at the deftness of Jones's touch while men laugh outright at the [Bert] Savoy-like attack on the theatrical reputation of such actresses and beauties as Tallulah Bankhead and Bette Davis. The roar of applause that greets Mr. Jones when he doffs his wig at the evening's end is a tribute to a performer carrying on a long theatrical tradition." It was perhaps the Savoy-ness of Jones's presentation, the outrageousness and high femininity, that made him nonthreatening to straight men, thereby allowing his success to continue. In fact, Jones was so convincing as a woman that a female audience member once quipped after Jones removed his wig, "Oh, the poor dear, she's bald."

That Jones was able to ascend to such star status at a time when both homosexuality and cross-dressing were held in contempt is anomalous and groundbreaking in its own way. Because of his highly curated public image, however, his stardom helped drag exist outside of the underground. But it would be decades until more people—beyond just those who appeared to be straight in public—would be afforded the same artistic consideration.

When Jones left the Jewel Box Revue for *New Faces*, another of the troupe's brightest drag stars took the helm. Lynne Carter, also a World War II navy veteran, first gained notoriety in Chicago, when famed singer and actress Pearl Bailey waltzed into the strip joint where Carter was performing an impression of her: vocals only, as Carter wore a blond wig when doing the impression and never performed in blackface. Not only did Bailey officially give him her blessing, she also supplied costumes and sheet music, and wrote letters of recommendation on his behalf. Bailey became a friend: twenty-five years after they first met, she *still* referred to the female impressionist as "the road company Pearl." Similarly, Josephine Baker loved Carter's impression of her when she saw him perform in San Francisco. She not only sent him three cabs full of her Balenciaga and Dior gowns to wear onstage but also taught him French pronunciation and supplied him with her own musical arrangements.

Carter wanted to be known to audiences and the press as a "female impressionist," not a "female impersonator." Talking in the late 1970s to *The Emerald City*—which billed itself "the world's first television show for gay men and women" when it aired on Manhattan Cable's Channel J ("Gay on J," as it was known)—he said,

> There's a great difference because a female impersonator just does a woman, doesn't do character work. I do impressions of actual people. In other words, if a guy just puts on a dress and he did a strip, it's just a girl doing a strip, you see, that's just impersonating a female. But I impersonate famous ladies and they are impressions of these ladies and they're satirical, so I do impressions, I don't just do just an impression of just a woman.

It's intriguing to consider the underlying hierarchy in Carter's statement, that in his own perception, a female impressionist is more elevated than a female impersonator. It's not far from the argument made by the Jewel Box Revue, that their work was art, not a gimmick. With Carter's desire to be called a female impressionist, it's almost as if he wanted to be as far removed from "drag queens" and their reputations as he could get. Carter had to find a way to make himself as palatable as possible to earn a living. This was still a time when "drag queen" meant a cross-dressing or transgender sex worker or an amateur who wore drag for fun at balls or other liberal venues; "female impersonator" and "female illusionist" were the phrases used by people who made a living performing onstage in drag, a designation of an internally designed hierarchy.

"I really wasn't harassed, but it was tough," Carter said to *The Emerald City*, reflecting on his earlier club days in the female impersonation genre. "You were subjected to the less than attractive clubs, they were a lower caliber. You were looked on as something, well, like, let's go slumming and let's see this show, this is gonna be skanky. Today, if you have something to offer, you can be presented in a decent room, people come to be entertained, and that's really where it's all at."

On January 20, 1971, Carter became the first gender impersonator to perform on the main stage at Carnegie Hall (Francis Renault had performed in the adjacent chamber, not the main hall). The show, *It's Lynne Carter*, boasted fourteen costume changes and included his famed impressions, comedy, song, and dance, all accompanied by a sixteen-piece orchestra. The one-night-only event was sold out and followed by a standing ovation. Throughout his career, Carter would also perform off-Broadway, on film, and on television, including shows hosted by Merv Griffin, David Frost, and Mike Douglas in the 1970s.

But Jones and Carter were outliers of their era. Homosexuality and drag still faced high levels of policing, and some performers were part of the criminal underground. Stealing, also called mopping, was not uncommon. "Brooks Costumes was the biggest contributor to drag queen-ism in America," former drag queen Claudio Diaz, who performed as Claudia, would say in Michael Seligman's excellent documentary about the 1950s drag scene *P.S. Burn This Letter Please.* Some queens outright mopped items from the store that also supplied costumes to high-end Broadway productions. Stage greats like Gertrude Lawrence and Helen Hayes were fitted for costumes there, and several costumes produced by the organization are now in the archives of the Metropolitan Museum of Art. Claudio remembers his friend Robert Perez, who performed in drag as Josephine Baker, running from the store after mopping a massive white fan made entirely of ostrich feathers.

On September 15, 1958, Josephine and Claudia simply walked through a gate accidentally left unlocked at the original Metropolitan Opera House on Broadway and West 39th Street. They made their way to the wig room on the fourth floor and promptly stole thirty-three wigs, in a variety of hair colors, worth a total of $3,000. They had no trouble leaving as they entered. Josephine and Claudia kept their favorites and offered the others to their fellow queens across the city at a discounted rate. Knowing their quality, the girls snatched them up. But the wigs would soon prove too good to be true.

The theft made the papers, and the FBI arrested nine queens at Club 82. Over three months, seventeen of the thirty-three stolen wigs were recovered. Josephine and Claudia gave the wigs back (or so the authorities thought; they were actually synthetic duplicates, and none were ever the wiser), but they were ultimately imprisoned for breaking and entering, which meant a year at Rikers Island. Claudia kept one wig from Rigoletto for sixty years, she says in *P.S. Burn This Letter Please*: "Part ego, part 'here New York Police, you couldn't find your way out of a closet and two faggots have both outsmarted all of you and you still don't know how we got in.'"

Henry Arango, another drag performer, was working in the wig department at the Met at the time. He'd arrived from Cuba in 1956 at the age of eighteen after performing as a female impersonator in a Havana club called Montmartre, which had permanently closed after a raid that left people dead. Arango lined up an audition for Club 82, got on a plane, nailed it, and joined the cast. He became known by his stage name, Adrian, a nod to his mother Adriana, and was acclaimed at Club 82 for his striptease version of Salome's "Dance of the Seven Veils."

Arango met photographer Avery Willard in the audience of Club 82, where Willard was a regular patron. He would also emerge in the late 1940s as one of the few drag historians of his era. Between the late 1940s and 1960s, Willard photographed the likes of Nat King Cole, Jayne Mansfield, Bea Arthur, Gwen Verdon, and more. He would find himself photographing at Brooks Costumes on more than one occasion. In his spare time, however, Willard photographed and filmed at his studio at 109 East 12th Street, or his home on West 56th Street. In addition to drag, Willard was interested in photographing men in the leather scene and made experimental gay porn.

Willard approached Arango at Club 82, asking to photograph him in drag. Arango agreed, and together they developed *Salome and the Dance of the Seven Veils*, a ten-minute color film of Arango's performance. Willard's capturing of drag on film was ahead of its time, making him among the pioneers chronicling drag and drag history. It is one of the few live drag performances by an actual drag performer captured on film from the era, but there would soon be more.

When Minette published her 1979 book *Recollections of a Part-Time Lady*—rather, when friend Ray Dobbins photocopied and disseminated it to her friends—she was fifty-one years old. She had been performing in drag for thirty-five years.

Minette was born on the Bowery to French parents. Her name, she writes in *Recollections*, "means many things: 'pussy-cat,' 'pussy,' or 'suck me.' It isn't too easy to translate and it's not a word used in polite company I've heard."

Minette, who went by female pronouns and dressed in drag on and offstage for most of her life, dropped out of grade school. "The principal decided I was 'too nervous,' a code word for gay at that time. I was sent to a psychiatrist," she wrote. "At the end of our meetings together she said to me that I would one day become a female impersonator." The psychiatrist was right: by age sixteen, in 1943, Minette began performing in drag. As a young person in show business, Minette was able to blossom and begin to find herself. "I felt so liberated finally working in drag," she wrote. "To be me, to be feminine. It felt gorgeous."

Minette settled in New York in 1949, becoming a sex worker in Times Square in addition to performing in drag in dive bars around the city, including Sammy's Bowery Follies, which *Life* magazine referred to as an "alcoholic haven for the derelicts whose presence has made the Bowery a universal symbol of poverty and futility."

Minette lived in Greenwich Village for two months as a woman named Rose Revere because she ran out of male garb and found it easier to get johns when in drag. She later moved to Paddy's Market, which is now known as part of Hell's Kitchen. She rented an apartment for $10 a month, making her way past herds of street vendors.

When Minette wasn't singing—she also played piano and could accompany herself in small club rooms—she also worked as a costume seamstress or "stitch bitch," as she'd say, to make extra money. In 1955, while sewing costumes at The Actor's

Playhouse, she met Avery Willard. They became friendly, and Willard invited her to a Halloween party at his home where guests all dressed in drag, Minette included. In a 1920s cocktail gown covered in black beads, her realness so stunned the host that he immediately asked to photograph her. She obliged, cementing her status as his muse. She even gave Willard the name for his production company: Ava-Graph.

Minette would also become a regular Ava-Graph player, appearing in ten films between 1957 and 1967. But Willard was very selective about who he'd show his films to, only assembling audiences of up to thirty-five people for screenings in his apartment or a familiar bar. This selectivity may have been artistic apprehension, but it certainly also could have stemmed from a fear of police raids—this did happen one time in 1958. Minette was in drag selling tickets at one of Willard's screenings and was placed in jail for two days. But she'd be out again soon, back on the road, in clubs, and making films with Ava-Graph.

Ava-Graph's early films starred female impersonators alongside actors out of drag until Willard transitioned his work to more erotic imagery. Or, as Minette writes, "After a while, Avery started filming the leather boys so he could no longer get me to work for him." But she would remain influential in queer theater and drag history throughout the 1960s and 1970s.

While it wasn't her ultimate goal, another artist working in New York at the time would become a chronicler of drag history. Diane Arbus, today known for her transgressive portraiture, began photographing drag from the audience of Club 82 in 1958. Arbus's work was often intimate. By establishing real connections with her subjects, she made them comfortable in front of her camera. For her day job as a photographer, she was photographing women in various stages of beautification for fashion magazines. But a perpetual interest in outsiders continually drew her back to Club 82. Her 1961 photo "Two Female Impersonators Backstage, N.Y.C." remains one of her most iconic images from this period. In it, two performers, Terry Noel and Ronnie Morales, lean against one another, half in drag and mid-laugh. In 2019, it sold at auction for $32,500. As she once said, "I really believe there are things nobody would see if I didn't photograph them." Later on, iconic photographers like Peter Hujar and Nan Goldin followed in her footsteps, while Chantal Regnault and Gerard H. Gaskin, among others, would immortalize the uptown ball scene.

Though Club 82 drew a line between "female illusionist" and "drag queen," mostly to appease straight audiences, Caffè Cino created room for performers to live the fullest expression of their identities.

In 1947, at sixteen years old, Joe Cino abandoned his native Buffalo, New York, for New York City to become an actor and a dancer. But by 1958, he had given up. After ten years of classes and odd jobs, it was time for something new. "He worked for 10 years and saved every cent, because he had this dream of having a little art gallery and a little Italian café," friend and artist Magie Dominic said in 2015. "He wanted to show art. That was it. That was his dream."

In December of that year, Cino—who was openly gay, an exceptional concept at the time—and a former boyfriend opened a space at 31 Cornelia Street in Greenwich Village. The Village was still gay and bohemian then, and the venue, called Caffè Cino, fit in nicely among the beat bookstores, art galleries, and (still illegal) gay bars in the area. So nicely, in fact, that within its walls, queer theater—of which drag became a part—would continue to blossom.

By the time the venue opened some thirty years after the Pansy Craze, drag had become inextricably tied to the queer community. In creating a space for queer art, Joe Cino would alter the course of modern theater. "This [the Caffé Cino] is the beginning! This is it!" said experimental theater artist John Vaccaro later. "The major things done in New York were done there, and nowhere else. I don't give a shit what anybody else says. They're lying." Cino hadn't intended to make history, necessarily: he just wanted a place where he and his friends could share art.

Cino's giant, hand-painted red-and-yellow sign advertised espresso, but the machine was perpetually broken; he kept pots of coffee nearby to keep up the illusion. Patrons filled small wooden tables nestled under balloons, tinsel, and handmade mobiles dangling from the ceiling. The walls were covered with art by friends and pictures of gorgeous celebrities, and a jukebox spun opera classics. With the venue's one-dollar minimum, you got coffee, a pastry, and a show.

Cino originally intended the coffee shop—merely eighteen by thirty feet with a small stage—to feature poetry readings, small dance performances, and tarot. But in 1959 he invited performers to move tables and chairs out of the way to stage (unlicensed) works. His only rule for plays was that they had to be thirty minutes or shorter because the audience's chairs were uncomfortable. That, and he'd only consider working with people whose astrological signs he liked ("Cancer…was supreme," said Magie Dominic). Electricity for lighting was stolen from the city, rigged from a streetlamp outside the club by Cino's new boyfriend, John Torrey.

The venue got so packed that patrons grabbed seats wherever they could, even on top of the cigarette machine. In full violation of fire codes, and with no theater, liquor, or cabaret license to speak of, Cino learned how to pay off the cops and fire inspectors (with money, sex, or both), as well as the Mafia. He also learned how to throw snitches off the scent with deceptive or purposely vague advertising—if you knew the code, you knew where to be and when. It didn't always work, and raids were frequent, but the venue somehow managed to stay open for ten years, becoming a favorite haunt of Tennessee Williams and Andy Warhol. Before each show, the affable Cino, portly with dark curly hair, took the stage in a cape. With a swirl of the garment, he would announce, "It's magic time!"

By 1960, theater artists began to produce work on the Caffè Cino stage, thereby birthing what would become known as off-off-Broadway theater, a space to challenge existing ideas of what theater was and could be. Caffè Cino anticipated re-nowned venues like La MaMa Experimental Theatre Club by unapologetically embracing queer themes and drag as a part of queer storytelling.

One play in particular put drag in the spotlight. *The Madness of Lady Bright* by gay playwright Lanford Wilson was born of a question: "Well, can we write a play about a screaming queen going crazy alone in her room one afternoon?" The answer, it turned out, was absolutely yes. Wilson found a typewriter and banged out the play in just a few days. Staged for the first time at the venue on May 18, 1964, *The Madness of Lady Bright* fol-lows drag queen Leslie Bright as she reflects on aging, mortal-ity, and the fleeting nature of relationships. Wrapped up in her contemplation is a universal struggle with both self-loathing and loneliness alongside the desire for beauty and self-acceptance. In her monologue, for example, she says to herself: "You. Are a faggot.... You're built like a disaster. But, whatever your dreams, there is just no possibility whatever of you ever becoming, say, a lumberjack. You know?"

Lady Bright became one of the longest running shows at Caffè Cino, with over 200 performances in three years. Its success led to an official off-Broadway run that more firmly established Caffè Cino as a credible venue for new work. Actor Neil Flanagan, who originated the role of Bright at Caffé Cino, would go on to win an Obie Award, or Off-Broadway Theatre Award, for his performance. Lanford Wilson would ultimately win a Pulitzer Prize for Drama in 1980 for his play *Talley's Folly*.

Indeed, many of the playwrights who moved through the Caffé were queer and poised for success—among them Gerome Ragni, later of *Hair* fame, and Tom Eyen, who'd go on to win a Tony for the book and lyrics for *Dreamgirls*. In their work grew a space for queer theater onstage: many stories were about gay men living in the world, just as mainstream theater featured heterosexual stories. Lanford Wilson remembered "the incredible freedom of being able to be yourself in that place... You could do just anything and it made me want to experiment like crazy." They had a wealth of talented young performers to draw on, too: performers like Fred Willard, Harvey Keitel, Barry Manilow, and Al Pacino would all cross the Cino's stage; at eighteen, a young actress named Bernadette Peters would also star in the Cino's original musical production of *Dames at Sea*.

At Caffé Cino, freedom reigned in all of its forms, until everything came quite literally burning down. A fire devastated the venue in 1965, and there was a fundraiser to repair it, but this was the beginning of the end. Upon the accidental death of his boyfriend, John Torrey, in 1967, Cino attempted to take his own life in the café itself, leaving his blood on the floor. He was taken to a hospital but ultimately died three days later. The venue struggled on until 1968, when it closed, but it is still designated by a plaque on Cornelia Street. In the decade it existed, the Cino set the stage for the presence of drag-infused queer theater across New York and beyond.

While the 1950s were paved with conservatism and conformity, a spirit of rebellion was brewing. In the next decade, drag would flourish in queer spaces for queer audiences, eventually moving away from the solely straight crowds that had populated its audiences for decades. The changes were incremental at first, but gained traction against the backdrop of liberation.

5

1960–1969

While the 1950s were on the whole conservative, currents of rebellion ran underneath. Queer liberation efforts picked up more steam during the more progressive 1960s, inspired by civil rights activism in the South. Both movements sought equality and integration into society. As the Vietnam War escalated, antiwar protests swept the nation. Martin Luther King, Jr., decried the war in March 1967, and over 100,000 people protested it in front of the Lincoln Memorial in Washington, DC. Peace demonstrations were regular occurrences, and many people didn't understand why the war was being waged at all. Vietnam also became a queer liberation issue: some queer civil rights groups across the country protested for the ability to serve openly in the military, seeing denial of service as another method of disenfranchisement as opposed to a support for the war. By the end of the 1950s, many queer people who, with other disenfranchised minorities, had borne the brunt of that decade's conservatism, had tired of conforming. This was also true for drag. Performers grew increasingly less interested in convention in terms of gender, race, performance, or aesthetic. More and more, these artists wanted to take up space, to live and/or perform in the world as they pleased. And as restrictions were either loosened or torn down, drag's reach, while still niche, expanded to larger audiences through artists, entrepreneurs, and activists who made names for themselves during the decade. In doing so, these individuals would also knock down walls not just for drag, but for the entire queer community.

For female impersonators in the style of Club 82 and the Jewel Box Revue, the nostalgia of Hollywood glamour persisted into the 1960s. And while performers continued to mystify straight audiences, this aesthetic became dated. These queens, still bedecked in sparkles, didn't embody the significantly more toned-down, casual look that was becoming popular in fashion and culture. The Warhol scene, for example, was more mod, minimalist, and rock and roll–inspired. This look, alongside the development of the natural hippie aesthetic, was a challenge for gender impersonators to achieve, especially when towering wigs and pancake makeup provided the illusion of femininity in the first place.

Drag was also affected by evolving nightlife trends. The floor show, the cocktail, and the steak dinner waned in popularity as patrons took to bars and discos. Audiences at once-packed venues like Club 82 shrank, and some venues eschewed live bands for more cost-effective music options. This led to the incorporation of lip-synching, now a tried-and-true part of the profession. It was initially met with skepticism if not downright contempt, especially by those who had built their careers on their talents for live singing, dancing, stripping, or comedy. Suddenly, for better or for worse, the field had become more democratic, the barrier to entry lowered: you could perform in drag as long as you had something to lip-synch to, which would later become an art in its own right. This also meant that venues once incapable of hosting vast musical setups could now show drag. But established drag doyennes who considered themselves artists felt their work was becoming devalued. If anyone could do drag anywhere, how would that change the nature of the form moving forward?

"A drag queen is an amateur—a female impersonator is a professional," Tish said. Joseph Touchette, Tish to his friends, performed in drag in the 1950s and 1960s. His viewpoint was common among performers at the time and decades into the future. Even in the 1990s, the legendary female impersonator Charles Pierce, also based in New York, discussed the phrase. "Up to the late eighties, the performers who worked the clubs and theatres in drag…were never what you would call drag queens. Then, a drag queen was not an entertainer but someone who had a job other than showbiz, who came home from work, got himself up in some outlandish costume or frock and went sailing off to a party or a drag ball. There is an odd line there, I know, but I will always draw it."

Overall, the 1960s saw growing entrepreneurship among drag performers, who would put together revues, publications, or like Tish, their own troupes. For his French Box Revue, Tish wore a blond flip wig and pale pink lipstick overdrawn with dark liner. The French Box Revue performed six nights a week at Crazy Horse, a coffee house up a flight of stairs at 149 Bleecker Street, today the club Terra Blues.

"No prudes will like it," a 1965 edition of *Female Mimics* magazine said of the Crazy Horse. "Well, go soon and see for yourself!" Presented as a sister venue (even though it wasn't) to Paris's famed high-end Crazy Horse known for its luxurious and scintillating showgirl stripteases, the club featured female impersonators who stripped, sang, danced, and did comedy.

Like Caffé Cino, the Crazy Horse billed itself as a café rather tenuously: people would regularly show up with alcohol in brown paper bags, and managers frequently dealt with police fines. But business went on as usual. The experience of the Crazy Horse was not unlike what you'd see in a gay bar's backroom today. Despite the Crazy Horse's potential for violence—one night in 1965, for example, a fight broke out, leaving five injured and three in the hospital—it found a healthy patronage, often peddling queerness to straight audiences. "Any woman can strip—there's no talent in just showing off a body," venue manager Lew Manx said in the magazine *Female Mimics*. "But when a man can create the illusion that he's a woman *even* when he's stripping, he really has talent." Venues like this wouldn't have openly advertised to queer people, whose existence in the city was still persona non grata—rather, bars and venues catering specifically to queer crowds often grew patronage by word of mouth. To get a straight crowd, you had to pose a certain amount of sophistication, whether or not you actually had it, as well as artistry and novelty—in other words, some fifty years later, the Eltinge principle endured.

Still, the Crazy Horse had stars of its own, including Pudgy Roberts. Roberts was known for his comedic striptease numbers but later became a self-proclaimed, outspoken historian of drag, though a troublesome one. His makeup was purposely clownish and grotesque, black eyebrows drawn to his hairline, mouth an overdrawn smear, eyelashes dark, thick, and high as if made of construction paper. During his striptease, he peeled off his overwrought tulle, rhinestone, and feather constructions into ratty fishnets and droopy tassels. It was not the way drag was done at the time, and it made him an anomaly. "I knew I could do a pretty glamorous job as a pretty stripper," he wrote in 1973, "but I feel that perhaps I could do it all better comically." Roberts would also perform successfully in burlesque. He had even trained his husband, Johnny, to do his act on nights with multiple bookings. "And it was a fabulous act," Minette told *Ladylike* magazine in 1999. "Funniest comedy strip I've ever seen in my life." It was a parody of drag, itself a parody of femininity.

"When I'm billed as 'The World's Funniest Stripper' it's pure clown pantomime, strictly for laughs," Roberts said in a 1968 *Female Mimics* interview. "When I work straight—noncomedy, that is—my audiences know that I'm not actually a girl, but merely one who builds an illusion of femininity."

This particular interview is riddled with transphobia, and at one point the author refers to transitioning as "a tragic farce." It's unfortunate that the magazine made statements like these, but these views were also a reflection of the era. Many in the female impersonation field resented fellow performers who took hormones, had surgeries, or transitioned in general, and this challenging perspective would endure for decades.

Roberts worked on some of the first periodicals for drag performers, like *Female Impersonators*, which published its first issue in winter 1969 after rebranding from *Female Mimic* (singular). It's worth noting that *Female Mimics* (plural) was a separate magazine, started in 1963, which ran under a few different names (*New Female Mimics, Female Mimics International*) and displayed increasing degrees of fetishism into the 1990s.

Meant for professionals in the field but aware of its potential fetish appeal, *Female Mimic* came with a warning label: "Sale to Minors Forbidden." Roberts, as the magazine's editor, wrote in his first editor's letter that he was "more than pleased to take over the reins of the leading publication dedicated to the art of female impersonation...with both a sense of happiness and joy at the chance to put out a publication that will fulfill the needs of our people." The publication included service-oriented content aimed at moving the art of female impersonation forward. The cover of the first *Female Impersonators* issue, for example, features "How to Dress as a Female Impersonator" and "Album of Impersonator Bests!" as well as the promise of images from a drag pageant on Fire Island. In 1967, Roberts created the *Female Impersonator's Handbook*, offering over 120 pages of tips, tricks, and secrets to success in the field. It includes everything from posture to punctuality, fabric choice to face shape, hair removal to hand positions, and more. Roberts urges readers to consider the art of female impersonation as a whole as they develop their acts and careers. "Hard work and constant striving for perfection is a trait that all the 'Greats' had in common, plus good wardrobe and a particular outstanding talent. These are things to keep in mind…" he wrote. "For not only do you decide what your fate will be, but you also decide what the fate of all impersonation will be." It was as much a call for representation as it was for respectability in the form.

In 1973, Roberts would also put out a magazine-length book called *The Great Female Mimics*, billing himself, ego ever-present, as "the world's leading authority on cross-dressing." Roberts would highlight some of the great "female mimics" of his time, including Frankie Quinn, Arthur Blake, and more. In the first few pages, always an entrepreneur, Roberts includes mail-order forms for his previous handbook and for Avery Willard's book *Female Impersonation*. By this time, Roberts's views of transgender performers had somewhat evolved, and the magazine would also include articles related to individuals of this experience.

But Roberts and Tish were not the only entrepreneurial spirits building drag's presence in New York. By 1962, Day Zee Dee would start an event of her own that would soon become a staple of New York drag nightlife for the next thirteen years.

By day, Day Zee Dee was a hairdresser named Lennie. As of this writing, Lennie lives with his family, and they do not approve of his past in drag, so he is referred to by his first name only. He was also unavailable to speak about his time in drag for this reason, but was previously interviewed by documentarian Michael Seligman for the film *P.S. Burn This Letter Please*, and Seligman was kind enough to share some of Lennie's story.

The very first time Lennie did drag was in 1954, when he served in the navy during the Korean War. "The other sailors had thought a real woman had gotten onto the ship, and so he had to get an escort back to his dressing room because these horny sailors were like, 'Oh my god, I have to go meet this beautiful, beautiful woman,'" says Seligman. Back in New York, Lennie did drag again on Halloween as a young man in his twenties. Halloween was one of the few nights when you could wear attire of the opposite sex and avoid police confrontation. "[Drag] happened in such volume that the cops couldn't really do anything about it so they would turn a blind eye on Halloween and New Year's Eve and, of course, around the drag balls," Seligman said. "It would be hard for the cops to arrest thousands of people at one time." Lennie, however, was a little more brazen. He and Tish would go out in drag for just a regular night out and pass as women, something that could have gotten them arrested or even killed if anyone found out their sex; indeed, they were among the comparatively few to do so. But because they mostly went out in the Village, where they were well-known in the nightlife scene, Tish believed, they'd rarely face trouble even if people knew they were in drag. As Tish told historian John Strausbaugh, "You are never going to be a lady if you weren't a gentleman first."

While Phil Black's was one of the most famous drag balls in New York, more and more would pop up throughout the next two decades: Frankie Quinn's Paris in the Spring ball at the Manhattan Center, the Art Students League's annual themed Dream Ball, Lee Brewster's Mardi Gras Ball, and many others. Lennie never performed in drag—he is what we'd today call a "look queen," Seligman says—but realizing the popularity of the drag ball, he wondered if maybe he couldn't get in on the action himself as an entrepreneur. In the early 1960s, he and a friend secured a 39,000-square-foot space in Brooklyn called Cotillion Terrace and decided to throw a drag ball on Thanksgiving Eve. They printed 1,600 tickets and thought if they sold 600 or 700 they'd have done well. But instead they sold out. "Day Zee Dee's Thanksgiving Eve Costume Ball" became a hit.

"Anybody who was anybody in the drag world went," Terry Noel said later.

Tish was the evening's emcee. Performers both amateur and professional, cis and transgender, competed at midnight for prizes of best hair, gowns, Queen of the Ball, and more, parading across the runway stage like the royalty they were, the audience cheering them on. "You walk up, you smile, you bow, you twist, you bend over, you give them what they want. It's called hip, lips and fingertips. They love it," former drag queen Dario Modon remembered in 2007. Terry Noel herself was a winner one year. On film and in images from the balls, queens are dripping in sparkles, their hair towering above them, chandelier earrings twinkling, long gowns at their feet, fringe at their hips, feathers and flowers and tiaras in their hair. It was a "once-a-year funfest freak-out," according to a 1975 edition of *Female Mimics* magazine, "a throwback to the days when only women wore make-up and gowns…and as such, it is a fantastic success."

Charity Charles loved getting into drag on special occasions like Day Zee Dee's ball. She had been doing drag in Boston before she moved to New York in 1964, and actively referred to herself as a drag queen. In the 1960s, she didn't want to do drag full-time and considered herself an amateur even though she did perform from time to time—once in the chorus of the 82—and she was the second ever Miss Fire Island in 1967, among other accolades (she appeared in the second issue of *Female Impersonators* in 1969 as well). But she looked forward to Day Zee Dee's every year.

I loved going to Daisy Dee's balls! I mean that was a special thing. You know, I had a group of friends who would all get in drag. We would get a hotel room, like four of us in a room, and we're all trying to put our makeup on, getting in gowns, bumping into each other, but it was always so much fun because we all loved each other and we always had escorts, so sometimes the escorts were in the room, too. It would be very busy. And we'd be zipping each other into our gowns and fixing each other's hair and it was so giddy and fun. But when we made our entrance, honey, we made sure we made fabulous entrances. We always made sure we would go in when the ball was already going. Society always arrives late. So we would be noticed. We would always walk in and be noticed. And of course, you know, drag queens, some can be sweet but some can give you this look when you walk in there like, "Who the fuck is this bitch? Who does she think she is?" Or they know who you are, and they go, "Oh, there she is." But yeah, we always made a splash there and it was exciting. It was a very exciting thing to go to. It was just something if you were into New York and you knew what you were doing, you had to be there. If you were part of New York gay society, you were at that ball. It was very important.

Charity did drag on and off throughout her career, but went full-time in the 1990s, becoming a well-known mainstay on Fire Island at venues like the Ice Palace and Cherry's, and later at Lips's Fort Lauderdale, Florida, location.

As they had been for decades, the balls were a space for members of the queer community to gather for themselves, not to perform for straight people as they would at places like Club 82, and Lennie's ball was no exception. Straight people still came to get a sense of the styles, but this time they were in the minority. "You had gay people performing for each other and trying to impress each other, and trying to outdo each other, and it was more of a family affair, if you will," Seligman says. Tickets regularly sold out. In fact, one year the street in front of the venue had to be closed down because so many people who couldn't get tickets had gathered to see the arrivals, cheering and applauding the way they might at an awards show red carpet. Permits still had to be acquired to throw the ball because otherwise being out in drag was a crime; incidentally, with the permits came police protection of the event. However, there were still some payoffs and mafioso involved.

While judges were typically Broadway-related writers, producers, or actors, one year Lennie thought it would be fun to have some of the mafiosos' wives be the judges. What he didn't expect, though, was that they'd throw the event in favor of all of his friends—they collectively figured that's why Lennie had asked them to judge and made the calls without a discussion. He was mortified, and all the categories had to be rejudged.

What's interesting is that—as with the other drag balls like Harlem's Hamilton Lodge Drag Balls or Phil Black's ball—even in a time when these events (without permits) were illegal, a massive crowd still gathered. Day Zee Dee's was considered one of the more high-end, well-respected drag balls of the year. All of the balls at that time were still mostly segregated, however, though it seems more by circumstance than preference. Everyone was welcome, but Day Zee Dee's ball in South Brooklyn drew mostly white queens, and Phil Black's ball in Harlem drew mostly Black queens. Phil Black's ball in particular was the height of drag society, and getting an invite as a white queen was considered a high honor, Charity Charles said. She remembered queens there had more pizzazz, and she cherished her invitation to be among them.

At the same time, traveling drag revues, which still performed to predominantly straight audiences, continued to expand the geographic reach of the form. Besides the French Box Revue, another noteworthy touring troupe was the Pearl Box Revue. One artist, Dorian Corey, performed with a live boa constrictor. The troupe would wind through the Northeast for several years. Jaye Joyce was the group's leader, daughter Dale Sharpe Jenkins recalled in a 2017 letter to website Queer Music Heritage. Joyce's mom served as a den mother of sorts "at a time when drag queens were seen as a subset of strange and somehow deformed individuals without much value to society," Jenkins wrote. "Many of my father's associates and friends had been thrown aside and disowned by family."

The Pearl Box Revue recorded a spoken word and comedy album called *Call Me MISSter*, which covers topics ranging from buttholes to sex work to bullying to transitioning. At times there's a sense of the queens' internalized homophobia as they discuss their own queerness. But there are also calls for a more inclusive path toward gay acceptance.

The fight for queer liberation was well underway at the beginning of the 1960s, and it would escalate alongside the Civil Rights movement. Members of homophile groups like the Mattachines, in their more conservative iteration, as well as individual queer activists adopted protest tactics like picketing, sit-ins, and more from the Black freedom movement taking hold in the South. In New York, such activism was distinctly quieter in the early 1960s than it was on the West Coast, but picked up around the time of the 1964 World's Fair.

Mayor Robert F. Wagner, Jr. had been elected in 1954, and though he was a decidedly liberal Democrat for the time—he quit the chic New York Athletic Club in 1962 because it refused to allow Black or Jewish people—he began a campaign prior to the World's Fair to shutter gay bars across the city. Really, any bars found catering to a queer clientele would soon have their liquor licenses rescinded. The 1964 fair, like the one twenty-five years earlier, would cost some $1 billion and was expected to draw 250,000 attendees on opening day alone. The mayor felt he had to make the city as hospitable as possible to outsiders. He didn't feel gay bars were part of that equation, and initiated regular shutdowns and (even more) raids to rid the city of queer life. Though it perhaps goes without saying, it was still illegal to appear in drag in the street, and it was rarely, if ever, allowed in bars.

Some queer activists in New York thought their situation might improve in 1965 with the election of liberal Republican mayor John Lindsay, but they were only partially right. Shortly after his election in November 1965, Lindsay, like his predecessors, targeted queer spaces again, raiding bars and cruising areas. Entrapment was still in use at this point, though the Mattachines fought to end the practice by 1966. Other forms of police harassment would unfortunately continue, and it could be dangerous to walk down the street alone for fear of an unprovoked police attack.

On April 21, 1966, Mattachines staged a "sip-in," inspired by the Black freedom movement's sit-ins, to protest the New York State Liquor Authority's laws banning "disorderly conduct" in bars. "Intimate encounters between two men," writer Thaddeus Morgan shared, were part of this, though many bars declined to serve queer people in general.

The State Liquor Authority still wouldn't admit that laws banning "disorderly conduct" shunned queer people, so Mattachines Dick Leitsch, Randy Wicker, John Timmons, and Craig Rodwell took it upon themselves to prove it. They called press to accompany them and watch what happened when they sat down at a bar and told the bartenders they were gay. It took five tries: at the last venue, Julius at 159 W 10th Street, they were denied. It was, Wicker would say later, a way to entrap governing bodies like the police and the SLA that had been entrapping gay men for decades. The SLA still rejected the premise of discrimination. But by then the Mattachines had reported the incident to the New York City Commission on Human Rights, who called foul—there was indeed discrimination involved—and the case went to court in 1967, where a ruling stated "the SLA needed 'substantial evidence' of indecent behavior to close a bar and not just same-sex kissing or touching," according to the Greenwich Village Society for Historical Preservation. This ruling made it easier to own a bar of any kind, especially a gay bar. The mob and its exploitative practices in gay bar owner-ship would be on their way out as well.

This era also marked the beginning of fearless queer repre-sentation onstage. A radical gender politic matched the radical social politics of the time—the ideals of antiwar, pro–civil un-rest, feminism, Black Power, gay liberation, and more trick-led into drag, pushing it into ideological spaces where it hadn't previously existed, or been allowed to exist. According to per-formance icon Penny Arcade, drag's goal then "was to be out-landish, which is very different from the goal to pass." Many found the possibility of being outrageous, of taking up space, a tantalizing prospect.

Rene Rivera's career started with another tantalizing pros-pect: meeting artist and filmmaker Jack Smith. Smith worked as a photographer out of his Hyperbole Photography Studio near Cooper Square. "The studio was less an opportunity to take commercial photos, than a chance at incorporating passersby into Smith's elaborately staged, exotic and erotic photo shoots," wrote historian Marc Siegel.

Rivera immediately wanted to work with Smith and shortly after asked to sit for the photographer in drag, which was his first time wearing women's clothes for any purpose. The Puerto Rico–born Rivera had moved with his family to New York City at eight or nine years old, in the mid-1940s, and lived in East Harlem, El Barrio, on East 111th Street. Rivera was a devout Roman Catholic and maintained his practice throughout his life. But when he went downtown, he could be anything he wanted.

Rivera and Smith became lovers and creative partners. In 1962, Smith cast Rivera in his film *Flaming Creatures*. On the tar-paper roof of what was then the Windsor Theatre on the Lower East Side, they filmed in the summer swelter. Among the cast members were denizens of the downtown and under-ground artistic worlds, including Judith Malina, cofounder of experimental theater company The Living Theatre. The often inflammatory and later paranoid Smith would insist, "you can't get artistic results with 'Normals.'" Artist Tony Conrad, who also composed the film's score, helped lug set dressing from their apartment on East 9th Street; he remembered, "there were lots of weird substances being consumed and strange people arriving on the scene. And boy, was I surprised when it turned out that people took three hours to put on their makeup; I was very [sic] more surprised when people took several more hours to put on their costumes."

In accordance with Smith's interests in transformation, drag appears throughout the film, with many performers donning wigs, gowns, and makeup. The look of the drag is deliberately, unapologetically rough and ready. It was by no means intended to make its wearers "pass," in direct opposition to much of the drag happening in the city at the time, especially at venues geared toward straight audiences.

On a budget of $300, with film pilfered from a store called the Camera Barn, Smith made the forty-five-minute movie. He was assisted by the playwright Ronald Tavel, of Caffé Cino, who at one point tossed plaster onto the cast to invoke an earthquake. Rene Rivera appears, credited as Dolores Flores, "The Spanish Lady." At the end of the film, he is a whirl of black fabric and fans, with a black mantilla, a flower in his teeth, a twinkle in his eye.

Flaming Creatures is a spasmodic cacophony of gender-bending imagery: people in drag applying lipstick to hungry mouths offset by an occasional penis; a collective howl into the sexual ether; a succulent, vampiric drag seduction all heavily inspired by classic Hollywood, the films of Josef von Sternberg, the non-conformity of the artistic and sexual underground in 1960s New York. The non-narrative film, though at once mind-boggling and mind-expanding, was originally intended to make people laugh. "I started making a comedy about everything that I thought was funny. And it was funny. The first audiences were laughing from the beginning all the way through," Smith told *Semiotext(e)* in 1978.

Flaming Creatures officially premiered at the Bleecker Street Cinema at midnight on April 29, 1963. But the film soon got caught up in a tornado of censorship lawsuits that eventually wound up at the United States Supreme Court. A March 1964 screening held by downtown film community arbiter Jonas Mekas was raided, the film seized by police for obscenity. The film then became even more of a sensation, making its way into an op-ed by Susan Sontag in the April 13, 1964, edition of magazine *The Nation*, her first for the publication. "The only thing to be regretted about the close-ups of limp penises and bouncing breasts, the shots of masturbation and oral sexuality in Jack Smith's *Flaming Creatures* is that it makes it hard simply to talk about this remarkable and beautiful film, one has to *defend* it," Sontag wrote. "But even if *Flaming Creatures* were pornographic, that is, if it did…have the power to excite sexually, I would argue that this is a power of art for which it is shameful to apologize." Her thoughts on *Flaming Creatures* would also incite one of her most well-known works, "Notes on Camp," published later that year.

People of the State of New York v. Kenneth Jacobs, Florence Karpf and Jonas Mekas was tried in the New York State Court beginning on June 2, 1964. Some of the greatest minds of the intellectual and artistic worlds were called upon to speak for the film's artistic validity—Allen Ginsberg, Sontag, and director Shirley Clarke among them—but to no avail. Mekas and projectionist Ken Jacobs ultimately did time in the workhouse (though their sentences were later suspended). They filed an appeal with the Supreme Court in 1966, which was dismissed as "moot because appellants' suspended sentences had lapsed and because the trial court properly found *Flaming Creatures* obscene." This, plus the film's later ban in four countries and twenty-two states, only led to a surge in popularity.

Smith never intended for *Flaming Creatures* to become so intellectualized: "then *that writing* started—and it became a sex thing. It turned the movie into a magazine sex issue... Then it fertilized Hollywood. Wonderful. When they got through licking their chops over the movie there was no more laughter. There was dead silence in the auditorium," he told *Semiotext(e)*. Even so, *Flaming Creatures* influenced creators like Andy Warhol, John Vaccaro, Nan Goldin, Cindy Sherman, and John Waters. It remains an iconic work, all made in New York City.

Rene Rivera's next collaboration with Smith after *Flaming Creatures* would bring him a new name. Both Smith and Rivera were mega-fans of 1940s Dominican actress and camp icon Maria Montez, and Smith suggested the name "Mario Montez" in homage. Maria Montez was almost universally considered a terrible actress, but Smith and Rivera, among many others, only saw glamour, camp, and magic in her screen presence. Like many great divas of stage and screen, her essence was ripe for channeling: a penchant for classic film actresses and singers, often revived through drag, reigned supreme in many queer creative communities in New York (and beyond) at the time, and still continues today. Smith described the actress's allure in his 1962 essay "The Perfect Filmic Appositeness of Maria Montez": "There is a (unsophisticated, certainly) validity there—also theatrical drama (the best kind)—also interesting symbolism, delirious hokey, glamour-unattainable (because once possessed) and juvenile at its most passionate." These were qualities in the actress also often ascribed to drag itself, then and now. Rivera adored his new name and kept it for the length of his career in drag.

Smith dreamed of having his own studio he'd call Cinemaroc, with his own stable of muses, which he'd call his Superstars. Andy Warhol and Smith both ran in the experimental filmmaking circles of Film-maker's Cinematheque, and Warhol would have been able to see Smith's work beginning in 1963. Montez had been a muse for Smith, and the director loved the actor because he felt "he immediately enlists the sympathy of the audience." Montez would become a muse for Warhol, as well as one of his earliest Superstars, an idea perhaps taken from Smith.

Warhol's own relationship to drag and to individuals we'd recognize as transgender today is regularly called into question. He was accused on more than one occasion of adopting drag queens into his coterie for their shock value and the clout of being seen with them, promptly dropping them once he was done. Even so, Warhol's massive cultural presence helped expose new audiences to the art form and by extension elevated his drag Superstars into legendary cultural figures.

Montez was the first. He appeared in his first Warhol film, *Batman/Dracula*, in 1964 alongside Jack Smith. But some of Montez's most famous moments on-screen are in Warhol's "Mario Banana" shorts. He wears a furry woman's bolero as a wig and bright red lips with darkly lined eyes. On-screen, he is both seductress and comedienne, peeling and eating bananas, teasing them with his tongue as if they were not bananas at all. Montez was "one of the best natural comedians I'd ever met," wrote Warhol in his 1980 memoir *POPism*. "He knew how to get a laugh every time... He had a natural blend of sincerity and distraction, which has to be one of the great comedy combinations."

But Montez never appeared in drag outside of his work on-screen. He didn't do drugs, and always kept a day job. "If you saw him in the neighborhood, you would pass him on the street and he was an attractive Puerto Rican man," performer and activist Agosto Machado said in Kembrew McLeod's book *The Downtown Pop Underground*. "But you would not know that he could transform himself into a goddess as Mario Montez, this goddess muse..." Montez also didn't want his family to know about any of his work in drag and instead referred to it as "going into costume," offended by the use of the word "drag." This had as much to do with Montez's Catholic family as it did with the negative perception of drag at the time. It's noteworthy, too, that Montez chose a man's name as his stage name, even though it was inspired by a woman. By the twenty-first century, however, Montez had no problem with the term "drag," understanding how its perception had adapted and changed since he had started in the form.

While today we know drag queens as entertainers who put on femininity and/or feminine garb for a performance, in the 1960s, as with years prior, the phrase "drag queen" was two things: it was a designation of amateurishness—a person who was a "drag queen" wore drag out or to balls for fun, while a "female impersonator" was a professional; and it meant a person assigned male at birth who donned typically female attire in the street. In the latter category there were "scare drag queens," who were described as "boys who looked like girls but who you knew were boys," and "street queens," often homeless queer sex workers assigned male at birth who wore feminine attire. Many were thrown out of or left their homes, shunned by families for being queer. While today some individuals of this description might be known as transgender, for some dressing this way was simply about adornment, a mode of gender nonconforming self-expression. The vocabulary around transgender identity was not the same then. Some 1960s drag queens would certainly identify as transgender now.

So despite Warhol's later adoption of drag queens, when he started working with Montez, he did not consider Montez a drag queen, nor did Montez consider himself one, though today we recognize Montez in that category. In the 1960s, Warhol referred to Montez as "a show business transvestite" and to drag queens as a "socialsexual phenomenon." The same rhetoric Julian Eltinge and the Jewel Box Revue used, associating with theater or showbiz tradition, is an attempt to elevate what was considered an unsavory behavior across all communities.

While Warhol eagerly adopted Montez into his stable of Superstars, featuring him in a number of films including the 1966 mainstream crossover hit *Chelsea Girls*, Warhol would not officially welcome drag queens into his famed Factory until the end of the 1960s. While he would have seen drag performed as part of experimental storytelling at the Caffé Cino, his reluctance at best and ire at worst toward drag queens was sadly not unusual, as there was bias against such openly gender nonconforming individuals running rampant through all aspects of culture, queer or not. "As late as '67, drag queens still weren't accepted in the mainstream freak circles," Warhol wrote in *POPism*, his language inflammatory then and easily labeled as transphobic today, that "people began identifying a little more with drag queens, seeing them more as 'sexual radicals' than as depressing losers."

Warhol goes on to write that as time went on and minds expanded, drag queens became accepted and even celebrated. He followed the vogue, embracing drag queens when it was chic or valuable or convenient for him to do so and not before. Despite his complicated relationship with drag, his association with it added its appearance to cultural conversations where it had not existed previously.

Montez continued to work with Smith and Warhol throughout his career, and became best known for these roles. He also worked with other underground film directors like José Rodríguez Soltero, whose 1967 film *Lupe* was a retelling of the life of tragic 1930s starlet Lupe Velez, the "Mexican Spitfire," with Montez in the title role. The film also featured a young actor named Charles Ludlam who played opposite Montez in drag as Lupe's lesbian lover. They would both appear in off-off-Broadway productions in the genre now known as Theatre of the Ridiculous, a foundation of modern queer theater.

Theatre of the Ridiculous was a distinctly 1960s phenomenon that emerged in America just as conservative '50s attitudes were fading, counterculture was brewing, and anti-Vietnam sentiment was rising. Defiance was in the air, and alternative youth culture would soon be at the forefront of American consciousness. The genre arose much as underground film did, in what were then New York's gritty downtown lofts, off-off-Broadway theaters, and unconventional performance spaces like art galleries or gay leather bars. By (even further) queering experimental theater and introducing non-actors, drag, fantastical stage constructions, and costumes to its productions, Theatre of the Ridiculous was a rebellion against the popularity of realist theater from decades prior. At the beginning there were no finished scripts or even finished shows, and each performance was different from the last, driven by improvisational whims and a dedication to chaos.

Theatre of the Ridiculous criticized realism and heteronormative society at large. It was always totally queer and occasionally camp, imitating and twisting great works of theater and literature with modern references, drag, and so, so much glitter. One of its founders, John Vaccaro, had found twenty-pound bags of glitter on Canal Street and asked performers to use it whenever and wherever possible. "We have passed beyond the absurd," playwright Ronald Tavel famously said of the genre. "Our position is absolutely preposterous."

Theatre of the Ridiculous was created by young American men who grew up queer in a world that didn't yet accept them, one that lay outside the liberated urban spaces they would come to occupy, according to Sean Edgecomb, an assistant professor of Theatre and Performing Arts at CUNY Graduate Center. In their youth, they sought out glamorous early Hollywood films and campy B-movies as an escape. "What the Ridiculous tried to do was to present queer culture without shame," Edgecomb says. "Shame culture had been so much a part of queerness for most of history—frankly, most of the 20th century in America."

Ronald Tavel's plays *Shower* and *The Life of Juanita Castro*, which opened in 1965 and in part initiated the Theatre of the Ridiculous movement, featured "a willful incoherence enhanced by non sequiturs and an emphasis on lewd jokes and bawdy behavior," as author David Kaufman wrote in his book *Ridiculous!: The Theatrical Life and Times of Charles Ludlam*. Both plays were directed by John Vaccaro, who went on to found The Play-House of the Ridiculous Theatre, an avant-garde theater troupe partially responsible for making New York's off-off-Broadway a fountain of subversive creative energy.

Vaccaro himself was regularly described by company members and colleagues as difficult and confrontational, and his theater was the same. The Play-House performed plays like Kenneth Bernard's *The Moke Eater*, about a man who arrives in a small town to have his car repaired only to be subjected to various humiliations and tortures by the townspeople before escaping. "It was very raw, it was very repulsive. It was very intense," according to actress and former Play-House performer Lola Pashalinski. She also remembers a 1969 play by Tom Murrin called *Cock Strong* that featured "this big cock on the stage that eventually spurted out sequins." The works were heavily ensemble-driven, according to performer and former Play-House member Penny Arcade: "It was 30 people on stage with John Vaccaro's dictum of 'you will not bore the audience.'"

Vaccaro frequently used drag in his performances, "simply to upturn propriety," Arcade said. "It was really cultural criticism…it was like searingly political but not feather boa camp. It was camp in terms of showing where you stood." The Play-House was constantly challenging to both audiences and actors.

"John Vaccaro was dangerous," Leee Childers said in Legs McNeil and Gillian McCain's *Please Kill Me: The Uncensored Oral History of Punk*. "He used [characters like] thalidomide babies and Siamese triplets joined together at the asshole… People loved that kind of visually confrontational theater." The work also became synonymous with glitter, which led glitter to be directly associated with outrageousness. Drag queens had been wearing it in the street previously, but when Vaccaro encouraged it, the sparkly substance became fused into other aspects of expression. The Play-House would also eventually become the house theater company of legendary experimental off-off-Broadway theater La MaMa.

Theatre of the Ridiculous gained recognition when Warhol began working with Vaccaro and added artists like Tavel to his Factory—Warhol turned the plays *Shower* and *The Life of Juanita Castro* into films. When Theatre of the Ridiculous first emerged as a genre, it was camp, but at the time, "Camp had so much to do with point of view, outsider status, and the idea that someone who is ridiculed and demeaned by society has the wherewithal to present their own position," Penny Arcade said. Similarly, Theatre of the Ridiculous was culturally irreverent, Edgecomb says, and "completely liberated from any social norms." It was a genre into which drag fit perfectly and became an element of storytelling. Theatre of the Ridiculous also allowed queer people the joy of seeing themselves represented onstage, a radical concept before the Stonewall Uprising, that tied the genre to queer liberation. "Straight people could come in and queer themselves," Edgecomb says. "Rather than coming out of the closet, you could go to the closet and dress up."

John Vaccaro was told to meet a young actor named Charles Ludlam. Their interview went well—Ludlam had actually seen *Shower* and *Juanita Castro* when they opened—and Ludlam soon joined Play-House of the Ridiculous in April 1966 alongside Mario Montez. As Peeping Tom in Tavel's play *The Life of Lady Godiva*, Ludlam was nude save for his sequin-covered penis ("It was quite stunning," quipped actor Lola Pashalinski). Ludlam first appeared in drag onstage in a Play-House show, bursting forth from the audience with his best Gloria Swanson-as-Norma Desmond-in-*Sunset Boulevard* impersonation. Some performers told Ludlam to avoid drag, fearful it would ruin his career, but Ludlam paid them no mind. "Drag came naturally to me. I daresay female impersonators are born not made," he'd write later.

"It's that teetering on the edge of being a man and a woman that throws the audience. I believe that I am Norma."

Ludlam and Vaccaro fought often, and Ludlam eventually left to create the Ridiculous Theatrical Company, a name suggested to him by Jack Smith. Ludlam and Vaccaro's disdain for each other lasted decades, but also contributed to the continued growth of queer theater in New York. Ludlam decided drag was central to his work: it was "always supercharged with theatricality, and theatricality is the hallmark of the Ridiculous Theatrical Company," he'd say.

Ludlam's RTC audiences were mixed, straight and queer, and by design. His sensibilities, his relationship to camp and drag in particular, were meant to transcend communities. Partly because of Ludlam's work, drag and queerness took up space on a more "serious" stage than the cabarets, gay bars, and sex clubs where they appeared previously, beloved though they may have been. For example, Ludlam's most famous role came in 1973 with the RTC's production of *Camille*. In it, Ludlam played lead Marguerite Gautier, a role he felt born to play. Ever one to upend norms, in wigs and low-cut dresses exposing a hairy chest, Ludlam never tried to hide his offstage identity. His reinvention of the show was both comedy and tragedy, and the goal was to convince the audience of the character's reality, no matter who was playing the part. Ludlam believed in the groundbreaking nature of his work. "I pioneered the idea that female impersonation could be serious acting, an approach to character... I became known as the actor who does real acting in drag," as author David Kaufman quoted the artist.

The RTC's fame escalated: they'd have a theater, be photographed by Richard Avedon, tour the world, cover the *New York Times* Arts & Leisure section. Some, Jack Smith among them, felt Ludlam had sold out by producing works that appealed to larger audiences. But Ludlam believed he was just getting the recognition he deserved and always wanted. By the late 1970s, the

RTC had become the crème de la crème of off-off-Broadway, a jewel in the heart of downtown, all with drag and gender non-conformity regularly on display. Characters throughout Ludlam's plays bent and twisted and broke and struggled with and celebrated the multiplicity of their existences in and out of traditionally ascribed gender roles.

This would also describe the work of Jackie Curtis, who would follow in these Ridiculous footsteps as the decade went on.

John Holder, Jr., dressed in drag for the first time as a teenager in 1963, assisted by his friend Penny Arcade in the confines of a New York apartment. Two years later, he'd change his name to Jackie Curtis, graduate high school, and complete his first play, *Glamour, Glory, and Gold (The Life & Legend of Nola Noonan, Goddess & Star)*. This was all while living with his grandmother, the tough former taxi dancer Slugger Ann, in an apartment behind her bar of the same name in the East Village.

Tall with shoulders like a linebacker, Curtis had aspirations of being an actor, and in 1965 appeared for the first time on-stage in a La MaMa production of *Miss Nefertiti Regrets* by playwright Tom Eyen, also of the Caffé Cino. Curtis played Ptolemy, brother to Nefertiti, portrayed by a nineteen-year-old singer and actress named Bette Midler, also in her first onstage role.

Curtis regularly auditioned but wasn't getting the results he wanted. He had a plan, though. "I transformed myself into Jackie Curtis because I wasn't getting enough attention," he'd say later. "Nobody took me seriously when I went to auditions. But when I walk in as a girl, I am immediately accepted on a creative level. And that's true everywhere I went dressed as a girl. I actually put on a woman's dress, in one sense, to ward off evil spirits." Curtis appeared in drag publicly for the first time in 1966, at a Halloween party with two friends, Candy Darling and Holly Woodlawn, and would also periodically tend bar at Slugger Ann's in drag. Should any staff or customers give Curtis a hard time, Ann would show them exactly how she got her name. Curtis would also try female hormones in 1966, but by his own description had no ambitions of transitioning. As he and friends would regularly say, Jackie was just Jackie.

Curtis had no intention of trying to pass, either. There was stubble, there were ripped tights and thrift store gowns, haphazard makeup, chaotic eyelashes and wigs, and always some glitter. In Craig Highberger's 2005 documentary and accompanying text *Superstar in a Housedress: The Life and Legend of Jackie Curtis*, Penny Arcade estimates he inspired a new era in drag. "Jackie ushered in that period of not trying to look real," she said. "What everybody was going for in drag up until Jackie Curtis was realness. That was the criterion, how 'real' did you look? Jackie could never hope to look real...so Jackie didn't use falsies. Jackie used his own eroticism." With Curtis, the delicious androgyny of the next decade's glam rock and genderfuck drag aesthetic was in its embryonic stages; indeed, today he is considered one of its forebears.

But Curtis also got attention because he was talented. In September 1967, at the age of twenty, he had his first play produced. The aforementioned *Glamour, Glory, and Gold* was a sendup of the classic Hollywood starlet trope, performed at Bastiano's Cellar Studio, a belowground theater at 1 Waverly Place in the Village. A few months earlier, Curtis had been shopping in Greenwich Village when he sighted Andy Warhol and asked the artist for an autograph on a shopping bag. Warhol was curious about the bag's contents. "Satin shorts for the tap-dancing in my new play, *Glamour, Glory, and Gold*," Jackie responded, according to Warhol's recollections in *POPism*. "It opens in September; I'll send you an invitation."

Glamour, Glory, and Gold also starred Candy Darling, who for a time in the 1960s was living in an apartment behind the Caffé Cino. Even as a young child she had dreamed of becoming a glamorous Hollywood actress, memorizing lines and gestures of the great 1930s and 1940s film starlets. Raised in the conformist suburbs of Long Island, the person who became Candy Darling escaped to Greenwich Village as soon as she was able. She began speaking in a breathless voice like Kim Novak and eventually bleached her hair Jean Harlow blond from its natural brown. Jackie cast her in *Glamour, Glory, and Gold*, a performance that garnered her rave reviews, her favorite of which was in the *New York Times*: "A skinny actress billed as Candy Darling also made an impression; hers was the first female impersonation of a female impersonator that I have ever seen." To reviewer Dan Sullivan, Candy was just an actress, which is all she ever wanted to be. In the parlance of the time she was often called a drag queen, but it was not an expression she liked. Diary entries reveal she struggled for words to describe her gender experience. The term "transgender" had only just emerged. "I am not a genuine woman, but I am not interested in genuineness," she'd write in her diary. "I am interested in the product of being a woman and of how qualified I am."

Warhol attended *Glamour, Glory, and Gold*, and gave the play a blurb it could use for publicity—"For the first time, I wasn't bored." The play ran successfully for six months with positive reviews. It would see another production in 1968 with a young actor named Robert De Niro and more positive press in *The Village Voice*. More impactfully, the play put Curtis firmly on Warhol's radar. That summer, Curtis began filming his first on-screen role in the Warhol-produced *Flesh*, alongside Candy. *Flesh* secured their place in the Warhol Factory, earning them the "Superstar" moniker. Jackie then starred in a number of off-off-Broadway productions and even graced the cover of the *New York Times* Arts & Leisure section in 1969. "Grooving down St. Mark's [sic] Place in miniskirt, ripped black tights, clunky heels, chestnut curls, no falsies ('I'm not trying to pass as a woman'), Isadora scarf gallantly breezing behind her, is the newest playwright to make the Off Off Broadway scene."

At a time when queer and gender nonconforming people were still subject to oft-unregulated brutality and ridicule, a cover story in the *Times* Arts & Leisure section was an extraordinary feat. But Curtis was extraordinary. Few drag stars before Curtis had been recognized for their talents *offstage* as well as on. "Jackie was a wonderful writer," said Ellen Stewart, founder of La MaMa. "And he said that being a drag queen brought him more fame, but he wish[ed] that his work as a playwright would establish him as a very great writer."

Just as Curtis made his film debut in *Flesh*, another legendary drag moment was also moving toward the silver screen.

After buying an expensive ticket to a drag show in his native Philadelphia, Jack Doroshow saw a business opportunity. Then nineteen years old and studying psychology at the University of Pennsylvania, he decided to host a drag pageant with some friends. The event was successful, but the queens were suspicious of Doroshow's motives because he wasn't in drag himself. Shortly after, his drag persona took flight.

Her name was Flawless Sabrina, and she had a look and demeanor Doroshow later described as "bar mitzvah mother" with big swoops of blond hair and thick black cat eye liner. The goal was to be nonthreatening to the pageant contestants, to let them know she was "Mother," not competition. Like other queens who came before her, Sabrina would also be photographed by Diane Arbus.

Flawless Sabrina—or Mother Flawless, as Doroshow became known—embarked on a journey hosting pageants throughout the decade. At one point, her company, the Nationals Academy, was big enough to hire 100 people. The contests took place in cities large and small around the country, promoted through word of mouth in gay bars and by hired gossipmongers in each city. Though cross-dressing was illegal in some cities where the contests took place—Sabrina herself was reportedly arrested over 100 times—she often met with city officials beforehand and offered to donate some of her proceeds to charity to garner an exemption. Even audience attendance at the events required a certain amount of discretion. The Nationals Academy would hang sheets so attendees could discreetly enter and exit.

In 1967, Doroshow moved from Philadelphia to New York specifically to make a documentary about that year's Miss All-America Camp Beauty Pageant, a drag pageant known affectionately as "Mind-Blow U.S.A." to its participants. *The Queen* was arguably America's first insight into the lives of drag queens. It follows the days leading up to the pageant—the arrival of contestants, rehearsals, the ever-important unpacking of wigs—as a host of performers gathered to compete. In the process, we also see the lives of the people behind the drag personas, those who were out long before it was ever acceptable or even legal. Andy Warhol helped secure funding to make the documentary through his connections with Hollywood producers.

The 1967 pageant at Town Hall in New York generated much more publicity than previous events held by the Nationals Academy. Linking it as a fundraiser for the Muscular Dystrophy Association, it attracted sponsors like Sammy Davis, Jr., Senator Robert Kennedy ("Bobby Kennedy was what you'd call a tranny-chaser, or...whatever," Sabrina told writer Hugh Ryan in 2015), and even Lady Bird Johnson, wife of President Lyndon B. Johnson, but Davis and Johnson dropped out once they found out the event was actually a drag pageant (Kennedy's support continued). Judy Garland had judged the event in years past. Ultimately, the judging panel included Andy Warhol, writer George Plimpton, songwriter Jerry Leiber, writer Terry Southern, and artist Larry Rivers, all prominent cultural figures at the time. Mario Montez, Minette and the Jewel Box Revue also gave performances. But the event itself wasn't as stocked with supporters as perhaps Sabrina would have hoped—only the theater's first six rows were filled. The evening still became legendary.

Upon its release in 1968, Renata Adler, then chief film critic at the *New York Times*, praised *The Queen* for the way it "shows us another America," how "all these gentlemen in bras, diaphanous gowns, lipstick, hairfalls and huffs" are "much more entertaining than the conventional Miss This or Miss That." The film, despite its X-rating, broke records for the box office at the Kips Bay Theatre in New York. It was selected for screening at the Cannes Film Festival, and its performers became small-scale celebrities.

Though the pageant served as a template for others to follow, the notion of pageants in general was a contested one. The 1968 Miss America pageant faced backlash from feminists who burned bras and makeup outside the Atlantic City venue in protest. Yet the drag version continued to follow a similar structure and celebrate feminine realness, even as times and styles changed around them. The traditional style of drag eventually inspired an aesthetic rebellion led by a new generation of performers.

After *The Queen* came out, pageant winner Miss Rachel Harlow couldn't go anywhere without being followed by cameras: "Usually it's naked women, but that year it was men in drag," Harlow told the *New York Times* years later in 1993. She would later transition and open a nightclub of her own in Philadelphia.

Moving to New York, Sabrina became "Mother" to a new crop of performers and artists. From her home at 5 East 73rd Street on the Upper East Side, she held court to a bevy of people who became her children throughout the decades. Many of them celebrated her at the 2018 event "A Flawless Night: Long Live the Queen," commemorating the fiftieth anniversary of *The Queen*. Artist Zackary Drucker was among them. "If she didn't exist, we'd have to invent her," Drucker said. "She was constantly dialoguing with young people, that was really her passion," Drucker said later. "She was forward, she was not at all looking back. I think if she had been it would've been too painful. She would've felt too bitter about life and the antidote for her was to look to the future and to surround herself with young people."

That night, burlesque performer Tigger! also described Sabrina's impact. "She demanded of all of us that we be flawlessly ourselves," he said. Drucker shared some of Sabrina's most famous idioms—"Normal is a setting on the dryer"; "Wherever you are is the center of the universe"—then called out to the audience, many of whom knew Sabrina, and asked them to share some of their favorites. Hands popped up throughout the darkened theater. "If it doesn't make you nervous, it isn't worth doing," one voice said. "If you don't think you're the most interesting person in the room, nobody will do it for you," said another.

Sabrina's boldness and entrepreneurship with *The Queen* led to further work in the film industry in the 1970s, where she functioned as a storytelling consultant on films like *Butch Cassidy and the Sundance Kid*, *Midnight Cowboy*, and *Myra Breckenridge*. After moving to Europe in the 1980s, she returned to New York and became a part of nightlife once again—go-go dancing or reading tarot or wearing a fabulous outfit she concocted, ever a pillar of the community. After she passed in 2017, Town Hall was bursting with people who came to pay their respects, well beyond just the six rows of people present some fifty years earlier.

In the background of *The Queen*, there's a dirty-blonde youth, an ingenue who in the next two decades would become a beloved showgirl. International Chrysis was just sixteen when she competed in Flawless Sabrina's Miss All-America Camp Beauty Pageant. It would be one of many drag performances that would make her an icon across New York and beyond.

Chrysis had been out and about in New York's underground queer scene as a teenager before she even appeared in *The Queen*. Performer and director Kim Christy, who'd also later become the publisher of *Female Mimics*, remembered meeting her one

Halloween in the Village at the Tenth of Always, another Mafia-owned gay bar. "I recall that her outfit bowled me over: white go-go boots and white vinyl trench coat with boxer shorts underneath. She had the cutest little Twiggy haircut," Christy told *The Advocate* in 2011. "We both pretended to be older than we were—even to each other; then we figured out we both lived in the Bronx. We both were out way later than we should have been and we both needed to figure out how to de-drag and get home."

Shortly before meeting Chrysis, Christy had been outed by *Life* magazine. A 1964 photo series on juvenile delinquency in Times Square revealed Christy in drag, the edges of her button-down Catholic school uniform shirt knotted at the waist, with curtain rings for earrings, eyebrows shaped with lead from a pencil, and hair teased into an updo. "I was famous! My parents were not as charmed," Christy said. "The irony is that I was a little wild at the time, but this image forced the issue. I was out of the house within a year or two." She eventually moved in with Chrysis, who had run away from Bellevue Hospital after her parents attempted to institutionalize her.

Chrysis and Christy shared a studio apartment on Mott Street in what's today known as Nolita. Sometimes they'd model in lacquered leather and corsets for fetish magazines, but they ultimately wanted to become top-tier gender impersonators. "The street gave you a great dress rehearsal to see what worked, what didn't, if you could pass or not," Christy said. "And if you actually had talent and made a success on the stage, you could command high prices." Eventually, they did.

The Queen also launched a new era of drag history with another of the pageant's contestants, Crystal LaBeija.

"I'll sue the bitch… She won't make money off of my name, *darling*. She can make it off of Harlow and all the other fools that will flock to her, but not Crystal, *darling*. Anybody but her."

With fire and fury, these now-famous words sprang from La-

Beija's bright pink lipsticked mouth as chronicled in the documentary. Every *darling* that flies from Crystal's glossy pout is a saber, spearing the pageant's winner Harlow and Flawless Sabrina, decrying what LaBeija felt was a racist, fixed competition. A glimmering tiara sits atop her sky-high nest of jet-black hair. Sabrina vehemently denies the accusation in the film and says the decision was purely left up to the judges. But LaBeija punctuates the end of the film with such electricity that, even in the few short minutes she occupies the screen, she practically steals the show. The third runner-up, she walked off the stage in a fit of rage. For years before and after, she had felt drag pageants favored white queens, and was fed up with the discrimination her Black and Latine sisters faced. Within the decade, she would go on to become the mother of the legendary House of LaBeija, thereby laying the groundwork for today's ball culture.

A few years after Crystal's Miss All-America Camp Pageant participation, a drag queen named Lottie asked her to help promote a ball in Harlem specifically for Black queens. Crystal, who was well-respected in the drag community, had won a Queen of the Ball title. Crystal agreed, on the condition that she could be the focus of the event. Lottie acquiesced, and suggested Crystal also create a group called the House of LaBeija, with Crystal at the helm as "Mother." Together, Crystal and Lottie created a ball in the 1970s that would give birth to the house system still in place today. As the flyer wrote, "Crystal & Lottie LaBeija presents the first annual House of LaBeija Ball at Up the Downstairs Case on West 115th Street & 5th Avenue in Harlem, NY."

One of the first balls specifically for Black queens was hosted in 1962 by Marcel Christian, though balls, as previously discussed, had existed since at least the mid-1800s. At the balls organized by white people before the 1960s, people of color were often expected to whiten their faces to fit in. This was not necessarily the case at the balls like the Hamilton Lodge Ball in

Harlem and Phil Black's Funmakers' Ball, though there were often queens in attendance who called out the organizers in the press for colorism.

Crystal and Lottie's ball was the first of its kind to be held by a "house"—a specific, distinctly queer group that would come to provide not just support for those seeking family structure outside their homes (each house has parental figures, with its members as their children), but even protection and medical attention for members. The instant success of the House of La-Beija Ball inspired the formation of other houses, including the equally legendary houses of Xtravaganza, Ninja, Dupree, Wong, Pendavis, and Corey, among many others, which people could join and adopt the last name if they so chose. Marcel Christian later adopted the LaBeija surname for himself as well. "Houses" became communities of refuge for queer youth of color in the area and later other parts of New York, and even around the world. The structure still exists today.

At a typical house-led ball, members compete in dance categories like voguing and hand performance, as well as in presentation and/or drag categories like Butch-Queen Up in Pumps, Legendary Runway, and Town and Country—all of which were popular in the 1980s, among others. The House of LaBeija played a central role in Jennie Livingston's 1990 documentary about New York ball culture, *Paris Is Burning*. At the time, the house was run by Pepper LaBeija, who had taken over from Crystal in 1982. The house continues to thrive today.

The founding of the House of LaBeija and the many houses that followed gave decades of young people, especially queer youths of color, a place to belong, and Mother Crystal's words in *The Queen* ring just as true now as they did back then: "I have a *right* to show my color, darling," she snaps. "I *am* beautiful and I *know* I'm beautiful." Onstage at Town Hall at *The Queen*'s fiftieth anniversary, before the House of LaBeija shared a voguing performance, Freddie LaBeija discussed the importance of Crystal's moment in *The Queen*. "It created an entire scene where we didn't have to worry about it being fixed for Harlow," he said. It would not be the last time drag had a direct relationship to community activism and social change.

Marsha P. Johnson moved to New York in 1963 with $15 and a sack of clothes to her name. From Elizabeth, New Jersey, she'd worn dresses periodically as a child, but after bullying and sexual assault, she stopped at age thirteen.

Marsha didn't know exactly what she was looking for when she got to New York, but she was determined to find herself. She waited tables, adopted the name Black Marsha, and later became a sex worker in Times Square. Far from the tinsel-toned corporate theme park it is today, Times Square in the 1960s was filled with sex shops, peep shows, adult film theaters, and sex workers soliciting clients. Marsha's last name is also a nod to the Times Square Howard Johnson's. The *P*, she'd famously quip, would stand for "Pay it no mind!" Marsha was tall and strapping, and she discovered she could make more money with a small dash of makeup—"a butch makeup queen," she called herself. But it was when she wore drag, she'd say, that she felt her most powerful. "I was no one, nobody, from Nowheresville until I became a drag queen," she said. "That's what made me in New York, that's what made me in New Jersey, that's what made me in the world."

Marsha cobbled together her drag from whatever she could find, wherever she could find it, but by her own admission she never took it seriously. Nothing was off-limits, whether it was a transparent miniskirt worn sans undergarments, fresh flowers given to her by vendors in the Flower District, gold lamé, faux fur, discarded gowns, or what have you. Her face might be brushed with giant sweeps of bright blue eyeshadow, hot-pink rouge rubbed into her cheeks, red lipstick, or all of the above. She suffered from mental illness and was often homeless, but was also, and by design, a sight, a smile, a beacon of light. "Hello, everybody! What a wonderful morning!" was her usual shout.

She'd become a drag mother to the incoming young street queens and hustlers, teaching them how to survive. "All of us who did drag or partial drag always admired her and thought of her as a patron saint," said artist and activist Agosto Machado, a former street queen protégé of Marsha's. Stay off drugs and alcohol when you're working, she'd say. Don't bend into car windows lest someone hit you with a brick. Get the money first. Marsha would become a well-known figure on Christopher Street, doing whatever she had to do to get by. She'd ask for money on the street, but would also give it to someone else who needed it.

A typical haunt of hers was the Stonewall Inn on Christopher Street, the only bar in all of New York City where queer people were allowed to dance together. On the evening of June 27, 1969, she arrived a little after 2:00 a.m. But she didn't find dancing when she got there.

Like other gay bars at the time, the Stonewall Inn was run by the Genovese family, who paid off policemen. Any planned raids were typically known about in advance. It was considered the sleaziest bar in the area, frequented mostly by people who were not allowed elsewhere, whether it was because of demeanor, race, age, or appearance. The bouncers at Stonewall were selective about allowing drag queens. The clientele was mostly people of color.

Patrons had to sign in because the Stonewall had billed itself as a "private bottle club" to evade the law. Well aware of the consequences that could befall them if their real names were discovered, the guestbook was filled with noms de plume. That night offered a rash of Judy Garlands. The iconic singer and actress had passed away the week before, and her funeral was held earlier that day on Madison Avenue and East 81st Street. She was a well-known gay icon even then, and some 21,000 fans, many from the queer community, had gathered to pay their respects. But one fan in particular was too emotionally spent to attend. Her name was Sylvia Rivera.

While Sylvia didn't love the term "drag," she did love to dress in drag, and early on referred to herself as a drag queen. Rivera was born in the Bronx to a Venezuelan mother and Puerto Rican father in 1951. After her father abandoned her and she lost her mother to suicide, she was taken in by her grandmother, who frequently beat her for her effeminacy. She shaved her eyebrows and wore makeup to school beginning in fourth grade, and by the time she was ten years old left home and began life as a sex worker, hustling near Times Square. As a street queen, she gave herself the name "Sylvia Rivera" in a ceremony attended by some fifty of her friends and peers. Later in her life she referred to herself as transgender.

Rivera was no stranger to standing up for herself. She and her peers on the street were regularly beaten up by cops, johns, or even each other. Rivera would eventually serve ninety days on Riker's Island, sent to a cellblock kept for perpetrators of "gay crimes," as scholar, activist, and author Jessi Gan noted in 2007.

By 1:20 a.m., an unplanned police raid at Stonewall stopped the evening in its tracks. But this time, hundreds of people fought back. A crowd began to form, filling up the West Village's Sheridan Square. There was shouting and jeering as people were thrust into a paddy wagon. Queens in handcuffs railed against cops. As legend has it, police cuffed a lesbian for violating the three-piece rule, then attacked her. Some believe this woman was Stormé DeLarverie. "Nobody knows who threw the first punch…but it's rumored that she did, and she said she did," friend Lisa Cannistraci told the *New York Times* in 2014, upon DeLarverie's death. Whether this woman was DeLarverie is unclear, but seeing this fellow traveler brutalized, the crowd retaliated, fighting back against decades of police brutality and oppression. At one point, historian Martin Duberman writes in his comprehensive book *Stonewall*,

"...police found themselves face to face with their worst nightmare: a chorus line of mocking queens, their arms clasped around each other, kicking their heels in the air Rockettes-style and singing at the tops of their sardonic voices:

> We are the Stonewall girls
> We wear our hair in curls
> We wear no underwear
> We show our pubic hair
> We wear our dungarees
> Above our nelly knees!"

By some accounts, both Johnson and Rivera were there— dropping bags of cement on cop cars and throwing Molotov cocktails, respectively. Other accounts claim they weren't there until the riots started, if at all. Either way, the event would spur both of them to participate in the fights for queer civil rights moving forward.

While the Stonewall Uprising was by no means the beginning of the gay rights movement, it became an inflection point for queer liberation. Drag, specifically worn by people of color, was the riot's beating heart.

6

1970–1979

Despite its role in the Stonewall Uprising, drag would still occupy a tenuous place in many parts of the queer community for decades. It was as if those hoping for equality had forgotten who agitated for change that night: specifically, Black and brown trans women of color, drag queens, and street queens. Indeed, for many years after Stonewall, drag was excluded from what became the annual Pride parade. Some people didn't want to be associated with drag and didn't want mainstream straight culture to think "that" was what the queer community was about.

Initially when Mayor John Lindsay was elected in 1965, gay liberation was not on his mind. In fact, he openly refused to institute antidiscrimination laws based on sexual orientation after he was elected for a second term in 1969, just after the Stonewall Uprising. But after gay liberation activists continually bombarded him with "zaps," public confrontations at events in places like Radio City Music Hall and the Metropolitan Opera, he signed those laws into existence in 1972: jobs at public agencies would no longer be able to engage in discriminatory hiring practices based on sexual orientation. It was slowly becoming safer to be a queer person existing in New York City. Indeed, the word "homophobia" entered the lexicon in 1969, courtesy of a straight psychotherapist named George Weinberg. Homosexuality was officially removed from the American Psychiatric Association's list of disorders in 1973, meaning a gay person would no longer be deemed mentally ill based solely on their sexuality. Also that year, the *Roe v. Wade* decision had established women's right to privacy, citing the Fourteenth Amendment—"No State shall make or enforce any law which shall abridge the privileges or immunities of citizens of the United States; nor shall any state deprive any person of life, liberty, or property, without due process of law"—which would ultimately protect others' right to privacy as well, at least until it was overturned in 2022. The "three-item rule" for clothing was mostly disregarded after Stonewall. Plus, the Mafia had unhooked its claws from nightlife, thus creating space for legal gay bars, which popped up throughout the city. People wanted to dance and mingle, but were often less inclined to engage with the bars' performers, least of all those in drag.

As television ascended, traditional nightclub floor shows continued to dwindle. Club 82 was reinvented as a punk venue, catering more to artists and young people than those looking to see drag shows. As New York teetered near bankruptcy, parts of downtown became more dangerous. Bridge and tunnel crowds, tourists and uptown straight people were less inclined to venture below 14th Street, where drag had thrived.

Drag balls, too, were held less frequently downtown. This could be attributed to the cost of putting on an event, to the decreasing safety of the neighborhoods in which the balls were traditionally held, and to decreasing attendance. The changing ways people dressed—that is, fewer and fewer people attired themselves in luxurious ball gowns to go out as culture became more casual—and the changing perception of drag in the city were also factors in drag's declining popularity. "Whereas it was once considered vogue and chic to be a participant in a drag ball," *Drag* magazine wrote in 1976, "it is now considered passé."

For some people, drag became stale. It required reinvention. Barbra Herr took to the stage in drag for the first time in the Bronx in 1973 with a drag group called the Cherries. "Back in those days, impersonations were the big thing. That's what you did, that's what they expected from people, from entertainers," Herr said, recalling queens who did Diana Ross and Barbra Streisand. The look was "a lot more showy and Broadway," she said. Local legend John LaFleur performed in drag as Marlene Dietrich and as Streisand, for example. He also owned a hustler bar on West 42nd Street and recorded a disco album called *It's a Wonderful Thing*, donning a massive black curly wig reminiscent of your favorite aunt from Long Island. But for many performers, Herr included, that showy look would soon change. "I broke that mold because I didn't look like anyone and I refused. So I used voices and I just did my own look for myself," she said.

Drag did in fact continue to thrive in theatrical settings like cabarets and theaters, though gay bars and the newly emerging discos weren't too far behind. Nor, incidentally, were portions of mainstream culture that adopted drag's aesthetics with open arms, despite its overall rejection of queerness. Those in drag continued to fight for their validity as they dealt with scorn and exploitation, and some still became legendary.

Lee Brewster had nothing if not initiative.

A West Virginia native, he later moved to the small, 851-person town of Honaker, Virginia, and left at seventeen to become a file clerk at the FBI. But after he was found kissing a man, he was quickly dismissed for being gay. Brewster arrived in New York and joined the Mattachines, where, much to the chagrin of the conservative organization, he threw fundraising drag balls. "They were very conservative, pushing the masculine, macho image," Brewster said of the Mattachines. "Any other image was negative."

Brewster had been approached by a young transgender woman named Barbarella who had served in Vietnam and was being threatened with a dishonorable discharge—she had breast augmentation surgery while still a soldier, and this was considered destroying government property. Brewster thought the Mattachines would want to use some of their funds to help her, but the organization vehemently declined. "They didn't want to use the money that I had raised from drag, drag balls, drag social activities, to help," Brewster said in 1995. "So I took it on myself." Brewster got Barbarella honorably discharged and left the Mattachine Society permanently. In February 1969, Brewster began throwing his own annual drag ball, Lee Brewster's Mardi Gras Ball, and began to advocate for the role of drag queens, transgender people, and cross-dressers in the queer civil rights movement.

Brewster's independent foray into civil rights began with the Queens Liberation Front, cofounded with then self-described "heterosexual transvestite" Bunny Eisenhower. Their mission was "to legalize the right to dress in the attire of the opposite sex in public without fear of arrest or police harassment." It was in part because of Brewster's work that citywide bans on public drag were dismantled. He also served his community by selling drag items in safer ways. Those who didn't feel they could simply walk into a store and buy women's clothes for whatever reason— be they cross-dressers, drag queens, or transgender individuals— could purchase them through Brewster's new mail-order business. The initiative proved so successful that people began showing up at his door, hoping to buy directly. So he decided to open a store on the second floor of 400 West 14th Street at 9th Avenue.

Today this address is next to a Lululemon in what's now the luxurious Meatpacking District, but at the time it was indeed a meatpacking district: in the 1950s, there had been some 3,000 employees working in the industry, but by the end of the 1960s, when supermarkets became popular and many butchers decamped to Hunts Point Market in the Bronx, the area grew more desolate. By the 1970s it was a hotbed for crime, gay bars, sex work, and what the rest of New York might have called the underworld.

So it was a perfect place for Brewster's drag emporium, Lee's Mardi Gras. Previously a kink-friendly gay bar known as The Toilet, this 5,000-square-foot space had everything from false eyelashes to breastplates to corsets to wigs to dresses in size 30 and steel-enforced heels in size 13. Some of the merchandise skewed more toward cross-dressing men—traditional women's suits and pumps, for example—as opposed to the glitter and sparkle of drag performance, but Brewster kept the store on the second floor for a reason: so anyone going in could be protected. There was no lobby, just an elevator right on the street, and a friendly staff member escorting patrons upstairs. Staff would also assist people getting into drag if they needed help. "Make your boyself into your girlself," with "drag consultants," one of the store's advertisements read, "Private, Discreet, Reasonable."

Lee's Mardi Gras was at odds with prevailing opinions of drag in the queer community. Dorian Corey laments the disconnect on the Pearl Box Revue's *Call Me MISSter* recording: "It stinks," she says, noting the movement's lack of inclusivity as it pertained to drag queens. "It's the closet bunch that are gay liberating," she says, "and when they get it for themselves, they will still be looking at the drag queens saying, 'No, no, no, not you'…you haven't seen a drag queen represented."

What became a more conservative homophile movement, bolstered by organizations like the Mattachine Society, was at odds with the new gay liberation movement. The former sought acceptance via moderation, and the latter sought total revolution. Some gay men, many of them upper-middle-class white gay men, even decried the events at Stonewall. Randy Wicker, an activist and participant at the "Sip-In" at Julius in the West Village, later said that "screaming queens forming chorus lines and kicking went against everything that I wanted people to think about homosexuals...that we were a bunch of drag queens in the Village acting disorderly and tacky and cheap." Wicker later changed his tune and acknowledged his errors publicly, also becoming a longtime friend and roommate of Marsha P. Johnson, but his thoughts then represented many at the time.

Indeed, on the first anniversary of the Stonewall Uprising, supporters held an event called the Christopher Street Liberation Day March, which evolved into what we now know as the annual Pride parade. Organizers, fearing negative attention, asked drag queens to march in the back. Marsha P. Johnson and Sylvia Rivera refused—instead, they marched at the very front of the parade with fellow queens, leading what became to that point the largest open presentation of queerness in the history of New York City.

The parade organizers' fears about drag went unrealized— nobody was arrested. "They wanted drag to be invisible," Brewster said. But like Marsha and Sylvia, he wasn't about to let that happen. The following year, 1971, Brewster's Queens Liberation Front, then called Queens, showed up proudly in drag, walking the three-mile parade route in heels. "The most satisfying thing about the demonstration was that a drag queen and a heterosexual T.V. [transvestite] for the first time marched under the same banner," Brewster wrote in *Drag*, a magazine he produced in the 1970s and 1980s to reflect the Queens Liberation Front's "desire to be treated as full-fledged American citizens."

The Queens Liberation Front would continue to march in the Pride parade, and Brewster maintained a lifetime of activism. His ball, which ran from 1969 to 1974, became so popular that it also drew the likes of Shirley MacLaine and Carol Channing. Lee's Mardi Gras remained open for thirty years. In that time, it also became a go-to for costumers working on films like *Tootsie, To Wong Foo, Thanks for Everything! Julie Newmar,* and *The Birdcage.*

★ ★ ★

Marsha P. Johnson and Sylvia Rivera were inspired by the wave of queer activism that swept the country after Stonewall. But some gay men and gay women involved in the feminist movement resented the way they presented themselves. In response, Sylvia and Marsha became activists, forming a group to help young queer people who lived on the street. "Marsha and I just decided it was time to help each other and help our other kids," Rivera said in a 2006 interview with activist and author Leslie Feinberg. It was 1970, and Marsha and Sylvia, then twenty-five and nineteen, were often homeless themselves, but they knew others, some as young as ten or eleven, who also needed help. They formed Street Transvestite Action Revolutionaries, or S.T.A.R.

S.T.A.R. was the first organization to provide housing and advocacy specifically for young street queens. It was also, according to the Village Preservation Society, "the first LGBT youth shelter in North America, the first trans woman of color-led organization in the US, and the first trans sex worker labor organization." Marsha and Sylvia didn't have much, but what they could give, they did. The first S.T.A.R. house was the open back of a trailer parked in Greenwich Village and became home to some twenty young people. They weren't required to perform sex work for money if they didn't want to, Sylvia would say, but if they did choose to, they were asked to contribute part of their funds back to S.T.A.R. Later, one of the queens went to a friend in the Mafia, who helped her procure a building at 213 East 2nd Street, between Avenue B and Avenue C. It would be theirs as long as they gave a down payment and paid rent.

While today renting a building in the East Village/Alphabet City is no small feat, New York in the 1970s was a very different place. The United States was in the throes of a financial crisis, and Mayor Lindsay had issues with his $7.8 billion budget (nearly $60 billion today). It included funds for programs ranging from the TKTS booth that still stands in Times Square to the Department of Consumer Affairs to the start of more air-conditioning in the subway, and the creation of 911 for emergencies, among others. Other programs didn't work as well as he had hoped, and he had resorted to shady borrowing and banking techniques to keep the city above water.

By 1974, the newly elected Mayor Abraham Beame inherited a budget of close to $10 billion with a $1.5 billion deficit. The city was less than two hours away from declaring bankruptcy on October 17, 1975, a crisis only averted when the teachers' union decided to invest $150 million in city bonds to cover the remainder of debts due that particular month. While Beame left the mayor's office in 1978 with a $200 million surplus, throughout the 1970s crime surged, schools were abandoned mid-construction, hospitals removed thousands of beds, residential buildings were deserted, people skipped town to the suburbs yet again, and some landlords purposely set their buildings aflame to collect insurance money. President Gerald Ford was unsympathetic. In October 1975, he gave a speech at Washington DC's National Press Club in which he fully refused to bail the city out. This prompted the *New York Daily News*'s now famous October 30, 1975, headline, "Ford to City: Drop Dead." To outsiders, life in the city was treacherous at best.

But for S.T.A.R., all of this made inhabiting a building for a mere $200 a month a possibility. S.T.A.R. members hustled for the money, and soon they were in, fixing the place up to be their own. Marsha and Sylvia hoped the young queens could foster community, connect, and work their way out of the life if they wanted to. But failing to pay their rent after about eight months, they were back on the street in July 1971. S.T.A.R. itself existed for another three years, later moving to 640 East 12th Street and collaborating with other activist groups like Lee Brewster's Queens Liberation Front.

After the 1973 New York Pride March rally, however, Sylvia

put her activism on hold. She went onstage despite boos from the crowd. "I had to fight my way up on that stage...people that I called my comrades in the movement literally beat the shit out of me," Rivera said later. She was banned from New York's Gay and Lesbian Community Center, for example, after she destroyed a desk in the lobby, enraged because she felt the center did not address the needs of transgender homeless youths who slept in front of it. Some people called her a liar. This homeless gender nonconforming person who struggled with mental illness and addiction was an anomaly to some of the cis, white, middle-class people whose voices dominated the movement, something she would later criticize. As always, she made her voice heard, and stood up for those who were too often absent from the gay liberation narrative: the imprisoned, the gender nonconforming, and people of color.

On the microphone, she called out the movement for what she felt was their failure to assist their comrades in jail, what she felt was their unchanging white middle-class point of view that left little room for people outside their experience. "I will no longer put up with this shit," she screamed into the microphone. "I have been beaten, I have had my nose broken, I have been thrown in jail, I have lost my job, I have lost my apartment for gay liberation, and you all treat me this way? What the fuck's wrong with you all?... I believe in us getting our rights or else I would not be out there fighting for our rights."

At the same rally, activist Jean O'Leary of the Gay Activists Alliance and Lesbian Feminist Liberation refuted Sylvia's speech, calling her "a man," while also publicly decrying what she and other women felt was the misogynist nature of drag, its perpetuation of stereotypes she felt women hoped to escape. Reading from what she said was a statement supported by 100 women, O'Leary stated, "When men impersonate women for reasons of entertainment or profit, they insult women. We support the rights of every person to dress in a way that he or she wishes, but we are opposed to the exploitation of women by men for entertainment or profit." O'Leary and the LFL saw Sylvia and her fellow queens, street, drag, or otherwise, as offensive caricatures. Lee Brewster rejected O'Leary's ideals and called her out—"you're celebrating what was the result of what the drag queens did at the Stonewall. You go to bars because of what drag queens did for you...screw you!"—but Sylvia had had enough. She might not have known it at the time, but she'd already made her mark on history.

For decades, Fire Island had been a queer enclave and summer retreat for New Yorkers. By the 1970s, however, drag queens and transgender women were still not welcome in the island's Pines hamlet. "From my perspective, from where I was, the Pines was very closeted," said activist Thom Hansen. "There were a lot of gay people who were gay in the Pines who were straight in the rest of the world." Unlike the neighboring community of Cherry Grove, which was more bohemian and had a decades-long history of drag performances, Pines visitors were typically more conservative. They were also on average more affluent and therefore, Hansen says, maybe had more to lose if outed. Drag was not a part of their lifestyle. "Some looked down on [drag] because they felt it wasn't the way they wanted to portray the LGBT community to the general public," he says.

In 1976, Hansen won Cherry Grove's Homecoming Queen contest as his drag alter ego, Panzi. His friend Teri Warren, a drag queen who'd also be called a transgender woman today, went over to the Pines' chic restaurant Botel in drag, but was refused service. In response, Hansen and his friends created what would become an annual tradition, "Invasion of the Pines." On July 4, 1976, Hansen and his friends all dressed in drag and took a water taxi from Cherry Grove to "invade" the Pines and avenge the wrong done to Terri, but all in good fun.

"The premise was that the Grove was the center of the world

and the Pines was a comedy of the Grove, so the queen was going to bless the comedy," Hansen says. Rather than getting rejected, though, Hansen and his friends were cheered on by Pines-goers, much to the chagrin of closeted property owners in the area. The Grove group waved hello, "blessed" the area, and were welcomed by patrons to establishments like those that had rejected Teri not too long before. Business owners were flustered, but tensions later subsided. Hansen and friends had so much fun they decided to do it again the following year. The "Invasion of the Pines" on July 4 became a major event, with hundreds of participants in drag arriving via ferry from Cherry Grove to herds of excited onlookers in the Pines, everyone waving and cheering. Hansen still organizes it every year.

After Stonewall, gay liberation also invited a gay sexual revolution. What had been underground sex scenes of the 1960s emerged unapologetically in the 1970s.

At the same time, some gay men embraced a hypermasculinized aesthetic, like a living Tom of Finland drawing. Finnish artist Touko Laaksonen, who went by the moniker, became famous for his illustrations of swarthy men in work gear, an image that now dominated the scene. A tight pair of Levi's, the crotch worn down to show off the goods, work boots, flannel, and a thick mustache were some of the visual cues of what would become known as the "clone" aesthetic. It was an evolution of sorts from the Brando look of the 1950s (popular among both gay and straight men). This new look was even more aggressively masculine, exaggerated to the point of almost being drag itself, though its wearers would have balked at such a statement at the time.

Drag directly countered this depiction of masculinity, and many men who took on the clone look wanted nothing to do with drag. "The gay boys didn't want that image," said drag queen Ruby Rims, who performed for the first time in the

1970s. "They loved to come see the shows but they didn't want to be associated with the drag queens because they didn't want to be associated with a bunch of guys dressing up in women's clothes."

Such an experience was captured in a June 25, 1979, *Village Voice* article by Edmund White entitled "The Politics of Drag." On the tenth anniversary of Stonewall, White chronicled the space drag occupied in the queer community. He recalled men seeking to challenge stereotypes of effeminacy, men threatened by drag's open embrace of the hyperfeminine and forceful rejection of the form. He wrote, "The gay drag is also more despised than ever because she reminds the new macho gays of what they once were, or might have been." This needed to change, he said, pointing out where the real revolution began: "Only the most oppressed outcasts of gay life—the drag queens—dared to speak openly of their sexuality. Contemporary drag is a reminder of our beginnings."

While female impersonators from the previous generation continued to perform at upscale cabarets, theaters, and ballrooms throughout the city, these acts weren't necessarily considered hip or cool, especially as youth culture embraced a more subversive energy. And while female impersonation was certainly a taboo embrace of gender nonconformity onstage, Judy Garland and Barbra Streisand impressions were far from edgy. Still, one of the most beloved and influential in this style of drag was Charles Pierce. He referred to himself as a "male actress," and first made a name for himself in San Francisco, where his shows featured classic camp diva impersonations of Joan Crawford, Bette Davis, and Tallulah Bankhead, among others. Pierce brought his comedic stylings and impressions to New York in 1975 with great aplomb, zingy one-liners populating his performances with polished patter in *The Charles Pierce Show*. The show was so successful it ran for five months and won Pierce an Obie Award. His career continued successfully into the next decades, and he even had a stand-up special in drag on the Play-boy Channel in 1984.

The *New York Times*'s theater critic Clive Barnes, a straight man who by his own admission "detest[s] drag performers," praised Pierce's performance in *The Charles Pierce Show*, in a review that reveals as much about the performer as the prevailing negative perception of drag. "To call Charles Pierce a female impersonator is a little like comparing a Rolls Royce with a Toyota," Barnes wrote in 1975. "To start with, one is cheaper than the other." Barnes goes on to evoke drag's theatrical antecedents in Shakespeare and raise questions of "psychiatric concern" regarding drag queens. "He might even give transvestitism a good name, and have perfectly normal sailors riffling through their mother's closets." These are all challenging sentiments to read now from the longtime "paper of record," even though at the time they were ultimately meant to positively reinforce Pierce's work.

Ruby Rims's first drag performance was at The Anvil, a sex club that opened in 1974 at 500 West 14th Street near 11th Avenue, just down the street from Lee's Mardi Gras. The club was filled with clones, and for the most part didn't allow women, unless it was a Monday night or unless you were Liza Minnelli or Lee Radziwill, sister of former first lady Jacqueline Kennedy. Drag only entered the venue when Ruby Rims did, in January 1977: she was the first drag queen to ever perform there, and the manager had initially hired her as a joke. This subset of gay men did not initially embrace drag. Nevertheless, she took to the stage at 5:30 in the morning after a fistfucking show that left behind a wake of Crisco. "They wiped down the stage and I went up and started to do my act and all I was thinking to myself was 'Dear God, don't let me slide off this fucking thing,'" she laughed. But she didn't slide off: on the contrary, she slid right into the hearts of all the well-muscled men in the audience. What had started as a joke became a beloved act, noteworthy for helping to shatter the stigma of drag among certain groups of gay men. The bar's manager hired her to work five nights a week.

Ruby normally lip-synched, but on Christmas Eve she sang "O Holy Night" live, in her real voice, and the bar went silent, "which brought a whole new interpretation of the words 'fall on your knees,'" Ruby laughed. "And when I finished singing, they were half applauding and the other half had their mouths open because they didn't know I could actually sing." Ruby later left The Anvil to start a career as a cabaret performer. She made appearances on *Geraldo* and *Donahue* and even did a commercial with the New York Yankees and Adidas. She still performs today and runs events for charity.

Seeing Ruby's success, The Anvil continued to hire gender nonconforming performance artists, among them now-iconic performers like the Amazing, Electrifying Grace, a transgender woman and lip-synch artist; The Amazing Yuba, who imitated Grace Jones; and countless others. Ruby didn't know it at the time, but her and her drag comrades' infiltration of this aspect of gay life created more space for drag in the community.

After witnessing performer Michael Norman in drag as Tanya Ransom—performing as German punk icon Nina Hagen— performance artist John Kelly was inspired and made his drag debut at The Anvil in 1979. He performed Maria Callas's "Habanera" from the opera *Carmen* "in my own version of punk, genderfuck drag with high heels, no tits, you know, eye socket, '20s silent screen makeup, teased out hair," he said. "I was embodying this other creature. And it became this huge Vesuvius of energy pouring out of me...fucking with gender provided me with a way to process a lot of pent up rage and anxiety, and it was the biggest social fuck you I could think of mustering, toward my father, toward the city, toward the culture generally, toward America, toward 'masculinity' and it worked. And it really led me on the path that I'm still wielding."

Jackie Curtis's next triumph—of sorts, anyway—opened at La MaMa on May 26, 1971. *Vain Victory: The Vicissitudes of the Damned* was a musical of some twenty numbers that follows the story of Blue Denim, played by Jackie Curtis and based on James Dean—Jackie was not wearing feminine drag at the time on or offstage—and Donna Bella Beads, a mermaid played by Candy Darling, as they graduate from Taylor Mead High School (Mead himself was an underground performer and Warhol star). They embark upon a journey that takes them from a circus to a Hollywood hotel to a ship, the *S.S. Vain Victory*.

The show was different every night, the cast was always changing, and many people just didn't learn their lines. It was largely panned: the *New York Times* called it "unabashed trash," and *The Village Voice* proclaimed it "awful, abominable, execrable, beyond description and beyond belief." But Jackie took it all in stride, especially since it drew packed houses and was beloved by John Lennon, who called it "the best play I've ever seen." Even with a panned play, Jackie had created a scene in all the right ways.

It's not surprising, then, that Andy Warhol continued to embrace drag throughout the 1970s for reasons sincere, opportunistic, or both. It seems by the time the decade began, Warhol referred to drag queens positively as "living testimony to the way women used to want to be, the way some people still want them to be and the way some women still actually want to be."

"I never thought I could be famous," Holly Woodlawn wrote in her memoir *A Low Life in High Heels*. "I was Harold Ajzenberg, a shy, skinny kid with buck teeth who happened to have a passion for tight pants, mohair sweaters, and mascara. Which was unheard of in the Sixties...for a boy!" Arriving in New York from Miami Beach at sixteen, she changed her name to Holly

Woodlawn, part Holly Golightly and part cemetery heiress. She was, she quipped, "a high-spirited goddess with a bottle in one hand and a pill in the other."

Holly met Andy Warhol because she lied (which, incidentally, she did a lot): she tried to put a $2,000 camera on Andy's tab then told a newspaper she was a Warhol Superstar. She was summoned to the Factory, not for reprimand but admiration. She had chutzpah. Arrests for grand larceny would come at a different time.

Warhol brought Holly Woodlawn to the screen for the first time in his 1970 film *Trash*. She was praised as the film's bright spot and quickly became a downtown persona. Her kookiness was a signature: "Holly was a delight but I knew that she had stolen $100 from my pants," journalist Michael Musto laughed. "She was so hilarious that I always forgave her and even spoke at her memorial." Holly's visibility, her desire to live unapologetically and undefined, make her a significant torchbearer in the cultural history of gender nonconforming presentation. Upon the occasion of Holly's death in 2015, Penny Arcade remembered for *Out* magazine her friend's appearance on a 1976 episode of Geraldo Rivera's news show *Good Night America*, where the television host seemed desperate to understand if Holly was gay, straight, transgender, or a cross-dresser, and pestered her with questions in hopes of getting her to respond. But Holly was unbothered, Arcade shared, and simply responded, "'But darling? What difference does it make as long as you look fabulous?'"

Warhol worked with Jackie, Candy, and Holly again on the film *Women in Revolt*, a 1971 satire of the women's liberation movement inspired in part by Valerie Solanas, a feminist who shot and severely wounded Warhol at his studio in 1968. The film, which the artist started working on that year, starred the three performers as a teacher, an heiress, and a model, respectively, who reject men and join a radical feminist group called

Politically Involved Girls, or PIG. While Warhol and (notably right-wing) director Paul Morrissey originally intended the movie to make fun of the burgeoning feminist movement, the unscripted film had the opposite effect and produced what was actually a very feminist film that analyzes the state of modern womanhood through its three gender nonconforming stars. Called a "madcap soap opera" by the *New York Times*, the film made its New York debut at the Ciné Malibu on East 59th Street, which also showed porn.

Despite helping usher drag into the spotlight, Warhol didn't work with Jackie, Candy, or Holly ever again. It didn't help that Jackie and Holly helped themselves to filet mignon and lobster dinners at Max's Kansas City and signed his name to the bill, or that they shut off the breakers in his studio, screamed at him and demanded money. "Don't get involved with drag queens," he was known to say afterward. This was not before they were all immortalized in Lou Reed's 1972 hit song "Walk on the Wild Side."

Candy Darling found other work as an actress periodically, including a role alongside Rue McClanahan in the 1971 film *Some of My Best Friends Are...* about New York gay life. She was also regularly photographed by some of the best image makers of her day like Robert Mapplethorpe, Peter Beard, Cecil Beaton, and Richard Avedon. Tennessee Williams, who had seen her in *Vain Victory*, even wrote a vehicle for her called *Small Craft Warnings* that ran off-Broadway. Even then, it was challenging— she wasn't allowed to use either male or female dressing rooms. "They gave her a broom closet, and she put a star on the door," said biographer Cynthia Carr.

Candy thought her career would take off, but she sadly passed away from lymphoma at twenty-nine in 1974, an illness later attributed to using apparently carcinogenic hormones. On her deathbed, she asked Peter Hujar to photograph her. In the image, she lies in her hospital room, gorgeous, clutching a rose. It remains among the photographer's most noteworthy images, which is fitting: she would never allow us to forget her. Though she may not have had the language to describe it at the time, her work makes her an early pioneer of transgender representation on film and in theater.

Despite his stated misgivings, Warhol did continue working with gender nonconforming models, discussion of exploitation always lurking. In 1974, Italian art dealer Luciano Anselmino extended a $1 million commission to Warhol for "impersonal, anonymous" images of people he then called "transvestites," but who today we'd call drag queens and transgender women. The series, Anselmino decided, would be called *Ladies and Gentlemen*.

Anselmino's idea was that the subjects would be a far cry from the screen-printed stars the artist typically used. Warhol asked a friend to go to The Gilded Grape, a Times Square haunt favored by drag queens and trans women of color, to recruit potential models, never mentioning Warhol's name. Interested parties were picked up in a cab at 10:00 a.m. and taken to Warhol's studio, where they had their Polaroids taken, much like their celebrity counterparts. They were compensated $50 for their time. Of the fourteen subjects ultimately featured, Warhol made some 268 works. Many subjects didn't know who he was, but at least two of them did: Marsha P. Johnson and Wilhelmina Ross, both of whom would also perform in the drag troupe Hot Peaches.

In these portraits, the subjects look beautiful and glamorous, but the work can be difficult to look at knowing what happened to the models after they left the studio. *Ladies and Gentlemen* was completed in 1975, four years after Marsha and Sylvia lost the S.T.A.R. house. "Andy Warhol silkscreens of Marsha sell for $1400 in a Christopher Street gallery while Marsha walks the sidewalk outside, broke," Steve Watson wrote in the June

15, 1979, issue of *The Village Voice* commemorating the tenth anniversary of Stonewall. The juxtaposition was stark: being painted by Warhol meant you'd be known around the world, but that didn't come with meaningful financial compensation, except for Warhol.

The artist experimented with drag himself in the early 1980s, donning wigs and makeup for a series of self-portraits made with artist Christopher Makos. His interest in cultural manufacturing is present in the shine of his synthetic wigs and the powder white of his skin. His red lips don't so much conceal as reveal the simulated nature of identity, the drag of it all. This time, he is the vulnerable one in drag.

Interestingly, the legacy of drag in Warhol's work lives on in a new, arguably more informed way today at The Andy Warhol Museum in Pittsburgh, Pennsylvania, which offers a School of Drag for teens "to learn about the history, culture, and practice of drag and gender-bending performance."

The unapologetic nature of drag embodied by the Ridiculous Theatrical Company, the Play-House of the Ridiculous Theatre, and later the Cockettes and the Hot Peaches, would heavily influence both punk and glam rock throughout the 1970s and beyond.

Prior to 1969, George Edgerly Harris III was a downtown New York theatre staple, sandy blond and sweet in sweaters. After 1969, he was Hibiscus, founder of a glitter-drenched theatrical drag rebellion known as the Cockettes.

They began in San Francisco, the opening act for the Palace Theatre's midnight movie experience known as the "Nocturnal Dream Show." In all of their own wacky ensembles pieced together with fringe, vintage gowns, pompoms, and feathers, they were a wild, kicking, prancing chorus line of friends at play, their senses of both abandon and humor deliciously intact.

Audiences couldn't get enough, and soon they were performing every week in all of their anarchic imperfectionism, a thrill of the underground that also later featured Sylvester, now of disco fame, and the irrepressible drag force Divine. The Cockettes also charmed nationally syndicated film critic Rex Reed, who declared the troupe "a landmark in the history of new, liberated theater." Soon, the Cockettes were everywhere, including a two-page spread photographed by Annie Leibovitz in *Rolling Stone.*

Based on Reed's enthusiasm, the Cockettes were booked for a month in New York at the Anderson Theatre in the East Village, at 66 2nd Avenue at East 4th Street. The gig inspired a split in the group between getting paid and performing for free. Hibiscus was incidentally among those who wanted to give free performances, and left the Cockettes to revive his original project, The Angels of Light Free Theater Collective. Poet Allen Ginsberg would make his first drag appearance with this group. The rest of the Cockettes went to New York.

The Cockettes' new show opened at the Anderson on November 1, 1971, the same night *Vain Victory* closed at the WPA Theatre. The performance attracted the likes of Angela Lansbury, Diana Vreeland, and other chic city dwellers who expected to see capital-T theatre in the vein of Charles Ludlam. Instead what they found was the Cockettes' brand of glittery chaos and they weren't having it. Press lambasted the show, but later audience reactions, people who really got it, were more significantly upbeat. John Kelly remembers seeing the troupe at the Anderson in high school, taking the PATH train from New Jersey "to go to the dark and mysterious East Village to see the Cockettes" the night after the opening, when the troupe performed their show "Pearls over Shanghai."

"The theatre was maybe a third full and it was mostly populated with these genderfuck creatures who had beards and glitter and these long, silky frocks, and it was just amazing, and it was patchouli-scented everywhere, so I was agape at the whole spectacle," Kelly recalled. "Basically, I knew in that moment that this chasm opened up and I saw a world of possibility which was a complete reversal and antithesis from what I had been experiencing growing up in Jersey."

The Cockettes broke up shortly after, but Hibiscus and other members continued to perform in drag or use drag in their artistic expressions. Sylvester became an icon of gender nonconformity in his ascension to disco superstardom. Other Cockettes joined a troupe called Savage Voodoo Nuns at a newly opened bar at 315 Bowery called CBGB & OMFUG, which stood for Country, Bluegrass, Blues, and Other Music for Uplifting Gourmandizers. At one show, they received top billing above two other bands, who are mentioned at the bottom of the poster, practically an afterthought: Blondie and the Ramones.

As in the 1920s, it became stylish for members of mainstream culture to consume work from "the fringes," drag of course included, hence the hype of the Cockettes in New York. Yet as mainstream interest in the counterculture continued in the 1970s, there was still a hesitancy to interact with drag, along with an occasional unwillingness to identify one's own work as drag or as queer. Toward the end of the decade, however, that began to change.

In his memoir *My Dear, Sweet Self*, Jimmy Camicia, the founder of New York drag theater company Hot Peaches, remembers neither the Cockettes nor the Angels of Light Free Theater actively describing themselves as gay theater companies. "Post-Stonewall liberation crawled slowly into the theatrical world," he wrote. "In legitimate theater at that time, you could be the swishiest, campiest, most outrageous queen imaginable, like Liberace or Paul [Lynde], but you could not say you were gay. Coming out was considered career suicide in 1972."

Jimmy Camicia's Hot Peaches sprung from the Cockettes'

wake in 1972. Camicia had been living in Berlin with Angie
Stardust, formerly of Club 82, and upon his return to New
York saw an Angels of Light show. Inspired, he formed Hot
Peaches. They rehearsed in Jackie Curtis's loft on 2nd Avenue
in the East Village, a ragtag group of hustlers and street queens
excited to be on a stage of any kind, especially in drag. Marsha
P. Johnson, Mario Montez, Peggy Shaw (who'd later become a
regarded theater artist in her own right), and Wilhelmina Ross
also starred in several productions.

What started out as fun became a real theater company, and
Camicia decided Hot Peaches would continue to be unapologetically queer and perpetually genderfucking in its approach. They
were among the comparatively few theater troupes that catered
to queer audiences. Hot Peaches also became an outlet for drag
queens, transgender women, and gender nonconforming individuals to perform onstage beyond drag clubs, which was then
unusual. Minette became a fan and even performed with them
herself in 1977. Camicia remembers turning down an invitation to be on a television show about gay life that went against
the Hot Peaches mission. "When we showed up for the initial
meeting, the producers asked us if we would dress as straight
as possible for the actual broadcast," he wrote. "We demurred,
and that was the end of that." The Hot Peaches formula worked
for two decades. The positive reception the troupe experienced
took them across Europe and the US, and later afforded them
their own theater and cast income as well as theatrical runs in
respected off-off-Broadway theaters like La MaMa.

"David Johansen borrowed the outrageousness of the ridiculous theatre and put it into rock and roll by starting the New
York Dolls," actress Cyrinda Foxe said in *Please Kill Me: An Uncensored Oral History of Punk*. "The ridiculous theatre was much
more exciting than rock and roll."

Johansen first saw Charles Ludlam's Ridiculous Theatrical Company in 1968 and later worked at a store on St. Marks Place that made costumes for the company. He eventually got involved in Ridiculous shows himself, with lighting, guitar, sound, and roles onstage. The experience inspired the aesthetic for his band, the New York Dolls. Formed in 1971, the Dolls—all cis men—became known for their glam raunch sound and visuals. The look was doubtlessly influenced by the queer downtown, underground worlds the musicians inhabited. With teased hair, wildly overwrought makeup, and platform boots, they became—if only in appearance—prominently gender nonconforming members of the punk scene, a look that would later influence all manner of glam rock and hair metal performers. But to them, it was nothing new. "We weren't trying to be confrontational," Johansen said later. "It's just what was going on in the Lower East Side. We were representing our constituency." But even as some straight rock stars played with gender nonconformity, others wanted nothing to do with it. Drag was often still unacceptable if donned by artists who were actually queer.

The worlds of drag and punk would converge again in the persona of Jayne County. "I wanted to make records and get out there and become a pop star. I wanted to become the first drag queen pop star," she told the *QueerCore* podcast in 2020. But before Jayne became the first openly transgender rock star in the US, she got her start in downtown New York's theater scene.

After seeing John Vaccaro's production of Ronald Tavel's *The Life of Lady Godiva* in the late 1960s, Jayne's world turned upside down. "It was real, organized theatre but using freaks and drag queens," she'd write in her 1995 autobiography *Man Enough to Be a Woman*. "I was never the same after seeing [it]. It completely clicked with me." Jayne realized drag didn't have to be confined to the street or the dive bar, and her wheels started to turn. She wrote and performed a play, *World—Birth of a Nation*, which contemplated male castration. Theatre of the Ridiculous ideologies animated her stage work and music. She embraced the highly sexualized, the naked (in any sense of the word), the vulnerable, the trashy, the sense of visual attack.

County met David Bowie in London during a 1971 traveling production of Andy Warhol's *Pork*. At that point, Bowie was still in his folkier, long-haired, *Hunky Dory* era, but Jayne said that would soon change after meeting her. Fortunately, they shared the same management company. "After us, David started getting dressed up," Jayne remembered in *Please Kill Me*. "I'd gotten the shaved eyebrows thing from Jackie Curtis, and David started shaving his eyebrows, painting his nails, even wearing painted nails out at nightclubs, like we were doing. He changed his whole image and started getting more and more freaky." Jayne's and Jackie's influences on Bowie were unmistakable, though the Cockettes also made such claims, and it's important to note Bowie was also spending time with other members of the Warhol and Ridiculous Theatre crowds. In London, too, theater artist Lindsay Kemp, whose work warped gender, sexuality, and their corresponding appearances, served as a mentor to Bowie, which the latter actively acknowledged.

Bowie's influence from these boundary-pushing gender-and genre-bending sources would inform his various public personas for decades. His take on gender nonconformity first appeared in his 1971 album *The Rise and Fall of Ziggy Stardust and the Spiders from Mars*. Ziggy Stardust would become his own drag persona of sorts, an exercise in glam androgyny that would itself influence legions of performers after him.

Incidentally, starting in the early 1980s, Hibiscus also created a glitter rock band called Hibiscus and the Screaming Violets with his three sisters. They performed in purple beehives and bouffants while Hibiscus dressed in a wild metallic drag ensemble. In performances at Theatre for the New City on 1st Avenue, they'd count among their fans John Lennon and the Osmonds. Above the Village Cigar Store by the West Village's Sheridan Square, Hibiscus also purchased a giant billboard covered in purple sequins advertising the band, which stayed up for several years.

Dressing in drag, Jayne County became a DJ and performer at Max's Kansas City. In 1972, she formed a band called Queen Elizabeth, and in their first performance, held at NYU, Jayne, dressed in a rainbow wig, made use of a highly lubed dildo that sent a university gay rights organization into a tizzy. The band was kicked off the school's stage that night, the performance deemed degrading to women. Such an experience would not be foreign to Jayne through the rest of her career. In her memoir, she remembers a New York Dolls show at the Mercer Arts Center, to which she arrived in drag:

> There was a demonstration outside the gig by lesbians and gay men calling the Dolls "transvestite scum" and saying that people like us were causing women to be raped on the streets. The liberation movement at that time was very anti-transvestite... Why should drag queens be picked out as a representation of the oppression of women? Some people try to use their ideas of "liberation" to suppress others... Gay or straight, an asshole is an asshole.

Indeed, Jayne was right about the gay liberation movement's rejection of drag at the time, but she'd also made not giving a fuck part of her existence. In the meantime, that controversial NYU show got Queen Elizabeth more gigs. The punk scene blew up and Jayne soared with it, once referred to as a "drag rock Lenny Bruce." But for Jayne, something was still missing—dressing up was fun, but she had always felt she was truly a woman. She transitioned in the mid-1970s, and adopted the name Jayne in the early 1980s.

Jayne was vibrantly, unapologetically visible—always in towering blond wigs; deep, dark eye makeup; lashes for days; and at least once, a dress made entirely of condoms. At one point she came onstage and would "fuck [her]self with a pitchfork." She'd waggle her tongue at the audience. "Gene Simmons said he got that from me, the tongue thing," she told *Interview* in 2018, once and still a trailblazer.

"U.S. Ballet Soars," said the cover of *Time* magazine in 1978. Performers of all stripes in New York recognized this appetite for dance, and some sought to make the most of it.

Larry Rée performed with the Cockettes on pointe in the classic "Dying Swan" solo from *Swan Lake*. His alter ego, Ekaterina Sobechanskaya, also appeared in an intermission of Charles Ludlam's play *The Grand Tarot* and in Jackie Curtis's *Vain Victory*. Shortly after, in 1972, the drag ballet troupe Trockadero Gloxinia Ballet Company was born. A most unusual concept at the time and even still today, Trockadero Gloxinia continued to perform until 1992.

"The credo of Larry was, it wasn't about technical excellence, it's about effort, and it's not about camping," said John Kelly, who performed with the company. "It's about aiming to achieve honesty, and in that, there will be both poetry and of course hilarity."

For some members of Gloxinia, this wasn't enough. In 1974, Peter Anastos, Natch Taylor, and Anthony Bassae, all trained dancers, started Les Ballets Trockadero de Monte Carlo, with more of an emphasis on ballet. They hired trained dancers, only a few of whom had ever actually done drag. That August, the Trocks, as they've become known, made their debut at the West Side Discussion Group Center, a queer community center, at 9th Avenue and 14th Street. "The parody company we've been needing may have just arrived," wrote the *New Yorker*'s dance critic Arlene Croce. "Its debut…could not have been more of a success." Anastos, Taylor, and Bassae were able to access their own Greenwich Village queer community while bringing uptown's Lincoln Center crowd to downtown spaces, even ones that were decidedly gritty. They used drag to transcend boundaries between highbrow and lowbrow, queer and straight, in a notoriously conservative art form.

Anastos laughed that at first "the pointe work was really terrible," but the ideas translated. "People wanted to see us because we were funny. And we used history, we used ballet, as a tool for laughter," he continued. "We did it with a lot of love and a lot of knowledge. And I think that got people interested in us. Again, I don't think a guy in a tutu is very funny. You gotta do something with it." And "do something" they did.

For the 1975–1976 season, they participated in the National Endowment for the Arts Touring Program, growing into a full-fledged ballet company. A ballet mistress taught daily classes, with rehearsals in a loft on West 24th Street that Taylor and Bassae had crafted into a dance studio. It had a wooden floor that Anastos called "Splinter City" with a chuckle. There were tours, appearances on Broadway, a photo shoot in *Vogue*, write-ups in the *New York Times*, and television appearances with the likes of Dick Cavett, Shirley MacLaine, and more. Their success only continued: in 2023, Les Ballets Trockadero de Monte Carlo celebrated its forty-ninth anniversary.

Just like the birth of punk, the dawn of disco provided another platform for drag. One of the first true disco hits, Gloria Gaynor's version of "Never Can Say Goodbye," arrived in 1974, and the genre began to thrive on the city's newly minted dance floors. Venues like the Sanctuary, the Loft, and G.G. Barnum's, a disco and trapeze club that served as haven for trans women and for drag, provided a safe dance space for a heavily queer contingent without fear of the police raids that still took place, in part because the venues were open to guests of all kinds (the first gay-only disco in New York, The Flamingo, opened in 1974). It was at the Loft that legendary DJs Frankie Knuckles and Larry Levan were thrilled early on by spaces like these—incidentally, the two had met through the world of Harlem drag balls, where Levan was in the House of Wong and Knuckles's drag name was Setter.

The most famous of these clubs was doubtlessly Studio 54. Steve Rubell and Ian Schrager opened the club in 1977 at 254 West 54th Street—it had been an opera house converted into a sound stage for CBS, then abandoned. Rubell, who was gay, created the club's clientele in his own vision: only the most beautiful, fascinating people in the world would pass through its signature velvet ropes. Short and balding, he'd famously quip that he couldn't have gotten into his own club. Just as with punk and glam rock, queerness and thereby drag had cachet in the disco sphere. People of all stripes clamored to get past the club's notoriously difficult door, to cavort in a partially queer-owned space—Schrager was straight—and live in its freewheeling existence.

Studio 54's patronage included some of New York's most beloved in drag. Hibiscus was among them, as was Rollerena Fairy Godmother, who by day worked on Wall Street and by night coursed through the club in roller skates, magnificent 1950s pillbox hats with giant shimmering earrings, and rhinestone eyeglasses. Also among them was Divine, who had relocated to New York after his success in John Waters's 1972 cult hit *Pink Flamingos*. Divine had already been a muse to Waters for several years when *Pink Flamingos* made him a star. In the film he portrays Babs Johnson, the "filthiest person alive," with shocking blue eyelids, fiery red lips, and eyebrows well past her forehead. After the film, at Waters's suggestion, Divine began deliberately destroying drag's previous beauty standards as the "Godzilla of drag queens," and in doing so informed future generations of drag artists. The hair was wild, the makeup hair-raising, the skirts short, the clothes bold, all unapologetically leading the eye to every inch of his bountiful figure. "His legacy was that he made all drag queens cool. They were square then, they wanted to be Miss America and be their mothers," Waters told *Baltimore* magazine in 2015. "Divine frightened drag queens because he would show up with a chainsaw and [makeup artist] Van Smith would put fake scars on his face… He broke every rule. And now every drag queen, every one that's successful today is cutting edge."

Still, like Charles Ludlam before him, Divine saw himself as an actor first and wanted to be accepted as such. He just happened to play female characters. "I'm a character actor," he told Terry Gross of NPR's *Fresh Air* in 1988. "I never set out in the beginning of my career just to play female roles."

And while Divine appeared regularly at Studio 54 alongside the likes of Bianca Jagger and Halston, so too did Potassa de la Fayette. In her lifetime, the model would become a muse to both Andy Warhol and Salvador Dalí, the latter of whom referred to her as his "house drag queen." Potassa was a Dominican transgender woman who also performed in drag in the decade prior and competed at some forty drag balls across the city beginning in 1969. It was at the balls that Potassa honed her high-fashion aesthetic. "Every queen in New York used to wear like ten wigs, a lot of curls, like banana curls and all that," she told *Interview Magazine* in 1977. "And when I went [to Studio 54] I went with my hair pulled back in a little bun like Halston [does] now, you know…so now they say Potassa came, she going to wreck, you know what I mean."

By the time most people met Potassa in the early 1970s, she no longer referred to herself as a drag queen and used only feminine pronouns. "I am not a man," she told *Women's Wear Daily* for a 1974 profile. "I am not a woman. And I am not a drag queen... I am a person who loves beautiful things." Potassa's gender identity was no secret among the elite circles in which she ran, though at the beginning of her career nobody knew. She had a successful career as a model first for fur companies and then for magazines like *Harper's Bazaar*, designers like Stephen Burrows and Valentino, and of course artists Dalí and Warhol. However, there were designers she called close friends, like Halston and Giorgio di Sant' Angelo, who wouldn't put her in their shows or feature her in their garments because they were afraid of how their clientele would perceive clothes worn by a "drag queen." A gay man was acceptable, but a transgender woman, a drag queen, or both, was not; among many people, drag was still seen at worst as freakish and at best as déclassé.

But for Potassa, reveling in her body was both an aesthetic pleasure and an act of power, something she learned, scholar Kara Carmack says, from drag. "She joyfully weaponized her garments and her body to affect turmoil through a sequence of poses—a skill honed on the stages of drag clubs and couture catwalks," Carmack wrote in a 2020 *Journal of Visual Culture* article on the model. And she did so with aplomb, becoming a toast of the town in New York—Grace Jones referred to her in a 1984 issue of *Interview* as "Gorgeous still, and *bones*, cheek-bones."

Potassa's story is an unusual one for the time, especially given the career of Tracey "Africa" Norman—Norman, also a veteran of the ball scene, covered a box of Clairol hair color in 1975 but upon being outed as trans in 1980 suffered a career fallout. But Potassa was very open about her identity, flashing her genitals with unapologetic abandon at Studio 54 while dancing in fringe, bangles, sheer fabrics and more. Dripping in designer finery, she was a regular in the fashion pages of *Women's Wear Daily*.

★ ★ ★

Potassa came up through a drag ball scene that by the 1970s was thriving. Crystal LaBeija's House of LaBeija was born in 1972, as was Dorian Corey's House of Corey. Leading houses Dupree, Dior, Pendavis, Omni, Ebony, and others soon followed throughout the decade, with even more to arrive in the 1980s. For queer youths of color living in New York, the houses were a saving grace. This was particularly true in parts of the city experiencing higher than usual economic devastation.

Throughout the 1970s, the South Bronx was quite literally burning as it became mired in crime and poverty. Landlords set fire to their buildings for insurance money, just as they did downtown. Harlem faced overcrowding and high unemployment rates for the underprivileged. Its more well-off residents had retreated to the suburbs the decade prior, leaving behind abandoned real estate that made the area rife with crime. By March 1978, though there was always beauty in the culturally-rich neighborhood, its state at the time was front-page news in the *New York Times*. In an article entitled "In the Last Decade, Leaders Say, Harlem's Dreams Have Died," the neighborhood's Black leaders mourned the current state of their home, the lack of assistance from the government, the gang violence, and how its citizens were failed by forces meant to help them.

Many young queer people from Harlem and the Bronx who were thrown out of their homes faced real danger on the street. The House of LaBeija and others became a refuge. Many also found kinship in the Village, still a hotbed for queer life of all kinds, including on the piers by the Hudson River, where people could cruise for sex, among other places. But the uptown balls continued to be a stabilizing force. After the 1960s, queens of color were prioritized, and there would be no more whitening of the skin as in competitions of some fifty years earlier. It was from this foundation of drag queens and transgender women of color that ball culture as we know it today would flourish.

Participants could compete in even more categories, from dance (this would become voguing in the 1980s, but originated as "pop, dip, and spin," a subsection of break dancing) to runway to performance to style to, of course, drag. Categories could be Butch Queen First Time in Drags at a Ball, or Executive Realness, or High Fashion Eveningwear, and more. You'd walk the runway for judges according to your category of choice, hoping to snatch trophies. "Realness," the ability to pass as a woman, was prized, but there was also an underlying racial aspect to the presentations.

"It was our goal then to look like white women," Pepper LaBeija, who became mother of the House of LaBeija after Mother Crystal, told writer Michael Cunningham in 2000. While there were certainly markers of Black beauty and glamour, like Diana Ross and model Beverly Johnson, they were still the minority. Though queens of color were in the spotlight, their style choices then are sometimes criticized today for catering to ideals of whiteness. Regardless, the ball scene, independently and with Black culture as its driving force, would have an indelible impact on fashion, music, and culture over the next few decades.

7

1980–1989

On July 3, 1981, the *New York Times* ran its first article on a little-understood illness with the headline "RARE CANCER SEEN IN 41 HOMOSEXUALS."

"Gay" was not yet an accepted word in the paper's style guide. The medical community usually only found this "rare cancer," Kaposi's sarcoma, and *Pneumocystis carinii* pneumonia, in patients with weakened immune systems. By 1981, however, these illnesses were detected in otherwise healthy young gay men in New York and California.

By January 1982, the virus had a name: "gay-related immune deficiency" or "GRID." But when straight members of Brooklyn's Haitian population began contracting the illness, the Centers for Disease Control renamed it "acquired immunodeficiency syndrome" or "AIDS." Early on, it was also known as "Saint's Disease" after the massively popular, members-only gay club at 102 2nd Avenue at East 6th Street in the East Village. The space boasted its own planetarium, brought in musical acts like Tina Turner and Grace Jones, and was also host to some of the earliest iterations of the famed BDSM-forward Black Party (where at least once Robert Mapplethorpe photographed guests). It seemed like so many of the men who caught this disease were among its patrons, those regarded as clubland's most beautiful. The medical community was stymied and scared, as was the rest of the world. Panic ensued.

Gay men would carry the stigma of AIDS as fatalities increased through the 1980s and into the 1990s, though anyone could contract HIV, or human immunodeficiency virus, the virus that can cause AIDS. *New York Magazine* reported on June 20, 1983, that "AIDS victims have been fired from their jobs, driven from their homes, and deserted by their loved ones. Any homosexual or Haitian has become an object of dread..." Anger and anxiousness came from within the gay community and created movements, raising money and awareness to help those affected by AIDS.

In New York, performers were creating a new, dynamic drag that also served as a vital, healing, artistic force amid great tragedy. At AIDS benefits, drag performers, DJs, and performance artists would take the stage all night long, raising money for patients' medical and living expenses. They performed with the fervor of time running out, still hoping that something, anything, would stop the constant funeral procession the city had become.

"I didn't do theater until I was 31. I was raised in theater by drag queens," Peggy Shaw told *Bomb* magazine in 1999.

Shaw moved to New York in 1967 and soon after was bowled over by Charles Ludlam's play *Bluebeard*. A few years later, she stumbled upon a Hot Peaches performance on the street in the West Village. "I went, Wow, I want to do this, and I went up to 'em and said, 'Can I follow you around?'"

Shaw initially made sets for the troupe before making her official onstage debut in 1975. "Hot Peaches taught me how to perform, and be aggressive, and do cabaret," Shaw told *The Rumpus* in 2017, but her look was different from their sequined, feather boa-ed extravaganzas. "I'd do monologues about being butch, and rolling cigarettes, and cowboy stuff, and I'd get booed because I was with a drag group," she said. She wished for a different experience, where she could be herself among women, but stayed for a few more years. While living in London and performing with Hot Peaches, she met theater artist Lois Weaver. By 1979, Weaver would become not just her romantic partner but her collaborator for more than four decades.

In 1980, Weaver and Shaw, with Deb Margolin, created the theater troupe Split Britches, inspired in part by Hot Peaches as well as by Indigenous performance group Spiderwoman Theater. "Nothing that we saw in traditional theatre reflected us as lesbians or [people as] Native American or as drag queens or gay or anything," Shaw said in 2018. "And we all learned together at the same time how to make a new type of performance that wasn't based on the old." Split Britches, they decided, would feature the work they felt was missing from theater spaces: work that questioned and confronted gender, sexuality, and theater canon. Shaw's work was also heavily influenced by drag on a performance level. In the documentary series *Theater of Desire: The WOW Aesthetic*, she says, "When you perform with drag queens, you learn very quickly. You make sure you're loud enough, you make sure you're standing in front of them, you make sure you have a glittery thing on, you make sure you hold the interest of the audience."

In May 1980, Weaver and Shaw met with performers Pamela Camhe and Jordy Mark at the restaurant Dojo on 24 St. Marks Place. Hoping to attend women's theater festivals in the States like they had in Europe, they decided to start their own. Together they cofounded the Women's One World Festival, or WOW Festival, for women's and international theater troupes over the course of eleven days that October. The festi-

val ran in various East Village venues, ultimately settling in a
loft on East 4th Street in 1984. This became the WOW Café,
a driving force for lesbian and queer theater in the downtown
New York arts scene. Like La MaMa and Caffé Cino, WOW
was and is a theater space for new and experimental work, but
specifically dedicated to the work of women and gender nonconforming individuals that sometimes happens to involve drag.
As *Curve* magazine editor Merryn Johns wrote, it is "a paradise of playwriting and acting established by a group of daring
dykes." The work created at WOW would mark a revolution
in feminist, lesbian, and transgender representation in theater.

While some critics dismissed WOW as cultish, the venue introduced a generation of women and gender nonconforming individuals to male drag and drag kings—poet Eileen Myles saw
their first ever male drag show at the venue and once appeared
on WOW's stage naked save for a dildo—pushing the evolution and presence of male drag in the downtown and theater
communities. Male drag at WOW had a layered complexity.
In her book *Lady Dicks and Lesbian Brothers*, scholar Kate Davy
defines this as a "desire for women to be visible *as women* impersonating men [that is] in part about the ever-present scarcity
of such portrayals."

Davy cites scholar and performance artist Holly Hughes's
assertion that WOW's relationship to male drag was to have
women play men "in quotes." Hughes, now a decorated avant-
garde performance practitioner, got her start at WOW by accident. "If I hadn't found that particular collective of people who
had been kicked out of other feminist collectives, I don't think I
would have started—it was peer pressure that drew me into performance," she said in 2007. "If they'd been doing skeet shooting or soccer league, I'd be doing that as well because I wanted
to hang out with this group of really smart bad girls, who were
really good, but good at being bad." It was there she found she
could tell stories she had always hoped to hear, which inter-

estingly enough was "inspired more by a lot of drag and camp theater than by feminist theater," she'd say. Indeed, she'd recall later, drag was a style of theater all its own.

The roles that did involve drag contained suggestions of men, but women's bodies and choices would not be sacrificed while bringing them to life. Many roles at WOW played with butch/femme aesthetics—this is to say, they were not drag, but portrayed more stereotypically masculine or feminine aspects of appearance in lesbian culture. Just as Gladys Bentley was not a drag king, there were times when "masculine" appearance at WOW did not dictate "man" or the desire to portray "man" unless the script called for it. There were, however, notable instances of male drag that affected the outcome and presence of drag in New York today.

In 1982, for example, Alina Troyano arrived at the WOW Café "looking for girls and found something more long-lasting: theatre," she said in 1995. She developed the persona of Carmelita Tropicana, who Troyano herself has discussed as a drag persona parodying femininity, sending up the stereotypical lusty Latine spitfire trope with a lesbian twist. As Carmelita, however, Troyano also performed in another layer of drag as Pingalito Betancourt, the "Socrates of [Havana's] M15 bus route," in a 1987 play she wrote entitled *Memorias de la Revolución*. In the play, Pingalito (which, for context and comedy, is slang for "little dick"), offers a history of Troyano's native Cuba through a comedically machismo-infused monologue, all while wearing a traditional Cuban man's ensemble of fedora and white guayabera, a cigar balanced on the fingertips. Such a performance allowed for an expanded vision of what drag could look like on the stage in terms of appearance, storytelling, and ethnicity.

Among the most influential WOW performers in the world of male drag, however, was Diane Torr. A native of Scotland and all of five feet three inches tall, Torr first performed in drag in 1982. She continued learning how to transform her petite

frame into that of a suited, mustachioed gent from the transgender musician, makeup artist, and postmodern drag king pioneer Johnny Science.

While the earliest appearance of the term "drag king" is believed to be in Bruce Rodgers's 1972 gay lexicographical text
The Queen's Vernacular, Science himself claimed to have developed the phrase as well. Science, who was also an art director
at Max's Kansas City, used his skills as a trained special effects
makeup artist to develop techniques for what he called male
makeovers. By 1987 he was conducting what he called "Drag
King Workshops" at seminars like the International Foundation
for Gender Education Annual Symposium.

After getting done up by Science for a photo shoot in 1989,
Torr wrote, "I had such a strong sense of a male identity, that
I went out to the streets of New York, and to an opening at
the Whitney Museum, and managed to convincingly pass as a
man!" While Torr taught classes on gender performance at colleges previously, she wrote that it was through Science's makeup
and facial hair she really felt herself transformed. And while Science as an artist knew how to successfully create a masculine
visage—from facial hair to chest binding to creating a bulge
and more—Torr found he needed help instructing his students
in movement and character, the creation of a persona. They decided to team with performance artist Annie Sprinkle and host
Drag-King-for-a-Day workshops. "I was encouraged [to] serve
the new 'boys' beer and rub my cleavage in their faces," Sprinkle wrote. "It was a blast."

In 1978, Club 57 opened in the basement of the Holy Cross
Polish National Church at 57 St. Marks Place in hopes of generating extra income for the church. The East Village at the
time was littered with trash, covered in graffiti, facing an influx
of drugs and homelessness. "I always say it looked like Berlin

after World War II," writer and drag artist Charles Busch said. "There were a lot of buildings that were just half demolished."

Neglected and in many cases deserted, the neighborhood became a refuge for artists seeking cheap rent or a place to squat. The infusion of creative energy led to new performance spaces and galleries. The East Village had been a "counterculture hotbed" in the 1960s, with "a mix of artists, writers and musicians, drawn by the cheap housing and casual street life," the *New York Times* wrote in 1983. The same would be true again in the 1980s, but added to that mix was a host of performers who would change the way we interact with drag today. The neighborhood became a breeding ground for a world of experimentation. "The East Village sensibility of celebrating drag was actually kind of radical, sort of punk rock," said drag queen and historian Linda Simpson. "But it was done in a very tongue-in-cheek, self-conscious kind of way because drag itself was being parodied." The idea was not necessarily to impersonate a woman or a man, but to joke in a visual format with the idea of what it meant to do that in the first place.

Club 57 in particular became a haven for creative types. There were concerts, poetry readings, theatrical productions, movie screenings, and so much more for people who, in the late 1970s, were merely local artists like Jean-Michel Basquiat and Keith Haring. The space nurtured a spirit of artistic freedom and experimentation that would become the foundation of New York's downtown scene. In the 2010 documentary *Arias with a Twist*, former Club 57 manager Ann Magnuson discusses the time as one not focused on careerism. Living in New York became easy, she says, because it was so cheap—you could just keep making art with friends and living inexpensively, not worrying about money; you didn't have to make money to make art.

While drag wasn't the main focal point of Club 57, Holly Woodlawn and Alexis del Lago would star in some of its fabulously low-budget productions, from *The Sound of Muzak* and

Peter Pan to *Nude Faces* and *Trojan Women*, all of which were composed by a young musician named Scott Wittman, who'd later win a Tony for the score of Broadway's *Hairspray* with another former Club 57 denizen named Marc Shaiman.

Transgender cabaret star Alexis del Lago had arrived in New York from Puerto Rico in 1956, and enrolled at Parsons as a fashion design student. Shortly after, she dressed in drag for the first time for the campus ball; she won, but the joy wouldn't last. "They didn't like that I expressed myself like that and I was told I couldn't continue in the school," she said. Her mother found her a program where she could be herself, however—"My mother used to tell me, darling, everything you do is art!" She later worked with star designer Pauline Trigère. But Alexis's attire of choice was not welcome there, either, however. "None of this Marlene Dietrich thing here. Curb that! You have to become a gentleman here," Alexis recounted in 2018—but Alexis made it work just the same. She'd go to parties dressed as Marlene instead, favoring the glamorous actress's tuxedo ensemble from the 1930 film *Morocco*. She became involved with the Theatre of the Ridiculous scene, later working with Jackie Curtis and Charles Ludlam, and appears briefly in Jack Smith's *Flaming Creatures*. But she famously didn't want to work with Andy Warhol. "I never made a movie with Andy Warhol because I didn't want to make movies about common people," she said. "I wanted to make movies with glamour like Dietrich and Garbo." She'd also refer to his films as "tacky" and "boring."

Alexis left New York in 1975, but upon her return the following decade re-created herself as a glamorous cabaret star. "In the 80s I wasn't doing campy drag anymore, but focused upon presenting an image of sophisticated glamour, and people started treating me like a star," she said, and Scott Wittman was among them. They were introduced when Alexis played one of the Siamese cats in a Disney-themed show called *When You Wish Upon a Star* with the Club 57 crew at the Limelight nightclub. "Once

I met Alexis, Alexis was in everything," Wittman said. "Alexis came to see Holly in *The Sound of Muzak* so after that we never sort of left each other's side for quite a few years."

In April 1980, performer John Sex started a night at Club 57 called "Acts of Live Art." John Sex incorporated aspects of high camp male drag into his work, embodying what author Steven Hager would later call "a glitter, Las Vegas version of the All-American kid—a handsome, fun-loving sex maniac with a foot-high shock of blond hair." His series featured a range of wild, mischievous, edgy performances, people doing really whatever they wanted onstage: Ann Magnuson tap-danced in a majorette outfit and twirled a baton to Donna Summer's "Hot Stuff," for example, while Sex did a matador burlesque. "Acts of Live Art" became one of the most important events in the club's five-year history and spawned some of the 1980s' most iconic artists and performers.

Joey Arias was one such performer. But when he first arrived in New York, he wanted nothing to do with drag. "I didn't like it. I didn't find it exciting. I just thought yuck, yuck, yuck," he said. That year, Arias drove cross-country from Los Angeles to New York with his friend Kim Hastreiter, who'd become the cofounder and co-editor-in-chief of *Paper* magazine in 1984. After arriving in New York, Arias became a frequent Club 57 denizen and downtown star.

He also made a name for himself working at the fabulous Fiorucci clothing store. Beloved as the "daytime Studio 54" and known for its bold neons, glitters, and animal prints, Arias made the acquaintance of everyone who walked through its doors, from Andy Warhol to Jackie Onassis (and a young actress named Cassandra Peterson who worked the espresso bar in her pre-Elvira days). Through Fiorucci customer and artist Katy K, Arias met Klaus Nomi, and the two began performing together in a band at Max's Kansas City and Hurrah. Word spread, and soon they were singing with David Bowie on the December 15,

1979, episode of *Saturday Night Live*, Arias wrapped in red latex and Nomi with his signature white face paint and blackened lips. Back at Fiorucci that Monday, there were lines of people hoping for Arias's autograph.

Befriending Warhol through Fiorucci, Arias was invited to the artist's annual Halloween party, for which drag was required. He wore a black rubber Vivienne Westwood top, water balloon breasts, and huge cat eyes, and everyone loved it. But he hated it and swore he'd never do drag again. In the next decade he proved himself wrong.

Drag was reinvented and reinvigorated in the East Village, moving away from mimicry and resemblance and toward the dismantling of the gender binary entirely. "It was social commentary," RuPaul said in 1993. "It was wearing ratty wigs and combat boots and big old water balloon falsies and saying, 'Look at me, I'm just as freaky as any Reaganomic Tipper Gore nightmare.'" DIY punk aesthetics moved drag performers away from the diva impersonations of yore, when eyelashes and eyebrows were never out of place.

From the time it was constructed in 1876, the building at 101 Avenue A hosted everything from labor meetings to weddings for the neighborhood's vibrant local German-American population. That population moved uptown in the 1930s, however, and by the early 1980s, the German community space had devolved into a decrepit bar run by building owner Richie Hajguchik. Old Polish men would arrive bright and early in the morning to pound fifty-cent shots of vodka. Nightclub coworkers Alan Mace (aka DJ and drag artist extraordinaire Sister Dimension), John Tucker, Bobby Bradley, and Victor Sapienza approached Hajguchik about doing a party in the bar's abandoned backroom to attract the neighborhood's new crop of artistic spirits. It was so successful it became a regular nightly event with dancing, performances, and music. The Pyramid Club had officially arrived. Brian Butterick was there, and he was astounded by what he saw. He had not been a fan of drag previously.

At a gay bar in Yonkers, Butterick saw a troupe of drunk, abysmally lip-synching drag queens called the Cherries. (By then Barbra Herr, who had started doing drag with the troupe, was not among them and had moved to Puerto Rico.) He thought he had seen all the drag he needed to see. However, artists David Wojnarowicz and Peter Hujar insisted he try again. "They [told] me, 'You guys gotta see this drag queen. Her name is Ethyl Eichelberger,' and I was like, 'Ugh, drag,'" Butterick said. "And they're like, 'no, no, no, it's not like a drag act. It's not like you might have thought a drag act should be. Wait till you see this.'"

Butterick saw Eichelberger perform for the first time in 1978, and he was completely floored. "She sang her own songs, she played six instruments, she played the accordion, she tap danced, she wrote these classically-inspired performance pieces... For some reason, I never had the luxury of doing [that kind of drag], so I was just blown away."

Ethyl was not just some celebrity impersonator. By his own description, James Roy Eichelberger wormed his way into the Ridiculous Theatrical Company by sewing costumes. He eventually joined the company as a guest artist in 1974 and changed his first name to Ethyl the following year. Eichelberger performed regularly with the company until he left in 1978—partly because an affair with Ludlam had gone awry, but mostly to perform his own work, though he'd return to RTC on occasion. He described himself as a "serious tragedian, club and drag performer." Toying with the boundaries of camp and drag in the 1970s and 1980s theater space, Ethyl became one of the era's most respected experimental theater performers, often regarded as a genius. "The conceptual construct of the narrative that she was embodying or taking over—putting over the top or taking shots at—was very much drag. And the idea of deconstructing and reconstructing was very [much] a part of that time," renowned performance artist Karen Finley said.

In place of female impersonators walked people like Eichelberger who saw drag's potential as experimental performance art and an act of rebellion, a medium to tell a story while subverting gender constructs. The experimental drag we have today is in part rooted there.

Arriving at the Pyramid Club on its opening night, Butterick saw the first of many performances that would come to characterize the space. John Kelly presented his piece "The Martyrdom of Saint Sebastian" wearing "an upside down-like bustier…a teased out red wig and black eye sockets," Kelly told writer Tricia Romano in 2014. "[Saint Sebastian is] considered the gay patron saint because he was shot with arrows… And then the arrows were actually sounds that I reacted to physically. I did a front flip over the railing, and that's how I died at the end."

All this time, drag has remained very personal to Kelly. "It was character driven but it was also this holy irreverence. Drag is a sensation-oriented gesture, in that when you show up in drag, you're going to cause a stir," he said. "There was this weird gender, or drag-ophobia, even in the gay community at that point, and I understand it, because gay men were trying to assert themselves in a world which detested them… I just wanted to create my own road, for being a gay man, a queer man, an outsider, and drag was part of that, and it was a tool. It was ammunition. It caught people off guard. But even as I was doing it, every step of the way, I was trying to circumvent people's expectations." Saint Sebastian would be his first of many performances at the Pyramid, where he also became famous for his character study of Joni Mitchell. Many saw Kelly's work and amplified their own drag accordingly, thinking as he did beyond the transparent, continuing to challenge drag norms.

Butterick was enthralled. He joined the Pyramid team and later became bar manager, a beloved creative force of its underground current. Heavily informed by Eichelberger, he later donned drag himself and became Hattie Hathaway, often in Victorian drag ("which is great for someone who doesn't tuck," he said later), performing in bands and hosting onstage. Drag parties were specifically reserved for Sundays. The Pyramid was music, performance art, genderfucking. It was punk drag, it was art, it was trash, it was irreverent, it was kitsch, it was cabaret, it was glamour. It became a playground for the artistry of gender nonconformity in all of its theatrical forms: skits, comedy, video, song, dance, monologue, and more.

The club opened in an era of mainstream social and economic conservatism under President Ronald Reagan. "Really, the thing we all seemed to be saying most frequently was, 'America, we aren't buying it.' And we weren't. Not one bit," Butterick wrote in 2015. Rooted in these punk ideals, the Pyramid's drag was not about pretending to be a woman. It was about questioning what a woman was, what identity was, what drag was. Or, as author Tom Eubanks wrote in his memoir *Ghosts of St. Vincent's*, "They loaded their feminine illusion with feminist allusions."

Eichelberger performed often at the Pyramid, doing solo drag shows celebrating famed women of history, commenting on being a gay man through stories of strong women like Nefertiti and Clytemnestra. "I try to tell the great stories. But they've been done. So I do my own versions," he said in 1987. He also upended classic theater pieces, flipping gendered roles on their heads, and added his self-taught circus background of fire-eating and acrobatics. It was still a new world for open queerness onstage, but Eichelberger received critical acclaim nonetheless. "He is an original interpretive artist—and his revels are boundless," the *New York Times* wrote. Eichelberger began performing at powerhouse venues like Lincoln Center, then expanded to film, television, and Broadway. His plays are still performed today and have inspired a generation of queer theater artists for whom drag could act as both medium and message.

It was also at the Pyramid that John Epperson found his voice, so to speak. Epperson had realized the breadth of what art could be at Club 57, that wearing a dress and lip-synching could be part of it. In August 1980, he made his New York drag debut at "Acts of Live Art," lip-synching to Patti James's "Pepper Hot Baby" in a dress of blue-and-white polka dots with gold lamé pedal pushers. "Why did I want to perform at Club 57? Well, because I could, because it was there, because I wanted to be noticed," Epperson said. In 1984, John Sex told him about the Pyramid Club, then open for less than three years.

John Epperson learned of AIDS and wondered if he might have it. "I thought to myself, but that means you're going to die if you have it, and there's so much I wanted to do that I hadn't done," he said. Epperson began assembling snippets of classic songs and films into narratives, inspired by the cultural mash-ups in Bette Midler's work and San Francisco's long-running play *Beach Blanket Babylon*. Soon he was Lypsinka, stylized in part like 1950s actress Dolores Gray, performing regularly at the Pyramid. He'd eventually leave the clubs, first for off-off-Broadway, then off Broadway. Lypsinka gained a cult following after the now-classic 1988 show *I Could Go On Lip-Synching*. Epperson was not crazy about the term "drag queen" and has never used it to describe his work. The 1990s saw Lypsinka on the runway with Thierry Mugler, as a face of l.a.Eyeworks and Gap campaigns, photographed by legendary photographer Francesco Scavullo, appearing in George Michael's "Too Funky" music video, and more. Lypsinka lives on today as Epperson pleases, heralded by *New York Times* theater critic Ben Brantley in 2014 as "the greatest chanteuse who never sung a note."

In the height of the AIDS epidemic, the Pyramid became as much a cultural workshop for performers like Epperson as it did a respite and battleground. "I think the performance art aspect of the 80s [drag] came about largely because of AIDS. It was a way to funnel all those emotions...the rage, the grief, the terror, into some kind of creativity onstage. And it was political. Drag is political as an act in itself. It became our way of making the clubs more politicized and bringing the whole community to share enjoyment of something," said journalist Michael Musto, who has spent decades covering the downtown and drag scenes in New York.

Such was also the case for Dean Johnson, "a 7-foot-tall drag queen with a bald head, a huge cock, and a rock band," as artist and Pyramid drag regular Tabboo! would say. The Pyramid Club's genderfucking punk spirit was a perfect match for Johnson. Brian Butterick was working the door and "immediately whisked him in," he said in 2007. "He had long red hair, like this Renaissance beatific child."

Johnson became known for attiring his six-foot-six frame in black dresses, red lips, bold earrings, sunglasses, and size 14 heels. His bald head towered above everyone as he go-go danced on the Pyramid's bar. Later, he started hosting "Rock and Roll Fag Bar," a Tuesday night party at The World on 254 East 2nd Street at Avenue C. The deliciously sleazy scene was beloved by the likes of Prince, Madonna, Lady Bunny, and Carolina Herrera.

"Rock and Roll Fag Bar" was a specifically gay night promising "live bands • drag queens • hot go-go trash," with drag artists Tabboo! and Lily of the Valley as emcees. "Everyone here is just so good looking that I get dizzy," Johnson quipped in an interview with Michael Musto for MTV in 1988. "It's really fun, we have lots of pop stars and drag queens and half-naked boys running all over the club and it's always such a good time every Tuesday. We're thinking of doing it every night!"

Jayne County and International Chrysis performed. Dean's band, Dean and the Weenies, regularly took the stage. It was at "Rock and Roll Fag Bar" that his song "Fuck You," earned him a record contract with Island, but he was quickly dropped. "They signed me based on my performance of 'Fuck You' but when they realized I was a gay activist and a drag queen, they freaked out and found an excuse to dump me," Johnson said later. The label still produced the single, but threw it in the garbage. "Homeless people pulled them out of the garbage and sold them for a dollar on St. Mark's [sic] and it became a huge phenomenon. That's how I really established myself as a performer back in '87."

Johnson's party was a night of punk-inspired debauchery that would make him a New York nightlife legend, especially as he continued to take to the stage with his band, the Velvet Mafia. An architect of the city's gay rock and roll scene, he'd make space for queer rock bands at venues across New York, including at CBGB's HomoCorps event. A regular sex worker, Johnson died under mysterious circumstances—many believe it was murder—while entertaining a john in 2007.

From 1984 to 1989, the Pyramid also held the famed "Whispers" disco party on Sunday nights. "Whispers" was jokingly meant for "hairdressers, display queens, theatre folk, fashionistas, florists, and sensitive straight people" because most hair salons, flower shops, and theaters were closed on Mondays. It was hosted by adored New York drag emcee Hapi Phace in full housewife drag, ratty blond updo, chunky bead necklace and all. The party promised "The Complete Suburban Gay Experience," a commentary on New York's increasing gentrification and sterility. Every so often there would be a voice in the speakers: "Whoever has the Subaru, your lights are on!" No matter the event, however, there were always drag queens dancing on the bar.

The Pyramid Club also hosted AIDS fundraisers, including one for Madonna's close friend, artist Martin Burgoyne—in 1983, he designed the cover of her second single, "Burning Up/Physical Attraction." The party hosted some 500 people, raising close to $6,000 for Burgoyne's medical care, and featured performances by John Sex and a relative newcomer to the New York scene named Lady Bunny. But it could only help so much. Burgoyne passed away two and a half months later. He was twenty-three.

"[It was] everybody on our block. You'd have like three, four friends at a time… The president wouldn't even mention it," said artist Tobie Giddio, a former Pyramid regular. "This created a need to try to create your own family, your own community. And we did! That was the great thing that happened." The Pyramid became a place to laugh at a time when so many vibrant lives were being lost. It wasn't "escape laughter," Giddio says, but "survival laughter." There was deep despair, grief, and sadness, but people counteracted that by helping each other, visiting friends in need, bringing people meals, and also by being creative, putting beauty and humor into a world that often felt absent of both. "It was a guaranteed death sentence at that point if you came down with AIDS," said Michael Musto. "We were losing people every day. We were all torn between mourning and grief and terror and rage against the government for not doing anything. But somehow the nightclubs were booming bigger than ever. Because we needed to cling to each other every night."

Indeed, President Ronald Reagan did not discuss AIDS in the public eye until a press conference on September 17, 1985. The political silence was monumentally negligent and only augmented the trauma. While the Reagan Administration created a National Commission on AIDS in May 1987 "to ensure that we are using every possible public health measure to contain the spread of the virus," that October, Republican senator Jesse Helms—who later called homosexuality "deliberate, disgusting, revolting conduct"—pushed through what became known as the Helms AIDS Amendments, which prohibited Centers for Disease Control funds from "being used to provide AIDS education, information, or prevention materials and activities that promote, encourage, and condone homosexual sexual activities or the intravenous use of illegal drugs." The following year, over seven years from the first mention of AIDS in the *New York Times*, Congress established the Health Omnibus Programs Extension (HOPE), a portion of which featured a $1 billion initiative to create programs for the education, prevention, research, care, and treatment of AIDS.

In response to government inertia early on, activist Larry Kramer founded the Gay Men's Health Crisis on January 12, 1982. By April 1982 they had raised $50,000 to offset financial costs for those in their community. But by the end of 1985, a few short months after Reagan's announcement that AIDS was a "top priority" despite having taken so long to address it, 3,799 people in New York alone had died of AIDS. They accounted for nearly one third of the 12,529 total AIDS deaths in the US that year.

By 1986, almost one third of all AIDS cases in America continued to come from New York. Kramer founded the militant activist group ACT UP, AIDS Coalition to Unleash Power, in 1987. Tired of government inaction and the apathy of gay men toward the disease, ACT UP held demonstrations and protests in some of the city's most ubiquitous areas, like Wall Street and the New York Stock Exchange. They also used drag in their demonstrations, memorably at an event inside the tony Republican National Women's Club on West 51st Street.

"ACT UP provided not only a way to express your anger or whatever; it could channel and focus your ideas," artist Hunter Reynolds told Sarah Schulman's ACT UP Oral History Project in 2012. Reynolds had been involved with the organization before he learned of his own HIV-positive status in 1989, but afterward took his activism into his own hands with the creation of Art Positive, a group focused on countering homophobia in the art world. Reynolds also channeled this into his drag alter ego, Patina du Prey, influenced by his time at the Pyramid.

As Patina, Reynolds sought to explore what he then called a third gender as well as queer hostility toward drag artists and trans individuals by moving through public spaces like art gallery openings and street fairs. Patina was not designed to "pass," as it were. Rather, she was assertively gender nonconforming: Reynolds wore no wig but painted his face in full makeup, and donned a dress with his chest hair on display.

Among the most well-known of Reynolds's works, however, are the dresses he crafted and then wore during activist performance art pieces. His 1993 "Memorial Dress" featured the names of 25,000 AIDS victims printed in gold on a black ball gown. He'd wear the dress and spin slowly on a platform edged in fabric also printed with names. "I want to express, reflect my life, how AIDS has affected me, but on a more emotional level," he said to Schulman. He saw Patina as a healer, and indeed when the dress debuted at Boston's Institute of Contemporary Art, he found patrons experiencing deep emotions upon witnessing him in it. "I wasn't prepared for the intensity of it. People found the names of their friends on the dress and began crying, having cathartic events in front of me," he told *AnOther Man*'s Miss Rosen in 2019. "I did six weeks of performances almost daily and it changed the direction of my work, connecting to the body and spirit, with the dress as a spiritual vortex to the universe."

While many drag artists joined ACT UP's protests, the group's militancy wasn't for everyone all the time.

Lady Bunny moved to New York in 1984 as the AIDS crisis was tearing the city apart. The first time she performed at the Pyramid, in a voluminous blond mane, and dark, batting lashes not unlike a draggier Dusty Springfield, she lip-synched to Gloria Gaynor's "I Will Survive," and fell over, losing her wig and a shoe. She got back up and replaced the wig by the time the song ended, and she had arrived.

Bunny wondered how to offer reprieve from the darkness of AIDS. "I thought, 'What can I do?'" she said in 2018. "I can be silly. I can be a clown. I can make people enjoy themselves and maybe lighten the burden of a blight." In the face of death, the drag festival Wigstock became a celebration of life, love, laughter, and wigs that continued to draw thousands through the end of the decade and beyond.

The idea for Wigstock emerged in 1984 after a night out at the Pyramid. Bunny, Brian Butterick, and other regulars grabbed beers from a nearby store and tottered to the bandshell at Tompkins Square Park. The fifteenth anniversary of Woodstock was coming up, they realized. What if they did a festival here? Not quite Woodstock, but a little different, and with very tongue-in-cheek hippie vibes. A little more Pyramid. It started as a joke, but the next day, Bunny got a permit for the event. Tompkins Square Park had been rife with heavy metal bands every weekend. "I can do a better show than that," she said on RuPaul's podcast *What's the Tee?* in 2018. "Honey, I used to pull a sheet between trees when I was a kid and put on shows with the neighbors."

Two years prior in Atlanta, Bunny met a then-unknown RuPaul Charles for the first time. They go-go danced together for a new-wave band called The Now Explosion and paraded around midtown Atlanta in punk rock attire, or anything they could find at thrift stores like the fishermen's wading boots Ru wore with a ripped T-shirt, thinking of themselves as Warhol disciples. "[Warhol's] mentality and his philosophy was what we had based our whole lives on, which is this postmodern, punk, create-your-own celebrity. Anyone could be a celebrity with the right clothes and the right attitude," RuPaul said in 2015. Drag in Atlanta at the time had been the height of pageant-style perfection with flawless coiffures and dazzling gowns. The first drag queen RuPaul had ever seen, however, was a New York girl: in 1978, he saw Crystal LaBeija perform a Donna Summer lip-synch in a "black bustier bikini thing with black fishnets and big black hair," he wrote in his 1995 autobiography *Lettin' It All Hang Out.*

Meanwhile, Bunny walked the streets carrying a stray tree branch like a scepter, Ru at her side, as the pageant queens offered them a barely tolerant eye roll. At Atlanta new-wave spot 688 Club, Ru was actually the first person to put Bunny in drag, for the venue's "Miss 688 Contest." It was "Do You Really Want to Hurt Me?"-era Boy George drag, all long hair and colorful scarf and fedora and exaggerated eyebrows.

In 1984, Ru joined Bunny in New York. Making $40 a night, they go-go danced at the Pyramid as drag queens. Ru was homeless for a time, sleeping in Tompkins Square Park, the Hudson River Piers, or Central Park when he wasn't on friends' couches. He stored his costumes in the Pyramid's basement. In the daytime, Bunny also answered phones in the Pyramid's office.

Later they'd live in an apartment they shared in the Meatpacking District, long before the neighborhood boasted high-end boutiques, restaurants, galleries, and an art museum. It was still known then for its proliferation of drugs, sex workers, and flourishing sex clubs alongside at least one actual meat shop. The neighborhood was also home to "The Drag Queen Stroll," an area west of 9th Avenue between Gansevoort Street and West 17th Street where sex workers tended to hustle. Though many of them would be known as transgender today, they too at the time were known as drag queens.

The proliferation of activity in the area also proved beneficial for Restaurant Florent, or just Florent as it was known to its denizens, a twenty-four-hour French diner opened in August 1985 by restaurateur Florent Morellet at 69 Gansevoort Street. Maintaining the chrome-and-green exterior left over from its previous truck-driver-friendly establishment R&L Restaurant, Florent was the place you went after the clubs closed, just before the sun rose. "Seemingly overnight, Restaurant Florent on Gansevoort Street has become one of the hottest spots in town, packed like a saucisson nightly with a mostly young and convivial crowd decked out in retrograde fashions," the *New York Times* wrote in its February 21, 1986 edition.

This "young and convivial crowd" consisted of drag performers, whether they lived in the area like Ru and Bunny, worked the area like the girls of the Stroll, or were simply looking for a fabulous, late-night meal on a budget—at the time, you could get a flank steak for $7.75 and an onion soup gratinée for $3.50. "Florent at night was just so glamorous," John Cameron Mitchell said. "All the performers would go there after and they were in their outfits, and everyone was cool and Florent was welcoming and friendly and had no attitude." It was a beloved space, day or night. "In *Cheers* everybody knew your name, right? Well, in Florent, everyone knows your name *and* your drag name," former city councilwoman Christine Quinn quipped in 2008. On Bastille Day in particular, Morellet would himself get in drag as Marie Antoinette, and hire drag performers to entertain outside the restaurant.

Nelson Sullivan lived around the corner from Florent at 5 9th Avenue, a crumbling three-story townhouse that became a revolving door of nightlife dwellers. Sullivan began documenting the scene with his video camera in 1983, in the process creating an archive of downtown royalty. Nelson and his camera were everywhere: at Florent, the Pyramid Club, Club 57, birthday parties and backstages, nightclubs, dressing rooms, concerts, and any other place you would have wanted to see in 1980s New York. The Meatpacking District and the East Village in all of their grit and glory, apartments you always wanted to be invited to, windows you always wanted to look inside.

In all of his curiosity, Sullivan created priceless documentation of an era. RuPaul eating a prune cake Nelson made from his mother's recipe. Lady Bunny performing at The World on 254 East 2nd Street. John Sex as Peter Pan at Danceteria. John Kelly performing "Air" from the musical *Hair* at The Saint. A parade of Judy Garlands in the West Village. The videos show these performers becoming legends in real time. Simply by following his own interests, Sullivan created a chronicle of drag history in the city in addition to all of his other recordings. Some found the bright light of his video camera invasive, especially when it was capturing illicit activities. But the videos, now collectively called *The 5 9th Avenue Project*, offer a unique insight into life at the time. Many have been uploaded to YouTube and reside in the archives of NYU's Fales Library for both viewing pleasure and posterity.

Nelson Sullivan also chronicled Wigstock. The festival drew together all the drag and downtown performance artists flourishing in the city at the time. While Bunny still loved the pageantry of the Atlanta queens, she felt the Pyramid performers had something they lacked. "I got a little bit bored by the celebrity impersonation, and New York queens tend to form their own character," she said on *What's the Tee?* in 2018. "I was so wowed by the kind of drag at the Pyramid. Drag queens were fronting bands, one had a dance troupe, or doing stand-up comedy, or singing live or impersonating offbeat people like Joni Mitchell or Janis Joplin. I wanted to showcase that talent that I was wowed by."

Co-sponsored by the Pyramid, the first Wigstock was held on August 18, 1985, and assembled on a budget of just $1,000, which included a sound system brought in from out of town and a $50 bribe to the New York City Department of Parks and Recreation. In Sullivan's video of the event, Lady Bunny dances to The Isley Brothers' "Live It Up" with fellow Pyramid drag performer Tangella DeVille in front of a sparse crowd, bicyclists moving past quizzically. She wears dark lipstick and eye makeup to match a black jumpsuit covered in fringe that swishes with every shimmy and shake. Later, she introduces the event— "Hello, everybody! Welcome to Wigstock! Stop the pigs and give 'em wigs!"—while singing a rendition of Carole King's "I Feel the Earth Move." The crowd starts to grow.

A black feathered wig perched atop her head, Lypsinka executes a tribute to 1960s icon Mrs. Miller, who performed jazz standard versions of pop songs. John Kelly, in a ratty, banged blond wig and exaggerated rouge, debuts a Joni Mitchell performance he still does to this day (to the delight of Mitchell herself), altering the lyrics from her song "Big Yellow Taxi" to "They paved Tompkins Square and put up a beauty shop." By the time rock band The Love Delegation takes the stage, the park is a mass of bodies, many of whom are adorned with wigs.

The event got bigger and bigger every year. "The Pyramid and I put on Wigstock every year just because there's so many housewives and children that can't always make it to the nightclubs!" Bunny quipped at the second Wigstock in 1986. The festival drew a beautifully bizarre crowd. "We, a wayward band of Fellini extras, would wander back and forth from the Pyramid Club to the Tompkins Park bandshell, getting drunk and having dirty sex in the backs of cabs. It was the solidarity of circus freaks—but instead of wading through peanut bags and cotton candy, we were making our way through beer bottles and tufts of wig hair," Wigstock performer Tangella DeVille said years later.

In its Tompkins Square days, Wigstock also drew Alphabet City locals who just happened to be passing through. "I can also remember looking out from the stage, when Wigstock was in Tompkins Square Park, and watching the incredibly diverse audience: bag people, neighborhood children, ancient Ukrainian babushkas and tattooed rock-n-rollers, all of them smiling and enjoying a show they would never have gotten to see," Butterick told Bunny.

Wigstock came at the right time, a time when New York, the queer and artistic communities in particular, needed a breath of fresh air. By the end of 1986, there were 6,458 AIDS deaths in the city. By 1988, Wigstock was so popular that surrounding costume stores sold out of wigs and passing bicyclists could no longer pause in front of the stage, as the area around the bandshell was swarming with people.

The Imperial Court system, an international queer charitable fundraising body founded in 1965 by José Sarria, also centered drag in its activism. The San Francisco–born Sarria was the first openly gay person in the country and in the world to seek election four years prior, to the city's Board of Supervisors. Sarria had been a drag performer in the 1960s, singing during the intermission for Lynne Carter's shows, and after winning a drag ball took on a title of his own divining: "Empress José I" of San Francisco. Later, he added "The Widow Norton" to his title as well and appeared as a judge in the film *To Wong Foo, Thanks for Everything! Julie Newmar* with this name.

Today there are close to seventy chapters of the Imperial Court across the world. Founded in response to AIDS in 1986, the Imperial Court's New York branch fundraises for queer organizations promoting AIDS/HIV health care, services for queer youth, and more. "We raised money back then to help those living with HIV, because they didn't have anything," said former president Gary Cosgrove in 2015. "As the years went on our mission started to include other LGBT direct-service organizations, LGBT homeless youth, and then we started giving away youth enrichment scholarships to LGBT kids going away to college."

Drag remains a large part of its fundraising. Many members take on drag personas—Queen Mother of New York Coco LaChine, Witti Repartee, Panzi of Fire Island's Invasion of the Pines fame, and Sybil Bruncheon, for example—and don drag for the organization's annual Night of 1000 Gowns gala. But charity is always the focus. "It's not all about looks or anything, it's about service that you do," Panzi says.

A young actor named Charles Busch found himself, literally and figuratively, in the audience at the 1972 Ridiculous Theatrical Company production of *Eunuchs of the Forbidden City*. By then, Busch was studying theatre at Northwestern, but with little luck. "The theater department wasn't quite ready for me," he wrote. "I was too light (euphemism for gay), too thin and just too...too much." But in *Eunuchs*, Busch found himself, seeing a celebration of queerness in Ludlam's work. Maybe there would be a place for him on the stage after all. "Being exposed to the work of Charles Ludlam made me think, 'Oh, well, there are no limitations. I can write my own roles,'" Busch said. "Seeing Ludlam gave me the permission to dream." In the next decade, Busch would indeed build a career of his own drag roles onstage. He even leased RTC's theater at One Sheridan Square for midnight performances of his one-man show *Hollywood Confidential* and appeared in some RTC productions.

But after *Hollywood Confidential* in 1984, bookings dried up. So he wrote a play. Soon after, it went up at Alphabet City's Limbo Lounge, a narrow after-hours bar and art gallery, at 339 E. 10th Street. Called *Vampire Lesbians of Sodom*, the play starred Busch and actress Julie Halston as lesbian vampires-turned-actresses, bitter rivals for a millennium, their careers everywhere from silent film to the Las Vegas stage putting them constantly at each other's throats.

Meant more as a party than a serious performance, the production cost about $35 to put on, most of which was spent on postage. "We sent out a flyer that I Xeroxed from my temp job," Busch said. "We just had a really great time and each person invited six people so we were sold out."

The play became an underground hit. "The camp comedy began to attract a wide cross-section of theatergoers, their curiosity piqued by the good reviews and a Theda Bara-meets-Jackie Susann title that promised the theatrical equivalent of slumming," the *New York Times* wrote in 1989. Busch and production partner Ken Elliott raised money to show it off-Broadway at Provincetown Playhouse in the West Village. It ran for five years, still making it one of off-Broadway's most enduring works all these years later.

John Cameron Mitchell made his way to the show during his time as Dickon in *The Secret Garden* on Broadway. "I was in awe, so between Charles [Busch] and Ethyl and Charles Ludlam, who I never saw but certainly knew about, it seemed like a great interface between drag and theater," Mitchell said. "So it was always in my back pocket. It was always something that thrilled me, so as I was doing my traditional acting, that's the kind of stuff I would go see."

Busch's creative spirit has been in full force ever since, both in and out of drag, from camp classics like *Psycho Beach Party* to *The Tale of the Allergist's Wife*—a comedy which earned Busch a 2001 Tony nomination for Best Play—to the 2003 cult classic film *Die, Mommie, Die!* With wigs and without, Busch became an indelible cultural juggernaut, Northwestern theatre department be damned. "What will people think?" he wrote in the *Times.* "That's a question that has luckily never concerned me."

Ira Siff once described himself as "dragophobic." He recalls gay men in the 1970s saying drag "gave them a bad name." But after seeing Charles Ludlam in *Camille*, he was a changed man. "I was completely subjugated. By the final scene, I mean I really was in tears from laughing and crying. He was so brilliant," Siff says. He put together a company of his own in 1981. "Without him, I'm not sure I would have... I thought, *hmm*, [opera is] bland, so somebody should do something colorful about opera, the way he did about theatre, and the way the Trocks did with ballet." A classically trained tenor, Siff and Mario Villanueva, the head of the Hunter College music department, founded La Gran Scena, adding drag to opera to both reinvigorate and lovingly spoof the highbrow form.

Like the Trocks and Gloxinia, La Gran Scena featured a host of fictitious divas played by Siff and friends all singing classic works in falsetto. Siff himself became Madame Vera Galupe-Borszkh to Villanueva's Celestina Della Glück. In November of 1981, La Gran Scena debuted at the Orpheum Theatre in the East Village. Madame Vera, dripping in jewels, velvets, and a towering orb of curls, performed the aria "In Questa Reggia" from Puccini's *Turandot* in her signature Slavic accent, to great effect. "The audience went berserk… I thought it would just be a sort of an arch, wry, entertaining evening that a few people would get, and now I'm going to have to hold for laughs during arias, which utterly delighted me, because it gave me a chance to rest," Siff said in 2004. "But I had no idea it would be that funny." What Siff also did not expect was a review from the *New York Times*, let alone one that was overall favorable.

"La Gran Scena Opera Company at the Orpheum Theater on Second Avenue asks—and answers—the question: If there are no more great women to sing dramatic soprano roles, why not men?" wrote critic Bernard Holland, touching on not just their "spectacular gowns" and "terrifying falsettos," but "subtle humor," "outrageous" gags, gifts of comedy and authenticity. Audiences who usually found themselves at the luxurious Lincoln Center made their way into the depths of the still bombed-out East Village—"you know, with paper bags over their heads incognito," Siff laughs—but never regretted the trip. "It was a guilty pleasure," Siff says. "When people from the Met started to come, they would tell each other about it, but it was still this thing of going to an 11 o'clock show in the East Village of drag queens singing opera." Eventually even more people came out of the woodwork, including opera greats like Joan Sutherland and Leontyne Price. Price herself once said in an interview, "La Gran Scena is UNBELIEVABLE!… They have EVERYTHING that is top-drawer in an opera ambiance. I JUST ADORE THEM!"

La Gran Scena's audiences expanded to larger New York theaters and then to Europe. Siff remembers the thrill of educated opera consumers laughing at inside jokes. But when AIDS decimated a portion of their audience and some of their company, Villanueva included, the show's reception changed. Siff remembered the audience getting "older and straighter." But La Gran Scena performed across the country for the next thirty years, at Lincoln Center and the Kennedy Center, and beloved international opera houses in Rio, Berlin, London, and more. The company ended its run in 2002, and Siff's solo work doing Madame Vera Galupe-Borszkh's "Annual Farewell Recital," ended in 2009. While certain New York queens are still known for their operatic stylings today—Shequida, Jasmine Rice LaBeija, and Monét X Change are all trained vocalists, for example—La Gran Scena remains a unique pioneering opera company, another artistic development proving drag's versatility.

Drag also made a splash on Broadway in the 1980s with Harvey Fierstein's *Torch Song Trilogy* and Jerry Herman's musical *La Cage aux Folles* (for which Fierstein also wrote the book).

In February 1978, Fierstein's play *The International Stud* went up at La MaMa. Fierstein had an extensive off-off-Broadway career before that, often appearing in drag in works by John Vaccaro, Jackie Curtis, and Andy Warhol (as a teenager, he also performed twice in drag at Club 82). He felt women's roles gave him more to play with. "Have you *seen* men's roles?" he said to writer Don Shewey that year. "They are so *boring*… Women get the last bow and the nicer clothes and the softer moments. A lot of women's roles are underwritten so there's more to play with; you have to bring your own strength to them, while men's roles are often so overwritten you can't put anything in them." By 1971, Fierstein started writing his own work, and would put on several plays in which he also appeared drag, like 1974's *Freaky Pussy: A T-Room Musical*, a meditation on gentrification with queer sex workers; and 1975's *Flatbush Tosca*, a retelling of Puccini's *Tosca* set in Brooklyn in which Fierstein played drag queen Flo Tosca.

Blending his theatrical and life experiences, *The International Stud* became the first of three plays where lead character Arnold Beckoff, a gay Jewish man from Brooklyn and professional drag queen, navigated the crosscurrents of love, family, joy, and tragedy in New York. With *Fugue in a Nursery* and *Widows and Children First!*, it became the *Torch Song Trilogy*.

The play was significant not just because it centered on a gay man's quest for family, but because it featured a character who played a drag queen. In *Torch Song Trilogy*, the drag queen is not the court jester, the drag queen is Arnold Beckoff, aka Virginia Hamm. The play upended both the dominant view of gay men in theatrical works—Fierstein was not interested in portrayals of gay men as tragic figures solely because they were gay, nor of drag queens solely for comic relief. Indeed, drag is one vehicle for character development in the play, where Arnold actively embraces an "alternative" life, but still aches for aspects of a "traditional" life, like a family. Unlike prevailing gay narratives of the time, *Torch Song Trilogy* showed these two pathways weren't necessarily mutually exclusive.

Despite the play's deftly crafted nuances, it took a while for all three works to get produced at once. "People would say, 'Fabulous writer. Fabulous play. But gay. Goodbye.' The idea [was] that a gay play couldn't make money," Fierstein said in 1982. That the AIDS crisis made for an uptick in homophobia was an understatement. But eventually the show did come together in October 1981, off-off-Broadway at the Richard Allen Center on West 62nd Street, where Divine once performed in Tom Eyen's *The Neon Woman* when it was still the club Hurrah. A rave review from the *New York Times* filled seats that could barely be given away before. "Three plays that give us a progressively dramatic and illuminating portrait of a man who laughs, and makes us laugh, to keep from collapsing. The evening is a double tour de force for Mr. Fierstein, who, with his throaty Tallulah voice and manner, stars in his own touching triptych," raved critic Mel Gussow. Soon bigger venues were in the cards.

Torch Song Trilogy opened at Broadway's Little Theatre on June 10, 1982, and ran for nearly three years. It garnered two Tony Awards, for Best Play and Best Actor in a Play for Fierstein. Still, it was not without its criticisms. Some felt Arnold's quest for "middle-class" goals of a home and a family were overly heteronormative. But in a world where gay men were often portrayed as desperately sad or hedonistic, Fierstein's play reflected a more nuanced form of representation.

Fierstein's next foray into the then-oft-uncharted world of queer joy onstage came the following year, in 1983. Based on the smash success of the 1973 French play *La Cage aux Folles*, then the 1978 film of the same name by Jean Poiret (later the source material for the 1996 film *The Birdcage*), Broadway's version of the work would be a musical, the book of which would be composed by Fierstein. And it would be no small musical indeed: on a $5 million budget, the show would feature at its center a drag club owned by a gay couple, drag performer Albin and his partner Georges, the club's director. Their son Jean-Michel comes home and announces his engagement to a woman, and not just any woman: the daughter of a conservative politician who would undoubtedly reject the young man as a son-in-law if his parentage came to light. Jean-Michel and Georges attempt to hide Albin from the future in-laws, and chaos ensues.

The show was groundbreaking for its time, its success astonishing even to Fierstein. After all, *New York Magazine* reported in 1983, he'd come from the downtown performance world where for some fifteen years he witnessed drag queens endure brutality and was even arrested himself. Some members of the queer community still found drag queens distasteful and insulting. But the Broadway success of *La Cage aux Folles* allowed it to be seen anew.

This was not to say, of course, that drag queens all of a sudden experienced better treatment—despite some changes in the way drag was perceived, it still was by no means safe to walk the streets, take the subway, or exist in drag outside of a club. But with Fierstein's work, drag had cracked the mainstream, an achievement made even more significant during a moment of intense homophobia spurred by the AIDS crisis.

With Fierstein writing its book, *La Cage* would humanize its characters, add shape and complexity to their lives. It's worth noting, though, that both starring roles were played by straight men, not queer men or even drag pros (though the show brought in Lynne Carter to prep actor George Hearn). Fierstein had raised his own objections about this to the director, saying, "'The greatest young actress in the world cannot fully express the role of a grandmother. There are things that life has simply not taught her—the gravitas of age, the price of getting older...'" as he recounts in his autobiography, *I Was Better Last Night*. But director Arthur Laurents, queer himself, wouldn't hear of it, fearing the show's public rejection by mainstream audiences if queer actors or drag queens appeared. Over time Laurents brought in gay actors for the lead roles. Eventually he called up Fierstein and admitted his mistake.

Still, the show was an instant smash—ticket sales exceeded $4 million before the show even opened. Like *Torch Song*, *La Cage* was critiqued for pandering to straight audiences. "The glitz, showmanship, good cheer and almost unflagging tunefulness of 'La Cage aux Folles' are all highly enjoyable and welcome, but, in its eagerness to please all comers, this musical is sometimes as shamelessly calculating as a candidate for public office," theater critic Frank Rich wrote. But these highs and lows aside, the show was a historic one: it was one of the first ever Broadway musicals focused on a gay couple's love story with queerness and drag as its backdrop, an explosion of sequins and sparkles and long-legged gender-bending showgirls. It won six Tony Awards (Best Musical, Best Score, Best Book, Best Performance by a Leading Actor in a Musical, Best Direction of a Musical, Best Costume Design), has been revived twice on Broadway, and is now considered a modern musical theater classic.

But there were even more stages in New York ripe for drag. One of them was BoyBar, launched by Paul McGregor in 1984. At the urging of hairdresser Matthew Kasten, hairdresser Paul

McGregor turned his bar at 15 1/2 St. Marks Place into a gay bar, BoyBar. "Gay men, [McGregor] said, are less quarrelsome than heterosexual men," the *New York Times* wrote in 1992 (even though one time a BoyBar patron bit off another's ear). But Kasten wanted to do a drag night at the bar specifically. Despite the success of the Pyramid, pre–Wigstock, drag was hardly popular outside of the two venues.

"At the time the worst thing that you could do in New York was be a drag queen," laughed David Glamamore, Kasten's former roommate and one of BoyBar's earliest drag performers. "It was the lowest thing on the totem pole. Nobody wanted it. There had been all these bigger drag queen celebrities earlier on in the '70s, but it had a die-off time. That's when we decided, let's do drag! It was the wrongest thing that you could possibly do."

BoyBar had started as a "weird little dive bar," Glamamore says, but Matthew Kasten, who became the bar's creative director, was dedicated to putting on a good show. Soon, Thursdays were packed with people ready to see full-fledged drag stage shows, with a more variety-style setup on Friday nights (other nights it was just a cool, dive-y place to hang). "Every week the BoyBar show would be a mini-spectacular," DJ Johnny Dynell said, complete with skits, songs, Glamamore's costumes, makeup by Bobby Miller, rapid-fire quick changes, and choreography by Raven O. The venue quickly became beloved by celebrities like Thierry Mugler and a young fashion designer named Marc Jacobs. Kasten also developed an in-house troupe for BoyBar known as the BoyBar Beauties, who were to BoyBar what the Rockettes are to Radio City Music Hall.

"The reputation that drag had at that time…was unorganized, slapped together with spit and polish at the last minute," said artist and model Connie Fleming, who performed at BoyBar as Connie Girl beginning in 1985. Kasten instead wanted the shows to be "slick, professional, put together, choreographed,"

Fleming says. He wanted the Beauties to know "we were professional performers, and that we could take our craft anywhere and have it be perceived as entertainment, which it is," Fleming continued.

HRH Princess Diandra joined Fleming in drag at BoyBar, but was hesitant at first. "One of the holdouts for me when I was initially asked to be a drag queen was that...if you'd say you were a drag queen, people would turn their noses up. They'd go 'ughhhh, drag queen,'" Diandra said. But when she arrived at BoyBar, she *arrived* and quickly became celebrated for deft renderings of Diana Ross and Patti LaBelle. Toward the end of the decade, the popularity of BoyBar, Wigstock, and the Pyramid contributed to the changing popular opinion of drag in and out of the queer community. In fact, BoyBar's Codie Ravioli and Chicklet, aka Gina Varla Vetro, later appeared on MTV show *Liquid Television* in the ongoing short "Art School Girls of Doom."

"We started to perform at really prestigious events and we had this semi-cultlike following," Diandra said. "People were like, 'Oh my god, drag queens were at the party!'" But this time, they meant it in a good way.

And while there wasn't an explicit rivalry between BoyBar and the Pyramid, they both had distinctive styles. Kasten was a perfectionist, and every queen's look was enhanced by his knowledge of fashion, hair, film, and theater. The list of "Kastenisms" was ongoing: always wear lashes, nails, and earrings (even if wigs cover the ears); makeup shouldn't match the ensemble but should accentuate hair color; never wear lingerie as an outfit; and don't wear too much black. In fact, 1968's *The Queen* also informed their aesthetic and Flawless Sabrina herself emceed the very first Miss BoyBar Pageant in 1984. The BoyBar sensibility caught on.

"Pat Field wanted anyone who worked at BoyBar to work at her store as well," New York drag legend Perfidia told *Paper* magazine in 2016, though girls from the Pyramid worked there, too. "It became this weird symbiotic relationship." Field gave drag queens, transgender individuals, and queer kids jobs "because they were visually interesting," Field said in 2016. "The way they put themselves together, they were stylists of their own kind, and they exuded fashion. I never looked at them as 'you're gay,' 'you're straight,' 'you're underage,' whatever. It was totally creative and visual." The boutique became a haven for gender nonconformity as well as self-identified freaks and artistic folks. Blondie's Debbie Harry and Madonna were among them.

Pat Field's, BoyBar, and the Pyramid formed a glittering triangle of downtown grunge and allure. "We would stop in to use the bathroom or shop or talk to the transsexuals at the makeup counter," Lady Bunny, who performed at both the Pyramid and BoyBar, said in 2015. "You lived in the East Village for the scene and went into the West Village for sex, so we were frequently going back and forth, and Pat's spot was right in the middle."

The BoyBar Beauties also performed at innumerable AIDS benefits, as did Pyramid performers. Glamamore remembers visiting friends in the AIDS wings at hospitals with Connie Fleming, bringing in lunch trays left in front of rooms nurses were too scared to enter, performing in elevators and common rooms on their way through. Because in its own way, glamour can be insurrection and resistance: when death looms large, it becomes a subversive celebration of beauty and life. Few knew this better than International Chrysis.

As the 1960s ended, Chrysis entered high-end cabaret spaces and revues across New York, particularly at nightclubs like Rockefeller Center's Rainbow Grill. The 1970s and 1980s saw a resurgence in the kind of elaborate drag revues popular in decades prior, often among straight audiences. In the 1970s, Chrysis became regarded uptown and internationally. She was also a muse to Salvador Dalí and sometimes accompanied him to

Studio 54. By the 1980s, BoyBar and the Pyramid Club were delighted to host a queen of her stature. She became a legend, though, because she used drag as a jumping-off point to kick-start other aspects of her career. In doing so, she paved the way for other transgender performers starting in drag to move past the form if they wanted to, and became a drag mother to performers across BoyBar and the Pyramid Club.

"She literally was the first person to put me in full drag and encouraged me to go out and entertain at the BoyBar, where I was crowned Miss BoyBar 1986," Perfidia told *The Advocate* in 2019. Perfidia, today an Emmy-nominated wig stylist, was known for her intricate lip-synchs to Peruvian coloratura soprano Yma Sumac. With a 1960s-inspired bouffant and thick black swathes of cat-eye liner, she became one of Chrysis's many children. Connie Fleming was another.

Chrysis had forged her own path when it came to understanding her relationship to drag as a transgender woman. She elevated drag and transgender identity in her work, both of which had been demonized in one way or another. "For many trans women…being on the stage and being a performer is a way to embody the self that you were maybe not necessarily born in or offered the chance to be from birth," says performer, writer, and Chrysis archivist Jordan King, who is herself transgender. "When you get on stage and you get to fully embody the persona and the being that you imagine yourself to be, that's where you're sort of born in a sense, and so that's where I think it allowed Chrysis to come into existence as herself."

Chrysis also knew that might not be the path for everyone. "She came up in a time [in the '60s and '70s] where the lines hadn't been drawn between drag and trans. She was such a forerunner in the two worlds meeting and the two worlds existing because that's the only way one could survive," Fleming says. "She saw the way the world was changing in the '80s and the '90s and saw that there was this kind of avenue for girls to go to in the straight, heteronormative world, and wanted me to know that it was okay and you weren't turning your back."

Throughout the 1980s, Chrysis was everywhere in downtown's nightlife, bedecked in chain mail, polka dots, sequins, and leather. She developed her own cabaret acts, *Jesus Chrysis Superstar* and *The Last Temptation of Chrysis*. She also joined Hot Peaches, and it was during her time in the troupe she found she had contracted liver cancer, due to either prolonged unregulated hormone usage or the silicon in her breasts. But it wouldn't stop her from taking the stage, a space she had fought so hard to occupy for over two decades and even parlayed to the silver screen in Sidney Lumet's 1990 film *Q&A*. Chemotherapy left her weak, but when Hot Peaches founder Jimmy Camicia began to devise a benefit show for her, she immediately asked what she could sing. She wouldn't be left out of the show, and "somehow dragged herself across town and up five flights of stairs to the rehearsal hall," Camicia wrote in his 2013 memoir, *My Dear, Sweet Self*. At the show on February 20, 1990, she brought the house down, Camicia wrote, and "performed brilliantly, never dropping a stitch."

One month later, Chrysis passed away from cancer. Transgender model Joey Gabriel remembered over 400 people in attendance at her memorial, all wearing costumes in her honor, her name written in glitter on the sidewalk by those who loved her. It was through Chrysis, Gabriel would say, that she learned a glamorous life was possible.

Upon *Q&A*'s release one month later, Vincent Canby of the *New York Times* declared Chrysis's performance a "standout." It would be no surprise to those in her orbit because she always did that. In his 2020 memoir *The Cobbler*, even footwear sovereign Steve Madden remembered meeting her. Noting her glamour, he referred to her as "one of the great, original transgender entertainers who epitomized the beauty and glamour of the 1980s downtown club scene." He also remembered the way she entered a room in extravagant, sparkling dresses whose long trains were carried and fussed over by scads of gentlemen. And yet, he wrote, "her exterior was over the top, but on the inside she was humble and generous."

"I was cold because we had to walk all the way towards the water and it was November and I went up those cute little stairs, turned, and when I entered that room, I always describe it as when Dorothy arrived in Oz," said Luna Luis Ortiz. Ortiz had arrived at the Institute for the Protection of Gay and Lesbian Youth on East 23rd Street. He'd come out at fourteen, in 1986, receiving an HIV-positive diagnosis the same year. When a friend invited him to the Institute's Thanksgiving festivities, he saw a room filled with queer youth, drag queens, and transgender women, also known in the ballroom community as femme queens. He met people from the House of Ovahness, Ebony, and Xtravaganza, but ultimately joined the House of Pendavis on December 5, 1988.

Avis Pendavis became his mother. She had performed in drag at the Club 82 alongside International Chrysis and had started her own house in 1979. Avis lived in an apartment on West 157th Street, which became the Pendavis clubhouse of sorts, her bedroom the headquarters. "Avis had these really great costumes and sometimes she would let us play with the feather boas and touch the fabrics," Ortiz said. He remembers one time trying to dress in drag with the other children, Avis correcting their form, fixing their makeup and lending them hats before they got on the train to go hang out in the Village. "We just thought we looked like the ultimate drag queen women, and we went downtown like that. We got on the train and people were looking at us but we were so unbothered," he laughs. "We were so excited to be in drag, and we were in broad daylight by the way, and this was in the 80s when it wasn't safe... We had a lot of nerve to be doing some of the things we did in terms of being so bold."

By the 1980s, Harlem faced a host of systemic issues in part rooted in the departure of many residents to the suburbs, the emergence of crack, and the neighborhood's declining economic climate. There was an increase in crime, dilapidated housing, crippling unemployment, and a great deal of homelessness. It was not a safe place to be a young queer person, physically or culturally. Ortiz remembers an episode of popular 1970s sitcom *All in the Family* featuring a drag queen named Beverly LaSalle, played by San Francisco drag impresario Lori Shannon. In the episode, Beverly was murdered in a gay bashing incident, and Ortiz recalls hearing people laugh about it. Although the episode inspired empathy in many, violence against queerness and drag was still a joke to some people across the country when Ortiz was growing up, even as people he knew were also murdered.

The house system remained a haven for queer youth. Ortiz, who later performed in drag himself, remembers finding safety in numbers at the House of Pendavis. "We had to go through tough neighborhoods, and I remember, it felt unsafe sometimes walking up, and we came in groups, so there were drag queens and femme queens with us," he says. "A lot of them could fight, and they didn't care if somebody called them a name, they would speak back. And so I was hanging out with a group of people where basically you don't fuck with them, and so I felt safe."

The house mothers and fathers influenced each other, too. In 1979, Dorian Corey brought Hector Valle to his first ball. He competed in categories like "'Leather vs. Suede' and 'Model Body vs. Muscular,'" *Dazed* shared in 2017. Valle started the House of Xtravaganza in 1982 to make space for Latine ballroom participants, who previously hadn't been as welcome. Drag was at the foundation of ball culture, and the early balls were created by femme queens, says filmmaker and ballroom historian Felix Rodriguez of Old School Ballroom, aka Felix Milan. But anyone who did drag, whether they were a femme queen or a butch queen up in drag (a gay man who did drag), was called a drag queen at the time. Drag categories were numerous, but specific categories for butch queens weren't added until later.

Because some femme queens faced discrimination from venue owners when assembling events, butch queens sometimes took on the responsibility, but that meant after a while there were more categories for butch queens than femme queens, which femme queens didn't appreciate. "[Butch queens] only wanted to see femme queens walk for face and walk for body and walk for best dressed…it kind of reverted to that, and now it's still run by butch queens," Rodriguez said. "In the '90s that still wasn't as inclusive. It had started, there was some kind of inclusion, but it was mostly male run with a lot of butch queen categories." Rodriguez has seen categories expand since then and become more welcoming. "Now I think there is some consideration for those who identify as trans, like no, we're not going to put you in this category with drags when you identify as a woman," Rodriguez says. Now there are categories specifically for femme queens, butch queens, trans men, gender nonconforming individuals, and Open to All categories, which aren't defined by gender identity. Indeed, today there's an entire weekly ballroom event called OTA held regularly at Brooklyn club 3 Dollar Bill.

Drag was also a fantasy, an escape. "In a ballroom you can be anything you want," Mother Dorian said in *Paris Is Burning*. "You're not really an executive but you're looking like an executive. You're showing the straight world that I can be an executive if I had the opportunity because I can look like one, and that is like a fulfillment."

It's worth noting that the eras of ballroom prior to the 1990s—the Gold Era (1967–1973), White Era (1974–1985), and Red Era (1986–1990), as coined by ballroom historian Tommy "Dee" Murphy—can sometimes be difficult to nail down, in part because so many of the stories are oral histories and details get lost. Many of the founding participants perished in the AIDS and crack crises before their stories were chronicled in full. Others may have not believed what they were doing was truly historic and didn't chronicle it or save memorabilia from it the way they might have if they thought otherwise. This is not necessarily a unique phenomenon to ballroom and describes many subcultures' early days. Luckily there are enough people who do remember the early days and have chronicled their experiences. There are also a host of historians working to keep these memories alive, talking to the elders and children, getting their stories, making sure any story told about them features their voices.

"One of the missions that I have is that I would like the ballroom culture to be Googleable," Rodriguez said at his annual Know Your History ball in June 2021. "Ballroom when it started, it was underground, it was clandestine, it was something that nobody really wanted to be a part of. And now look at it. And if somebody wants to know what happened in the '60s, what happened in the '70s, what happened in the '80s, there's no documentation. Besides [documentary] *Paris Is Burning*, what else do we have? Not much. So my mission is to make sure that our names are not erased and not forgotten…that we can go online and we can find Hector Xtravaganza and Roger Milan and so many."

Houses would compete at balls, many of which were held in churches and Elks Lodges in the neighborhood at hours when they'd be cheapest or easiest to procure: often three, four, or five o'clock in the morning to two or three o'clock in the afternoon, weekends, weekdays, it didn't matter. You always had to be on your toes, ready to be called to the runway. "Your category says number eight and you should probably be ready by number four, because suppose nobody walks five, six, and seven, guess what number's next?" says legendary drag queen Harmonica Sunbeam, who started in ballroom with the House of Adonis and later became its mother. "I've been asleep and people have had to wake me up for my category because sometimes the order of the categories aren't done in the order that they're presented on the flyer," she says. The flyer was the ultimate guide to the ball, and if your ensemble didn't match the description you'd be chopped—cut from the competition—immediately. In the the 1990s, downtown also became a ballroom destination as community centers and clubs like the Red Zone on West 54th Street, the Marc Ballroom at Union Square, Tracks on West 19th Street, or occasionally the Roxy on West 18th Street hosted balls. Many members of the ballroom community also hung out at a place called Sally's Hideaway.

Sally's Hideaway, named for proprietor Sally Maggio, a man, opened in 1986 at 264 West 43rd Street in Times Square. The area was still gritty, a site of sex work and peep shows. Managed by femme queen Jesse Torres, Sally's featured many transgender performers of color in showgirl numbers and pageants, draped in beaded gowns and furs, with long legs and sparkling heels. But make no mistake, there were girls at Sally's who were not drag queens, nor did they want to be considered such. "The trans women who performed these shows did not want to be compared to drag queens," said Barbra Herr, who began performing there herself in the early '90s. "They would always say, 'I'm not a drag queen. That's a man in a dress.' There was so much discrimination from the gay community itself against trans women that it was pretty much jaded. The same way that the drag queen didn't want to be associated with the trans community, it worked both ways." The girls did perform in ways that later became closely associated with drag, lip-synching, and participating in pageants, but "showgirl" was the appropriate terminology. Dorian Corey was a regular performer—though throughout her career she would regularly refer to herself as a drag queen—as were Angie Xtravaganza and many of her children.

Sally's catered to the people who loved the showgirls, or hoped to just for the evening, and it became known as a hustler bar. Some of the girls made extra money by doing sex work. Other times transgender sex workers came to hang out, looking for clients. When Barbra Herr worked at Sally's, only as a performer and bartender, she remembered everyone from Wall Street types to Orthodox Jews coming in to meet one of the ladies. The original Sally's burned down in 1992, then reopened as Sally's II on the same block until it closed in 1997.

Beyond Times Square, a nightlife scene developed in the Meatpacking District, queer nightlife in particular, and drag would follow suit. "Now people live there, but back then it was awful…it was dangerous," Luna Luis Ortiz said. "New York used to stop at Ninth Avenue at that time. It was considered bad to go to Tenth, Eleventh, Twelfth Avenue. You had to be insane to go that way. And that's where the balls were."

All of the houses had a particular month when they'd host a ball—they were fewer and further between than they are today—and always with a theme. For example, Avis Pendavis was known for her Viva La Glam ball, not to be confused with cosmetics company MAC's Viva Glam charity initiative. Paris Dupree threw her legendary Paris Is Burning ball beginning in 1981 in Harlem. People always wanted to walk Dupree's balls because she had the biggest trophies—at the time, you rarely competed for money, and a massive trophy was a sign of prestige—and thereby some of the biggest crowds, the highest number of contestants. Dupree herself was lauded for her participation in the Butch Queen Up in Drags category. By 1990 Dupree's ball would become synonymous with a documentary so lauded and controversial that it exposed the entire world to ballroom culture; much footage shot for the film takes place at the Imperial Lodge of the Elks on West 129th Street.

Harmonica Sunbeam walked the Paris Is Burning ball in 1989 with the House of Adonis. At the time, though, her category was Butch Queen, First Time Up In Drag at a Ball, and despite her lack of experience, she doused the competition. "This is where

The JULIAN ELTINGE COLD CREAM makes me look like these.

JULIAN ELTINGE
IN
"THE FASCINATING WIDOW"

...dvertisement for ...nge's cold cream, ...the performer ...g and in four ...drag looks.
...:
...eatre Division,
...k Public Library
...rming Arts

...ublicity photograph ...avoy and Jay Brennan, ...s.
...:
...eatre Division,
...k Public Library
...rming Arts

THIS PAGE:

Top: James Bidgood entertains in drag as Terry Howe at Club 82, 82 East 4th Street in the East Village, ca. 1950s.
Photo Credit: © Estate of James Bidgood (1933–2022)

Bottom: Street Transvestite Action Revolutionaries, with Marsha P. Johnson on the left and Sylvia Rivera on the right, at the Christopher Street Liberation Day, March 1973.
Photo Credit: Leonard Fink Photographs, The LGBT Community Center National History Archive

OPPOSITE PAGE:

Top: In 2021, Panzi is introduced by dancers at the annual Invasion of the Pines on Fire Island, an event held since 1976.
Photo Credit: Elyssa Goodman

Bottom: International Chrysis performs at a Hot Peaches benefit the troupe held at La MaMa Experimental Theater Club to raise funds for her cancer treatment, 1989.
Photo Credit: John Simone Photography

Top: Linda Simpson and Glennda Orgasm, aka Glenn Belverio,
ride a city tour bus while filming an episode of *Glennda and Friends* in 1993.
Photo Credit: Linda Simpson

Bottom: The 2021 Drag March begins at Tompkins Square Park,
twenty-seven years after its first iteration in 1994.
Photo Credit: Elyssa Goodman

Top: Ever a club staple, Kevin Aviance poses at Tunnel, 220 Twelfth Avenue in Chelsea, in 1995. **Photo Credit: Linda Simpson**

Bottom Left: Hattie Hathaway, aka Brian Butterick, was a downtown drag legend and a champion of genderfuck and punk drag. Here she is at Mother, the home of Jackie 60, in 1992. **Photo Credit: Linda Simpson**

Bottom Right: Mona Foot, aka Nashom Wooden, was famous and beloved for her Wonder Woman number, which she performed across New York. This photo is from Wigstock 1996. **Photo Credit: Linda Simpson**

A 1996 flyer from
the Click + Drag party,
themed "2000 A.D."
Photo Credit: Rob Roth

Drag kings at
a 1998 event at
The Lesbian, Gay,
Bisexual & Transgender
Community Center,
including Brad Clit,
Dred, Murray Hill,
Mo B. Dick, with
Stormé DeLarverie
on the microphone.
**Photo Credit:
Efrain John Gonzalez,
Hellfirepress.com.**

Horrorchata, later
Chata, performs at
Bushwig, 2017.
**Photo Credit:
Elyssa Goodman**

Merrie Cherry
performs at
Bushwig, 2021.
Photo Credit:
Elyssa Goodman

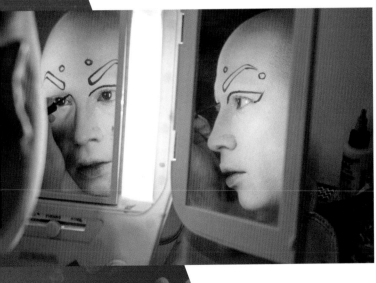

Untitled Queen applies
makeup before a night
out at Metropolitan Bar,
2018.
Photo Credit:
Elyssa Goodman

Ambrosia Alert
performs at
Bushwig, 2017.
Photo Credit:
Elyssa Goodman

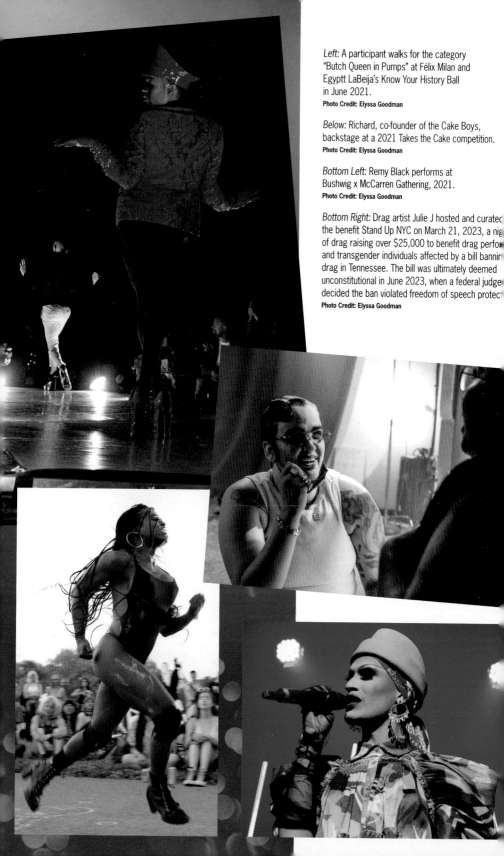

Left: A participant walks for the category "Butch Queen in Pumps" at Félix Milan and Egyptt LaBeija's Know Your History Ball in June 2021.
Photo Credit: Elyssa Goodman

Below: Richard, co-founder of the Cake Boys, backstage at a 2021 Takes the Cake competition.
Photo Credit: Elyssa Goodman

Bottom Left: Remy Black performs at Bushwig x McCarren Gathering, 2021.
Photo Credit: Elyssa Goodman

Bottom Right: Drag artist Julie J hosted and curated the benefit Stand Up NYC on March 21, 2023, a night of drag raising over $25,000 to benefit drag performers and transgender individuals affected by a bill banning drag in Tennessee. The bill was ultimately deemed unconstitutional in June 2023, when a federal judge decided the ban violated freedom of speech protections.
Photo Credit: Elyssa Goodman

the magic of the house members comes in because they put me all together, you know," she says. "Someone made an outfit for me. One of the house members did my makeup, my hair. They dressed me. And the only thing I had to do was go out there and sell it, and…to this day there are bitches out there still bitter that I won," she laughs. Sunbeam began booking shows as a drag queen the following year, and has been a working drag queen since then. "I still to this day bring a lot of ballroom with me," she says. "I credit everything that I've learned as far as stuff on stage and things like that to ballroom, for giving me the confidence to do my thing because it's not easy…"

More ball categories were added throughout the decade. Judges rated the performance of each participant or chopped them. The expression "10s across the board" is actually an ode to Nadia Comăneci, the Romanian gymnast who achieved the Olympic Games' first perfect 10 on the uneven bars in 1976. In Comăneci, the ballroom community saw a kindred spirit—she was considered an underdog who overcame adversity to achieve greatness. "We remember or pay homage to Nadia Comăneci by using the term in our categories, '10s, 10s, 10s across the board,'" veteran ballroom emcee Junior LaBeija told *Vogue* writer Nicholas Boston in 2021. "That means that you are legendary, iconic, a statement, up-and-coming."

Voguing also emerged in the 1980s, though its origin story remains murky. Some trace it to break dancing, where it was originally known as "pop, dip, and spin," and others to Paris Dupree and a club called Footsteps on East 14th Street. According to legendary DJ David DePino, also of the House of Xtravaganza, Dupree flipped through a copy of *Vogue* magazine while dancing and started duplicating and holding the poses to the music. Some queens came up and tried to outdo her. "It soon caught on at the balls," DePino said. "At first they called it posing and then, because it started from *Vogue* magazine, they called it voguing."

★ ★ ★

When the kids began voguing at downtown clubs like Chelsea's Tracks, uptown ballroom culture, driven by Black and Latine people and youths in particular, entered downtown's consciousness in a bigger way.

The House of Field, founded in 1987, was the only house based downtown and with many white members. When you started working at Patricia Field's eponymous boutique, you'd also get a membership card to the iconic members-only queer dance club Paradise Garage. The Garage, at 84 King Street in Manhattan, was presided over by legendary DJ Larry Levan and frequented by many members of the ballroom community. The Pat Field kids met and became friendly with the ballroom crowd. With the support of the store, Patricia Field employees Perfidia and Myra Christopher decided to establish the House of Field. Field was connected to the fashion world, so balls thrown by the House of Field drew the attention of 7th Avenue's fashion industry, downtown trendsetters, and eventually mainstream culture. These were connections the House of Field had that uptown houses didn't have yet, whether because of socioeconomic status, race, or just industry alone.

The House of Field's Grand Street Ball, on September 25, 1988, marked a shift in ball culture. The six-and-a-half-hour event featured uptown houses like Xtravaganza, Pendavis, Omni, LaBeija, Ebony, Magnifique, and Adonis, and influential judges from the ballroom world like Willi Ninja. There were also judges from the fashion world like Andre Leon Talley, Betsey Johnson, and Steven Meisel, some of whom had never seen a ball before, according to Myra Christopher. Marc Jacobs, two months before joining Perry Ellis as vice president of women's design, and Cesar Valentino, a founder of houses Ninja and Magnifique, walked the ball in the "Innovative Male" category. Models Lisa Marie and Veronica Webb walked the Face category. For the first time, the ballroom community and the fashion industry had coalesced, and ballroom's influence continued to reverberate. Ballroom also appeared on national television for the first time in 1988, when House of Magnifique father Cesar Magnifique Valentino and his house daughter Michelle Visage vogued on the program *The Latin Connection.*

Among the earliest large-scale publications to cover the ballroom scene were *The Village Voice* and *Details.* The *Voice* ran an article entitled "Venus Envy" by Donald Suggs in May 1988, making it the first mainstream publication to cover the ball scene. It was an article that also inspired filmmaker Jennie Livingston to produce her ball documentary *Paris Is Burning. Details,* which typically focused on downtown's arty and avant-garde scenes, published the article "Nations," in their October 1988 issue. Writer and nightlife impresario Chi Chi Valenti offered an introduction into the most noteworthy houses of the day, like Extravaganza (as it was originally spelled before becoming Xtravaganza), LaBeija, Dupree, Field, and more. Thanks to the articles, ballroom continued to take up more space in the cultural consciousness.

Swiss club promoter Susanne Bartsch noted the connection between ballroom culture, drag, and fashion. She began to hire drag performers and voguers to attend and perform at her parties at Sauvage, a club beneath the Chelsea Hotel. In doing so, she gave them a stage outside of venues that were specifically queer-oriented, expanding their audiences further. Indeed, she became one of the first people to give RuPaul a stage.

Bartsch also established The Love Ball, a successful AIDS benefit. By the end of 1989, AIDS would take over 19,000 lives. "So many of my friends had died of AIDS and not enough was being done about it to bring awareness and support," Susanne told *Paper* magazine in 2016. AIDS took a major toll on the ballroom world. Because the scene was still relatively small, Ortiz says, you'd see someone at a ball one month, and a few months later they'd be absent because they had died. House members were constantly being buried. Beginning in 1989, the Gay Men's Health Crisis had started teaching house parents about how to talk to their children about AIDS, the importance of disclosing your status, and the importance of condoms, but the stigma of AIDS was pervasive. The Love Ball worked to dismantle these stigmas, especially among the ballroom community. "The epidemic had just swept through, and very few people wanted to raise their voices for us or nevertheless give money for funding and programs and research," Jose Xtravaganza said in 2020. "So it was a very big deal; the Love Ball was an event that was the first of its kind."

Designers and fashion houses came out of the woodwork to walk the ball, many in drag, with the uptown ballroom kids, at the now-shuttered Roseland Ballroom on West 52nd Street. Legendary yet now-defunct department store Barneys got involved, along with designers like Donna Karan, Armani, and more, paying $10,000 for a table. Madonna and Calvin Klein showed up, and East Village queens participated as waitresses and models. Artists like Keith Haring and Kenny Scharf created trophies.

"The evening had all the elements that make New York City night life remarkable: beauty, pageantry, celebrity and gender confusion," the *New York Times* wrote. It's a fine assessment, but it also begs the question of whether or not the *Times* ever attended or covered balls when they were held by people of color.

The evening raised $400,000 for the Design Industries Foundation for AIDS to combat the disease, making it so successful that Bartsch produced another two years later. The collision and collaboration of the ballroom and fashion worlds would skyrocket ballroom to even higher levels of cultural awareness. The dawning of the next decade would bring it front and center to screens around the world.

AIDS ravaged all corners of the queer community. Not only did a generation of artists and creators disappear, but so did their core audiences. Yet as the decade came to a close, surviving drag performers pushed forward, continuing to be unapologetically visible, to claim space, and to leave an indelible mark on a culture they would soon change forever.

8

1990–1999

By 1994, some 50,000 New York City residents had passed away from AIDS, the majority of whom were queer. Among them were drag artists, arts and culture staples, and nightlife icons like Hibiscus, Ethyl Eichelberger, John Sex, Angie Xtravaganza, Charles Ludlam, Lynne Carter, Jack Smith, and Dorian Corey, among too many others.

While that number would drop significantly after November 1995 when the FDA approved an HIV-curbing drug cocktail of AZT and 3TC, and protease inhibitors, the virus continued to claim lives at alarming rates. By the end of the decade, over 75,000 people in New York would perish.

Alongside fundraisers and memorials, a rebellious spirit animated the community as drag performers sought to reject fear and live in the moment. But New York's nightlife soon had a new enemy to contend with, this time in the mayor's office.

Republican candidate Rudolph Giuliani won New York's 1993 mayoral race, promising "quality of life" changes for the city. As scholar Alex S. Vitale wrote in his 2008 book *City of*

Disorder, "quality of life" at the time referred to "a desire by urban residents to be free from the dirt, disorder, and incivilities that were widespread in the 1980s and 1990s." The problem was, Vitale wrote, that "'quality of life' created a stark division between residents' reasonable desires to be free of fear and harassment and the belief that the way to achieve this is by systematically removing anyone perceived to be a potential source of these problems."

Mistress Formika knew something was in the air during the election and tried to rally her community to stop it. "Every microphone I got on, the first ten minutes were like, 'Hi everybody, welcome to—now have y'all registered to vote, because I'm gonna tell you something, we cannot let Giuliani win, we cannot let him become mayor of New York,'" she said. "'Because if he's the mayor of New York we're gonna lose everything we love... He's gonna turn [New York] into everything that we got away from...'" With other drag performers, she became part of New Yorkers for Cultural Freedom, a group of nightlife individuals mobilized to vote against Giuliani (posters included "Rudy Gives Disney Blow Jobs for Free!"), but to no avail. "And he won and after that I was just like, 'Okay, everybody you'll see.'"

Giuliani's crackdowns began almost immediately and continued into his second term. In hopes of making the city more hospitable—in large part for new, wealthy inhabitants and wide-eyed tourists (and their money)—Giuliani and thereby the NYPD began attacking what they called "the small things," among them truancy, missed court summonses, public urination, public drug deals, and more. "Behind the announcement," the *New York Times* wrote at the time, "is the idea that leniency toward even these minor infractions lowers New Yorkers' quality of life, raises fears and leads to greater crimes." Enforcement of these laws might not seem negative, but they became a jumping-off point for a broader suppression of nightlife, queer nightlife especially. As downtown neighborhoods gentrified, their nightclubs became a nuisance to powerful, wealthy community boards. "That kind of behavior" was no longer welcome, and boards developed zoning restrictions to curtail the scenes.

Giuliani also reinvigorated New York City's controversial cabaret laws. These laws had largely lain dormant since the 1960s, and at that time, they were mostly used against gay bars. While the cabaret card itself had been done away with by 1967, and the laws against musicians lifted by 1988, the laws against dancing held. If more than three people were dancing, or even swaying by accident, in a venue without a cabaret license, the bar would be fined or temporarily shuttered. And the cabaret licenses were difficult to get. "Obtaining one is costly and time-consuming, requiring the approval of several agencies, and only businesses in areas zoned for commercial manufacturing are eligible," the *New York Times* wrote.

In 1995, Giuliani created a hypervigilant task force, the Multi-Agency Response to Community Hotspots, or M.A.R.C.H. According to the New York City Office of Nightlife, M.A.R.C.H. is "led by the New York City Police Department (NYPD) and supported by inspectors from the NYC Fire Department (FDNY), NYC Department of Buildings (DOB), NYC Department of Environmental Protection (DEP), NYC Department of Health and Mental Hygiene (DOHMH), and the NY State Liquor Authority to conduct unannounced inspections at nightlife establishments." M.A.R.C.H. still exists, but in the 1990s, it began conducting raids and issuing tickets for exceedingly minor offenses that ended up costing venue owners much more than mere tickets. The task force infiltrated the clubs, scouring for everything from fruit flies to swaying to low Exit lights.

While in four years, Giuliani's mayoralty led to a 56% decrease in violent crime, nightlife dwindled. In May 1997, both *New York Magazine* and *Time Out New York* signaled nightlife's impending doom with these headlines on their covers, respectively: "Nightlife Under Siege: With clubs being padlocked, Times Square sanitized, and dancing forbidden, is there anyplace left where anything goes?" and "Club Crisis! How bad is the crackdown? And where is it still safe to party?" People wanted to go out, but they didn't want to deal with police raids. With clubs and bars fined and closing, lounges emerged, filled with seating and expensive cocktails in the once-artistic neighborhoods that yuppies soon dominated. Discrimination against queer spaces, queer spaces of color in particular, ran rampant. "If anyone hadn't heard the death knell for creative nightlife yet, the ascent of bottle service rang it loud and clear," Michael Musto wrote in 2017. "Eighties clubs like Area had been focused on art, performance, and dance, but now, sitting down and paying way too much for a drink was considered the height of expression." When Times Square was "cleaned up," Sally's II, Edelweiss, and other venues where trans showgirls and sex workers of color thrived were shut down for good.

Edelweiss, similar to Sally's, was a beloved spot for gender nonconformists of all stripes, drag queens included. It had opened in 1994 but endured frequent raids and shutdowns. A year-long padlocking of Edelweiss's doors came in 1999 at the hands of an undercover cop in drag, Detective Gerard McMahon, and his alter ego, Cindy, "in her sporty combination skirt-shorts, white top, and fiery locks." It was the first time the police department assigned a case to a male police officer in drag. Still, the club was unfairly targeted, according to Hal Weiner, the defense attorney of Edelweiss proprietor Constantine Eliopoulos. "You can probably find the same number of drug dealers and prostitutes at the Waldorf-Astoria bar, if you put the kind of effort the [NYPD] put into this," Weiner told *New York Magazine*. "All the drug arrests were stings; the sex was agreed to; and if lap-dancing is all they saw, they might as well raid fraternity houses." It would not be the only venue to endure such treatment.

★ ★ ★

The 1990s also brought into focus the club kid, as gender-fucking nightlife denizens in ensembles studded, shining, and salacious were known. Some considered their appearance drag, others did not, but their collective presentation embraced gender ambiguity. Boots might be sky-high; makeup might be thickly painted and Kabuki-esque; hair might be all manner of neons; piercings and tattoos might abound; but really, every club kid had their own signature look, whether they were heavily mohawked, covered in fishnet and glitter, or all of the above. Soon they appeared everywhere from print publications to television screens. Drag artists added additional flair to nights that drew club kids, and for a time the two existed and thrived in tandem. Some drag performers loved club appearances while others found them at best boring or at worst exploitative—some were paid to be walking mannequins more than they were to actually entertain—but money was money, and at that time club owners had a lot of it.

The decadent and raucous club kid culture took a turn in 1996 when Limelight promoter Michael Alig and clubland friend Robert Riggs killed club kid Angel Melendez, who Alig then dismembered. The event was chronicled in part in James St. James's 1999 memoir *Disco Bloodbath* (later republished as *Party Monster*), which also became the 2003 film *Party Monster*. The murder drew negative attention to the club scene, which had previously been a sweaty, sexy, creative way for people to blow off steam and escape their lives for a while. It was in some ways the final nail in the nightlife coffin, and soon clubland's glitter would turn to dust. Despite the rapid razing of nightlife venues in which drag had thrived, the art form would be resilient yet again and find new, consistent stages across the city. "The drag became stronger, actually," performance icon Joey Arias remembers. "Drag to me at that point was the real punk of the gay scene... Drag also became the forefront of fighting for rights.

Not just the gay guys, but it was the drag queen with the can of hairspray and the pitchfork and the match."

By the mid-1990s, drag was everywhere, and not just in New York. While the form still faced subjugation, it flourished creatively, generating full-blown careers for queer performers who never thought such a life was possible, drawing attention to the possibilities of the form and the queer community itself.

Voguing was part of the nightly scene in Washington Square Park. In the late '80s, Jennie Livingston was transitioning out of a short-lived career as a photographer, taking a filmmaking class at NYU in hopes of creating a new path for herself. She saw these nimble, artful dancers and asked to photograph them. Permission granted, she snapped, and began chatting. Soon she'd attend an uptown ball with a sound operator to film what she saw, struck by the way participants played with gender and personal expression. She returned consistently over the next few years and edited some seventy-plus hours of raw footage into the documentary that became *Paris Is Burning*, named after Paris Dupree's annual ball.

Paris Is Burning followed the lives of uptown ballroom participants like Dorian Corey, Willi Ninja, Pepper LaBeija, Octavia St. Laurent, Venus Xtravaganza, and Avis Pendavis. At the balls, the documentary revealed, they could create their own worlds of glamour and beauty, worlds to escape poverty, homelessness, violence, addiction, and other issues they saw in their communities. The film was a sensation, winning the 1991 Grand Jury Prize at the Sundance Film Festival. It was picked up by Miramax for distribution for $250,000 and made close to $4 million at the box office. Now a part of the National Film Registry and the Criterion Collection, it is considered among the most important documentaries of the last forty years, if not ever.

By the late 1980s, Dorian Corey was performing at Sally's II, where she hosted her "Drag Doll Revue" as well as many other clubs in Midtown Manhattan. She also served as guide and mother to performers in and out of the House of Corey. Barbra Herr remembers Corey from their time working at Sally's. "She dragged me off to Fire Island to do the pageant, the best professional pageant. It was so crazy because I won. After that she became my mentor here in New York. She was always booking me, always finding me work. She made me clothing... She was very, very special," Herr remembers. Dorian, a transgender woman herself, also helped Barbra through her transition. "I wasn't used to dealing with trans people because I had just [undergone] my transition," Herr said. "If you were talented, that would be enough for them to hate you. So with Dorian, she taught me that, screw them! You're talented, you are who you are... She actually pushed me to get better gigs and do better things." Barbra Herr was only one of the many people Dorian would mentor and help throughout her lifetime.

During her time in the ballroom scene, Dorian snatched approximately fifty grand prize ball trophies. She also had a successful business as a costume designer, making ensembles for off-Broadway productions. In *Paris Is Burning*, Mother Corey is forever nonplussed. Through her practical and sardonic wit, we get some of the film's most telling lessons. "Shade is, I don't have to tell you you're ugly, because you know you're ugly," she masterfully drolls. She also explains how she tempered her expectations as she aged:

Everybody wants to make an impression, some mark upon the world. Then you think, you've made a mark on the world if you just get through it, and a few people remember your name.... If you shoot an arrow and it goes real high, hooray for you.

Though a critical success, *Paris Is Burning* was not without its controversies. While all of the participants knowingly signed agreements noting they wouldn't get paid for their contributions, Livingston split $55,000 of the film's distribution money among thirteen members of the cast. Many were still indignant, believing they should have been paid more. Others felt Livingston was not the person to make the documentary at all, herself queer but white and Jewish, and felt her viewpoint othered and exploited participants instead of respectfully chronicling their stories.

In 1993, two years after the film's successful yet contentious release, the *New York Times* ran an article called "Paris Has Burned" highlighting the issues the film faced. "I love the movie, I watch it more than often, and I don't agree that it exploits us," Pepper LaBeija said. "But I feel betrayed." She recalls the thrill of signing whatever papers she saw, basking in the camera's attention, the "couple hundred dollars" Livingston gave them for interviews with the potential of more. LaBeija hoped the documentary would change her life. "But then the film came out," she said, "and—nothing. They all got rich, and we got nothing."

"I wasn't as bold as some of the people who spoke in the documentary, but I was there," said Harmonica Sunbeam. "It's funny because people say those kids were exploited, but we were hungry for attention. Somebody's coming to talk to you and ask you a few questions about yourself, of course you say 'I do this and that,' because who else could you get the attention from, in a sense? I couldn't go home and tell my family 'I'm this and I'm this, oh, you should see me when I do this.'"

The film came out, the *Times* reported, and many went back to their lives as they had been. Pepper LaBeija lived with her mother in the Bronx. Octavia St. Laurent went back to being a peep show dancer. Many of the participants died, some of AIDS. Venus Xtravaganza was murdered in the course of the film's production. Paris Dupree attempted to sue for $40 million, but upon realizing she signed a release, her lawyers abandoned the case; later, *New York Magazine* reported, the performer said she was "on a college-circuit tour," doing talks at places like Brown University.

Dorian Corey retained her signature pragmatism. "I'll tell you who is making out is those clever Miramaxes. But I didn't do it for money anyway: I did it for fun. Always have," she said, reflecting on the fame the film brought her, even if it felt at the time short-lived: the limousines, hotels, free cigarettes, young fans fawning, the hope of a sequel. "Once you do something big, you want to do it again," she said. "But what I got was plenty, and the rest is just bitter onions."

Livingston didn't "get rich," per se—as she said at the time, "The truth is I live about the same as I did, except that I used to be chronically about three months late in paying the rent, and now I'm more or less on time." But she was able to forge space for herself as a filmmaker and establish a career in ways many in the film did not. Willi Ninja was among the exceptions, becoming an internationally successful choreographer as he had hoped.

And in some cases, the film also brought notoriety. Dorian Corey died of AIDS in August 1993 at the age of fifty-six. Her final performance took place at Sally's II just a few months prior, in May 1993. She performed "If I Could" by Regina Belle, a song that personifies a mother's letting go. Corey's ears glittered with jewels. She wore a gown of pearls with dark lips and a coat of white marabou. After her death, friend, caretaker, and drag sister Lois Taylor hoped to sell some of Corey's famed costumes. Amid swaths of sinuous fabric in Corey's West 140th Street apartment, Taylor discovered a garment bag that revealed not an elaborate gown, but the mummified corpse of Robert Wells née Bobby Worley, a bullet through his head. He hadn't been seen since 1968 and was possibly a former abusive boyfriend of Corey's.

News of the body rang through New York's tabloids and drag circuits. The May 2, 1994, issue of New York Magazine ran a feature on the mysterious event called "The Drag Queen Had a Mummy in Her Closet," in which writer Jeanie Russell Kasindorf sought to track down evidence of the alleged crime. She came upon Worley's brother, who remembered Dorian's name and his brother's tendency toward violent behavior. Lois Taylor mentioned finding one note possibly about Worley asking Dorian to have "a sex change," and another where the words "revenge" and "murder" appeared. The case was never solved, and years later it became fodder for the television show *Pose*, with the character Elektra also hiding and mummifying a body. However, Corey's contributions to her community as a mother, a friend, and a performer were and remain much greater than the literal or figurative skeletons in her closet.

Paris Is Burning preserved the lives and legacies of ballroom icons, most of whom have since passed on, for audiences who may have never known about the phenomenon otherwise. One of them was Felix Rodriguez, who saw *Paris Is Burning* when it arrived in theaters. "I literally went to see *Paris Is Burning* on a Friday and that Sunday was my first ball in 1991," he said. He became a member of the House of Milan in 1993.

Many people in ballroom felt exploited by *Paris Is Burning*, he said. A filmmaker himself, he was quickly made aware that cameras were no longer allowed at balls. But *Paris Is Burning* and the release of Madonna's "Vogue" in 1990, which also stirred appropriative controversy but featured the House of Xtravaganza's Luis Xtravaganza Camacho and Jose Gutierez Xtravaganza in its video, Marie Antoinette–inspired performance of the song at the 1990 MTV Video Music Awards, and on Madonna's Blond Ambition World Tour, brought the ballroom world fully into the public eye. "Before *Paris Is Burning*, not so many people wanted to go to a ball because they were considered trash," Rodriguez said. "They were at 4 o'clock [in the morning] at a cheap hole up in Harlem. You had prostitutes, you had pimps, you had all these people that were considered from the underworld being a part of it, and not too many people wanted to be associated or to be a part of it, but then after *Paris Is Burning* and Madonna's

'Vogue,' they were like wait a minute, I'm missing out on something and maybe I can become famous, too." In spite of or because of its controversies and complexities, *Paris Is Burning* has remained an introduction to drag and ballroom for generations and cemented ballroom's place in American history.

Ballroom was devastated by AIDS, Rodriguez says, in part because of the stigma attached to the disease. Some people didn't want to disclose or even acknowledge their status, and some in denial refused medication. Ballroom was a way to escape, to live a fantasy, so it wasn't often discussed there. "Part of the glory of a ball was to be able to disconnect from your reality, so you had this night where you were a superstar and on Monday you had to deal with the fact that you were HIV positive, or that you were homeless, or that your family hated you," Rodriguez says. By 1995 he had to stop going to the balls because he estimates about 90 percent of his friends in the community had died and going back was just too painful.

Rodriguez remembers getting a job in 1994 and being told about a 401(k), that when he'd turn sixty-five he'd have access to money he saved. "They lost me, because I didn't think I'd get to that age. Nobody that I knew had. All the gay men that I [knew didn't] get to thirty," he said.

Ballroom house mothers and fathers like Avis Pendavis, Hector Xtravaganza, and Derek Ebony, among others, approached the Gay Men's Health Crisis to offer the ballroom community education on sexual health, AIDS transmission, treatment, and prevention. The GMHC House of Latex program started in 1989 with peer educators and information tables at balls. "Between '89 and '94, it was just GMHC teaching the Mothers and the Fathers and some other members, whoever would show up, about safer sex, this is how you have sex, this is how you negotiate sex, this is how you bring it up," said Luna Luis Ortiz. He helped organize the House of Latex Ball, thrown for the first time in 1994, an event that brings attention to safe sex practices and AIDS/HIV awareness, a process it continues today. The House of Latex has also expanded into the House of Latex Project, which "offers year-round programs for LGBTGNC youth and young adults of color within New York City's House & Ball Community regardless of HIV status. Members of the H&B community, including houses and groups, have access to meeting spaces three evenings per week to conduct house practices, mini-Kiki ball competitions, and vogue lessons." Similarly, GMHC's Project Vogue, for which Ortiz is also the program coordinator, has taken steps to close the gap between young Black men and HIV prevention. The program is "about dance, self-expression, community, and being fabulous. It's also about linking young Black men who have sex with men—the most at-risk group for HIV infection in New York City—with HIV treatment, prevention, and behavioral health care."

Kevin Aviance moved to New York from Miami in 1992 at the behest of Mother Juan Aviance. The House of Aviance didn't compete in balls, but Kevin found an audience on the dance floor of the Sound Factory on Saturday nights, a regular hangout for the ball crowd. Kevin started doing drag, hosting parties at Chelsea bars like The Break, known for (mostly white) muscle queens. But he soon took the Sound Factory by storm in drag as well.

I had this body suit and these platform shoes and I had [put] the eyebrows on, and I'm up against the wall. I didn't realize the light was on me and I hear the song start, *"My back is against the wall..."* And I love this song, and so I start doing it, and then I open up my eyes and people are staring at me, and they're like, "Girl, if you're going to do it then do it," and I'm like, "Oh, shit." You know the phrase "it's time to take the bull by the horns"? Well, you couldn't have told me anything more.

Kevin became a regular drag performer at the Sound Factory after that. He made his way around town performing at clubs like BoyBar, Area, the Roxy, and Tunnel. But Kevin was no ordinary queen. He had no interest in tucking or wigs or tits. A sleek, bald head was his signature. He had long, muscular legs accented by dizzyingly high heels, skin cloaked in a bodysuit, nails like glamorous claws and a face beat for the gods. As renowned scholar José Esteban Muñoz wrote in his essay "Gesture, Ephemera, and Queer Feeling: Approaching Kevin Aviance," "Aviance does not work in illusion; he becomes many things at once." He plays with ideals of masculinity, femininity, and drag itself, reimagining what the form can be.

It was in 1994, however, that Aviance says his life truly changed: a one-night stand ultimately led him to appear in Madonna's music video for her song "Secret." And while Kevin is indeed bewigged on-screen in a leopard dress, he'd soon be able to make a living as himself. "I have one little snippet of [the video]," he said, "and honey, I was working everyday afterwards. So, thank you, Madonna!"

Kevin grew his own international career as a dance music artist starting with his song "Cunty" in 1996, the title of which came from overhearing ballroom kids dancing on the piers. DJ Junior Vasquez broke the song on the dance floor at the Tunnel that year, and more Aviance classics soon followed, like "Din Da Da" and "Rhythm Is My Bitch." Songs like "Cunty" were known as "bitch tracks," fierce house anthems to hype the ballroom crowds, drag audiences, and dance floors.

Many more New York drag artists got in on the game. Moi Renee's 1992 "Miss Honey" features the lyrics, "Where's the bitch, she's got some nerve/Here I am and feeling fierce," playing over ferocious house beats perfect for voguing. Both Aviance and

Moi Renee were later sampled by Beyoncé on her 2022 album *Renaissance*. Other bitch tracks included Harmonica Sunbeam's "I'm Here to Work," Laritza Dumont's "Body to Body," and Ru-Paul's "Supermodel," featuring LaWanda Page. Jade Elektra, "the ballroom bitch bombshell of Avenue B," also became known as DJ Relentless. Relentless collected bitch tracks and "cunty beats" into a compilation after a record store owner said customers kept asking for the music. "I told [him] that I would make him a CD of some of my favorite tracks. I only intended it to be for him to listen to. I didn't think that he would want to sell my compilation. After a day or so, he called me and placed an order for 10 copies for the store," Relentless said. "A lot of these records and recordings were never released on major labels. Most were on independent labels or bootlegs. And a few were actually created by me."

Kevin Aviance released his debut album, *Box of Chocolates*, in 1999 and followed it with a national club tour, all the while maintaining his own artistic and aesthetic sensibilities. "I have no desire to be mainstream, a Midwest representative of our gay culture," he told *The Advocate* in April 2000. "I'm too into being a freak and being different." Aviance's reign in the dance world continued, with a collection of Billboard #1 dance hits, as well as performances alongside the likes of Whitney Houston and Cher. "I was [told] by my mother that I had ended up being gifted and Black, so I was doubly blessed," he said. "No one ever told me that I could never do something, so I didn't see things that way and I didn't want to see things that way."

Ballroom culture continues to inform culture, bridging dance, music, fashion, television, and even language—with the mainstreaming of words or phrases like "werk," "shade," "for your nerves"—and so much more. Its influence also appears in reality competition shows like *Legendary* (2020), groundbreaking dramas like *Pose* (2018), and documentaries like *Kiki* (2016), all of which were made *with* members of the ballroom community and not just about them. It's a world that continues to provide refuge and inspiration for its participants.

"It was the dive of dives, but you know, it was one of the few places that actually paid a living."

Barbra Herr performed at Escuelita, which catered to Black and Latine performers and audiences, as well as a few "blanquitos." Escuelita in its earlier days was "a rundown little place but it had its history," drag performer Laritza Dumont said. "I would do a split, I would feel the splinters up in my stockings and I was like, oh my Lord," she laughs.

When Escuelita closed in summer 1995 after thirty years, its community mourned. "All of the drag queens, the *transformistas*, and impersonators gathered on stage for the grand finale. They sang 'America the Beautiful.' They cried. Their makeup ran. An American flag unfurled...*upside down*," wrote club regular Manuel Guzmán. But it would reopen, slicker and updated for the '90s. "Things were changing, time was changing, music was changing, you know? People were much younger coming out to the clubs and things like that," said Nathan Tate, a former Escuelita cast member who since 1989 has been performing in drag as Victoria Lace. "And the music, you know, Deborah Cox was all the rage!" The club featured the incredible talents of Latine queens, showgirls, and gender illusionists, as some preferred to be called, like Angel Sheridan, Jesse Volt, Jessica Foxx, Karen Covergirl, and Laritza Dumont, as well as Harmonica Sunbeam, Victoria Lace, and many girls from the House of Xtravaganza. Like BoyBar, Escuelita had a cast of performers, the Escuelita Follies. They'd lip-synch to the music of Celia Cruz and La Lupe in addition to US pop hits. In the venue's new incarnation, Angel Sheridan became the show's director. Described as an old-school pageant girl and a veteran performer of high-end drag cabarets, Sheridan's shows became a little more showbiz. During her reign, the floor was shellacked and they got a curtain. Escuelita was also a beloved home of voguers and members of the ballroom scene before it shuttered for good in 2016.

Before she arrived at Escuelita, Harmonica Sunbeam made a name for herself at Two Potato in Greenwich Village at 143 Christopher Street and Greenwich Avenue, a bar beloved by queens and queers of color. It was a small bar with a small stage, but it boasted a vibrant and discerning crowd. "If you've ever seen like *Showtime at the Apollo*, I think a crowd of African Americans are going to really expect something to happen, to really be impressed...they're not easily impressed," Harmonica said. "There were some girls who were Black but had not performed in a lot of Black establishments who were afraid of the crowd. And there were also non–African American girls who were afraid to work there as well." Harmonica found learning how to engage the audience a positive challenge and an exercise in receiving constructive criticism. "I'm glad I started out with this particular crowd, because they either like you or they don't. It's kinda like the saying, *if you can make it here, you can make it anywhere*," she said in 2016.

Another among the most famous Escuelita performers was Puerto Rican drag artist and transgender showgirl Lady Catiria. Lady Catiria began performing drag in Jackson Heights, Queens, then as now a thriving queer neighborhood; she was only nineteen. By her early twenties, Catiria made her way to Escuelita, where she quickly became one of the club's most beloved performers. Actress Rosie Perez remembers seeing her there with John Leguizamo: "She'd do 'My Way' and take off all her clothes except her G-string and the tears would run down her face," Perez told *Out* in 2007. "I saw her show four times."

Laritza Dumont remembers how helpful Lady Catiria was to her. "She was the one that really took a kindness to me and [told] me, pay these girls no mind, be you, be who you wanna be." Laritza also remembers Catiria performing "Turn the Beat Around" with only her back—or rather, backside—to the audience. "She would perform, lay down, turn her rear end to the audience in a nice latex or something bathing suit…and one of her cheeks would move by itself like she was lip synching with her rear end," she laughs.

Lady Catiria would notably make an appearance in the opening scene of *To Wong Foo, Thanks for Everything! Julie Newmar* (as would Laritza), but arguably her most defining moment came at Chicago's 1995 Miss Continental Pageant—which, when it was founded in 1980, became the first drag pageant to allow transgender participants. Catiria discovered her HIV-positive status that year, and when she won the pageant, she knew by the end of her term that people would see the illness's effects. "I didn't want everyone saying, 'What's wrong with Mary?'" she told *POZ* magazine in 1999. "So I told them myself."

When passing her crown to Miss Continental 1996, she took to the stage in a custom gown, shining black and overlaid with a sparkling red rhinestone-encrusted AIDS ribbon. The performance told the story of her diagnosis and living with the illness at a time when few public figures were open about their status. She passed away in 1999 at age forty.

"If in my mind's eye I always knew I was going to be a star, I never thought it was going to be as a drag queen," RuPaul wrote in his 1995 autobiography *Lettin' It All Hang Out*.

The prevailing mood in New York's queer community was funereal when RuPaul returned in 1987. In Atlanta, he had been working his Bowie-esque, genderfuck fantasy look, covered in tinsel and cellophane and the occasional leopard loincloth. He was fronting punk bands like Wee Wee Pole and RuPaul and the U-Hauls, trying to make a name for himself. He wheatpasted posters across Atlanta that said "RuPaul Is Everything," always hustling to keep himself in the public eye. When Ru felt he had made the most of Atlanta, he packed up every wig and disco ball and instrument he had, got in a van with DJ Larry

Tee and drag queen Lahoma Van Zandt, and drove up to New York. "When we showed up, it was post-AIDS, which wiped out a whole generation of entertainers and DJs and creatives," Larry Tee told *Entertainment Weekly* in 2017. "We showed up, [Ru] in her Daisy Dukes and colorful tops, me as raver Liberace. We must have looked a sight for sore eyes at a time when there needed to be some optimism."

Ru began go-go dancing at the Pyramid Club. Rocking a mohawk with his punk/new-wave drag, he fit right in.

But it wasn't easy, to say the least. He worked coat check, danced, and appeared at Susanne Bartsch's parties, but it wasn't enough. In 1988, he gave up and moved out to Los Angeles, sleeping on his sister's couch and watching a lot of *Oprah*. He then moved to his mother's house in San Diego until Tee shook him loose. "Larry Tee called me and said, 'Ru, what the fuck are you doing? You are a fucking star. Get your ass back to New York. I will pay for your ticket. But get your ass back here and get your shit together,'" he said later. "And I did." He moved back to Manhattan in January 1989 with a renewed sense of purpose.

The genderfuck punk drag would be no more, he resolved. The new look would be "drag queen realness." He traded his mohawk for a blond wig that has since become his signature, shaved his legs and chest, added some rolled up socks for breasts. "If that's what the children wanted, then that was what the monster would serve them," he wrote. In what he would later call his "*Soul Train* dancer-slash-black hooker" look, he began go-go dancing at the club Sauvage. Something had changed. That year, 1989, brought not just a Wigstock performance (to Whitney Houston's "So Emotional" and Nicole McCloud's "Don't You Want My Love?" from the soundtrack to the 1986 Bette Midler vehicle *Ruthless People*), but an appearance in the The B-52s' "Love Shack" music video. In it, Ru is utterly eye-catching, shimmying in an afro, giant gold hoop earrings, a tiny white halter top, and hot shorts. He even taught the dancers on set how to do a *Soul Train* line. "Love Shack" won Best Group Video at the MTV Video Music Awards, and the song was nominated for a Grammy.

By the end of 1989, Ru was crowned "The Queen of Manhattan" by a panel of club promoters and owners. Though his reign came to an end after one year, his successes wouldn't stop there.

That year, five fresh-faced models—Cindy Crawford, Naomi Campbell, Christy Turlington, Linda Evangelista, and Tatjana Patitz—gathered with photographer Peter Lindbergh in the Meatpacking District of New York. They covered the January 1990 edition of *British Vogue*, and in doing so ushered in the era of the supermodel.

RuPaul noticed in part because he remembered arriving at Nelson Sullivan's stoop in the Meatpacking District after a night out, only to see models sitting there for a Chanel photo shoot. Newly sober, Ru came up with a new look. He wanted to be a supermodel too: gone were the days of "Black hooker." Larry Tee had written a song based on the supermodel phenomenon, one into which Ru would fit perfectly.

This moment crystallized into a demo called "Supermodel (You Better Work)." It was released on November 17, 1992— RuPaul's thirty-second birthday. In a moment when New York Fashion Week was getting more attention than ever, the song appeared on the runway and soon became an MTV staple. In October 1992, the video filmed all over Manhattan. "It was very New York," RuPaul wrote in his autobiography. "No one seemed to think anything of a drag queen prancing around in [The Plaza] fountain at sunset." It soared, and "Supermodel (You Better Work)" peaked at #45 on Billboard's charts in the US. RuPaul appeared everywhere from *The Arsenio Hall Show* to *Saturday Night Live*. He collaborated on music with Elton John, hosted a morning radio show (with cohost Michelle Visage), and became a face of MAC Cosmetics.

The RuPaul Show, a talk and variety show, premiered on VH1 on October 12, 1996, making its star one of the first openly gay national talk show hosts in the country. As he had predicted in his Atlanta days, RuPaul was, indeed, everywhere. "The only way that the mainstream had embraced drag was to have [men] in *Some Like It Hot* doing drag because they were hiding. *Tootsie,* [a guy] unable to find work. *Mrs. Doubtfire.* There was always a reason," Lady Bunny said in 2017, a phenomenon that hearkened back to Julian Eltinge. "Ru didn't need a reason. That was a huge benchmark for him to say, 'I want to do drag because I look gorgeous—don't you agree?' And for the world to say, 'Yes.'"

But there were many models who gave superstar turns in drag, some long before RuPaul. J. Alexander used to go out to Studio 54 in drag. He'd first take the Bx13 bus then the 6 train down from his grandmother's Bronx apartment, then hop into a cab at 59th Street. "I wanted to look beautiful and glamorous like a couture model," he wrote in his 2009 autobiography, *Follow the Model,* but he didn't want to be a drag queen. Miss J, as he became known, booked a Jean Paul Gaultier runway show in 1984, and afterward was signed to Elite Model Management in Japan with a $20,000 contract. He was sixteen, and modeled in drag on runways for years before becoming a runway coach for top-tier designers and the women who, many due to his tutelage, became supermodels. Later on, he also became known as a beloved runway coach and judge on *America's Next Top Model.*

Connie Fleming began transitioning in the late 1980s, and around that time walked the Runway Effect category at the House of Field's Grand Street Ball. There, photographer Steven Meisel saw her and hired her for an Azzedine Alaïa book. She'd later appear on the runways of Thierry Mugler, Vivienne Westwood, and more in Paris and New York. "Me being on Mugler's runway, that should have been the end of his business," Fleming told *Interview* in 2020. "People thought no one would ever buy from him anymore. But his business did not go up in smoke."

By the time the drag craze hit the runway, Fleming had already left drag behind. But she was grouped in with drag performers despite identifying as trans. "It was the look of the moment," she said. "But like Chrysis told me and taught me, the punches are going to come hard and fast and you are going to have to be able to withstand." She was still booked and busy, a stunning force on the runway. But as the trend for drag on the runway faded, Fleming found her demand as a model also decreased. Around 1995, she said, it was time to leave. "The pendulum had swung," she said. "Whether being put into the drag box or being trans, it was swept up into one pile and pushed out." Returning to New York, however, she found a new career in runway production and coaching, as a tough door person at clubs in the city, and as an artist. She continued print modeling for Mugler, *Interview*, *Australian Vogue*, *Candy*, and more, always legendary.

Billy Beyond, while working in management at the Pyramid Club, modeled for designer Todd Oldham in the early 1990s. He had started modeling in the late 1980s when David LaChapelle photographed him in women's clothes for a spread in *Interview*. "Everybody saw it, and that was it. 'Who's the new model?' And I started getting other modeling jobs in drag," Beyond said. "Once you're in it, you *can't* take it off. Sorry. I'm sorry, you're not allowed... And beyond that, you will always be a drag queen. *Always*. Whether you like it or not," he said.

Todd Oldham loved the precision of Billy's look, he said, and thought he had a great walk. "When you're doing a show or casting anything, or taking a photograph, it's all just about what and who can deliver in these moments, how is the best way to create this. So there was never really like, 'let's put a man on the runway in clothing.' That never ever, ever crossed my mind," Oldham said. "There was just something about him, especially in that moment, sort of looking back and looking forward all at the same time. And he really just seemed to kind of capture it all for me and made what we made look so much better. Like he could really sell it, so to speak."

Beginning in 1990, Billy appeared on eleven Todd Oldham runways, one of the hottest tickets in the fashion industry, alongside supermodels like Linda Evangelista, Cindy Crawford, Carla Bruni, Naomi Campbell, and Christy Turlington. While he was known as "the drag model," like Fleming he was really just…a good model. That's all he wanted to be. But not wanting to be pigeonholed and hoping to expand his creative pursuits, Beyond stopped modeling in 1997.

In the mid-1980s, Zaldy, a Filipino-American fashion designer, entered the Miss BoyBar competition at Perfidia's behest and promptly won. But he relinquished his crown and didn't get in drag again for several more years. Artist Mathu Andersen, later his partner of ten years, began photographing and putting him in makeup. Susanne Bartsch convinced Mathu, a six-foot-two white Australian, and Zaldy, a five-foot-nine Asian man, to appear at her parties as twins, an idea Zaldy finds hilarious even now. They rethought drag for themselves, skipping chest pieces, accentuating small waists and padded hips, envisioning an edgy "alien fashion drag," Zaldy says. Nightlife also led Zaldy to meet RuPaul, who he encountered for the first time at club La Palace de Beaute in the late 1980s. Zaldy and Mathu soon became the performer's de facto costume and makeup team (they appear in RuPaul's 1993 "Supermodel" video doing this).

In 1995, after turns on the runways of Paris, Zaldy starred in a commercial for Levi's. He's a shapely figure in jeans, long dark hair, and red lips who gets into the back of a taxicab, much to the delight of the driver. Shortly after, Zaldy takes out an electric razor and begins shaving his beard. "I couldn't grow facial hair back then… And so they had to clip my hair and glue hair to my chin so I had something to shave," he laughed. At his destination, Zaldy gets out and walks into a cloud of smoke coming from under a New York bridge, and the words "Cut for men since 1850" appear on the screen. The commercial was promptly banned in the US. "I'm American. I was born in America, and you're saying this is too much for you?" Zaldy said. "Give me a break! It's Levi's! Levi's is from America." Not long after, Zaldy reimagined his design career, which was always his first love. He has maintained a regular working relationship with RuPaul for some thirty years—he designs all the performer's costumes—and also designed for the likes of Lady Gaga, Britney Spears, Michael Jackson, and countless others in that time.

The issue of Zaldy and Levi's is an interesting one as it relates to the placement of drag in American culture. While there was so much discussion at the time of a drag boom in and out of New York, it was still considered fringe. Drag was by no means a respected art form, even among the gay community in New York. Zaldy remembers in the late 1980s there were still bars that didn't allow drag queens at all. "There was a stigma to saying 'I'm going to become a drag queen,'" he said. "It's like 'ugh, nothing else is going for you? You wanna focus on a career?'... It wasn't a career choice...now it's a *career* choice."

But some activists used drag to take up space and joyfully commandeer that negative stereotype for good.

In January 1992, Chicago drag queen Joan Jett Blakk announced her candidacy for president under the slogan "Lick Bush in '92!" She ran as a part of the Queer Nation Party, having helped found the Chicago branch of the activist organization. Queer Nation helped reclaim the word "queer," which had previously been relegated to a homophobic slur, transforming it instead into a descriptor of power and pride.

Joan became the first ever drag queen to run for president. In July of that year, she arrived at the Democratic National Convention, held in New York at Madison Square Garden. At that time, Joan appeared on *The Brenda and Glennda Show.*

Glenn Belverio, in drag as Glennda Orgasm, and Duncan Elliott, as Brenda Sexual, had developed *The Brenda and Glennda Show* on cable access in 1990. They wanted to offer what Belverio describes as a "political energy" without potentially estranging audiences, with drag inspired by the Pyramid. Belverio had been involved with ACT UP, but saw how polarizing its actions could be. "I noticed how the stridency of street activism was alienating a lot of gay and straight people. They were scared of it or it was too much for them, they didn't want to get arrested, so we wanted to do something that was fun and was on TV and was informative, and it brought issues to people but doing it in a campy, drag queen way," he says. Brenda and Glennda brought drag to the daylight, to the streets, with episodes filmed on the Circle Line, at the Empire State Building, and even at the Trump Taj Mahal in Atlantic City, where they'd speak to people on camera in hopes of creating "Gay, Lesbian, and Drag Queen visibility." This was a time when, aside from Wigstock, there was rarely a drag queen seen outside of nightlife, let alone on television, let alone during the day, let alone talking to people who had maybe never seen a drag performer.

When Brenda/Elliott departed New York, Glenn continued the show as *Glennda and Friends.* In one episode, later screened at the 1994 Sundance Film Festival, Glennda and scholar Camille Paglia traverse the West Village, perusing sex shops and arguing with feminist antipornography protesters. Glennda Orgasm would also be the face of Sonic Youth's CD single "Self-Obsessed and Sexxee" that year (Linda Simpson would also appear in the single's interior).

On Joan Jett Blakk's episode, Glennda asks, "What would you do about this police state, Joan?"

"Well, first of all I'd fire them all. All of them. Every single one of them," Joan says. "And I'd hire, probably Dykes on Bikes.

I mean, give them something really meaty to do, you know? I don't think we'll have much crime if people know who's really protecting them, you know what I mean? The cops aren't going to protect you, that's obvious."

Blakk didn't seriously expect to win, but in seven-inch platforms, a miniskirt, a blond wig, pearls, and a leather jacket, she managed to draw attention to queer rights. This was at the peak of AIDS activism, ten years after the disease was first reported, and activists like Blakk felt that not nearly enough was being done to help people who had it. She also vowed to start calling the White House the Lavender House; to abolish all student debt; to "make the Supreme Court more fun by making it the Supremes Court"; to move the nation's capital to someplace more interesting, like Palm Springs; to return Kennebunkport to Native Americans; as well as, of course, championing gay rights, universal health care, and a woman's right to choose. "You can watch the news and never hear the word 'gay' mentioned," Blakk said at the time. "That just unnerves me. But with this campaign, they'll have to say the word; I'll make them."

Despite having a press pass, Blakk was not allowed into the Democratic National Convention in drag. Instead she donned the press pass in "boy drag" as Terence Alan Smith, and then changed in the bathroom into a spangled red, white, and blue minidress covered in stars and stripes. She was the first person to ever announce a presidential candidacy on the floor of the DNC. It was an outspoken act of visibility for queer rights made ever more possible by drag.

Despite the many strides that had been made in queer rights and visibility to that point, there was still work to be done. ACT UP was regularly in the press, gay cultural groups thrived in New York, and Bill Clinton's 1992 presidential election campaign saw gay voters as a boon. He was beloved by many in the community—that is, until he signed the 1996 Defense of Marriage Act (DOMA), which ruled that the country would not acknowledge same-sex marriage (it has since been struck down). The presence of gays in the military—the "don't ask, don't tell" edict—was hotly debated during his administration as well.

In his book *The Gay Metropolis*, author Charles Kaiser posits that acceptance for the gay community in mainstream culture began with corporate outlets, and in part due to the launch of *Out* magazine in 1992. While queer publication *The Advocate* had been in existence since 1967, it featured an (often very explicit) personals section and related advertising, but *Out* would not. "Before Bill Clinton's election, not even a master of homoerotic images like Calvin Klein had ever purchased a single advertisement in a gay magazine," Kaiser writes. In *Out*, that changed, and high-profile advertisers like Apple, Banana Republic, and Absolut Vodka joined its pages. It became not just accepted but chic for large corporate entities to align themselves with gay culture, a pivot for many that in the past had refused to acknowledge, if not openly excluded, the gay community. But what many saw as corporate greed also made space for queerness in mainstream culture—whether queer people wanted it or not (and some did not). That space was conditional, however, especially when it came to drag.

The Stonewall twenty-fifth anniversary committee, for example, suspended drag and leather at its commemorating events, including the annual Pride parade. It was a harsh twist of irony given the prominent role drag queens played in the Stonewall Uprising. But the committee had secured its largest corporate sponsors to date and was concerned about scaring them off. "They wanted to normalize the image of gay America for a mass audience. They wanted to present a palatable image of gay men and women, men and women who were *normal*," activist Brian Griffin told the *Huffington Post* in 2018. It was as if 1950s-era respectability politics had returned. Griffin, a longtime drag activist, co-created the Drag March to respond to these happenings with none other than Gilbert Baker, creator of the gay pride flag, himself an occasional drag queen who adopted the name Busty Ross, a "gay Betsy Ross."

Some 10,000 people gathered at the first Drag March to protest its exclusivity on June 24, 1994—the Friday before the sanctioned Stonewall 25 Pride Parade. The march became an annual tradition. Today participants gather in drag in Tompkins Square Park and walk across town to the Stonewall Inn, where the crowd joins together in singing "Somewhere Over the Rainbow." The Drag March maintains its stance as an alternative to corporate-sponsored Pride events.

Drag's exclusion from Pride also happened in the face of the most prominent drag representation in nearly a century, with RuPaul's successes reverberating across the country. "In 1993, there were a dozen drag queens running the city. Thirteen on a good day. The moment that RuPaul made 'Supermodel,' every queen that could purchase a wig and a pump wanted to be a drag queen. It was like someone poured water over Gremlins and there they were all over the goddamn city," HRH Princess Diandra said. But Harmonica Sunbeam still remembers drag's polarizing nature within the gay community, let alone the mainstream. "Back in 1993, I couldn't go to a restaurant and say 'are you interested in having drag brunch or drag bingo?'" she said. "Even on a slow night they would say 'hell no, get out of here.'"

Still, more doors opened for drag. In 1994, the Australian film *The Adventures of Priscilla, Queen of the Desert*, turned the "road movie" genre on its head with two drag queens and a transgender performer taking their cabaret across the country in a converted, fabulized tour bus. It received critical fanfare, recognized by both the Cannes Film Festival and the Academy Awards. The *Wigstock* documentary premiered at the Sundance Film Festival in 1995, and HBO would produce its own drag documentary, *Dragtime*, in 1997.

To Wong Foo, Thanks for Everything! Julie Newmar, another drag queen road movie, also came out in 1995. "My inspiration for the script came from watching the religious-right videotape *The Gay Agenda*. There's a scene where they show drag queens going through a town, and the narrator is warning viewers that these people will take over your town, and I thought, *Well, that would be fun*," *To Wong Foo* screenwriter Douglas Carter Beane told *The Advocate* in 1995. "Drag is a part of the gay community that Americans still shut out a lot. But why is it that the people… who are not allowed to be part of the party that is America… [are] having a *better* party over here?"

The film followed three drag queens across the country, from their home in New York to Los Angeles, with a stop in a rural town aka "fair hamlet" that's different than expected. But the three drag queens were not portrayed by actual drag queens; rather, the film would star Patrick Swayze as Vida Boheme ("of the Manhattan Bohemes"); Wesley Snipes as Noxeema Jackson ("you know, Jesse's daughter"), and John Leguizamo as Chi-Chi Rodriguez ("I'm the Latina Marilyn Monroe; I've got more legs than a bucket of chicken!"). Though Charles Busch was also brought in to read for Vida, and Swayze and Leguizamo would both go on to garner Golden Globe nominations for their work in the film, ultimately the casting was a marketing decision. The film's executive producer, Bruce Cohen, who is himself gay, told *The Advocate* in 1995 that "We're hoping Americans who wouldn't see a movie about three drag queens will go because it's Wesley and Patrick. Our dream—which I think we'll achieve—is that people will change how they think when they see this movie. Despite themselves, they're going to fall in love with these guys."

While it's a challenging sentiment to stomach now—prioritizing the tastes of mainstream audiences over the community the story is actually about—it's also deeply reflective of the culture's relationship to queerness at the time: not always accepted, but tolerated. Actors who portrayed drag queens mostly weren't actual drag queens or openly queer at all. But at the time, the *To Wong Foo* team focused on just getting the story told; it helped, too, that Steven Spielberg was an executive producer.

The film's leads sought to learn from the drag scene in New York. Mona Foot inspired Wesley Snipes, and Girlina helped him with choreography. Candis Cayne and Coco LaChine became drag mentors to Patrick Swayze. John Leguizamo was paired with Laritza Dumont. LaChine also served as a script consultant and added production notes and props to the film, while Cayne provided assistance to choreographer Kenny Ortega. In salute to the New York drag scene, the film's opening and closing pageant sequences featured a host of New York queer icons as competitors and judges. RuPaul descends from the ceiling as the previous year's pageant winner, Miss Rachel Tensions, in a sequined evening gown decorated as a Confederate flag.

The film was number one at the box office its first two weeks in theaters, eventually grossing over $36 million domestic, but it still faced pushback. As screenwriter Beane told *Entertainment Weekly* upon the film's release, "People keep telling me, 'Oh, it's so great you're doing this mainstream film...' Excuse me, *mainstream*? I'm barely in the back door, honey. We could not even get makeup product tie-ins on this movie, that is how piss-scared people were." Similarly, corporate entities like McDonald's and Pepsi wanted no involvement, and scenes involving their products had to be cut. *To Wong Foo* was also not necessarily made for queer audiences, skimming the surface of the queer experience. The main characters' romantic desires are notably unfulfilled while straight characters have the opposite experience—indeed, Chi-Chi was originally supposed to have a kiss with a local (straight) rural fella, but the scene was deemed too edgy and had to be cut. A counter-interpretation is that these queens learn to put self-love first, that the world is too big and too fabulous, that they themselves are too fabulous, to be with people they'd have to hide from, and there's universality there: that everyone deserves to be loved for exactly who they are and shouldn't have to settle for less.

The film exposed a new generation to the power of drag. "It really felt like a lightning bolt through a lot of drag performers in New York because they realized there was hope for them to go beyond these $50 gigs," Michael Musto said. "It gave them a chance that they could go beyond the local club scene. Or keep a homebase in the club scene and then do other projects."

The July 17, 1995, issue of *New York Magazine* featured a cover story called "Every Man a Queen" written by Charles Busch. In it, Busch mentions that "Manhattan, at this moment, is the drag capital of the world." Drag performers were invited on national television talk shows (Joan Rivers, Sally Jesse Raphael, Jerry Springer) and appeared in music videos like Cyndi Lauper's "Hey Now (Girls Just Want to Have Fun)" and George Michael's "Too Funky." The demand for performers soon translated into several drag-forward spaces that bloomed across the city.

As the tides turned, nightlife started recognizing the achievements of its own. Drag performer Cherry Jubilee, who also worked in the office at Lips and later Lucky Cheng's, wanted a way to honor the community, with votes from their peers. On December 7, 1997, the Glam Awards, or the Glammys, were held at Barracuda for the first time and the event continues today.

Joey Arias performed in drag as Justine at Wigstock's second iteration in 1985, singing Led Zeppelin's "Immigrant Song." But Justine wouldn't appear again for another few years—Arias had been singing and in bands, but he was looking to make some more money. He called Susanne Bartsch, and she was happy to have him. "She was like, 'I've been waiting. Put on the tits and heels, bitch, and come.'" Justine thrilled audiences, so Arias performed as the character more often, even fronting a band called Justine and the Pussycats from Outer Space (Perfidia was one of the Pussycats at one point, as was Sherry Vine).

As Justine, Arias appeared at Wigstock several more times, but by Wigstock's 1991 appearance at Union Square, Lady Bunny was hoping for something new. Out of drag, Arias was channeling Billie Holiday—performing as himself with a jazz band but cultivating the singer's vocal stylings in homage. The voice had initially emerged as Arias was doing a sound check when hired to do backing vocals for Iggy Pop.

So there he was onstage at Wigstock channeling Billie, "tits and makeup," long earrings, gloves, and gown, and the crowd went wild screaming. "People were coming up and asking, 'How much are you? How can we book you? We'll offer you $2,000,'" Arias said. "I didn't say anything, but in the back of my mind I'm thinking, Joey as a boy channeling Billie Holiday is making $150 a show. Joey in drag channeling Billie Holiday is being offered $2,000. And I'm thinking I'm going to stay in drag now. It was like a no-brainer... It wasn't like I decided to do drag, it was more a means to a means."

In 1994, Arias assembled his show *Strange Fruit*, dedicated entirely to Holiday, with Raven O and Afrodite as backup singers. After high praise from noted *New Yorker* theater critic John Lahr, the show ran at the Astor Place Theater on Lafayette Street, next to restaurant Indochine, for more than a year. Arias had cemented himself as an avant-garde performance and cabaret icon, and remains one to this day.

Arias soon had another success on his hands with his work at Bar d'O, which opened in 1994 at 29 Bedford Street in the West Village. Bar d'O had previously been Glowworm, a tiny bar opened by Indochine restaurateur Jean-Marc Houmard. It wasn't doing well, and Houmard hoped to resurrect it with one last idea. He saw Arias's show at the Astor, where the singer tsked Madonna for talking in the audience. "He said: 'Hey you there! It's not all about you!'" Houmard told *Sidewalkkilla* in 2020. He then hired Arias to perform at Indochine's fifteenth anniversary and sat down with the performer to discuss the West Village bar's potential.

Cabaret was going through a revival in popularity at the time—a twelve-page spread on the genre in the March 1992 issue of *Town & Country* declared, "Nowhere is cabaret fever hotter than in New York. In the last five years...Manhattan's cabaret scene has expanded, buoyed by a legion of newcomers who want to make their voices heard—and audiences who want to hear them." The success of Arias's show at the Astor plus this ongoing interest in cabaret would give Houmard's venue new life.

It became a cabaret on Tuesdays, Saturdays, and Sundays, with Arias, Raven O, and Parisian chanteuse Edwige Belmore. Other times there would be DJs, including a young writer named Hilton Als. Edwige eventually went back to Paris, and in her place arrived a young drag queen named Sherry Vine.

Arias had seen Vine sing Edith Piaf's "La Vie en Rose" at one of Florent's Bastille Day celebrations and invited her to get involved. Vine had arrived in New York from Los Angeles in 1992—she had gotten an MFA in acting at the University of Southern California, studying under legendary theater artist Anna Deavere Smith—and started with friends the off-off-Broadway theater company Theatre Couture. Known for their high camp and drag comedies and parodies starring the scene's top drag performers of the day, the company ran for fourteen years.

Raven O had moved to New York in 1980 from her native Hawaii to be a dancer. She and Patrick Briggs, who would go on to cofound legendary drag rock and roll party Squeezebox!, performed in clubs as duo Tempest and Torment. They joined BoyBar's Miss Shannon for a performance, and later Matthew Kasten asked Raven to choreograph numbers for house shows. She started onstage in drag when another performer didn't show up one night, and quickly became house mother to Kasten's father.

Raven herself never took a liking to the term "drag queen," preferring "drag artist" instead. "I'm a māhū, which is a two-spirit person in the Hawaiian culture, and when I was dressed up in my feminine side, I was not a boy in a dress pretending to be a girl, I was a woman. I was Raven O's female counterpart to the male counterpart," she said. In fact, throughout her career, one of the few venues she'd play that was specifically a gay bar was BoyBar. She'd tour with Joey Arias at cabarets and jazz venues singing live, and Bar d'O became a natural progression.

Together Arias, Raven, and Vine—known in particular for their rendition of "Miss Celie's Blues (Sister)" from *The Color Purple*—created a glamorous, intimate, and raucous nightlife experience that was beloved by audiences for a decade. The three would also be accompanied by Flotilla DeBarge, veteran of both BoyBar and Pyramid, who would sing live at Bar d'O and in her own cabaret performances. She came to drag as actor Kevin Joseph. Since creating Flotilla DeBarge, she has had one of the longest-running careers in the New York drag scene with additional appearances on film and in television, making her a respected drag legend of the community. Sade Pendavis, hailing from the ballroom scene and *Paris Is Burning*, was also beloved as an incredibly talented live-singing drag chanteuse and ran her own show on Sundays at Bar d'O dedicated to gospel music. Additional rotating members of the cast would include Candis Cayne, Jackie Beat, Lady Bunny, and vocal impressionist Jimmy James, who would also impersonate Marilyn Monroe (in performance but also in a campaign for l.a.Eyeworks in 1989 that is still famously misidentified as Monroe herself despite the actress's death), and many others.

With the cast dressed in anything–but–basic black, standards like "My Baby Just Cares for Me" and "The Lady Is a Tramp" were the order of the day, and Arias continued to channel Holiday. The tiny space originally had a capacity for sixty or seventy people, with plush furniture and red walls. But after word of mouth and a few key press items, lines wound around the block—Arias estimates as many as 200 people packed in on some nights, famously sitting on the floor if there was nowhere else (and there often wasn't). Bar d'O became a rare place in New York to see drag artists and gender illusionists singing live, continuing to expand the possibilities of what drag could be in the 1990s. Purring into their microphones, crossing long legs on top of bars, bantering with the crowd, the audience was theirs.

The Bar d'O audience loved to be loved, and returned the favor twentyfold. The girls even recorded an album and went on international tours; after the bar closed, its reunion shows delighted year after year. All of its performers continued to thrive. Sherry Vine became one of New York's leading divas before departing for Los Angeles. She made a splash internationally with her parody songs on YouTube, with hits totaling almost 22 million as of this writing; hosted her own variety show, *She's Living for This*, on network Here TV; toured the world; and in 2021 debuted *The Sherry Vine Variety Show* on Canada's OUTtv. Joey Arias continued to cross creative spectrums and in 2008 debuted with puppeteer Basil Twist the extraordinary show *Arias with a Twist*, a blend of music, comedy, and puppetry that was ultimately nominated for a Drama Desk Award in 2009 and became the subject of its own eponymous documentary in 2010. Arias continues to be a respected force in avant-garde performance. Raven O continued her career in cabaret and song, and also became host to outrageous variety show and nightclub venue The Box when it opened in the mid-2000s. She moved back to Hawaii at the end of 2021.

What was interesting about Bar d'O and many other venues at the time is that there was an anything-goes atmosphere that simply can't be duplicated today, in both performance and audience. There was ribald behavior on and offstage that many only saw with their own eyes. Sherry Vine remembers Meg Ryan dancing on tables, visits from Liv Tyler, and Drew Barrymore dancing on the bar at Bar d'O, not to mention all manner of shenanigans in the bathroom. None of this can happen today in the same way, lest someone be captured on a camera phone, their activities shared online. So there was an even greater sense of freedom attached to experiences like this for people famous and not, whether you were attending or performing or both. Drag could be outwardly raunchy and mischievous without fear of repercussions, sometimes making it a deliciously taboo delicacy that was happily not meant for mainstream consumption. But as technology changed, drag would be affected as well.

Clinton Leupp would also ride cabaret's wave of popularity and create a show for himself as his drag alter ego, Miss Coco Peru. At that time, Leupp remembers, "Drag queens usually that were in the cabaret world were singing live or telling jokes. There weren't very many drag queens in the cabaret world, there's probably more now." There were female impersonators still in those spaces—Tommy Femia doing Judy Garland, James Beaman doing Lauren Bacall, Jimmy James doing Marilyn Monroe, and Steven Brinberg doing Barbra Streisand, among others—but original characters were fewer and further between. "I wasn't impersonating anybody and I was talking about politics, religion, the things that were current at that time and I wasn't just doing comedy, I was doing serious stuff as well," Leupp says. His approach inspired others, including Varla Jean Merman. To see a drag queen onstage performing a monologue at all was unusual, let alone one that also had serious content, in addition to singing live.

Stingy Lulu's opened at 129 St. Marks Place in 1992 with an unusual mission: to cater specifically to drag queens. Most of the waitresses at Stingy Lulu's were drag queens themselves and transgender women—though at one point among their ranks was a young actor and comedian named Zach Galifianakis. As writer Jeremiah Moss shared in 2008, owner Karazona Cinar was not in the business of catering to heterosexuals or tourists. Moss offered this Cinar quote from the *New York Post*: "We were serving drag queen customers first, and since we're always busy, there's no reason to change our clientele." Open twenty-four hours a day, Stingy Lulu's was known for its 1950 diner aesthetics, not to mention "midnight drag shows that usually ended with them eating your fries," according to *Gothamist*. You could count on performances from gals like Trixie Trash, Jacquée, and Krylon Superstar, alongside comfort food and watered-down cocktails. In a 2006 story for *GQ*, writer Alan Richman remembers Jacquée in particular, who, in Eartha Kitt regalia,

did a dozen push-ups, slunk along the tops of booths and strutted out the front door to tantalize men standing dumbstruck on St. Marks Place. I was out of my seat, applauding.

World Famous ★BOB★ also got a job at Stingy Lulu's in 1995. "You got $20 extra if you did a lip sync number in your shift break, and then people would tip you," she said. "I was a baby queen and I was very grateful to be there and not a great waitress at all. I don't think people went there for the service or the food, to be honest." She does remember, however, the drag artist Tina Sparkles, who'd perform Shirley Bassey's "Goldfinger" decked out in gold, then walk out of the restaurant still lip-synching, and finish the song on top of a cab. "It was the East Village equivalent of Florent," writer Tim Murphy told the blog *Bedford + Bowery*. Though beloved, by March 2006 it was closed.

Lucky Cheng's opened in November 1993 at 24 1st Avenue at 2nd Street. Cheng's exclusively employed Asian drag queens and transgender women as servers and performers, later expanding its staff to include performers of all backgrounds. One of the original girls on staff, Tora Dress, had been with Cheng's from its opening and curated its twenty-five-year anniversary party in 2018. "There was a close bond the staff developed," she told *Hornet* that year. "We became a sisterhood of sorts—another family that supported each other when your own blood family didn't. We were there for each other through the ups and downs of love and life…"

While upon its opening Cheng's drew attention for its "California-Asian"-style food from the likes of *New York Magazine*, *The New Yorker*, and more, the main draw was always the girls. It drew a celebrity-and-yuppie-filled crowd, and at one point even Barbra Streisand and Robert De Niro couldn't get a table. Their limousine had pulled up, but as Tora remembered in 2016, "we had just given away the last table. She waved her manicured fingers and told her driver to move on. Everyone was gasping!"

Many performers thriving today got their start at Cheng's, among them a young dancer named Laverne Cox and a drag queen then named Kitten Withawhip who later changed her name to Bob the Drag Queen. Cheng's sought to capitalize on its successes and the tourist/bachelorette party contingent, moving from its East Village home to Times Square in 2011. As of this writing, Cheng's carries on as a Friday to Sunday affair at the Secret Room event space in Hell's Kitchen, on West 45th Street at 8th Avenue.

In October 1996, Mark Zschiesche, née Yvonne Lamé, opened Lips at 2 Bank Street in the West Village. "The idea was to re-create a drag queen's hyper-decorated apartment," *The Washington Post*'s Paula Span wrote in 1997, a shrine to fabulosity in all of its glitter and animal-printed glory. It would be a drag take on Planet Hollywood, Span wrote, this time with drag paraphernalia under glass instead of drumsticks: Flotilla DeBarge's fan, Charles Busch's bustier, and even "what are those round foam-rubber things? 'Varla Jean Merman's butt pads,' the proprietor says with quiet pride."

HRH Princess Diandra was skeptical at first about the prospect of working at Lips. After years of performing, she didn't want to be a waitress. But the waitressing job there wasn't the same as a traditional restaurant and ultimately, she says, it was a lifesaver. At Lips, she said, "[we] were making money hand over fist." They would take orders and bring drinks, yes, but runners would bring out the food while the girls could make fun of customers, who loved it. Early on in the West Village, customers were queer, but like Cheng's, it evolved to cater to bachelorette parties, brunches, and more. In 2010, Lips moved uptown to 227 E 56th Street, and in 2021 it celebrated its twenty-fifth anniversary. There are performers who've been at Lips for decades, among them the legendary Gusty Winds.

At the larger mega-clubs earlier in the decade, performances themselves were sparse, and drag performers—usually queens—were hired as atmosphere. Really, gay bars were usually meant for cruising. Then, in June 1991, Bob Pontarelli opened the tiny Crowbar, not much bigger than a studio apartment, in Alphabet City at 339 E. 10th Street and Avenue B with business and romantic partner Stephen Heighton. They wondered what would happen if they offered drag performances every night, so they put in lounge seating, and soon a generation of other iconic New York drag performers passed through Crowbar like Sherry Vine, Miss Understood, Hedda Lettuce, and Mona Foot.

"For me, she was just always a powerhouse," Lina Bradford said of Mona. "She was a muscular man, but when she got up in drag honey, she gave it to you. Everybody loved Mona. Mona was the shit. She was the one."

Nashom Benjamin Wooden of Brooklyn, New York, had started his career as Mona Foot at BoyBar. "I wanted to be a rock star," Wooden told *Paper* magazine in 2017. "I never wanted to be a woman or dress up like a girl. It's just what happened." Wooden became known for his performance of Chaka Khan's "I'm Every Woman" (and later the Junior Vasquez remix of Whitney Houston's version) while dressed in a Wonder Woman costume. He also worked in the men's department at Patricia Field's, and learned how to do makeup from RuPaul when they were cast together in the 1990 off-Broadway play *My Pet Homo*.

"To say that Mona Foot lip-syncs is to say that the Plaza is a hotel, that Midas was wealthy or that Kiss was just a band,"

Julian Fleisher wrote in his 1996 book *The Drag Queens of New York: An Illustrated Field Guide.* "She doesn't simply mouth the words, she rides a song like a cowboy rides a bronco..." Dazzling the crowds at BoyBar, Wooden began to host a night at Crowbar. He came up with an event concept called Mona Foot's Star Search, a drag talent show based on the *Star Search* television show. Some say it is the basis of a very famous drag competition show that arose later on. Whether they knew it or not, Mona's Star Search performers continued building the foundation of our current drag culture. Crowbar was sold in 1996, but by then the owners had opened a new venue in Chelsea called Barracuda, and the show continued there.

While Star Search started with Mona, it also ran after her tenure and became a coveted gig. One of New York's most beloved queens, Shequida, helmed the program for eight years. Mona ultimately left drag behind to be Nashom the musician and DJ, but his legacy was and is a fierce one. There's hardly a person in the scene who doesn't remember his role in and out of drag in *Flawless* opposite Philip Seymour Hoffman, his buff shoulders squeezed into that Wonder Woman corset, or his wicked Space Cunt shows at BoyBar spoofing 1960s sexy space B-movie films (one of which is available on YouTube).

Mona Foot was Girlina's drag mother. Girlina, once the stage name of Lina Bradford, was not a drag queen, but rather a gender illusionist. "My family embraced me as a little girl from the age of four, and growing up in Manhattan, that was nothing but an eyelash flap," she said. "My grandmother being a dominatrix and taking me to Studio 54...I had a different perspective and understanding of myself and everything else around me." A trained dancer, she had performed at the Pyramid and at BoyBar, an easy commute because she lived above it. Later, Pontarelli invited her to create a Tuesday night party at Crowbar called *Swirl*, a show about a model returning to New York from a stint in Europe. "Crowbar was really where it was happening because it was a little fresher, it was a little funkier," she said. "It had more of what was going on in the moment and at the time."

A young dancer named Candis Cayne started at Crowbar, fresh from performing on a cruise ship, and she'd soon host Crowbar's Wednesday night party, Crisco Disco. Cayne, who had lived with Sherry Vine in Los Angeles, moved to New York seeking stardom. Like many of the girls, she lived in the Meatpacking District when it was still covered in meat, but also had a dance studio scholarship. Candis and Girlina hit it off instantly—in fact, after the two faced off in Mona Foot's Star Search, they vowed never to compete against each other again.

By 1994, the two were appearing together in performances with elaborate choreography. The *New York Times* in particular noted their "triple pirouettes in four-inch pumps" on the dance floor. But Pontarelli would never forget their duet to "Enough Is Enough" on a frigid Wednesday night at Crowbar:

> the front door opened and Naomi Campbell came sashaying across the plywood floor. The crowd went crazy and Lina and Candis kicked and whirled as though their lives depended on it.

Candis and Lina would perform as twins around town, dancing and working the runway for Dolce & Gabbana and Mugler into the 2000s. They both used drag as a springboard for their careers while also not being defined by it as transgender women. "When we met, it was just like, wait a minute, we're not like anyone else. We saw each other," Lina says. Lina was also among the first transgender women of color to become a prominent DJ, along with the renowned Jordana and Honey Dijon, the latter of whom also has a background in drag and appears in the *Wigstock* movie.

Candis was hosting Monday nights at Barracuda when she began her transition, and the bar held benefits to raise money for her surgeries, at a time when transgender lives in queer spaces weren't as visible or understood. "In the gay community, there wasn't a real acceptance of trans women. There might not have been a dialogue people had. They didn't really identify with us as part of the community," she told *Out* in 2015. "I got to transition and go onstage every week, and through my comedy and dance and my talk, it opened up a lot of people's minds about that side of our community." She went on to score roles in film and television, becoming the first transgender actress on a network television show, ABC's *Dirty Sexy Money*.

Barracuda opened in Chelsea at a time when the area was known mostly for "a hot muscled guy in a white t-shirt... It was the '90s version of the clone," owner Bob Pontarelli says. "A big part of that was, you gotta beef up because you want to be invulnerable to AIDS, and also to all the homophobia that was rising," said Michael Musto. "Of course it didn't work against AIDS, but it still was symbolic and it was a psychological thing." He remembered that too often drag queens bore "the brunt of internal homophobia. You know, 'oh, you're not a real man and we need to present this butch image to the public'... I don't think they were really as beloved by the community [then] as they were later on."

Barracuda was the first drag venue in the neighborhood. It was part of a new wave of gay bars where the backroom was more for performance and less for casual encounters, a change driven in part by Giuliani's campaign against nightlife as well as the ongoing threat of AIDS. As *New York Magazine* wrote in 2003 when it proclaimed Barracuda the best gay bar in the city, "The dim lighting and black walls give it a comfortable edge of sleaze—but you can settle into one of the many couches in the back without worrying about what you might be sitting in."

Some of the biggest names in drag got their start at Barracuda. "We wanted people to come to our bar. That's it. And drag [was] the way to get them there. And so we find the best drag queens we possibly can, and some of them are hit or miss, who have a kind of intellectual component and performing aesthetic that we think will be entertaining and innovative," Pontarelli said. "We presented girls that could stand up in front of a room for two and a half hours and hold that room and hold their own… It's hard as shit to do that. It wasn't 'get up and lip-sync your number and then go away,'" he went on. "It was the personality and charisma and the intellect behind their audience engagement that was so extraordinary. Whether it was Candis or Lina or any of them, they had that gift. They were true performers in that serious way, and yet all of the stuff was evil and funny and ironic and funny and smart and reality-based and clever."

But queens were not the only ones in demand.

Johnny Science and Diane Torr's Drag King Workshops became popular the world over. Through events at colleges, art schools, and gender conferences, they inspired a generation of drag kings. Though Science later departed for other projects, at the beginning he did participants' makeup, and Torr taught physical presence. Torr later changed the Drag King Workshop to the Man for a Day Workshop, largely because it was based on the experience of "passing." Accordingly, the style of drag that emerged from Torr's workshop centered on realness.

Buster Hymen took Torr's class and passed on the teachings to others. They danced and sat like men. They were taught to walk like they had "a three-foot moat around us, and that when we walk we can take up that much room and people have to respect that space if you claim it," remembers Tracy Blackmer, who performed as Hymen almost immediately after taking the workshop. "It changed my life," he said. Torr got Hymen his first gigs at the Pyramid Club, and took him onto *Jerry Springer* with her. Hymen ended up quitting his job to do drag full-time, becoming among the first drag kings to adapt the workshop's form for the stage. But he didn't know many other kings, so he had to convince people to get in drag with him. "You just book a show and then you find people to be in it," he said.

Drag kings, it would turn out, were on the rise, and were especially popular at lesbian bars, Hymen remembers, which were significantly more prevalent at the time than they are now. "Women loved us, and it was crazy because I could go up on stage and talk about my dick and women ate it up and it made no sense," he laughs. It was refreshing, Hymen says, noting that up until that point, drag queens had gotten most of the attention. For Hymen, drag became a political statement as much as a performative one. "Women doing drag involved taking on power not relinquishing power, and so it's like a real bold statement, and I think [women in the audience] caught on to that and the excitement," Hymen said. "And the drag queens loved us as well because we were sexy and we were masculine."

Mildred Gerestant first saw drag kings perform at the Pyramid Club. "I was like, wow! I'd like to come up and do that, and be a stud just like them, in drag," she told writer LW Hasten in 1999. "I kept running into Buster, and I kept telling her how I wanted to try drag. We made plans and she came over to my place one day and we put on the mustache, which was really cool. She showed me how to apply the facial hair and stuff, and then I experimented with it, how I wanted it." From Mildred emerged Dred, bald with strong dark eyebrows and a sharply lined beard and goatee, stylized as the smoothest 1970s mack daddy of them all and among the few Black kings on the scene.

"Dred blurred and blended gender lines; made you question masculinity, sexuality, identity; challenged racial, social, gender stereotypes; and provided memorable, world class entertainment," wrote fellow drag king Mo B. Dick. In a one-person show at the WOW Café, Dred performed Isaac Hayes's theme from *Shaft*, "It's All About the Benjamins" by the artist then known as Puff Daddy, and Aretha Franklin's "Natural Woman," all the while embodying the characters he had created for each song, a fluid lip-synch assassin, as Dick says. At the end of each performance, Dred would remove an apple from inside his pants and take a bite, Eve fucking with God with a wink and a smile.

Mo B. Dick came up alongside Dred. Having seen drag kings in Provincetown and inspired by an article about a bisexual woman like himself performing as a man, he was inspired to attempt drag on his own. He got his hair cut, then later at a Goodwill found a bowling shirt emblazoned with the name "Dick." The name stuck, and with the clippings from his haircut (and assistance from Mistress Formika), he formed a mustache with eyelash glue. Clocked as a man walking down Avenue B, Dick was ecstatic. "I went, 'Oh shit, there is power in this. I'm on the level with these fellas who create an unsafe environment walking down the street,'" he laughed.

Mo B. Dick launched a Sunday night party at Club Casanova at the Pyramid Club in 1996. It featured drag kings as the Beatles, with tunes by DJ Mike Hunt (say it faster), and kings go-go dancing on the bar. It later settled at a bar called Cake at 99 Avenue B. The party was indeed kings only, at the door, on the stage, lip-synching, in the DJ booth, performing skits, and more. Club Casanova was, in part, born from Dick's desire to create community among kings, and in part to prove wrong those who had negated kings' abilities in the first place. "When I first started Club Casanova, everybody was saying, 'Oh, I've seen drag kings. They're awful. I've never seen any good ones. Good luck.' Just a lot of resistance. So I was like, I'm gonna prove you wrong; this is a challenge to me. So I knew I had to do it," Dick told writer LW Hasten in 1999. Club Casanova found their crowd amid a growing appetite for drag kings in general, with performers like Dred, Mo, and others appearing regularly in television and film, including the influential documentary *Venus Boyz*.

Dick eventually produced a Club Casanova national tour and would himself appear in an episode of *Sex and the City*, as well as John Waters's film *Pecker*, in a role specifically designed for him. Today, Dick continues to perform and produce events while also chronicling drag kings of yore at DragKingHistory.com.

Before Club Casanova ended in the late '90s, however, perhaps the most famous drag king working today made his debut. Murray Hill appeared for the first time at the end of 1996 dressed to impress and ready, albeit (mostly) in good humor, to challenge Rudy Giuliani in the candidate's bid for mayor. A mustachioed gent with lacquered hair and rings on fingers hearkening back to the age of Borscht Belt comedians, Hill calls himself "the hardest working middle-aged man in show business." Today he's among New York's most beloved performers, a perennial downtown favorite who's also escalated to global renown.

When Hill arrived in New York and attended Wigstock, he noticed photographers snapping pictures of queens, but hardly anyone else. He had even been among them at one point, photographing Lady Bunny and Lypsinka while studying photography in college. But he wondered where the male drag was, wishing to embody the comedy and campiness of queens, but with his own twist on masculinity. He didn't see much of this—the goal for male drag then was to "pass," he told WNYC, not to make people laugh.

When Hill first showed up in clubs, part of his act included his 1997 mayoral campaign against Giuliani, or "Ghouliani," as Hill would refer to him, which started at Club Casanova that spring. "Mayor Ghouliani is trying to clean up our city, and I will not tolerate his behavior!" Hill said, as C. Carr chronicled in *The Village Voice* that year. "Ladies and gentlemen, I love New York, but I love the old New York better!" Hill didn't win his bid for mayor, but he did cement his status as a downtown New York staple, later deemed "the reigning patriarch of the downtown performance community" by writer Ada Calhoun in the *New York Times*. It was time for kings to have their moment.

Still, Hill just prefers to be…Murray. "I don't want to be known as a 'gay comedian,' or a 'transgender performer.' I'm old school—call me Murray, that's it," he told magazine *Vestoj* in 2021. "I guess I'm transgender by the literal definition, but I don't go around saying that I'm transgender—I feel it's reductive. Straight people don't go around saying 'I'm heterosexual.' To me, equality is when we can all just hang out."

Drag continued to thrive at legendary parties across the city.

By 1987, Linda Simpson had arrived in drag. "It was like this whole new way of looking at the world or having the world look at me," she said. That year she also began publishing an alternative queer zine called *My Comrade*. Now considered among the most influential queer zines of its day, it was a satiric call-to-arms response to the raging homophobia that the AIDS crisis had engendered. The parties Linda hosted in drag for *My Comrade* became her entrée to emceeing. In 1990, she began hosting her own party at the Pyramid called Channel 69, themed as a gay television station in a variety show format.

By the time Channel 69 started, the life and popularity of the Pyramid had shifted, partly due to AIDS, a changing interest in drag, and a change in ownership. But Linda made it work, and Channel 69 became a Pyramid revival effort. Every Wednesday, she hosted a generation of drag performers like Mistress Formika, Flotilla DeBarge, Ebony Jet, Afrodite, Mona Foot, Page, and Sherry Vine, alongside those who were already local legends. "It was like a vital clubhouse for a lot of people," Linda said. "It was really a kind of low, dark period right then in gay life… besides AIDS there was a lot of homophobia and even physical violence toward gay people that was going on back then, like gay-bashings, etcetera. So I think the Pyramid was this safe place to bond." She documented the time in a presentation and then photo book called *The Drag Explosion*, published in 2020.

Actor Daniel Booth gave birth to a new character at Channel 69, and soon became known across New York as "big titted, honky soul mama" Sweetie. She seamlessly moved across Manhattan's different nightlife scenes, always with a delightfully filthy mouth. Her dramatic lip-synchs paid homage to beloved singers but didn't impersonate them. Her "Light of a Clear Blue Morning" by Dolly Parton and "You Can't Always Get What You Want/I Shall Be Released" medley by Bette Midler (from the singer's 1980 Divine Madness concert) always killed. Sweetie's party Cheez Whiz, in the back of the Lower East Side's Parkside Lounge, also became a weekly intimate hang for performers of all stripes, drag and not. She worked in drag between 1990 and her passing from cancer in 2017.

Blacklips started in the summer of 1992 at Crowbar, but made its way to the Pyramid on Monday nights. It was founded by Anohni, Scott Jackson (aka Psychotic Eve and then Poison Eve), Johanna Constantine, and Michael Cavadias (aka Lily of the Valley). "It was the later years of the AIDS crisis, and so there's a lot of sadness around, and we were so young," Cavadias said. "This massive holocaust had happened and we had just sort of arrived there. There was this just mourning feeling everywhere and also all this really exciting stuff going on artwise." Blacklips was at once "beautiful and tragic and absurd and hilarious," Cavadias said, embracing the AIDS-fueled darkness that had filled the queer community.

The troupe's shows were "gory retellings of Jack the Ripper, audience members covered with blood and entrails, Tiki torches threatening to send the place up in flames, gender-bending prostitutes having pantomime sex, elaborately staged deaths, and the birth of Anne Frank reimagined as a twisted retelling of the Virgin Mary," writer Tricia Romano chronicled in 2016. "It was mayhem," Anohni wrote. "We screamed, cried, and laughed our fucking heads off, hemorrhaging reservoirs of fake blood." It was a backlash against the conservatism that had invaded the arts space. Four artists—Karen Finley, Holly Hughes, John Fleck, and Tim Miller—received National Endowment for the Arts grants, which were later revoked because the government said their work did not adhere to "general standards of decency and respect for the diverse beliefs and values of the American public." The defunding of this group, later known as the NEA 4, inspired Blacklips to channel their own rage into their performances. "Our flyers said things like, 'Be beautiful, worship the devil,'" Anohni said in 2019. "We were saying 'Fuck you' to what was happening in our community."

On Friday nights beginning April 15, 1994, there was a sign on the door at Don Hill's, way at the edge of SoHo at 511 Spring Street: "SqueezeBox! is a gay club run by gay people with gay performers for gay people and everybody else! If you don't like it, don't fucking come in, get the fuck out," recounted the party's host, Mistress Formika. Don Hill's wasn't a gay club; it was just a divey live music bar among a smattering of warehouses dotting the Hudson River. But when the club owners wanted to do a gay night, SqueezeBox! was born.

SqueezeBox! was a rock and roll drag party specifically for punk queers and the people who loved them, created by Patrick Briggs, lead singer of glam band Psychotica and manager of Don Hill's, and clothing designer Michael Schmidt. It featured a house band and Miss Guy, previously of BoyBar, was in the DJ booth. "We wanted a rock party that was mostly gay but anyone was welcome as long as they weren't an asshole," Guy said. Plus, drag performers were required to sing live, which many had never done before. But that was the beauty of punk: you didn't have to be refined.

The party also drew major rock artists like Jayne County, Green Day, Joey Ramone, Courtney Love, Debbie Harry, and Mark Almond, who'd all perform alongside other drag artists and gender-bending chanteuses. Formika remembers singing live while Courtney Love and Billie Joe Armstrong from Green Day played guitar; later they all went downstairs to get star tattoos on their wrists.

"I heard that SqueezeBox! was this rock and roll queer bar, which was what I liked," said Justin Vivian Bond. "I liked the sort of punk and rock and roll edge of the music in the '90s, and it was live music. I had been performing live music...I never felt comfortable lip-syncing. So, when I heard that they had drag queens singing live at SqueezeBox!, I went and I was like, oh my god...as soon as I walked in the door I knew this was for me and this was where I had to be performing." Bond was overjoyed the first time they were asked to perform at SqueezeBox!, and did so covering Marianne Faithfull's "Why'd You Do It?" The party became the place they launched their career in the city. "That was really how I started to establish my own audience and my own identity as a performer in New York," they said. "But it was so amazing because [you'd] meet all of these incredible rock stars that came there... It just became this amazing scene, it was so much fun." Shortly after in 1995, they made the New York debut of their famed cabaret act Kiki and Herb with pianist Kenny Mellman, with Bond as Kiki, a snarling, faded cabaret singer, and Mellman as Herb, her long-suffering pianist. The act later made its way uptown to Carnegie Hall and Broadway.

John Cameron Mitchell soon became a SqueezeBox! staple as well. "I was such a rock and roll fan but I didn't like how it was dominated by sexist, homophobic lunkheads...rock was very queer, you know," he said. "So it was exciting to see it come back around, with these queens and incredible drag and trans performers performing with the house band and then legends of that tradition later joined the party." Mitchell, by then an established theater actor in New York, had attended the party since it began and had been talking with SqueezeBox! house band music director Stephen Trask about developing a musical. But Mitchell's first SqueezeBox! performance came with some external resistance: he was a Broadway actor and not a drag queen. In fact, he had never performed in drag at all. But he soon won everyone over with a character from his musical with Trask. She made her debut at SqueezeBox! on July 29, 1994, and her name was Hedwig. A genderqueer singer/songwriter, she took to the stage in a blond wig, edges curling up in a flip so flouncy it might take flight, giant hot-pink sunglasses, the word "FUCK" written on her chest. "Don't you know me, baby?" she shouted into the microphone. "I'm the new Berlin Wall. Try and tear *me* down."

Mitchell, by his own admission often over-prepared, learned the art of letting loose at SqueezeBox! He remembers performing Yoko Ono's "Death of Samantha" that night, inspired by Formika in particular. "I ripped my drag off during 'Death of Samantha,' which I'd seen Mistress Formika [do]…her wig fell at one point and she tore the rest of her clothes off and it was very effective to me, so that became from the beginning a part of Hedwig's narrative."

Every six months, Mitchell and Trask debuted new Hedwig material at SqueezeBox! with the ultimate goal of performing it in a theater. "We invited a bunch of artistic directors from different theaters to come, and nobody wanted it," said director Michael Mayer in the 2003 documentary *Whether You Like It Or Not: The Story of Hedwig.* "I think at that point it was too rock and roll for the gay people and too gay for the rock and roll people…too music-y for the theater people and too theater-y for the music people." But ultimately, Mitchell and Trask got their wish. Mitchell came upon a dilapidated ballroom at a flea-bag spot called the Hotel Riverview located at 113 Jane Street. Today it's the Jane Hotel, but then it was still very much part of the Meatpacking District's more debauched days. At an early Hedwig preview, a corpse had to be taken down past waiting crowds. Nonetheless, the show formally opened there, at what became the Jane Street Theatre, on February 14, 1998.

Hedwig and the Angry Inch was a live concert performed by Hedwig and her band, the Angry Inch (played by Cheater, Trask's real-life band). The band also featured the character Yitzhak, played in drag by actress Miriam Shor wearing a beard with long hair. The show told the story of Hedwig's journey as young Hans, escaping East Berlin via a damaging forced sex-change and marriage, living an ignored existence as a put-upon songwriter in Kansas.

"[M]agnetically impersonated by the thrilling John Cameron Mitchell, Hedwig, the pouting headliner of 'Hedwig and the Angry Inch,' brings a theater alive with the pounding sounds of rock and the funny-sad voicing of a painful past," wrote the *New York Times*. It went on to praise Trask's "fresh and tuneful score" and Mitchell's "impressive achievement" of "transform[ing] what might have been just another campy drag act into something deeper and more adventurous." The paper also correctly predicted Hedwig would draw a cult-like following not unlike *The Rocky Horror Picture Show*. Some audience members—dedicated fans are called "Hedheads"—would go to see it some 400 times.

Mitchell and Trask ultimately preferred a cult status. "The people who cared about it and found it later loved it more than anything. Then the press picked it up as a 'cool' thing and suddenly celebrities started flocking," Mitchell told *Rolling Stone*, recalling people like David Bowie, Lou Reed, and Joey Ramone in the audience as well as Mike Nichols, Robert Altman, and Glenn Close. *Hedwig and the Angry Inch* became a film in 2001, with Mitchell starring and directing; it was also not a hit, but gained the same cult status as the show, garnering Mitchell a Golden Globe nomination. The film has since joined the Criterion Collection. *Hedwig* has since been reproduced on Broadway, for which it won the 2014 Tony Award for Best Revival of a Musical, along with Tonys for Neil Patrick Harris as Hedwig and Lena Hall as Itzhak.

In the depths of the Meatpacking District, another sign on a door let you know what you were getting into. Or at least it tried.

Jackie 60 is a club for dominant women, poets, gay men and lesbians, free-thinking heterosexuals, transvestites and transexuals, fetish-dressers, bisexuals, and those who love them. If you have a problem with this, don't come in.

—The Management

On Tuesday, November 20, 1990, at nightclub Nell's, the weekly Jackie 60 party kicked off with a host of deliciously bizarre and inventive themes in homage to or mockery of Bettie Page, Margaret Thatcher, and *A Christmas Carol*. But Jackie needed some danger. On March 19, 1991, the party moved to the still ungentrified Meatpacking District, back when severed beef limbs still bled into the street. For Chi Chi Valenti, husband Johnny Dynell, choreographer Richard Move, and fashion designer Kitty Boots, it was perfect. In 1996, Chi Chi and Johnny bought the venue and renamed it Mother. In artist and director Rob Roth's magnificent audio history "Night Paving: The Aural History of Jackie and Mother," Michael Musto refers to the club night as "a combination of Studio 54 and Lincoln Center for people who'd never even think of going above 14th Street."

Jackie 60 became a font of creativity, with inventive themes and shows every week including Night of 1000 Stevies, a salute to Stevie Nicks, which still runs today. "They did the whole club like a performance piece, complete with a dress code that was brilliantly loony with all these specific things that you could and couldn't do. So they were commenting on the club elitism while also embracing it," Musto said. Overhead, Paul Alexander was ever the emcee, "the Voice of the Night." Rose Royale was a Jackie cocktail waitress. A longtime downtown drag staple, AIDS activist, and artist, her work—as Edwin Shostak—appeared in exhibitions at the Museum of Modern Art, SculptureCenter, and the Chrysler Museum. She was also a former Warhol Factory denizen and roommate of Candy Darling, Jayne County, and Holly Woodlawn. "Rose was extremely hard of hearing because of injuries sustained in the Vietnam War and in a crowded, loud club like Jackie 60 it was almost impossible for her to get a drink order right," Johnny Dynell wrote. "So, of course we had to hire her."

The weekly Jackie dress code was listed on all the flyers, which you'd sometimes casually find muddied on the ground downtown. It went as follows:

Approved are leather, rubber, PVC, glam drag, full evening, Victorian & Edwardian, jockstraps, gothic drag, cyber-wear, religious garb & pagan robes, Jackie T-shirts & flannels, military drag & uniforms, traveler garb (burlap), tattoos, scars & piercings, butch drag for women.
ABSOLUTELY NO fur coats
NO suits, ties, dress pants or jackets for *MEN*.
NO rugby shirts *OR* rugby players.
NO droopy drag and NO banjy cliches.

And as ALWAYS—NO SKI WEAR!

At the door, if Kitty Boots didn't like the look of you, you wouldn't get in. As Jackie became more popular, this included celebrities who just didn't get it. "There were supermodel cat-fights every week and...Jack Nicholson getting thrown out with Robert De Niro and so, every week it was like a Page Six thing," Dynell remembers. It made the party all the more exciting.

As much fun as Jackie's wild themes were for its attendees, the Jackie team sought to push its performers past their artistic boundaries. Transgender nightlife icon Amanda Lepore once appeared as Sid Vicious, and Sweetie played Eleanor Roosevelt. Richard Move performed as choreographer Martha Graham at his dance series Martha @ Mother, which persisted despite cease and desist letters from Graham's estate (he'd later be invited to perform with the company).

But when Jackie ended in 1999, it was 100% deliberate. Jackie 60 didn't want to become part of a yuppie scene. On December 28, 1999, post-apocalyptically themed After the Blast, they started destroying everything at Mother because it was closing anyway. Jackie stayed behind in the twentieth century, save for periodic nightlife events throughout the years.

Jackie 60's daughter of sorts was Click + Drag, a party produced and creative-directed by Rob Roth from 1996 to 2000. Click + Drag's roots were at a Jackie Hacker night at Mother. Happening upon the club's fantastical nights as an art student, Roth was inspired to form a party of his own. He met Chi Chi Valenti and impressed her with an all-too-rare quality in 1993: he had an email address. Working in the new field of computer graphics, Roth pitched Valenti an InterJackie night, an interactive event that later grew into Click + Drag, a Saturday night party that ran for four years. "We introduced drag queens to the Internet," Roth says, smiling. "We would rent a computer to bring into the club for a night, and do you know what a computer looked like in '95? I mean, a huge fucking monitor, it was exhausting. And then she would hook up to the phone line a modem, and we would at 4AM, IRC chat [internet relay chat, a precursor to chat/instant messenger features] with someone in fucking Oslo or wherever." So much of what Roth and Valenti predicted with Click + Drag themes eventually came to fruition outside of the club as well, from surveillance to cybersex.

Click + Drag's dress codes were also intricate and, Roth says, "incredibly strict." But he believes this is what made the party so successful, with its rooms for performance, salon-style hanging, dancing, ongoing tech-inspired installations, and go-go dancers in costumes made of computer parts by Kitty Boots. One night, themed for Philip K. Dick's "Through a Scanner Darkly" called for "Bladerunner, Sci-Fi Fetish, Cyber, Imaginative Head-to-Toe Black, Genderhacking, Gothic, Silver, Classic Fetish or Access Denied! No Blue Denim/Khaki."

Roth explains, "Drag in the title of [the party], [is] very different than probably what people think about drag. I mean, of course drag queens came, many, but so many different kinds of drag. Butch drag, leather daddies, dominatrixes in their leather suits." He remembers Flawless Sabrina arriving at a party wearing a full-on hat box as a hat. "It was total art, it went beyond drag."

Performers included Debbie Harry, Mindless Self-Indulgence, Justin Vivian Bond, Jayne County, Joey Arias, Genesis Breyer P-Orridge, Anohni, Narcissister, and countless others. And it drew crowds from far and wide—Roth believes the night of the aforementioned "Through a Scanner Darkly" party, even the Spice Girls showed up.

But Click + Drag's end arrived at the hands of forces much bigger than Giuliani. The fateful events of September 11, 2001, enveloped New York in a mournful hush, the city's morale at a deafening low. Coupled with Giuliani's crackdowns, a quiet settled over nightlife, over New Yorkers. Few parties, Click + Drag included, could keep up.

After mainstream culture's interest in drag as a trend waned, the form's presence and demand decreased. But drag wasn't dead—it never was, and never has been. From the void a new force in drag emerged, invigorating the form in ways irreparable, interesting, or both, depending on who you ask.

9

2000 – 2022

"I went to the top of my building and watched it happen at Ground Zero, and thought it was so funny looking. I wondered why somebody would do that, that shit is really crazy," Kevin Aviance said. "I didn't know what to believe... And then that building fell. It was so quick. I was like, 'What the fuck?'"

He and Candis Cayne rode their bikes down 7th Avenue, watching frightened people slowly making their way uptown in a daze. Too scared to continue heading south, Kevin went home, locked the door, closed his windows, and prayed.

"The bars were closed but people just started hanging out," he said. "What else was there to do? We didn't know what else was going to happen."

Tuesday, September 11, 2001, began like any New York City workday, except by 8:46 a.m. a plane had crashed into the North Tower of the Twin Towers at the World Trade Center. As television coverage began, another plane crashed into the South Tower at 9:03 a.m. Another plane crashed into the Pentagon and one more in Pennsylvania after passengers fought back. The hijackers were members of militant extremist group Al-Qaeda, led by Osama bin Laden. Nearly 3,000 people died that day, though with injuries and related illnesses, deaths would increase. The events of September 11, 2001, were a defining moment in American history, in New York history, the worst attack the US ever experienced.

The city and the country were in mourning. Nightlife and performances halted. But ultimately when the show did go on, it returned with even greater purpose.

Justin Vivian Bond was supposed to have a show at Joe's Pub on the evening of September 11. It was postponed and became a fundraising performance. "Within a week, we were all mobilized and raising money," they said. "The bars and clubs and performances that happened after 9/11 were really major things as far as healing. It became a very powerful tool for all of us to come to terms with what had happened."

Writer T Cooper, formerly of drag king troupe the Backdoor Boys, remembers hearses driving through Alphabet City, a hush falling over the neighborhood. "The whole city stopped," World Famous ★BOB★ said. Venues closed, some permanently. But then, in true New York fashion, the city roared back. It was a feeling, Ana Matronic said, of "'Oh we're all going to fucking die. We are under attack. We have to make happen what we moved to New York to make happen now.' There was a sense of urgency unlike anytime I've ever felt in my life because there was this notion of, why did you move here, what is it for, are you getting there, what's the point?... Whatever you're living here for, make it happen. It lit a fire under a lot of people, and it also lit a fire under a lot of parties to just fucking party because there is no tomorrow." Almost like the AIDS crisis, there was a feeling that something horrible could happen at any moment, so if you wanted to create something, you should do it *yesterday*. Plus, there was a desire to escape through entertainment, to experience joy, not just to hook up. This translated across nightlife and made it once again a space ripe for drag.

Rudy Giuliani's citywide regulations had already left their impact on nightlife. The vast majority of mega-clubs closed. Yet downtown remained a site for creative experimentation, blending drag, burlesque, and the avant-garde/off-off-Broadway theater scenes together in a gorgeous grab bag of ideas, gender-fucking, and glitter. Gentrification spurred artistic souls to seek new homes in Brooklyn, drag performers included. These artists would keep drag's experimental punk streak alive as mainstream cultural forces began to prize a more polished version of the art form. Over the course of two decades, drag's cultural placement would both return to and surpass its '90s heyday, even as dramatic world changes disrupted its creative ascent.

A countercultural backlash against a new wave of American conservatism also reverberated through the scene. In a national address delivered on September 20, 2001, President George W. Bush stated, "Either you are with us or you are with the terrorists. From this day forward, any nation that continues to harbor or support terrorism will be regarded by the United States as a hostile regime." Declaring a "war on terror" after the 9/11 attacks, Bush set his sights on war with Iraq in September 2002, citing the country's possession of "weapons of mass destruction." Between August 2002 and March 2003, Gallup polls revealed 52% to 59% of Americans surveyed supported the war, while 35% to 43% did not. So there was a clear majority of support, but also an active opposition. When it became clear that war was imminent in 2002, antiwar protesters took to the streets.

Drag again became a vehicle for protest. Bernhard Blythe and Eric Mercer created GLAMericans to speak out against both the war and its profiteers, like private equity firm The Carlyle Group. As artist and designer Machine Dazzle said, the point

was "to give activism a little lipstick." The group's mission statement cheekily stated,

GLAMericans are a non-partisan group of funky Americans committed to non-violence and its promotion through
glamorous, media-savvy, cultural events. We believe in
America's potential to be a peaceful and powerful force in
the world. We believe that war is bad for our country, bad
for our environment and bad for our travel plans.

Downtown denizens like Justin Vivian Bond, Florent Morellet, and many others would join their ranks. Among them
were the Dazzle Dancers. Founded by Mike Albo and Grover
Guinta, the deliciously raucous group of often-naked and/or
glitter-covered individuals had been dancing together across
New York since 1995. "The original Dazzle Dancers were a re-
action to not being able to be naked in bars... And it was a way
of reclaiming our bodies, because we all have them. And it just
seemed absurd, in New York City that you weren't allowed to
get naked for the sake of entertainment," Machine Dazzle said.
Machine did their costumes, but also attired himself in what he
called genderfuck drag at nightclubs or at GLAMerican protests.
    On February 13, 2003, GLAMericans hosted an antiwar party
and fashion show at nightclub Marquee to benefit antiwar and
anti-Bush organization Not in Our Name. Two days later, on
February 15, 2003, they planned to join what became the world's
largest antiwar protest ever: there would be millions of people
across 600 cities internationally, and at least 100,000 other people in New York according to the NYPD, but what protesters
would recall as closer to 400,000. However, there was a snag:
with the city government's safety concerns still high after 9/11,
Mayor Michael Bloomberg wouldn't allow protest march permits. Police barricaded the intended protest route in hopes of

deterring people, but instead protesters gathered by the thousands to form their own protest groups across the city, convening—if they could make it through police barricades—at a single rally at East 51st Street and 1st Avenue. Meeting up with organization Reclaim the Streets at the main branch of the New York Public Library on East 42nd Street and 5th Avenue, GLAMericans protested the war while "draped in campy boas, carri[ying] signs that read 'War is Tacky, Darling,' and 'Peace is the New Black,'" according to scholar Marcyrose Chvasta.

On April 7, 2003, the GLAMericans also took to the street outside the Carlyle Group's offices at 520 Madison Avenue. Some dressed up in "corporate drag" like suits. Others draped themselves in dollar bills or held signs that said "More Blood for Oil." Machine Dazzle, in "a cowboy hat, golden high heels, a fake mink stole, lipstick and earrings," carried a sign bearing lines like "I Am a War Whore," and "I Come Fully Loaded." Despite being within his rights to protest peacefully, he was arrested that day, as were Linda Simpson, Mercer, Blythe, and many others.

The spirit of dissent also animated a show called *Live Patriot Acts: Patriots Gone Wiiiild!*, which was held during the 2004 Republican National Convention at Madison Square Garden. Part of the Imagine Festival, defined as a series of RNC-related yet still nonpartisan events, *Live Patriot Acts* was a "political vaudeville bringing together downtown subversives and spring break Americana." It featured Murray Hill tailgating on a George Foreman grill, Stars and Stripes beach towels, and "almost enough nudity to counterbalance the Madison Square Garden power-tie bonanza in honor of George W., just up the street." Its host and curator was Taylor Mac.

Mac, who uses the pronoun judy, had moved to New York in 1994 to attend the American Academy of Dramatic Arts. Judy performed at regional theaters upon graduating, but was frustrated with American theater at the time and so began developing judy's own work. It wasn't until visiting the gay summer haven of Provincetown, Massachusetts, that Mac began to play with drag onstage. Judy's work began to reimagine Theatre of the Ridiculous sensibilities for a post-9/11 world.

Mac's first work of cabaret performance art took place in 2003. *The Face of Liberalism* was held at The Slide, a queer nightlife hotspot on the Bowery named after the notorious nineteenth-century gay bar of the same name. In its three years of existence, The Slide would become a raucous site of drag, performance art, and cruising, sometimes all at once. Sweetie's High Life/Low Life party, for example, featured drag on its main floor—with Mother Flawless Sabrina go-go dancing, no less—and cruising in the basement. "A modern-day East Village mélange mingled at the bar," wrote the *New York Times* that year, with "Drag queens, punk rockers, muscled men wearing Abercrombie & Fitch T-shirts, even two men in white tie and tails. The plank floors and wagon-wheel chandeliers, on the other hand, summoned the vaudeville era." It was the downtown performance scene converging with a rowdy dance floor.

The Slide became a community nexus in many ways, especially during the blackout on August 14, 2003. For nearly thirty hours, New York City (and much of the Northeast and Midwest) was without power. New Yorkers, in true fashion, made it work: they helped each other out of subway cars and directed traffic; restaurants had cookouts; and nightlife kept the party going. Amanda Lepore "spent part of the blackout riding around the East Village in a rickshaw-like vehicle totally butt naked and offering photo ops to strangers," according to *The Village Voice*. Tompkins Square Park became a festival ground of sorts. The Dazzle Dancers took over The Slide with a battery-powered boom box. Some of them had been sitting outside on the sidewalk when performance artist Garrett Domina, née Jackie Bigelow, encouraged some of them to drive "naked in a station wagon all over the East Village, running into every bar and dancing on the tables, screaming and begging the bartenders for provisions. The next morning we noticed the car roof was covered in dents from Dazzle Dancer heels." If it hadn't already gone there, the evening later became a "raucous night of bacchanalia, culminating with everyone getting naked and go-go dancing on the bar at The Slide." The Slide's Daniel Nardicio also drove artists like Justin Bond and Lily of the Valley around the East Village in his pickup truck as they performed.

The Face of Liberalism ran at The Slide for six months, becoming "arguably the first theatre piece to interrogate and satirize the climate of fear and resultant xenophobia that Mac suggests came from the Bush White House following 9/11," according to scholar Sean Edgecomb. With fantastical Stars and Stripes makeup and a dress made of latex gloves, Mac's show critiqued the American government after 9/11 and the wave of patriotism it inspired. The *Live Patriot Acts* cabaret did the same.

Mac was both a descendant of Ridiculous theater and a drag child of Flawless Sabrina. "It wasn't her imperfectly-painted face that earned her the title of 'Flawless'—her flawlessness was found through fostering artistic expression as a form of civics. My time spent with Flawless lasted a little less than two years and yet, like the best mothers do for their children, she transformed me by inspiring me to transform myself," Mac would write later.

Judy's most well-known work from the decade was *The Lily's Revenge*. Directed by six different people, the five-hour play premiered at HERE Arts Center in fall 2009 and was written to oppose California's Proposition 8, which intended to ban same-sex marriage in 2008. It starred Mac, a California native, as Lily, a flower who hopes to become a man and marry, and a collection of downtown avant-garde, drag, and burlesque performers. Machine Dazzle did the costumes. Machine Dazzle, née Matthew Flower, originally got his name when he joined the Dazzle Dancers. It was one of these nights out that Taylor Mac approached Machine about some design work. "I was probably covered in glitter from a Dazzle Dancer gig...he asked me if I would make him a lily costume. And that's how it started," Machine said. They have been collaborators ever since, Dazzle's ensembles of fabulously extreme maximalist drag adding texture, nuance, and a whole lot of glitter to Mac's performances, not to mention Machine's own performance work. From 2022 to 2023, Dazzle had a solo exhibition of his costume work at the Museum of Arts and Design in New York.

In 2017, Mac became a MacArthur "Genius" Foundation grantee and a Pulitzer Prize finalist for Drama with the show *A 24-Decade History of Popular Music*. A Tony nomination for Best Play with judy's show *Gary: A Sequel to Titus Andronicus* followed in 2019. Mac continues to make theater heavily inspired by and including drag that addresses and questions history, art, society, and culture through a queer lens.

Earl Dax's *Weimar New York* also questioned neo-conservative values through drag and performance. Dax had drag personas of his own—queen Enya Buttox and king Indigo Earl, for example, the latter influenced by Mo B. Dick and Murray Hill—and had run regular queer performance parties downtown. Founded in 2007 during the Bush Administration's second term, *Weimar New York* featured drag troupe The Pixie Harlots, Justin Vivian Bond (then Justin Bond), Flotilla DeBarge, John Kelly, Julie Atlas Muz, Alan Cumming, Ana Matronic, and countless others. *Weimar New York* was meant to connect Berlin's decadent and debauched Weimar era—the time between World War I and World War II when culture and libertinism soared to historically prolific proportions—and New York's similar life at the time, using "the rubric of Weimar Germany to highlight unsettling parallels between the rise of fascism then and conservative political elements today," as Dax wrote. "The other fun thing about getting into drag at that time is everything we did felt important and it felt political. It wasn't just motivated by chasing celebrity," said former Pixie Harlot, Matt Crosland. "Sometimes even going out in drag felt…just walking down the street felt like a political statement back then."

When Mayor Michael Bloomberg took office in 2002, it seemed not much would change for nightlife. In fact, for a while, the new mayor had proposed bars and clubs close as early as 1:00 a.m. While this never came to fruition, he also discussed a Silent Night initiative, later known as Operation Silent Night, meant to quiet some areas of neighborhoods after a certain hour. This would also impact nightlife, increasing police presence in the East Village and Greenwich Village, as well as other areas across the city, some largely populated by people of color. Bloomberg also rezoned nightlife-heavy areas in Greenpoint and Williamsburg for residential buildings, forcing bars and clubs deeper into the borough by the beginning of the next decade.

As a result, smaller performance spaces also emerged, ushering in a burlesque revival. World Famous ★BOB★ had moved to New York in the 1990s from San Francisco and found the New York queer scene more accepting. "I hated, *hated* being called a faux queen or a fake queen," said World Famous ★BOB★, who identifies as nonbinary today and uses all pronouns. "I was like listen, there is nothing faux about my fucking drag." And indeed, there wasn't. At that time, World Famous ★BOB★ was identifying as a gay man, and later defined their personal identity as a spiritual transexual. In drag ★BOB★ referred to themselves as a female impersonator. "This confused most," ★BOB★ wrote. Or, as ★BOB★ explained to Ben Stiller when auditioning for a part in *Zoolander*, a female female impersonator. She wouldn't be the first or last to occupy such a space when it came to femme drag—Robin Tyler at Club 82, Sequinette, and later Miss Malice would chart similar terrain, all with their own unique approaches.

World Famous ★BOB★ came to burlesque by accident, through drag and topless performance art. In one act, she'd make a Jack and Coke in her cleavage with cherries she'd remove from her underwear and have the audience do body shots off of her, all to the tune of AC/DC's "Have a Drink on Me." But one day at a wig shop with her drag mother, the legendary Jackie Beat, World Famous ★BOB★ tried on a 1950s-style Marilyn Monroe wig, and something felt different. "I just saw everything in my life start to fall into place," she said. "So I bought that wig. It changed my life." She started making martinis instead. "I'd pull olives out of my panties. And the check had been written. I cashed it for sixteen years," she said. She didn't have a name for what she was doing until one night at East Village bar The Cock, a patron told her he loved her burlesque. She didn't know what "burlesque" meant, and he told her to look it up. She went to Tompkins Square Park library and realized this was most definitely who she was.

There was so much space for experimentation in the downtown scene at the time that no one batted an eye. "There was just this freedom to create numbers for the joy of it and not have to worry about somebody sitting there with a red pen making sure I did it right," World Famous ★BOB★ said. Because even in the midst of new nightlife regulations, there was still a sense of liberation inside the clubs. World Famous ★BOB★ began calling herself a burlesque revivalist at a time when neo-burlesque was still in its infancy. In recent years, the term "draglesque" has emerged as the drag-forward sibling of burlesque, where performers like Cétait BonTemps, Uncle Freak, Muscles Monty, and Theydy Bedbug continue to play with the form.

All the while, Justin Vivian Bond was still performing in a

variety of formats in addition to their work in Kiki and Herb:
as chanteuse some nights, and as a drag queen on the others.
"I basically created this drag character nightclub hostess that I
played, so I had no problem being called a drag queen because
that was what I was showing up to do on these crazy ass nights,"
they said.

One such night was Foxy. Every Saturday night, there would
be a Foxy contest, where everyone in attendance would get a
certain amount of Foxy Dollars, and the person with the most
at the end of the night would be declared the winner and get
something like $100 ("which in the mid to late-90s for queers in
the East Village was a decent amount of money to leave with,"
Bond said). But you didn't get the dollars for just being foxy.
Bond would auction off participants' talents, which would include acts like extracting a plastic-wrap-covered turkey leg from
one's vagina, playing the guitar naked, autofellatio, or allowing
guests to decorate a Christmas tree that had been summarily
stuffed into one's behind. It was magnificent chaos, fleeting and
ephemeral before camera phones, an act of rebellion in a time
of highly policed nightlife.

Later on, The Cock held a similarly subversive party called
Slurp. From 2006 to 2008, Slurp railed against the norms en-
forced by the mayor's office. "The party was insane—a hotbed of
creativity and sexiness. It was my final hurrah throwing weekly
parties and it was so great to go out on such a high note," wrote
its host, Linda Simpson. "It was 2006, the MySpace era. I don't
remember anyone having cell phones at the party and I think I
was the only one taking pix." Her photos include Miss Understood, openmouthed in a towering neon-pink wig enjoying a
go-go boy's assets; the performance artist Lee Adams in a ball
gag and polar bear suit; theater artist Glenn Marla mostly naked
in a cage as Divine; as well as clown nights, Ancient Rome
nights, and more. Slurp became an exciting space for both es-

tablished drag performers and new voices on and offstage, like Jiggly Caliente, the Dazzle Dancers, Lady Bunny, Milan, Sequinette, and even Flawless Sabrina. Indeed, Sequinette made her drag debut at Slurp, performing an electronica number she described as a cross between Depeche Mode and cats, with a lot of meowing. "Everything was so different before there was so much social media," she said. "You had so much more face to face interaction, and not everyone knew about everything, so things weren't destroyed or completely over-attended."

Cream started when Justin Bond and promoter Mario Diaz were trying to think of ways to get people to come to their party. "I said to Mario, 'Why don't we have a big load contest to see who has the biggest load?'" Bond said. So guests would jerk off into condoms, and Bond would bring them out and hang them from a clothesline over the stage. The condoms would be weighed at the end of the night, and the winner would get a prize like a double-headed dildo. "And then eventually, I was spending so much time in the bathroom waiting for these drunks to come," Bond said, that they tried a pretty penis contest, a "Say Hello to My Tits" contest, a "Hungry Hole" contest, all made possible with a Polaroid camera.

For Bond, these parties were also a certain kind of activism. In the midst of the ongoing AIDS crisis and Giuliani's quality-of-life campaigns that felt more and more anti-queer and anti-nightlife, Bond didn't want queer sexuality to become a space of shame or fear. "I thought it was very important to create a whimsical expression of sexuality so that people weren't so freaked out because gay people were so stigmatized and traumatized about sex," they said. "I wanted it to be a kind of playful exploration of sexuality and gender expression within the safety of our community so that it wasn't aggro or shame-based, but that was really funny and celebratory."

As expensive condos replaced crumbling buildings, and crime

dipped across the city, queer people were still subject to violence. The drag community in particular was rocked when on June 10, 2006, Kevin Aviance was assaulted by several young men after leaving Phoenix, a gay bar in the East Village. They beat him, kicked his head and legs multiple times, and left him in the street covered in blood. Aviance's jaw had to be wired shut in order to heal.

One of the first people at his hospital bedside was Flawless Sabrina. "She had a daisy with her. And she told me, she said, 'I had to be here right away. A lot of times you don't get to see the girl. Somebody gets beaten up and you don't get to say anything. So I made it a point to come over here and tell you that you did a fine job and that I appreciate you and I love you, what you've done for our community,'" Aviance remembered. While Aviance didn't know Sabrina well at the time, she became one of his mothers, he said. "She was one of the first people who ever called me an icon. She said, 'You are so important to us, you have no idea. Whether they say it to you or not, it doesn't matter. I said it to you. There's nothing like you. Not one thing.'"

And Aviance still performed during New York's annual Pride celebrations and spoke out as protests were held in June 2006 against a wave of gay bashings in the city. "It's been kinda hard," he said through his wired jaw. "But you know what, you can't keep a good queen down... We have to fight all of these people with love, every single day. Just watch out for each other and take care of each other, okay?"

By the early 2000s, as Giuliani's regulations stifled nightlife and rent rose, New Yorkers needed new places to go out and new places to live. Luckily, the L train meant Brooklyn was just one stop away.

Williamsburg had been an industrial neighborhood, with many local Puerto Rican and Dominican residents working at factories that dotted the area. Artists had been moving into the neighborhood since the 1970s, but by the late 1990s, it had become an alternative enclave to Manhattan's increasingly regulated nightlife and bottle service.

In 1999, Ana Lynch, who performed in drag as Ana Matronic, found herself immersed in New York's nascent electroclash scene. New parties cropped up around the genre, drawing influences from house, techno, indie pop, synth, and dance, inspired by gender-bending and performance art. Spencer Product and Larry Tee's Berliniamsburg party at Luxx on 256 Grand Street was among the most famous. "Finally my friends have some place to go where they like the music and we can dance all night and there's cans of Pabst Blue Ribbon for $3 and you can actually catch a cab right across the Williamsburg Bridge and be home in five minutes," Ana said. "That scene was basically a conduit for a lot of people to become expressive."

The electroclash scene in New York embodied the anticonservative backlash from George W. Bush's election in 2000. The aesthetic was, Ana says, "elements of Bowie and New Romanticism, definitely [the film] *Liquid Sky* and that fucked up, weird performance art, new wave, what-the-hell-is-this kind of shit." Drag diva Tobell von Cartier, aka fashion designer Steven Davis, and transgender nightlife icons Sophia Lamar and Amanda Lepore served looks that coalesced with the swirling smoke, neon, and synthesizer-laden decadence the scene loved. Drag queen Jackie Beat, club king Mario Diaz, and DJ Barbeau even got in on the fun with their own electroclash band, Dirty Sanchez. "The more queer you were, the more weird you were, the more you were elevated, or I guess the more you were seen as living the dream," Ana said. "To people like me who had moved there, who were inspired by the club kids, that was all we needed to take off and to make it happen for ourselves and our friends."

The scene was populated by bands toeing the line of gender,

punk, and electronica, like Fischerspooner and Peaches. Electroclash also owed its cuntiness if not its existence to bitch tracks
from the ballroom, house, and drag worlds, which inspired many
of its queer performers.

Ana Matronic and performer Xavier hosted drag party Knock
Off on September 21, 2001, just ten days after 9/11. There, a
young singer from Arizona took to the stage with a friend. Offstage they were known as Jason Sellards and Scott Hoffman, but
onstage they became Jake Shears and Babydaddy, and their band
was called Scissor Sisters. Ana joined the band that December, followed by Del Marquis and Paddy Boom, and later Randy Real.

Scissor Sisters were heavily influenced by drag, and not just
because Ana was in the band. Shears had started playing his songs
at The Cock courtesy of Mistress Formika. "Formika would
encourage me to throw one of the demo CDs on and get up
on the bar at one in the morning or whatever and grab the mic
and do a number that maybe I had just recorded or written a
few days before," Shears said. Sweetie was also a big supporter
of the band early on.

Drag played an essential role in the music as well. "That sort
of DIY ethos that drag has always had was central to who we
were as a band," Ana Matronic said. "We dressed in drag on
stage. We didn't go up in our street clothes and perform. There
was a ritual behind what we did and that was informed as much
by people like David Bowie and Brian Eno as it was people like
Divine and Ann Magnuson."

By 2004, Scissor Sisters released their self-titled debut album,
which peaked at #1 on the UK charts and became the top
Dance album in the US that year. It featured their song "Filthy/
Gorgeous," which was inspired by Ana's time in San Francisco
drag clubs and is "100% a love letter to drag culture," she said.
The music video, filmed over the course of twenty consecutive
hours at the former Zipper Theatre in Midtown, was directed

by John Cameron Mitchell. It featured an all-star cast from New York nightlife, including Mona Foot, Murray Hill, Taylor Mac, Sweetie, World Famous *BOB*, some of the Dazzle Dancers, and even the actress Charlotte Rae, who starred on the 1980s hit show *The Facts of Life* as Mrs. Garrett.

"All I can really say about that video is it is such a special snapshot of New York in 2004 and it's just a snapshot of all the nightlife people," Shears said. "Like, everybody's in that video... Anybody that wanted to come, people just showed up." Scissor Sisters released three more studio albums before breaking up in 2012.

As larger venues shuttered, Manhattan dance floors became smaller and more crowded. So where could you go dance and see something unusual without getting policed? The answer was Williamsburg, still in the throes of early gentrification, more warehouses than Whole Foods. Metropolitan Bar, or Metro, opened in 2002 at 559 Lorimer Street. It was one of the borough's first new gay bars, but didn't feature drag until 2007. Epiphany was the first drag performer to take its stage. "It was kind of at a time where drag was still a little bit weird in Williamsburg," she said. "It wasn't mainstream at all, so it was kind of like a mindfuck for me to walk to work and have all the truck drivers coming in off the BQE going to Bushwick." At the time, Epiphany was going back and forth between Williamsburg and Hell's Kitchen. It was an expensive cab ride, one venues didn't always cover. It would be great if a drag scene could develop in Brooklyn, too.

Aaron Kint moved to New York with friends from the bacKspace Performance Ensemble, a group recognized for their style of "gender fuckery and exquisite stage chaos," according to member Charmin Ultra. The troupe created shows filled with wild costumes, dance, drag, songs, videos, skits, and more. Kint, in drag as Krystal Something-Something, was "interested in creating unconventional beauty that's always enjoyable, but doesn't need to be understood," he told *Time Out New York* in 2010, when he was chosen as one of the city's 50 Most Stylish People. His drag was inspired by horror films and camp, rave culture and the avant-garde, electronic music and club kids, he said, decked out in black lips, black-frame glasses, a blond bowl-cut wig, a black-and-white houndstooth couture jacket, and sweatpants with the word "FAGGOT" printed on the front.

bacKspace's New York shows inspired a new wave of Brooklyn drag performers, though Kint didn't know it at the time. "We didn't understand really what we were doing, honestly. We just did it," he said in 2015. From there, bacKspace took to stages across Brooklyn, the most noteworthy of which was Williamsburg bar Sugarland. Much like Blacklips, bacKspace's weekly Sugarland show, *Sunday School*, offered new material every week for two years, often created in Kint's living room. They expanded their reach to a multitude of venues, even to the Big Apple Circus at Lincoln Center and a shoot with Bill Hader in *Rolling Stone*.

Harry James Hanson, who now performs as Ambrosia Alert, recalls bacKspace's influence. "They would actually have choreography. That is what stuck with me...I was like, when did they practice this? But Mary Jo and Diba [Lil' Kimchi] are both women, so it was cool to see women performing in a drag space, always," they said. "Krystal was just this incredible chameleon, and she was bald, so she really took full advantage of that. She'd paint all sorts of crazy things on her head. She'd have eye makeup that looked like Rorschach ink blots... She was super creative and one of the first queens I really saw doing art drag."

While the northern parts of Hell's Kitchen were dangerous in the 1980s and 1990s, the southern streets were often occupied by theater folk. By the late 1990s, Hell's Kitchen was a noted gayborhood, "gentrified by New Yorkers who yearned for West Side living but were priced out of Chelsea and the Upper West Side," as the *New York Times* wrote in 2007. Gregory Angelo, then the editor-in-chief of New York's gay events magazine *Next*, told the *Times* about the neighborhood's development: "'Go to Hell's Kitchen,' he says. 'That's where you want to be as a young 20-something gay man who wants to live and experience gay New York.'"

The move to Hell's Kitchen, drag icon Shequida says, was inevitable. "I remember living in the West Village, and seeing all the younger, gay people not being able to afford to live in the West Village, so they're like, 'Okay, well, we're gonna live West Village-adjacent. Chelsea.'" Hell's Kitchen was the next neighborhood up. "I think gay people would joke [that when] a gay person moves in…property values go up. But it is true!" she says. "When you're in college or you're super young, you can't afford to live in these neighborhoods where you have the established rich gays living. So you make your own neighborhood, and then that neighborhood becomes the next thing."

A slew of gay bars popped up in the neighborhood, including The Ritz, Vlada, and Therapy, which would help launch the careers of some of New York's brightest drag stars. Hell's Kitchen, so close to Times Square's famed Broadway theaters, would remain the go-to stomping grounds for people seeking a career on the stage, some of them finding their way in drag. "In the aughts, there were a lot of girls doing Britney Spears, Whitney Houston…it became less performance art and more production numbers," Michael Musto remembers.

Bob Pontarelli opened Industry on West 52nd Street in 2010, which became known for drag as well. Shequida opened the bar, but was initially hesitant about the location. "I was like, it's a little far up… I had already been doing Bartini, but Bartini was on like, 46 and 10. And now Bob wanted to open a club on 52nd and I was like, 'Oh, girl. Oh, no, honey, what are you, this is a disaster,'" she says, laughing at how wrong she was. "But, you know, I saw his concept. And I saw the space. And I was like, you know, people, the gays, will go to a destination." The club became a hotspot.

"It was a great time for drag queens, in [that] drag queens had to be performers," Shequida said. Amid nightlife restrictions on dancing, smaller venues continued to thrive. "The performing drag queens really had a boom, because now there was nothing else to do," Shequida said. "So you go to a drag show, and you watch and you would mingle and that was now your entertainment in the bar… It was the power of like, the gays needed something to do."

One of these performers was Peppermint, who had worked at Peter Gatien's club The Tunnel for $50 a week while still a student at the American Musical and Dramatic Academy. This was a time, she said, when you did drag simply for the love of it; the only person who really made a living doing it when Peppermint started was RuPaul. Plus as a performer you got into all the clubs for free. She also began to use her platform to advocate for transgender visibility, the first performer to compete from the beginning on *RuPaul's Drag Race* as an out transgender woman in 2017. "I've always believed that as an entertainer, and as a drag queen, and of course as a trans woman [who's] visible now, it's…I don't want to say it's a duty or responsibility. It's my passion to inform those who are uninformed or misinformed," she said in 2017. With her success on *Drag Race*, her profile continued to skyrocket, and in 2018 she became the first transgender woman to originate a starring role on Broadway as Pythio in *Head Over Heels*, inspired by the music of the Go-Gos. Her reign continues on stage and screen.

★ ★ ★

Queer activists across the country had long fought for marriage equality, and in 2011, a New York group called Drag Queen Wedding for Equality made a splash. Every week, queens like Kitten Withawhip—today Bob the Drag Queen—Frostie Flakes, Honey LaBronx, and Miz Cracker (then Brianna Cracker) held approximately twelve to twenty-four mock weddings for four hours every Saturday in Times Square to educate people about the disparities and injustices queer people experienced in regard to marriage in the US.

Bob, Honey, and Frostie had been arrested wearing full drag in 2010 in a collaborative protest with the organization Queer Rising. The groups obstructed traffic by Bryant Park, holding a large sign stating "New York Demands Marriage Equality Now." Cops waited in the park to arrest them for blocking traffic, but the protesters didn't care: the point was to get attention, Bob said in 2016, a goal they accomplished. They'd continue to draw press attention, particularly the following year when Drag Queen Wedding for Equality Members took to Grand Central Station, singing "Here Comes the Bride" walking down the steps. Cops told them to leave, and with Queer Rising, they walked to Governor Andrew Cuomo's New York City office at 633 3rd Avenue in Manhattan, the queens chanting, "I demand! Full equality! Right here, right now! I demand! Full equality! I am! Somebody!"

When New York's Marriage Equality Act became law on June 24, 2011, a crowd of some 600 people gathered outside the Stonewall Inn, making out, chanting, "Our streets!," flashbulbs crackling, fire dancers twirling, drums beating, drag queens dancing. *Gothamist* reported "a line of drag queens [telling] everyone in their path to 'watch out, we're legal!'"

Queer Americans gained broader rights and protections under the Obama administration. Among the positive rulings were the

Supreme Court's overturning of the 1996 Defense of Marriage Act, which had defined marriage as only between a man and a woman (2013); an executive order "prohibiting federal contractors from discriminating on the basis of sexual orientation or gender identity" (2014); the Supreme Court's legalization of same-sex marriage across the country (2015); dissemination of guidance that Title IX, which bans sex discrimination in schools, also includes the rights of transgender students (2016); and more. Not to mention that a Hedda Lettuce ornament even appeared on the Obamas' Christmas tree in 2009. The tree, designed by Simon Doonan, featured ornaments created by community groups; Lettuce volunteered with one such group and made a bulb of herself, which made the cut.

When in November 2016 the forty-fifth President of the United States was elected, fear, sadness, and rage passed through a multitude of communities. For queer Americans in particular, there was grave concern over the new president's remarks saying he would void all executive orders made by his predecessor, one of which included banning discrimination against queer individuals in the workplace. What would the United States look like under such leadership? The queer community instead vowed to "Make America Gay Again." New Yorkers would not take this president's victory lying down.

Marti Gould Cummings was among the many spurred to action. By the time the forty-fifth president had been elected, Marti had been doing drag for about six years, always incorporating drag into political action or vice versa. Interestingly, when Marti moved to New York in 2005 to attend the American Musical and Dramatic Academy, drag was not held in as high esteem by their professors. "I would hear, 'There is no work for someone like you. You're just going to end up a drag queen,'" they wrote in 2020. "I remember thinking at the time, what does that mean? Am I not going to be successful, am I not talented, what does that mean? Because the tone that they were using was all of those negative thoughts…so I was really devastated by it," they said later. Instead, they found inspiration in the likes of Peppermint, Sherry Vine, and Shequida. "So now when I think back on that moment of, 'oh, you'll just be a drag queen' and they said it as a negative, oh I'm so proud. I'm not *just* a drag queen. Every opportunity that I've had in my life is because of drag."

In 2016, Marti moved more purposely into the political space. "I thought oh, I have a microphone and I have to use it, and so to me it just felt very naturally the right thing to do," they said. The nature of the form was not lost on them, either: "The act of doing drag in itself, whether you meant it to be political or not, is political because you're going against societal norms." Eager to make change on a local level, Marti started Hell's Kitchen Democrats, or HK Dems, on January 14, 2017, in opposition to the McManus Midtown Democratic Club, which had reigned for 125 years. "I wanted to make sure that everyday people had a voice in local government because in my beliefs local government is the bedrock of democracy…what happens in New York City and on a state level affects your day to day life," they said. "We need to make sure we're electing people that are doing good things on your block, and so I really wanted to make it accessible to a lot of people." Marti felt the current Democratic club hadn't done enough for Hell's Kitchen. "Everybody was like 'oh, you can't overthrow them,' and I was like, 'well, fucking watch me.' Like, why not? Why should we just go with the status quo? Why should we just go because it's comfortable? We should just shake it up and really make a difference," they said.

In September 2017, HK Dems–supported candidates unseated their McManus club opponents for seats as district leaders in the New York State Assembly. Drag was always part of the process for Marti. Indeed, accessibility, they found, started with their active presence as a drag performer. "Education is power, so that's what I wanted to use my drag for, was to educate people about these issues, as I educated myself." Marti didn't stop with HK Dems. In July 2018, they became one of fourteen people chosen for New York City's first Nightlife Advisory Board—developed to "issue formal recommendations to the mayor and the Council about various issues affecting the nightlife industry, such as its regulatory structure, public safety concerns, zoning and the integration of nightlife into local neighborhoods." They served for two years. "I was really proud to be a drag artist in our city's government to help steer how things were going," they said.

In September 2019, Marti ran for the New York City Council's Seventh District, with a platform of "housing justice for all, equal education, integrating our school systems…and criminal justice reform," they told *Vogue*. Winning would have made them the first nonbinary person and first drag queen to hold public office in New York State. While Marti didn't win, they remain an active voice in politics. This includes supporting Drag Out the Vote, "a nonpartisan, nonprofit organization that works with drag performers to promote participation in democracy," ever an arbiter of drag's ongoing possibilities in New York and beyond. When President Joe Biden signed the Respect for Marriage Act into law, requiring the federal government and the states to recognize same-sex marriage even if performed in other states, Marti and fellow New York queen and Drag Out the Vote collaborator Brita Filter were among those invited to the White House to celebrate the occasion.

And it didn't stop with Marti. During the forty-fifth president's 2019 impeachment hearings—on the grounds of "abuse of power and obstruction of Congress" in dealings with Ukraine— New York area drag queen Pissi Myles made a splash as the Capitol Hill correspondent for news startup Happs, which had discovered her at Barracuda. "By the time I got inside and realized that I was literally steps away from the hall where they were holding the impeachment hearings, it hits you like a wave—you're standing in something that's going to be part of American history," Pissi told *Out* that year. "Not only that, but I'm making a social commentary by being there in drag and being a voice for queer and other marginalized people. It was really overwhelming."

After *The RuPaul Show* on VH1 was canceled in 1998, its eponymous star retreated from show business for nearly a decade, occasional album releases and the 2007 film *Starrbooty* aside. RuPaul relocated to LA and got sober as he planned his next move. Reality television seemed like a new option, but he wasn't interested and said he didn't want to portray drag negatively.

Randy Barbato and Fenton Bailey, RuPaul's longtime business partners, had started production company World of Wonder in 1991, and by the mid-2000s it was a successful enterprise. And a reality show idea proposed by World of Wonder's Tom Campbell, then head of development, got RuPaul's attention. He sensed a change in culture. "The Obama movement was happening, and I could feel it in my bones that it was time," Ru told *Vulture* in 2017. Filming on what became *RuPaul's Drag Race* started in September 2008. On February 2, 2009, the show debuted on Viacom's queer network, Logo.

While Nielsen did not track the first season's ratings, by season two the show was bringing in some 440,000 viewers each week. Bars across New York and the rest of the country held viewing parties hosted by local drag performers. This writer in particular remembers New York's Manila Luzon, *Drag Race* season three contestant and first runner-up, hosting regular viewings at Boxers in Chelsea. Boxers, a gay sports bar, would itself quip that *Drag Race* is a sport, airing the show on their many televisions and a giant projection screen. Viewing parties continued building community around the art form and created more opportunities for drag artists to gain work and visibility.

The show also provided a potential career path. Appearing on *Drag Race* could be one very public way to an active career in drag. It didn't always matter if contestants won or how they placed on the show: often, just attaching *Drag Race* to one's name brought instant clout. Plus, the more people watched the show, the more people wanted to see drag performers offstage as well. There became an even bigger demand for drag artists beyond local bars and clubs than before. As Linda Simpson said later, it had the "high tide raises all ships" effect as audiences began to clamor once again for drag wherever they could find it.

Two New York musicians also deserve credit for helping to mainstream drag and drag aesthetics. Stefani Germanotta had started as a singer in downtown New York, heavily inspired by nightlife and drag, not unlike Mae West before her. Living in the hipster paradise that the Lower East Side became by 2008, Germanotta became a local it girl, adopting the stage name Lady Gaga. From her apartment at 176 Stanton Street, she put herself in any limelight she could find, "running around in leotards and go-go boots, stumbling up the stairs at four in the morning," as author Maureen Callahan wrote. Early on she performed in gay bars, and in a full-circle moment, wound up affecting drag in New York City herself.

Shequida remembers hosting a performance of Gaga's at the former bar HK in Hell's Kitchen. "It was the shittiest place, like she had to perform on a staircase because there was no stage," she said. Gaga had them turn off the lights in the bar mid-song so she could dance with a light stick; rather, a disco stick. People shone flashlights on her. "It was an amazing moment," Shequida remembers. "She worked that staircase like nobody's business." After Gaga began making the rounds—her first magazine cover, incidentally, was New York's queer nightlife magazine *HX* in August 2008—Shequida said drag queens had started stepping up their game. "If you look at drag queens before Lady Gaga, it was very sort of cute, simple, real girl, like just a little skirt. Even myself, you look at pictures of me back at Bartini, it was like a little skirt," she said. In the '90s, many queens started rejecting the pancake makeup and diamonds and furs of the past, instead striving for a kind of minimalist supermodel realness. There were no hip pads or corsets or pantyhose. "And then once Lady Gaga came on the scene, it was like big shoulders and diamonds and furs and spikes," Shequida said. "I'm going to go to my grave saying that Lady Gaga made drag queens elevate at a certain point." Indeed, the look that queens like Shequida once considered antiquated—all glittery and sparkly and rhinestoned within an inch of its life—had returned. "To look at my closet now, if it doesn't sparkle, I don't wear it. But in the '90s if it sparkles, you would not put it on, honey."

Even so, by the time Lady Gaga's first album, *The Fame*, came out on August 19, 2008, the look had evolved (and would continue to). In fact, her extravagant outfits—a dress made of plastic bubbles, the infamous "meat dress," a captain's hat bedecked in pearls, an exploding bustier, blond hair twisted into a bow— could only be described as drag, an influence and a practice the performer has long acknowledged.

But her exploration of drag did not only extend into the hyperfeminine. In 2010, she also created a male drag alter ego named Jo Calderone. In a dark pompadour, dark suit and white T-shirt, cigarette, and thick New York accent—a modern-day James Dean via Queens—Jo made his debut in *Vogue Hommes Japan*'s October 2010 issue. Gaga and photographer Nick Knight had been able to convince the magazine, they said, that Jo was the next big thing in male modeling. He was on the cover. Gaga wrote about the experience in *V Magazine*'s winter 2011 issue, wondering, "how can we fuck with the malleable minds of on-lookers and shift the world's perspective on what's beautiful? I asked myself this question. And the answer? Drag."

Jo also appeared on the cover of Gaga's single "Yoü And I" from her 2011 album *Born This Way*, and its corresponding music video. When Jo took the stage at the 2011 MTV Video Music Awards, Gaga was in character the whole night. Jo opened with a monologue about Gaga, her mythos and their love affair, that both parodied and questioned Gaga's reality. "I want her to be real," Jo said. "But she says 'Jo, I'm not real, I'm theatre.'" Pop stars known for over-the-top acts sat with mouths open as Jo launched into "Yoü And I" in a growling register. And via Jo, Gaga proved that even stripped of glitter and sequins, she could still captivate an audience. In the process, Gaga also brought drag kings to a public sphere—12.4 million people would tune in that night. And when one of the world's biggest pop stars does drag, people listen.

"I have always really admired the craftsmanship that goes into what you all do," she told the queens of *RuPaul's Drag Race* when she was a guest judge on season nine's 2017 premiere. "Drag has for me been an opportunity to leave myself when I didn't want to be me. I felt so completely out of place when I was in high school. Drag has just been part of my life for the longest time." As inspired as Gaga was by drag, her own journey into the form would also inspire drag performers. Not only could you no longer enter a drag club without seeing at least one Lady Gaga number, her presence continued to challenge new performers to exist onstage as their most outrageous selves.

Nicki Minaj has also pushed drag aesthetics into the mainstream. Before her first album, *Pink Friday*, was released in November 2010, Minaj was already being clocked for her drag-inspired looks. "Hip-hop has always had a flair for the dramatic... But Minaj has taken the art to the next level with her drag-queen-like outfits (she's rocked Wonder Woman spandex and Freddy Krueger nails), wild-eyed rapping, and split personalities," *Out* wrote that year. Her debut album established her as a high camp, highly intelligent rapper, leading *Rolling Stone* to call her "The New Queen of Hip-Hop." She became as beloved by the music world as the drag world, and suddenly there were bright pink wigs with bangs and "Super Bass" lip-synchs popping off in clubs around the country.

Minaj was born Onika Tanya Maraj in Trinidad and moved to Queens at the age of five. She later attended the Fiorello H. La Guardia High School of Performing Arts. While dealing with a difficult childhood—one in which her father burned down her mother's house in an attempt to kill her—Minaj created characters to escape her reality. One of them was called Nicki Minaj. Others included Harajuku Barbie, or Barbie, and Roman Zolanski. Nicki would appear as Roman, an unpredictable, cocky gay man, on a multitude of tracks that made her a star, like "Monster" with Kanye West, as well as on *Pink Friday* ("Roman's Revenge") and on the album dedicated to him, *Pink Friday: Roman Reloaded*, released in 2012. Roman also appeared via Nicki onstage at the Grammys in 2012. In her performance of the song "Roman Holiday," she channeled both Roman and his mother, Martha, as Roman deals with the premise of conversion therapy. Like Gaga's performance at the VMAs, Minaj's performance was nothing if not drag, reaching the millions who tuned in.

In time for her debut as a guest judge on *RuPaul's Drag Race*, *Essence* magazine described Minaj's inspiration from queens: "She leaves it all on the stage as if she were lip syncing for her life, marrying her unapologetic rap lyrics with moves better than a perfectly executed death-drop," they wrote. "Her colorful lace front wigs are endless, her makeup is creative, she serves *bawdy* with no padding, and sis knows a thing or two about reading someone. She's everything we want in a drag queen." Like Gaga, Nicki would become and remains one of the most successful artists of the last twenty years, bringing her drag-inspired aesthetics with her into the spotlight.

And while *Drag Race* brought the form to new audiences, a different drag sensibility continued evolving off-screen in Brooklyn. By 2012, Macy Rodman started a show at Don Pedro's, a gritty rock and roll bar at the edge of Bushwick. "It was across the street from this housing project and people used to throw bottles at the drag queens from the balconies," Hanson remembered. Rodman's show was called Bathsalts, then named for a top headline of the day about the drug ingested by a Florida man who ate another's face. Rodman's Bathsalts was "a drag show for fuck-ups" and, in the same vein as bacKspace, often played with and tested the limits of what drag was and could be. That Don Pedro's was a rock and roll bar contributed to the event's "anything goes" ethos. "The important part of that, for me at least, was you were allowed to make a giant fucking mess. All the food, all the props, all the liquids on yourself. I had a giant dick that ejaculated green silly putty all over me. I remember once Macy Rodman killed a giant cockroach in the middle of her set without missing a beat," Hanson continued. Rodman's style, Hanson says, was "feral. Her signature look at the time was Pleaser heels covered in duct tape." There was room for messiness and experimentation and weirdness, and the growing crowd of performers would become foundational members of a new Brooklyn scene. "People just had permission to be weird," Hanson says. "Bathsalts perhaps not intentionally but by consequence was defined in opposition to mainstream drag." On the occasion of Bathsalts' third and final year in 2015, Rodman spoke to *Posture* magazine about the party. "Bathsalts will be survived by the rowdy, sloppy spirit that anyone with a sense of humor can tap into. It's a cheap, glamorous, stream of consciousness insanity that can infect anyone at any time," she said. "Just be careful not to eat any faces."

The same spirit animated nearby bars like Sugarland and Spectrum, the latter of which *Paper* magazine called a "nondescript sweaty room located in some godforesaken [sic] part of East Williamsburg...revered for its consistently wild parties that would only be attended by the most fabulous, messy queers this side of the East River had to offer." Williamsburg bar This N' That, or TNT, opened in 2012 and became a divey haven for alt-queer performance with drag almost every night until it closed in 2016.

What a concept that "mainstream drag" could even exist. The emerging drag counterculture, informed by decades of antiestablishment ideologies and presentation, stood in opposition to the success of *RuPaul's Drag Race*. Brooklyn became a hotbed for this kind of drag over the course of the next decade.

In 2011, Merrie Cherry founded the competition DRAGnet at Metropolitan Bar. "I just noticed there was an emptiness with creativity and performance art happening in Brooklyn," she said in 2017. Alongside other key players in the burgeoning scene like Horrorchata, Untitled Queen, and Macy Rodman, she would also help galvanize a community through which quirky, artistic drag could thrive. "Myself and Horrorchata, we were the second wave of Brooklyn drag. We weren't paid that well in the beginning. But we stayed and waited it out," she said. Merrie became known as the Mother of Brooklyn to Horrorchata's Mother of Bushwig. Merrie also founded the Brooklyn Nightlife Awards, the Brooklyn counterpart to the Manhattan-centric Glam Awards. Competitions popped up all over Brooklyn like Miss Williamsburg, later Mr(s) BK, and Mx. Nobody. "It's drag evolution," said Murray Hill in 2017. "The drag in Brooklyn, in my opinion, is more punk and gender-fucking than what I've seen before here."

Untitled Queen came to drag after dabbling in performance art while getting her MFA in Fine Arts at Parsons. She saw *Drag Race* and instantly became enchanted. A professor mentioned that another student was doing drag and that if Untitled was interested to get in touch. At the time, she was hesitant. "I was doing performance visual art stuff and doing costumes but not calling it drag," she said in 2017. But she ultimately did, and the other student was Macy Rodman. Untitled performed at Bathsalts and at the first DRAGnet, which she won. "It was so crazy back then. I had one friend who was in drag, but I didn't know anybody in the scene, I didn't have a [drag] mom," Untitled said. But she became fast friends with Horrorchata and Merrie Cherry, all three learning from and supporting each other. "Everyone and their mom, their aunt, and goddaughter wanted to be a drag queen," Untitled said. She calls this time "The Brooklyn Renaissance."

"For me, it was just amazing because I could be creative every day," she said. "I treat it like my studio practice." And her practice—drag incorporating cues from all corners of the visual art world, from Japanese Noh masks to Yoshitomo Nara drawings—was met with open arms by the tight-knit Brooklyn community. Untitled has since transformed her drag practice into solo shows in galleries and the queer venues that supported her work to begin with, much like Hunter Reynolds and John Kelly.

Horrorchata remembered performing to practically no audience. "When I first started doing drag, I did shows in Bed-Stuy and no one would come to them," she said in 2017. Horrorchata started honing what she called her Selena-meets-Morrissey persona in 2007. After moving to New York in 2009, she began performing at events like artist Colin Self's monthly Clump party, where there was "a lightness and a playfulness," Self said. "You'd have someone who showed up in their pajamas hanging out next to someone who showed up in like, a $3,000 gown." Horrorchata would also host parties herself throughout the borough, not to mention the epic drag festival Bushwig.

The heir apparent to Wigstock, Bushwig started as a single day in 2012 at underground (in spirit) arts and performance space Secret Project Robot, but in the last ten years has evolved into a two-day, often sold-out phenomenon at the 3,200-person-capacity Knockdown Center in Maspeth, Queens. The event, which features daylong stretches of back-to-back drag, music, and performance art shows from 2:00 p.m. to 12:00 a.m. (or later), gives performers both new and seasoned a chance to celebrate their community. "I was just happy I could bring everyone together," Horrorchata said in 2017. "There were so many people involved with Bushwig and the door is always open." Bushwig has since taken Horrorchata, now Chata, and cofounder Babes LaBeija around the world, with iterations everywhere from Berlin to Austin. And what's so entrancing about Bushwig is the same thing that brought people to Wigstock: the creativity and freedom, all to screaming crowds. It was a far cry from the days of performing for no one.

This is not to say, however, that Manhattan drag was staid or traditional. Rather, the girls living in Brooklyn were still going into Manhattan and brought their sensibilities with them to Hell's Kitchen and Chelsea. Over time, a loving rivalry even emerged between the two boroughs. Bob the Drag Queen almost exclusively worked in Manhattan and noticed the differences between queens. "I think the idea is that Brooklyn drag is more gritty and artistic, and Manhattan drag is more palatable and pretty, I guess. Or more showy. More show-based. Like a cabaret, where Brooklyn drag is a little more experimental." There were performers who bridged the gap and performed in both boroughs, but as time went on, they were fewer and further between. "Manhattan audiences don't wanna see you ripping out of a trash bag and covering yourself in blood; they wanna see four girls who all know the 'Single Ladies' choreography," quipped Ruby Roo, who still performs in both boroughs, in 2016.

Hanson recalls writer and adult performer Ty Mitchell's observation that drag in Manhattan was informed by Broadway, and drag in Brooklyn was informed by art, fashion, and the internet, though the two were not mutually exclusive. Brooklyn drag, as it became known, was given a national face of sorts after Sasha Velour's 2017 win on the ninth season of *RuPaul's Drag Race* with her combination of bold graphic design, high fashion, and art-inspired looks, always a proponent of gender nonconformity. "I just want to be able to get kings and queens and nonbinary performers working together and having discussions about what drag is currently, what it has been and where we can move it to that is truly new," she told NPR in 2017. "I think if we work together and have a conversation, we can really advance the art form."

Another font of artistic experimentation with drag emerged from troupe Chez Deep. Colin Self had been producing performances, but didn't realize they were drag until friend and performer Alexis Blair Penney pointed it out. Together, they founded a post-drag collective, along with Sam Banks, Bailey Stiles, and Hari Nef, in 2012. "Initially a drag collective of five gender-variant transhumans," Self wrote in 2014, "Chez Deep has transformed into a family creating ceremonial evocations, grievances, and celebrations of post-human living through collaged audio and spoken narratives." With performances at downtown hotspots like Niagara and Santos Party House, Chez Deep also welcomed drag performers, artists, and writers from across the boroughs like Merrie Cherry, Raul de Nieves, and Linda Simpson. Chez Deep's work continued to position drag as performance art, with full-fledged narrative performances. "Chez

Deep was so much a result of feeling in opposition or against the competitive rhetoric of drag, or this expectation of it being about competition and money and all that stuff," Self said.

Members occupied a former gallery on Atlantic Avenue in Bedford-Stuyvesant beginning in 2015. With the Long Island Railroad clattering in the distance, up to 200 guests gathered in the converted apartment space that became known as Casa Diva for some of the group's beloved underground drag parties. Entry was a modest donation ("Suggested $5–10" a sign read in 2016. "Dickheads $0 Free!"). They'd split the crowd and make a runway in the center of the room, then get on the microphone: "Shows, show shows, shows shows!" in three rounds, all under clamp lights, at around 11:30 p.m./12:00 a.m., 1:30/2:00 a.m., and sometimes 3:00 a.m. In addition to the Chez Deep crew, there was an annual Carly Rae Jepsen–themed CarlyFest, not to mention performers like Remy Black, Tyler Ashley, Momo Shade, and the queer art collaborative House of Ladosha, among others.

Charlene Incarnate had moved into Casa Diva by 2015, and by Colin Self's description had given it new life along with Remy Black. "Charlene I feel like is Casa Diva in many ways," Self said, that she carried the torch when she moved in. Similarly Remy, "the Carmen Sandiego of drag," also lit up Casa Diva's stages with electrifying performances when she'd come to visit.

Remy and Charlene met as students at NYU, and it was Charlene who put Remy into a look for the first time at a Casa Diva New Year's Eve party in 2015. "I'm not square, but at that period of my life, I really was. It was stepping out of my squareness and really into who I was and there was enough space and support in that specific space and magic for the egg to crack," Black said. That night, both Remy and Colin Self remembered Charlene performing Natalie Cole's rendition of "Lucy in the

Sky with Diamonds," bedecked in a bodysuit sequined with lightning bolts. "I'd never really seen good drag and I'd never really seen transformative drag and I [had] definitely never seen a trans woman do drag before. So Charlene was the first trans woman that I'd ever seen do drag," Black said. The song in itself was special, having been performed as a winning number by another trans showgirl, Paris Frantz, at the 1996 Miss Continental pageant.

For Remy, the experience of seeing Charlene was transformative as well. "I realized how she was performing the song. She was the woman of the future, but not just she, the trans woman was the woman of the future," Remy said. The experience resonated with her deeply, and she began her own transition in the years after. "When Charlene performed it was legendary. And it made me trans," she laughed. But Remy's own performances were legendary as well. Her electrifying performance of Janelle Monáe's "Cold War," for example, was captured onscreen in *Wig*, Chris Moukarbel's 2019 documentary chronicling the revival of Wigstock, along with Charlene and other performances at Casa Diva.

Charlene knew performance was beating through her blood. While a student at NYU, she "stepped out of the closet in a pair of heels." Incidentally, she had her makeup done for the first time at a MAC counter by none other than Sweetie. In *Wig*, Charlene also reveals her approach to drag, which places trans women like herself at the forefront of the medium: she took her first estrogen shot onstage at Bushwig 2015. At Bushwig 2017, she took to the stage completely nude save for a wreath of flowers and her signature heeled Timberland boots, a commanding force lip-synching to Melissa Etheridge's "I'm the Only One."

In 2018, Charlene published a *BuzzFeed* op-ed decrying RuPaul's unfortunate comments that year denying space for trans women in drag despite their perpetual history with the form. In a March 3, 2018, article in *The Guardian*, RuPaul had claimed he would "probably not" accept a transgender drag queen onto the show: "You can identify as a woman and say you're transitioning, but it changes once you start changing your body. It takes on a different thing; it changes the whole concept of what we're doing."

"By drawing a distinction between queens based only on whether the silicone bags hanging from their chests are on the outside or inside of their bodies…RuPaul is not only erasing present-day trans queens from the history of drag, but also abandoning the decades-long deification of drag queens into honorary womanhood regardless of their everyday presentation," Charlene wrote. While RuPaul later apologized for his comments and the show continues to expand its contestant base and honor its trans contestants and winners, trans women are and have always been a foundational part of drag and should be acknowledged as such both historically and currently.

"We're engaging in hyperqueer and non-normative lives, and that's what makes us drag queens," Charlene told *Out* in 2019 on the occasion of being named the magazine's Showgirl of the Year for their *Out 100* issue. "If you're not transgressing societal norms or heteronormativity with your body…you're just playing dress up."

The Casa Diva story of transgression and love concluded on New Year's Eve 2018. "Casa Diva was our queer family household," Self wrote on Facebook at the time. "It was nothing short of a miracle that we had this space together to learn, grow, survive, fight, think, make, and change. Thank you to everyone who came to our parties and performances and showed the resilience of non-biological family love." Sadly, as Brooklyn changed and rents increased, Casa Diva would not be the only queer space, underground or not, to lose its home.

★ ★ ★

It was around 2013 that Harry James Hanson noticed a tide turning for drag in the city, where girls were entering clubs with the goal of ultimately being on *Drag Race*. "They knew drag was happening here and they came to do drag here, rather than it being a coincidence we were all doing the same weird thing together," they remember. "Aja was always very up front, like, 'I'm going to be on *Drag Race*.' She knew from the jump," Hanson says. By that point a great deal of queens hailed from New York City, and there would only be more to come. And indeed, Aja joined the cast of *RuPaul's Drag Race* for season nine, in 2017.

Drag Race fever ran through the boroughs for some, while others still said they had no interest in the show. Queens who did made reels and refined talents they might need on the show—design, impersonation, comedy, dance, and more. A new generation of performers grew up with and on the show, and others found community at weekly watch parties. The show had become a regular and popular presence in queer life, and later even mainstream culture. Being on *Drag Race*, it seemed, could mean everything from your own cosmetics line (Trixie Mattel, Kim Chi) to your own reality television show (Bob the Drag Queen, Shangela, and Eureka on *We're Here*) to book deals (Sasha Velour, Alaska Thunderfuck) to television commercials (Jujubee, Miz Cracker) to Broadway (Peppermint, Jinkx Monsoon), and more. "There's a ton of full-time queens in New York. They're not making hundreds of thousands of dollars; 'Drag Race' girls are. You need somebody to guide you," said season seven finalist Pearl Liaison, formerly based in Brooklyn, in the *New York Times*.

This is not to say that working locally never led to success. Rather, there are legendary performers who started out in New York and never appeared on the show, building their careers as working drag performers. Many have already been mentioned in this book. But to some, *Drag Race* held the potential for next-level stardom. If they could just get on that show, maybe they could have the fame, money, and success they always wanted. Drag could be a career on a mass scale, and it would be something to work toward in the scene. "If you want to be on it, you better be damn good. And they're all perfecting their craft night after night and working their butts off," Michael Musto said. The show also helped ensure drag's continued existence. "The clubs know that that's what's gonna keep them afloat at this point is just putting drag queens on the stage," he continued. Drag was now a thriving industry. "It's almost like drag is an everyday thing now. And it's for those of us who've been involved since the get-go, it feels strange," says Gina Garan, who manages drag performers and owns MyBestJudyMerch.com, a website dedicated to selling drag queen merchandise. "We would just go to [drag shows] like an underground thing. I would often ask people, do you know what a drag queen is? Now of course, everyone knows what a drag queen is. So I don't know how that will affect things going forward."

Drag Race was indeed befuddling to some who had been with the form for a long time. "They do a lot of makeup that is time consuming to do and…why is that necessary for drag? I don't understand that," said Hattie Hathaway before she passed in 2019. "'Cause believe me, some of this is just in my roots… Marsha P. Johnson and Sylvia Rivera, who did drag but just barely, would find it in the garbage as they walked down Christopher Street…[now] no one can seem to have an original idea." At the Pyramid, fishnets were ripped and legs were hairy, but there was also room for a queen with big hair in a minidress and heels. There had rarely been a barrier to entry for drag previously. "We just threw anything or anyone that looked interesting up on the bar and could come up with a crazy look," Hattie remembered.

By 2022, contestants on *Drag Race* discussed shelling out tens of thousands of dollars for looks, going into debt for the opportunity. While drag pageants and costumes were always costly, it seemed like getting the best gigs could also cost you the most money, whether or not that was actually the case. Many performers still make little if any money on gigs, and tips are vital. Some do it merely for cab fare, if that. Others feel you have to do it because you love it, and it's subsidized with side hustles or day jobs or night jobs. There's also a long history of drag in sex work and vice versa. In previous decades, drag wasn't about how much money you had and it couldn't be, because for a long time, people doing drag were considered persona non grata by culture at large, not to mention queer culture itself. Shequida anticipates the pendulum swinging back, that the next generation of young drag performers will not be as interested in such theatrical visuals. Drag will return to its even more subversive roots, she says, when "The younger generation that doesn't have that kind of money and says, 'I don't need that kind of money to entertain or to jump up on the stage'… All of my costumes will be outdated," she laughs. "Like, 'oh, she has Swarovski crystals, she must be from the 2000s.'"

The cost of drag affects the audience, too. What would have cost you a few dollars in tips back at the Pyramid could set you back $30, $50, $150 or more today. In 2018, a ticket to Wigstock, revived that year by Neil Patrick Harris and Lady Bunny, started at $95. There are still free local shows, of course, and some shows that do charge for tickets have sliding scales. It's also important to note that at some venues, though not all, the ticket price also goes directly back to the performers. For people who have been a part of the drag world for decades, it was a wild phenomenon to witness. "These [*Drag Race*] girls can command money that's really crazy in terms of just their fees to perform. But also kids are willing to pay a lot of money to do meet and greets with them," Garan says. "Drag queens back in the old days didn't make a lot of money. But now these girls are living great lives because of their chosen profession."

Drag today is analogous to the birth of rock and roll—when the genre emerged, it was an umbrella term to encapsulate a variety of influences and sounds. As time went on, subgenres of drag emerged both influenced by and reacting to the status quo. Though subgenres of drag existed long before *Drag Race*—the punks and goths at the Pyramid, for example—*Drag Race* became a dominant, bubblegum pop–like force: sparkly, easy-to-consume fun that also came to define a particular look and style of drag, though multiple styles of drag would ultimately appear on the show. The genres of drag are never-ending, living everywhere from the "nerd culture" of video games and comic books, to high camp horror witches and ghouls, to surreal art-fashion aliens, to fierce around-the-way girls and baddies from the block, to triple-threat Broadway babes. There are at least as many genres of drag as there are music, and at the same time, it's all still drag, itself a powerful force of subversion.

"I do think things are a little more homogenized but there's still individuality," Bob the Drag Queen said. "There's tons of queens doing really cool stuff," he continued, pointing to innovative queens on the scene in New York like Pissi Myles, Kizha Carr, Pixie Aventura, and Jada Valenciaga. "Nothing against old queens, but I don't wanna become an old queen saying 'Everyone's beep-bop-boop and back in my day everything was great. Now it's all shit!' Old queens will always say that. And you know what? The thing is, somebody said it about them!" And while that may be true, Marti Gould Cummings would encourage performers to think beyond what they see, to not feel like drag has to be contained by network cable or streaming services. "I want people to know that the great thing about drag is you can invent the roles for yourself. You are your own director and producer and writer and storyteller. You don't have to do what you see on TV. Go outside of the box," they said. "That's the beauty of drag."

When the Backstreet Boys' "I Want It That Way" was released in 1999, T Cooper was working at *Teen People*, fact-checking the band's lyrics with their publicist. As a joke, Cooper decided the song was about anal sex, that there definitely had to be a parody performance. The Backdoor Boys were born. They practiced in Cooper's Alphabet City apartment, creating a performance to the song in question. "That song takes us through the journey of the sweet, heart-achy, I love you, I want to hold your hand stuff but then it goes all out and these guys just end up fucking each other onstage," Cooper laughs. The Backdoor Boys debuted in all of their butch glory at the book party for Jack Halberstam's *Female Masculinity* at Bluestockings on the Lower East Side, at which Dred also performed. They anticipated only doing one performance, but it snowballed.

"The more songs the Backstreet Boys would release, if it felt right we would choreograph it and make it basically as gay as possible," Cooper said. "It was a commentary on masculinity and gender and subverting that compulsory heterosexuality that the boy bands offered. It was actually very, very queer." Costumes came from the *Teen People* fashion closet, and members took on Backstreet Boy-esque personas: A-Jack, Billy Starr, T-Roc, and Harry Ballerina.

The Backdoor Boys performed up and down the East Coast—though Cooper once joked in an interview they had been booked as far away as Malaysia—with features in *The Village Voice* and *Jane* magazine, where they answered women's dating questions in an advice column called "Dear Man." That they were able to make such cultural waves at the time both in and out of New York was a feat considering that even now, over twenty years later, kings still don't get as much attention as drag queens. Throughout the course of the next two decades, however, more and more kings would make space for themselves.

Wang Newton remembers how difficult it was to perform as a king, even with four years' experience under their belt, when they first moved to the city. "The king scene was minimal in 2004, to the point where I didn't realize I was doing gender bending drag artistry," they said. That drag was the persona of a "1970s-Vegas-style emcee, a Taiwanese version of Wayne Newton…a giant red lace thong in their pocket to dab away perspiration." Wang was interested in both genderfucking and what they have called "culturefucking," parodying cultural stereotypes to reveal their absurdity like speaking in a pidgin accent or making Asian-centered puns and jokes as a wacky, horny, satin-jacketed emcee.

Lesbian bars, despite an unwillingness to feature kings early on, had become sites for king performances, though Wang remembers the demand for kings was still generally low. "When chatting with kings and friends in the lesbian nightlife scene circa 2000–2010, the general consensus is that it felt as if kings were not an absolute staple at every lesbian bar/party in the city," they said, much unlike the relationship between gay bars and drag queens. A number of lesbian bars also shuttered as the decades wore on, replaced by venues billed as more generally queer. But there's still an imbalance in the spaces occupied by kings versus queens. "Would you believe that in 2022 when asked 'Oh, what do you do for a living?' I still have half the people I meet completely blank and say they have never heard of [a] drag king?" Wang says.

When Goldie Peacock moved to Brooklyn in 2009, they also remember a much smaller drag scene for kings. "In 2009 kings were treated as a novelty and an oddity in comparison with queens," Peacock said. "Throughout my career I was often the only king on the bill, or the first king someone had met, or the one to teach people we existed." Peacock's drag embodied another style of king performance that would emerge, one known for its flamboyance, camp, and active flouting of gender norms. "I held up androgyny and was never exactly trying to pull the wool over anyone's eyes and pass as a butch cis man," they said. They remember one performance, for example, where they stripped in drag to Chelley's "Took the Night," some layers of which included "a sparkly pink ski mask, spiked blonde wig, my actual prom dress (floor-length, beaded and blue) and was binding with 'Police: Do Not Cross' tape (which I then unwound). I ended up topless, wearing some skimpy shorts which I'd packed."

Among the few places Peacock remembers drag kings could perform was with Switch n' Play. SnP was founded in 2006 by drag kings Trey Baise, Chaz Del Diablo, Max Satisfaction, and Mr. Peter Bigs. In the mid-2000s, the drag king scene in New York was small, so SnP became one of the focal points for the community, a convergence of drag and burlesque performers of all kinds. Many SnP drag king performances challenged the nature of masculinity. An old number, for example, featured a lip-synch to "Macho Man" with two performers flexing and pumping iron onstage, which then dissolved into a campy, rainbow feather-boa-laden make out session. The new wave of kings performed not just the traditional idea of masculinity, of men swaggering in suits or leather or cowboy boots (though they do that, too). They also dismantled the tropes around it.

K.James arrived at SnP in 2008 by accident, answering an ad for a queer/trans roommate on Craigslist placed by one of the original SnP members. "As a trans guy, I had spent a lot of time thinking about masculinity, but the group rehearsals held in the apartment introduced me to king culture and the local drag scene. Soon, I was itching to get on stage myself," he said in

2013. His first performance was to Color Me Badd's "I Wanna Sex You Up," and he was asked to join the troupe shortly after. When he performs in drag, he seeks to parody masculinity and make fun of gender stereotypes he was taught to believe growing up. For K.James, drag is a hyper-expression of the self, but also a deconstruction of what it means to have a gender at all. "Dealing with the patriarchy, taking them down a little bit, is always fun," he laughed in 2015. James's work in drag is heavily inspired by pop culture icons like George Michael and James Dean, and he remains among the most oft-cited kings performing today.

With regular shows in Brooklyn at Branded Saloon and with Sasha Velour's Nightgowns, SnP has expanded its reach across New York and the country: they were the subject of a 2019 documentary called *A Night at Switch n' Play* and have performed at the Brooklyn Museum and the Brooklyn Academy of Music. In February 2023, they presented their show *Vamp!*—"a celebration of all things queer, bloodthirsty, and decadent"—at Lincoln Center. Indeed, SnP's work continues to dissolve artistic and gender binaries. Amid a progressive cultural shift into the 2010s, SnP, alongside groups like The Cake Boys, would be at the forefront of drag. They embody ideals of inclusivity and representation, serving as a prominent site for the gender nonconforming drag that continued emerging throughout the city.

At the end of 2019, The Cake Boys—trans drag performers Richard, Muscles Monty, and Sweaty Eddie, and queer musician Senerio—took shape to help expand New York's drag and queer performance scene. Queens were everywhere, they noticed, and they wanted more space for drag performers across drag's gender spectrum, those they affectionately referred to as drag "kings and things."

"They saw a niche that was missing," said Mo B. Dick, who has also mentored the group, in 2021. "They said, 'wait a minute, where are the drag kings in New York City? There used to be a thriving drag king scene, we need to bring that back.' So they are a direct lineage of the New York drag king scene."

But the goal was not just to create space for themselves, so they also created a competition in August 2021 called Takes the Cake, adding yet another outlet for drag's multitudes. "I don't think [they have] to be a woman or a man, just anything," Senerio said during the show's first competition cycle that year. "It could literally be a fucking mythical creature as long as it's like, oh my god, like bitch, you work, you came here to let the girls know, like, 'hey, this is who I am' and fucking eat it."

Drag would, as ever, continue to live at the intersection of nightlife and activism. Papi Juice, the "art collective that aims to affirm and celebrate the lives of queer and trans people of color," was founded in 2013 by Mohammed Fayaz, Oscar Nñ, and Adam R. The parties became a sensation, often featuring as hosts drag performers like Serena Tea, Janelle No. 5, Chiquitita, and countless others. "Our collective's work is more intentional than just a party," Fayaz said in 2019. "Our mission is to affirm and celebrate the lives of queer and trans people of color who exist all 24 hours of the day, not just 10 p.m. to 5 a.m."

Bubble_T, a queer Asian dance party featuring Asian drag performers, was created in response to a community tired of feeling excluded from queer spaces. In the past, Midtown bar The Web had been a gay Asian bar, but was often frequented by those looking to fetishize patrons; Lucky Cheng's, created by white business owners, exoticized Asian culture. Bubble_T was by and for queer people of Asian descent, a space to feel appreciated and celebrated by each other first and foremost. Accordingly, its drag shows channeled the layered complexity of Asian culture in the US. Along the same lines, A+, "a Pan-Asian Drag Revue" begun by drag artist Emi Grate in 2017, also sought to uplift drag artists of all genders from across the Asian diaspora "for a stunning display of Asian excellence that transcends exotica and orientalism…[that] seeks to explore the intersections of queer identity, performance art, and being Asian."

Chiquitita made space for the trans drag experience with shows like Trans Excellence and her salute to the television series *Veneno* chronicling the life of trans icon Cristina Ortiz Rodríguez. A native New Yorker, model and drag artist, Chiquitita has performed in drag since she was fourteen. She develops events to support the community, be they her annual Met Gayla (later La Gala, now a regular event at the Brooklyn Museum), Lady Gaga tribute shows, or drag fundraisers for the nonprofit For the Gworls, an organization supporting the lives of Black trans individuals.

Performer Junior Mintt recalls a time in 2019 when a producer told her not to say "Black Trans Lives Matter" because "nobody wanted to hear it."

"Nobody wants to *hear* that? Nobody wants to hear that my life is in danger? Nobody cares that I could be murdered after this?" she said, incredulous. She said she felt that as a Black trans woman, she was part of a minstrel show, that the only reason she was brought on was to expand the diversity of the cast. She didn't want that, and she didn't want anyone else to have to feel that, either. She decided to create In Living Color, a "highly melanated & genderfully extravagant" evening, she writes, that "will nurture your soul with love, laughter, & SHOWS," ever a celebration of trans lives, lives of color, and those who love them. "Drag is about giving… Drag is not about hoarding. Drag is just expression and love and abundance. That's my activism, that's my drag," Junior Mintt says. "I don't think there's a way of doing drag and not [being] political. I think there's just a way of doing it and not be aware you're doing it politically." Troupes like The POC Drag Art Collective and Sylvester would follow, creating even more spaces for drag performers of color in Brooklyn and beyond.

★ ★ ★

In March 2020, the coronavirus pandemic reached New York, and the city shuttered. Some two weeks into lockdown, the virus took the life of a living New York drag legend, Nashom Wooden, aka Mona Foot. He was a handsome, strapping man of only fifty years old and was HIV-positive, but had been un-detectable for years. Having performed his swirling Wonder Woman number just eighteen months earlier at the 2018 itera-tion of Wigstock, his death devastated the nightlife commu-nity. "Mona was the shit, honey. Only a mother could do that. I miss her so much. The beginning of COVID was rough," Lina Bradford said. "She was really the first one in the family. But we didn't know anything. So if you had preexisting health is-sues, it was going to get you. She was something else, Mona." In the weeks and months after his death, a giant photo of Nashom adorned the exterior of The Cock on 2nd Avenue, where he was a beloved longtime staple. The death of Jackie 60's Rose Royale followed in April 2020 after she also contracted coronavirus at the age of 79. A memorial exhibition of her work, "A Queer Perspective From Postminimalism to Social Practice, Selected Works: 1963–2020," went on at New York's David Richard Gallery the following year.

When the pandemic began, drag performers of all stripes were suddenly without income. Unemployment websites were crash-ing regularly. Many would face severe financial hardship, become unhoused, or even leave the city entirely. But they did what they could, raising money via GoFundMe, collecting tips via apps like Venmo and Ca$hApp, selling merch, taking on remote work. And many took to the internet to make shows online—among the earliest was Charlene and Tyler Ashley's digital *Baby Tea Brunch*, shot and livestreamed from the roof of their apartment in Brooklyn. When it grew safer to congregate outside, people flooded Maria Hernandez Park in Bushwick for Horrorchata and Babes LaBeija's free, masked, outdoor iterations of Bushwig, throwing dollars and Venmo-ing coin to help the performers. The POC Drag Art Collective held a Prince and Janet Jackson–inspired show in the park, and others took to Twitch, Instagram Live, or Zoom to do shows and raise money for survival funds, for themselves and each other. Nightlife was dead for months as the pandemic raged, but some threw illegal parties to get by.

In the middle of the coronavirus pandemic, the murder of George Floyd by Minneapolis police officer Derek Chauvin on May 25, 2020, set the country aflame with rage. After Floyd was suspected by a store owner of paying with a counterfeit $20 bill, a white Minneapolis police officer put a knee to Floyd's neck for over nine minutes, cutting off his air supply and, despite Floyd's pleads that he couldn't breathe, led Floyd to a heart attack and death while three other officers watched and pushed back those who tried to stop them. A video of the attack circulated and, even in the midst of the pandemic, masked protests and vigils electrified the nation, forcing the country to reckon with its long unresolved systemic issues of racism and police brutality. People took to the streets to advocate for change.

Drag performers were in the streets, too, leading the way at community action events. "Drag performers are pillars of the queer community… When you walk into a space, you'll see us before you see anybody else in the bar. We are people who people look to for guidance. People look to us for how to process what is going on," Junior Mintt said. "It brings me so much joy because I watched so many drag performers and, whatever vocabulary they had or knowledge they had, speaking up for all of the causes that were being fought for at the time, like Trans Lives Matter, making sure people have housing, making sure people have healthcare, making sure people have everything that they need, and it was really beautiful to witness because I think a lot of people found their voice at the time and realized people care what we think."

In McCarren Park on June 4, 2020, Mother of Brooklyn Drag Merrie Cherry stood among a massive gathering of peaceful Black Lives Matter protesters in a green dress and a blond wig, a microphone in her hand.

This time has been a long time coming. We have been waiting for our brothers and sisters to join us. The time is now! Don't let this time go by, like a news cycle. Our lives depend on it. My life depends on it. George Floyd's life depended on it. Please call your representatives. Tell them you want police reform *now*! Call that relative that doesn't stand for progress and have a real conversation with them and call them again and again! And again! And one more time just for good luck, and again! Until they listen. Make sure to vote; if you are not registered, do it when you get home tonight. There is no time to waste. When you see injustice from a cop or regular citizen, stand up and protect your brothers and sisters. Stand up for what is fair and righteous. Stand up for trans rights, stand up for women's rights, stand up for queers' rights, and stand up for Black lives!

She brought people to their feet with applause. "POWER TO THE PEOPLE!" she wrote on Instagram the next day. "I will be there everyday until people stop showing up." She continued to assemble and speak to crowds by the hundreds in Black Lives Matter vigils nightly, *Time Out New York* reported.

Merrie Cherry also became an inspiration for her drag daughter, West Dakota. Along with editor Fran Tirado, activists Raquel Willis and Eliel Cruz, and some 150 other volunteers both in and out of the Black transgender community, West Dakota founded Brooklyn Liberation. The June 14, 2020, event called attention to the disproportionate number of Black transgender people murdered and attacked every year. Mere days before the event, the sitting presidential administration eliminated a law protecting transgender individuals from discrimination in medical settings.

Brooklyn Liberation ultimately brought together over 15,000 people to march in white clothing, like the 1917 NAACP march that inspired it, from Grand Army Plaza to Fort Greene Park. "West Dakota's idea blossomed into one of the most striking demonstrations that New York has seen since the killing of Floyd," the *New York Times* wrote on June 15, 2020, "a gathering of thousands of people in a sea of white clothing. Its size and intensity stunned bystanders, participants and the organizers themselves." Among the speakers was Ceyenne Doroshow, lauded author, founder and director of Gays and Lesbians In a Transgender Society, or GLITS, who was also a mentee and daughter of Flawless Sabrina, née Jack Doroshow. Brooklyn Liberation ultimately became, as *Out* magazine reported that year, the largest event of its nature ever. "I hope this shock to our system can push us forward in reimagining what our lives can be," Dakota told *Out*.

Drag would consistently face challenges, especially as a beloved children's event like Drag Story Hour sought to make strides in queer understanding. Founded in 2015 by writers Michelle Tea, Julián Delgado Lopera, and Virgie Tovar, Drag Story Hour brought drag to libraries with performers reading picture books to children. The series originated in San Francisco, but made its way to Brooklyn in August 2016. It has since expanded to all five boroughs, "[helping] children develop empathy, learn about gender diversity and difference, and tap into their own creativity." The event became a staple of young lives in New York, and by 2022 was producing some 200 events around the city. However, Drag Story Hour and similar events endured threats, bans, and protests, often from the extreme right.

There were, according to GLAAD, approximately 141 incidents of drag-related violence in general across the country in 2022.

On December 17 of that year, for example, angry protesters swarmed outside the New York Public Library's Flatiron branch as Harmonica Sunbeam read a story to children inside. "Today I witnessed pure hatred and bigotry outside Drag Queen Story Hour at a public library in Chelsea," New York City Councilman Erik Bottcher tweeted. "Inside, I witnessed a loving and peaceful reading of children's books to kids." Protesters later attacked his home. Members of the right-wing extremist group Proud Boys also protested a Drag Story Hour event in Queens shortly after, on December 29, and other New York City Council members who supported Drag Story Hour had their homes attacked. It was unfortunately not the first incident of this kind, and it is one drag performers at Drag Story Hour have also endured—some were even chased down the street. But Drag Story Hour events continue to bring their mission of positivity to the city. "DSH teaches children to follow their passions and embrace gender diversity in themselves and others," DSH NYC writes. "This helps to curb bullying of LGBTQ+ kids and kids who may be perceived as different in all kinds of ways."

Drag would be an active part of mainstream culture, yes, but the fight was far from over. At the time of this writing in February 2023, there are a number of states across the country seeking to pass legislation that limits or bans drag performances. Some seek to limit its exposure to children at events meant for families like Drag Story Hour, some to remove it from public presentation entirely, some to ensure venues presenting drag are registered for adult-only entertainment. New York drag artist Julie J decided to take a stand. On March 21, 2023, she and her team held the benefit Stand Up NYC, a night of drag raising over $25,000 for drag performers and transgender individuals affected by a proposed bill banning drag in Tennessee. Though the bill was deemed unconstitutional in June 2023 when a federal judge decided the ban violated freedom of speech protections, it remains another example of drag's role in activism and its artists' power to make change. In their ignorance, bills like these miss entirely the purpose of an art form that is meant to be about joy, while also treading on the rights of queer individuals, engendering harmful negative stereotypes, and limiting freedom of speech and expression.

Still, New York continued making strides. In September 2017, New York City established the Office of Nightlife, with the promise to protect community spaces. That same year, Mayor Bill de Blasio ended the nearly century-old cabaret law. This meant that venues without cabaret licenses could now let their patrons dance. And in queer spaces where there was room to dance, there was room for drag. In September 2021, the "Zoning for Dancing" legislation was introduced, which allowed dancing at venues with under 200 people in capacity. It would start helping New York nightlife back on its feet. "We can't let outdated regulations hold back our economic recovery from COVID-19," said then-mayoral candidate Eric Adams in 2021. "Our food and drink establishments have been hammered by the pandemic, and many are in dire financial straits. We took an important step in 2017 by repealing the Cabaret Law and combating years of discrimination against Black, Latine, and LGBTQ+ New Yorkers. Now, we must change the remnants of the law in our city's zoning code, and let New Yorkers break it down without breaking the law."

Queer nightlife would reemerge after the pandemic had waned significantly, welcoming a new generation of performers on new stages, new career opportunities at their fingertips. And now, in 2023, there's new ground waiting to be broken by drag performers the world has yet to see. In the backrooms of bars, on streets and stages, they smooth their mustaches or gloss their lips or pull their gloves a little tighter. The audience cheers. A lifetime of history glitters under their feet.

EPILOGUE

I wanted to speak to Bobbie Hondo about the history of drag in New York, how she came to it, how she embraced it and how it embraced her. I loved how she talked about New York drag legends bringing her into the fold in Chris Moukarbel's documentary *Wig*, and I wanted to include her perspective in the book.

But sadly this book ends as it began, with the passing of a vibrant star, and all too soon. Bobbie Hondo passed away on May 31, 2022, at the age of twenty-eight.

She had come to New York at sixteen to dance, having trained with the Pacific Northwest Ballet. She would also move for her health. After surviving sexual assault at fourteen, she had been diagnosed with HIV. She could receive better care here than in her native Texas, where she endured HIV-related medical complications and severe ostracism. While still in Texas as a young queer person, she sought out as much queer history and culture as she could find online, in film, and on television. The *Wigstock* documentary in particular caught her attention. "That's where I first saw these insanely vibrant personalities and their struggles as LGBTQ+ people," she told writer Fernando Cerezo III in 2021.

Still, after moving to New York, she had never planned on doing drag. "To be honest, drag was something I shied away from," she said in 2019. She remembered thinking "that would be the lowest moment of my career, if I ever did drag, because my god-given talent is dance. Movement is really where my strong suit is." She had seen drag in local gay bars in small Texas towns, but she wasn't impressed. "Then I heard drag queens could do Paris catwalk shows and I was like, wait, what?"

Bobbie loved drag history, learning about the people who came before her and made her own journey possible in drag and as a trans femme. She was driven to meet her Wigstock idols and, she would say, banged down their doors to have them sign an original Wigstock program she had procured. In the process, she met Mistress Formika, Hattie Hathaway, Joey Arias, and Lady Bunny, who would all further bolster her confidence in drag as they took her under their wing. "We treasure people like Bobbie…who is one of us and who doesn't do the obvious, who is not cookie-cutter," Lady Bunny said in *Wig*.

Bobbie went to Perfidia for wigs. She performed in one of Tabboo!'s plays. She worked with Linda Simpson at drag bingo events. "I think people were kind of tickled that they had a young person that knew their histories," Linda said. "It wasn't like an *All About Eve* situation necessarily," she continued with a laugh. "She was admiring of other people, but she wanted to carve out her own unique path also." Bobbie interpreted their influences as an artist would. Her makeup and presentation was '90s glamorous but not too contoured, not too pancake, not too YouTube. She wore no hip padding. "I think Bobbie liked being sort of contrary and a little unique. So I think she wanted to seek something out that maybe others weren't quite as involved with," Linda Simpson said.

Bobbie continued to hone her performances, becoming known in particular for dancing on top of magnum champagne bottles in pointe shoes or pumps, elegant and lithe as only a dancer can be. She made videos, she performed with bands, she acted in plays. "You know, she had a checklist and yes, was able to check off much of it. But she was restless, she wanted to do more also, all the time," Linda went on. "She was continually expanding her world and I think that she was able to always make an interesting impression on people."

I remember seeing Bobbie perform at The Jackie Factory's Low Life 8: Fairytale of New York event at the Pyramid Club in 2018. Her long limbs moved in a modern-dance-esque gesture atop sky-high black patent leather heels, a red mask painted across her face. They called her a rising star, maybe the only person performing that night under thirty. They all recognized her talent, and brought her into the rebirth of Wigstock in 2018. As chronicled in *Wig*, she wears an ensemble worn by Mistress Formika in the original *Wigstock* documentary, lent to her by Formika herself. She was doing it, drag, art, dance, you name it. She had plans. "I would want people to remember that she was a bright light that was extinguished too quickly," Linda says.

Profiled for *Paper* magazine's "Coolest Person in the Room" feature in 2020, she gave her drag forebears credit. "I came here as a little kid and I was so clueless and I was really fortunate that I was standing at the right place at the right time and I met all of the right people that would then become collaborators, co-conspirators and friends," she said. It was important to her to bridge the generational gap. "Unfortunately there was a bottleneck effect that had happened and separated us. You know, when you got to New York, all those people from the 80s had mentors from the 60s and 70s," she said. "I had all these curiosities in my mind that I wanted answered and I felt like these people would have the answers. So, I literally just said hi and one thing led to another and it just grew from there and I got a lot of support and help from them." But Bobbie also had the ambition and talent and willingness to learn. Like so many others who came before her, she was making space for herself, living as vibrantly and unapologetically as possible. And she succeeded.

Bobbie is a testament to the power of knowing your own history, yes, but also to the power of learning from the past to design your future; to the power of community to see strength and uplift it; to the power of what one person's passion and drive can lead them to accomplish. Like every drag artist in this book, Bobbie saw and learned and created and lived the life she wanted to live to the best of her ability. That is the power of drag, this art of invention and reinvention. I believe this book is for Bobbie and for people like her, people eager to connect to the world of drag as they craft their own paths, voices, and selves.

I think of sitting down with Junior Mintt at the Brooklyn coffee shop Love, Nelly, how she beams when she talks about drag, community, how she made a space for herself onstage when she saw none available. Junior calls herself a drag preacher, a title I love. How does one become such a thing?

"Well, you just be yourself!" She smiles broadly, hands popping into slender fireworks. "I realized...other people would find it easier to be themselves, and would find nuance and wisdom and a better future through me just being myself." Her friend Filthy June spoke about Junior's drag events as church. "To me, that's what being a drag preacher is. It's connecting people to a vision of themselves that they didn't even know that they had."

Through makeup, Junior first realized her own transness. "Taking the face off I'd be so emotional at night, and I was like, why am I so emotional taking off this makeup? And then realizing it was the only time I gave myself permission to be a woman," she said. Now she has her own makeup line, Mintty Makeup. It's available in 600 JCPenney stores across the country. Understanding the stigma, violence, and oppression drag queens and Black trans women have faced throughout history—thinking again about Tracey "Africa" Norman, a face of Clairol hair color until she was outed as a trans woman and the boxes were pulled from the shelves—the moment is utterly groundbreaking. "I have found new ways to uplift, support, and love my community, all the people who look just like me, to create opportunities for them, to show them how much I want to see them reflected in everything that we do," she said in a June 2022 speech.

"We're always stronger together… As long as one of us is thriving, we are all thriving," she said earlier that year. "The only reason I'm here is because of my community."

This is the same reason for the Know Your History Ball in June 2021, a Mini Kiki Ball organized by Felix Milan of Old School Ballroom and Egyptt LaBeija, drag powerhouse and Overall Godmother of the House of LaBeija. Participants walk in categories that embody the great legends of ballroom past like Egyptt herself (Lip Sync), Taifa Ebony Mizrahi (Vogue Femme), Danielle Revlon (Femme Queen Realness), Jose Disla Xtravaganza (Butch Queen in Pumps), Avis Pendavis and Paris Dupree (Best Dressed). At the end of each category, participants are asked to name a great inspiration from the past known for walking the category: some know their names and those who don't will learn. Or Felix hopes they will. The Know Your History Ball, which in June 2022 was hosted at Lincoln Center, is an important step toward this goal.

But true community doesn't need a bar, or a club, or a department store to thrive. On a Friday night in April, Wang Newton is having a party at their apartment, where people I've seen on stages across New York are out of drag for the night. Well, mostly: Emi Grate's nails are twinkling under purple and magenta lights as she sits comfortably on the couch in sweats. She is talking about her career in drag, when a DJ told her she should learn the song "This Is Life" by Grace Jones. And before long, the song is on the speaker and Emi is giving shows, the nails shining and the hands expressive while punctuating Miss Jones's lyrics, which are so crisply lip-synched it's as if she were singing them herself. Emi is powerful and captivating even in sweats, crawling like a jungle cat across Wang's wooden floors. It is magical to watch. The dynamic force of drag is in full effect, a power that runs so deep it's palpable even through fleece.

Calling out tenacity, optimism, and dignity, the song also reflects a history of drag in the city, its performers creating light
in the dark, relentless in their quests to be themselves onstage,
especially in times when they couldn't do so offstage. In drag,
they find a freedom of expression, a self-realization that isn't always possible out of it. They are truth manifested as creation.

New York has been an incubator for generations of drag artists who made history with their glamour and drama, talent and
wit, dedication and righteous rage. They were outlaws, design-
ing lives in the underground to escape an unsafe and unwelcom-
ing exterior. Whether in Bushwick or Hell's Kitchen, Jackson
Heights or Harlem, drag in its essence is an act of anarchy and
defiance, a flouting and parodying of gender norms. Drag is as
much a leotard and a Beyoncé megamix as it is a beard and a
Kate Bush number. The choice, the variety, and the freedom
are what give drag its power.

Now drag is on national and international stages. It has long
faced oppression—often in times when men in power feel
threatened—but its resilience and spirit have toppled such forces
decade after decade. In spite of ignorance and opposition, it is
still embraced by so many like never before, in ways that a young
version of myself and so many others wouldn't have thought possible. The day before I wrote this, there was even a drag performance at Radio City Music Hall with the Rockettes. And
while *Drag Race* is an industry juggernaut, that show couldn't
exist without the generations of performers that preceded it.
Drag did not need to be on television to be the powerful art
form that it is, that it has always been.

What a time to be alive, when one can go out every single
night in New York City and see drag. New performers arrive,
excited to make their own mark on the city that has become,
without question, a drag capital of the world. And while the fight
for queer equality is far from over, there are more possibilities
and more room to experiment with gender and performance

than ever before. I'm excited to see how the next generation of performers continue to push the envelope in ways even their dragcestors couldn't have fathomed.

In this city of millions of people charging ahead with the blood that makes and has always made New York move, drag stops time for just a few minutes to remind us of the potential of our own creation, of the triumph of wit, imagination, and community over oppression, of glamour as a potent force of resistance. For generations, performers have harnessed the power of drag to tell their own stories, stories that should not be lost, stories that, even in a city laden with concrete, continue to glitter.

★ ★ ★ ★ ★

ACKNOWLEDGMENTS

This book is nothing without those who lived the lives chronicled on its pages. I have been honored to tell your stories so that others may become as inspired, dazzled, and awed by your sparkle as I have been.

To the forthright and fierce Ross Harris, my first agent at the Stuart Krichevsky Literary Agency. I am not here without your open-mindedness, incisiveness, and savvy. I still remember our first phone call, when I sat outside the Metropolitan Opera in the cold and listened to this man tell me *Glitter and Concrete* could become a reality. I am grateful that you introduced me to Melissa Danaczko, who became my agent later on. Melissa, I don't know where I'd be without your kindness, generosity, patience, advocacy, and general unflappability. You are the epitome of professionalism, and I am so glad you are my agent.

To my editor, John Glynn, thank you for your enthusiasm for this book as well as your encouragement, for not being scared of this book's original length(!), and for helping me dig into the process of crafting my first book. I am thankful for the work of the whole team at Hanover Square Press, including Eden Railsback, Kathleen Oudit, Jennifer Stimson, and my wonderful publicists, Leah Morse and Sophie James. I appreciate your dedication and assistance in making the book come alive—I am honored that you gave *Glitter and Concrete* a home.

To the historians, sociologists, journalists, and documentarians whose shoulders I stand on, past and present, your work is monumental and I am so grateful you have chosen or chose this life so others like myself could learn from you: Joe E. Jeffreys, George Chauncey, Esther Newton, Gillian Rodger, John D'Emilio, Martin Duberman, Allan Bérubé, Charles Kaiser, Scott Sandage, Felix Rodriguez, Luna Luis Ortiz, JD Doyle of Queer Music Heritage, Jonathan Ned Katz, Hugh Ryan, Michael Musto, Linda Simpson, John Strausbaugh, Lisa E. Davis, Sean Edgecomb, Michael Seligman and Jessica Bendinger, Kathleen Casey, Ada Calhoun, Anthony Slide, Lynn Abbott and Doug Seroff, Lillian Schlissel, Nelson Sullivan, James F. Wilson, Neil Miller, Chad Heap, David Kaufman, Craig Highberger, Tim Lawrence, Kate Davy, Myra Christopher, Harry James Hanson and Devin Antheus, Julian Fleisher, José Esteban Muñoz, and the countless others who ever believed drag was worth chronicling.

Thank you to everyone who spoke to me for this book, for sharing and trusting me with your stories, your knowledge, your passion, and your insight: Linda Simpson, Connie Fleming, Harmonica Sunbeam, Joe E. Jeffreys, and Felix Rodriguez for your multiple conversations on the phone with me; Mo B. Dick, Wang Newton, Lisa E. Davis, and Jordan King for your time and your ongoing encouragement; as well as Alex Heimberg, Ana Matronic, Barbra Herr, Bernie Brandall, Billy Erb, Bob Pontarelli, Bob the Drag Queen, Bobby Miller, Brian Lantelme, Ben Sander, Charity Charles, Charles Busch, Chris Tanner, Coco Peru, Colin Self, Daniel Nardicio, Darrell Thorne, Dean Mathiesen, Epiphany, Esther Newton, Gina Garan, David Glamamore, Glenn Belverio, Goldie Peacock, HRH Princess Diandra, Harry James Hanson, Hattie Hathaway, may she rest, Ira Siff, Jackie Beat, Jake Shears, Joan Marie Moossy, Joe E. Jeffreys, Joey Arias, John Cameron Mitchell, John Epperson, John Kelly, Johnny Dynell, Jo Weldon, Junior Mintt, Justin Vivian Bond, Karen Finley, Kevin Aviance, Laritza Dumont, Lee Kimble, Lina Bradford, Luna Luis Ortiz, Machine Dazzle, Marti Gould Cummings, Matt Crosland, Michael Cavadias, Michael Economy, Michael Musto, Michael Seligman, Miss Guy, Mistress Formika, Myra Lewis, Nathan Tate and Victoria Lace, Penny Arcade, Peter Anastos, Raven O, Remy Black, Robin Tyler, Rob Roth, Ruby Rims, Scott Wittman, Sequinette, Shelly Mars, Shequida, Sherry Vine, T Cooper, Thom Hansen, Tobie Giddio, Todd Oldham, Tory Dobrin, Varla Jean Merman, World Famous *BOB*, Zackary Drucker, and Zaldy. Thank you also to Brian Paul Clamp and Jackson Siegal at ClampArt; Efrain Gonzalez; The New York Public Library; Lou McCarthy, Luis Rubio, and the team at The Center Archives; John Simone, and Linda Simpson for allowing me to license your images.

Thank you to everyone who's helped along the way when they didn't have to: Abbott Kahler, Adam Baran, Angela Di Carlo, Brian Ferree, Daniel Nardicio, Harmonica Sunbeam, Harry James Hanson, Hugh Ryan, Jasmin Hernandez, Jayson Littman, Joe E. Jeffreys, Lady Bunny, Linda Simpson, Lisa E. Davis, Machine Dazzle, Magali Duzant, Meena Ysanne, Michael Economy, Michael Seligman, Penny Arcade, Peter Corrao, Remy Marin, Robbie Manulani Soares, Scott Sandage, Susannah Cahalan, Tobie Giddio, Todd Snider, Untitled Queen, World Famous *BOB*, Sob Sisters, and the Queer History Meetup Group at the Center.

I am also grateful for the fact-checking royalty who is the amazing Haylee Millikan, as well as the assistant artistry and glamour of the phenomenal Rachel A.G. Gilman, and the transcription wizardry of Shayna Maci Warner, Julia Easterlin, Brianne Lugo, and Christian Zeitler.

Thank you to Susan Ludwig because your encouragement changed my life. Thank you to Jane Bernstein and Scott Sandage at Carnegie Mellon University for your insight, knowledge, and generosity, and for believing in me even when I have been full of piss and vinegar.

To Fran Tirado, who was so encouraging when I told them the idea for this book that I began working on it the same night we met for coffee in March 2018. To Gabriel Shane Dunn, who blazed a trail so I might understand how a career as a young writer might start. To Hannah Orenstein, who listened to my book angst and offered sage advice. To all of my friends and loved ones who put up with me, loved me back, and held me together for the last five and half years as I worked on this book: Adrienne and Lewis Waxman, Alex Marakov and Cassandra Chisholm, Alissa Sexton, Andrew Rizzardi, Ben Seagren, Dusty York, Erin Honcharuk, Hannah Rosen, Jenna Lawrence, Jocelyn Seidle, Magali Duzant, Morgan Boyer, Naomi Extra, Shannon Deep, Steven Jude Tietjen, Ted and Paulette Levine, and Todd Snider. To Christopher John Bittar—I am grateful every day for your love, support, laughter, and your invention of Arthur "Ralph" Baseball. Thank you for catching me when I fall.

Lastly, but never, ever least, to my parents, Rani Stevens Goodman and Jeffrey Goodman. Everything I am is because of you, and there would certainly be no book without you. There will never be enough words to describe the love and the gratitude I have for your hearts, your support, encouragement, comedy, and magic throughout my life and yours, not to mention for bringing me to drag shows, being excited about my interest in drag, calling me into the next room whenever *To Wong Foo* or RuPaul were on TV, taking me to Lips in Fort Lauderdale, watching drag documentaries, and always advocating for curiosity, the pursuit of knowledge, reading, writing, confidence, and a healthy disrespect for authority. I miss you every day and I hope Spain is the most beautiful vacation you have ever had.

RESOURCES AND SUGGESTIONS FOR FURTHER READING

Books

And the Category Is...: Inside New York's Vogue, House, and Ball-room Community by Ricky Tucker

The Big Sea by Langston Hughes

Bulldaggers, Pansies, and Chocolate Babies: Performance, Race, and Sexuality in the Harlem Renaissance by James F. Wilson

The Changing Room: Sex, Drag and Theatre by Laurence Senelick

Coming Out Under Fire: The History of Gay Men and Women in World War II by Allan Bérubé

Disco Bloodbath: A Fabulous but True Tale of Murder in Clubland by James St. James (later republished as *Party Monster*)

The Downtown Pop Underground: New York City and the Literary

Punks, Renegade Artists, DIY Filmmakers, Mad Playwrights, and Rock 'n' Roll Glitter Queens Who Revolutionized Culture by Kembrew McLeod

The Drag Explosion by Linda Simpson

The Drag King Anthology edited by Donna Jean Troka, Kathleen Lebesco, and Jean Bobby Noble

The Drag King Book by Judith "Jack" Halberstam and Del LaGrace Volcano

The Drag Queens of New York: An Illustrated Field Guide by Julian Fleisher

The Encyclopedia of Vaudeville by Anthony Slide

Fabulous: The Rise of the Beautiful Eccentric by madison moore

The Gay Metropolis: The Landmark History of Gay Life in America by Charles Kaiser

Gay New York: Gender, Urban Culture, and the Making of the Gay Male World, 1890–1940 by George Chauncey

Gender Trouble: Feminism and the Subversion of Identity by Judith Butler

Hidden from History: Reclaiming the Gay and Lesbian Past edited by Martin Bauml Duberman, Martha Vicinus, and George Chauncey, Jr.

A History of African American Theatre by Errol G. Hill and James V. Hatch

How You Get Famous: Ten Years of Drag Madness in Brooklyn by Nicole Pasulka

I Am Not Myself These Days: A Memoir by Josh Kilmer-Purcell

I Was Better Last Night: A Memoir by Harvey Fierstein

Just One of the Boys: Female-to-Male Cross-Dressing on the American Variety Stage by Gillian M. Rodger

Lady Dicks and Lesbian Brothers: Staging the Unimaginable at the WOW Café Theatre by Kate Davy

Legendary: Inside the House Ballroom Scene by Gerard H. Gaskin

Legends of Drag: Queens of a Certain Age by Harry James Hanson and Devin Antheus

Lettin' It All Hang Out: An Autobiography by RuPaul

Life and Death on the New York Dance Floor, 1980–1983 by Tim Lawrence

A Low Life in High Heels: The Holly Woodlawn Story by Holly Woodlawn and Jeffrey Copeland

Man Enough to Be a Woman: The Autobiography of Jayne County by Jayne County

Memories of the Revolution: The First Ten Years of the WOW Café Theater edited by Holly Hughes, Carmelita Tropicana, and Jill Dolan

Mother Camp: Female Impersonators in America by Esther Newton

The My Comrade Anthology by Linda Simpson

My Dear, Sweet Self: A Hot Peach Life by Jimmy Camicia

Out of Sight: The Rise of African American Popular Music, 1889–1895 by Lynn Abbott and Doug Seroff

Out of the Past: Gay and Lesbian History from 1869 to the Present by Neil Miller

Pansy Beat by Michael Economy

Please Kill Me: The Uncensored Oral History of Punk by Legs McNeil and Gillian McCain

POPism: The Warhol Sixties by Andy Warhol and Pat Hackett

The Prettiest Girl on Stage Is a Man: Race and Gender Benders in American Vaudeville by Kathleen B. Casey

A Queer History of the United States by Michael Bronski

Ridiculous Theatre: Scourge of Human Folly: The Essays and Opinions of Charles Ludlam by Charles Ludlam

Ridiculous!: The Theatrical Life and Times of Charles Ludlam by David Kaufman

Secrets of the Great Pyramid: The Pyramid Cocktail Lounge as Cultural Laboratory published by Howl! Happening

Sexual Politics, Sexual Communities: The Making of a Homosexual Minority in the United States, 1940–1970 by John D'Emilio

Slumming: Sexual and Racial Encounters in American Nightlife, 1885–1940 by Chad Heap

St. Marks Is Dead: The Many Lives of America's Hippest Street by Ada Calhoun

Stonewall by Martin Duberman

Striptease: The Untold History of the Girlie Show by Rachel Shteir

Superstar in a Housedress: The Life and Legend of Jackie Curtis by Craig B. Highberger

Three Plays by Mae West: "Sex," "The Drag," "The Pleasure Man" edited by Lillian Schlissel

Torch Song Trilogy by Harvey Fierstein

Vampire Lesbians of Sodom by Charles Busch

The Village: 400 Years of Beats and Bohemians, Radicals and Rogues, a History of Greenwich Village by John Strausbaugh

Voguing and the House Ballroom Scene of New York 1989–92, photographs by Chantal Regnault, text by Tim Lawrence, edited by Stuart Baker

When Brooklyn Was Queer by Hugh Ryan

Whiting Up: Whiteface Minstrels and Stage Europeans in African American Performance by Marvin McAllister

Wig Out! by Tarell Alvin McCraney

Film and Television

A Night at Switch n' Play, directed by Cody Stickels

Arias with a Twist, directed by Bobby Sheehan

Beautiful Darling, directed by James Rasin

The Brenda and Glennda Show/Glennda and Friends, produced by Glenn Belverio

The Brini Maxwell Show, produced by Ben Sander

The Cockettes, directed by Bill Weber and David Weissman

The Death and Life of Marsha P. Johnson, directed by David France

Die, Mommie, Die!, directed by Mark Rucker; written by Charles Busch

Flaming Creatures, written and directed by Jack Smith

Flesh, written and directed by Paul Morrissey; produced by Andy Warhol

Glennda and Camille Do Downtown, directed by Glenn Belverio

Hedwig and the Angry Inch, directed by John Cameron Mitchell; written by John Cameron Mitchell and Stephen Trask

How Do I Look, directed by Wolfgang Busch

I Am Divine, directed by Jeffrey Schwarz

In Search of Avery Willard, directed by Cary Kehayan

Kiki, directed by Sara Jordenö; written by Sara Jordenö and Twiggy Pucci Garçon

Legendary (HBO Max)

My House (Vice)

Paris Is Burning, directed by Jennie Livingston

Party Monster, directed by Fenton Bailey and Randy Barbato; written by Fenton Bailey, Randy Barbato, and James St. James

Party Talk, produced by Marvin Schwam

Pay It No Mind: Marsha P. Johnson, directed by Michael Kasino

Pier Kids, directed by Elegance Bratton

P.S. Burn This Letter Please, directed by Michael Seligman and Jennifer Tiexiera

The Queen, directed by Frank Simon

Rebels on Pointe, directed by Bobbi Jo Hart

RuPaul's Drag Race (MTV)

Stormé: Lady of the Jewel Box, directed by Michelle Parkerson

Superstar in a Housedress, directed by Craig Highberger

To Wong Foo, Thanks for Everything! Julie Newmar, directed by Beeban Kidron

Trash, written and directed by Paul Morrissey; produced by Andy Warhol

Venus Boyz, directed by Gabriel Baur

Whether You Like It or Not: The Story of Hedwig, directed by Laura Nix

Wig, directed by Chris Moukarbel

Wigstock: The Movie, directed by Barry Shils

Women in Revolt, written and directed by Paul Morrissey; produced by Andy Warhol

Digital Media

The Digital Transgender Archive

DragKingHistory.com

Felix Rodriguez's Old School Ballroom (on Instagram @oldschoolballroom)

The 5 Ninth Avenue Project (Nelson Sullivan's video collection on YouTube, @5ninthavenueproject)

Harry James Hanson and Devin Antheus's Legends of Drag (on Instagram @legendsofdrag)

The Luna Show (Luna Luis Ortiz's YouTube show about ballroom history, @thelunashowny)

Marc Zinaman's Queer Happened Here (on Instagram @queer_happened_here)

Mob Queens, a podcast by Michael Seligman and Jessica Bendinger

The NYC LGBT Historic Sites Project

Queer Music Heritage

Sidewalkkilla by Alexey Kim

Thotyssey! by Jim Silvestri

Village Preservation: The Greenwich Village Society for Historical Preservation

Endnotes

Prologue

1. **"Ready or not..."** *To Wong Foo, Thanks for Everything! Julie Newmar.* Directed by Beeban Kidron, 1995.

2. **"And wheeeeeere issssss the bodyyyyyy..."** Salt-N-Pepa. "I Am the Body Beautiful." *YouTube*, 1995, https://www.youtube.com/ watch?v=qq6NQv8wuyk.

3. **"Drag is an example..."** Butler, Judith. "Preface (1999)." In *Gender Trouble: Feminism and the Subversion of Identity.* Routledge, 2007, pp. xxiv–xxv.

4. **"Saying you love drag but..."** AfterBuzz TV. "Interview with Trixie Mattel: Aging, Dating, and Wanting to Look Like a Wind-Up Toy." *YouTube*, 24 Jan. 2017, https: //www.youtube.com/watch?v=-2OnPCYMcNk.

Chapter 1

1. **Ella Wesner is smoking.** Sarony, Napoleon. *Ella Wesner, Male Impersonator.* Albumen print, ca. 1880, Collection of George Eastman House. *Flickr*, https: //www.flickr.com/photos/george_eastman_ house/3334087530/in/photostream.

2. **Little Beauties Cigarettes.** Quinn, Anna. "See: First Exhibit Exploring BK's Queer History Opens This Week." *Brooklyn Heights-DUMBO, NY Patch*, 4 Mar. 2019, https: //patch.com/new-york/heights-dumbo/ first-exhibit-explor-brooklyns-queer-history-opens-week.

3. **smoke in public** Blakemore, Erin. "When New York Banned Smok-

ing to Save Women's Souls." *History.com*, A+E Networks, 7 Apr. 2021, https://www.history.com/news/when-new-york-banned-smoking-to-save-womens-souls.

4. **in 1870** Rodger, Gillian M. *Just One of the Boys: Female-to-Male Cross-Dressing on the American Variety Stage*. Urbana: University of Illinois at Urbana-Champaign, 2018, p. 35.

5. **serve as dresser** Senelick, Laurence. *The Changing Room: Sex, Drag and Theatre*. London: Routledge, 2000, p. 331.

6. **from England in 1867** Senelick, p. 329.

7. **curly mop top** Photograph of Annie Hindle. Senelick, *The Changing Room*, p. 330.

8. **only performer of her kind** Rodger, p. 35.

9. **shaving to grow facial hair** Senelick, Laurence. "Boys and Girls Together: Subcultural Origins of Glamour Drag and Male Impersonation on the Nineteenth-Century Stage." In *Crossing the Stage: Controversies on Cross-Dressing*, ed. Lesley Ferris. London and New York: Routledge, 2005, p. 93, https://books.google.com/books?id=qZyKAgAAQBAJ.

10. **"The Great Hindle"** Rodger, p. 32.

11. **"Protean"** Rodger, p. 28; Cullen, Frank, Florence Hackman, and Donald McNeilly. "Protean." In *Vaudeville, Old & New: An Encyclopedia of Variety Performers in America*. New York: Routledge, 2007, p. 902, https://books.google.com/books?id=XFnfnKg6BcAC&pg.

12. **songs to sing** Rodger, p. 34.

13. **only competition** Rodger, p. 35.

14. **Attired in a formfitting suit** Sarony, Napoleon. *Photograph of Ella Wesner*. Cabinet card, ca. 1880s, McClung Museum of Natural History & Culture, https://mcclungmuseum.utk.edu/object-of-the-month/ella-wesner/.

15. **well-to-do gentleman...an aspiration and a joke** Rodger, p. 39, p. 41, p. 43.

16. **afforded some of their privileges** Rodger, pp. 49–50.

17. **a man named Charles Hindle** Rodger, p. 140; Senelick, *The Changing Room*, p. 331.

18. **"The groom gave me her—I mean his"** Senelick, *The Changing Room*, p. 331.

19. **"the only living woman who has a living wife."** Rodger, p. 141.

20. **Helen "Josie" Mansfield** Ryan, Hugh. *When Brooklyn Was Queer.* New York: St. Martin's Press, 2020, p. 54.

21. **abandoning her stage work** Rodger, p. 55.

22. **"like a man"** Rodger, pp. 172–73.

23. **escapist forms of entertainment...distinctly more feminine** Rodger, p. 75.

24. **more for novelty than satire** Rodger, p. 169.

25. **manly... My dad was very... I wasn't considered... She might as well... Hippodrome.** Slide, Anthony. "Kitty Doner." In *The Encyclopedia of Vaudeville.* University Press of Mississippi, 2012, p. 134.

26. **The Passing Show** Westover, Jonas. "Putting It Together: The Creative Team and Players of 'The Passing Show of 1914.'" *The Passing Show: Newsletter of the Shubert Archive* 28, issue 2009/2010, pp. 1–2, PDF download, https://web.archive.org/web/20140606225717/http://www.shubertarchive.org/pdf/passingshows/PS2009Final.pdf.

27. **Al Jolson** Rodger, p. 167.

28. **"a wonder...a live wire"** White, Jr., Matthew. "The Stage: The Lure of Novelty." *Munsey's Magazine*, Dec. 1914, p. 558, https://books.google.com/books?id=fowmAQAAIAAJ&dq=.

29. **bristles...mustaches...gestures** Slide, p. 134.

30. **"If the police..."** "Clothes—and the Girl: A Word with Kitty Doner." *The Green Book Magazine*, Sept. 1916, p. 545, https://books.google.com/books?id=InvNAAAAMAAJ&lpg=PA545.

31. **"The Best Dressed Man on the American Stage"** Slide, Anthony. *Images of America: New York City Vaudeville.* Charleston: Arcadia Publishing, 2006, https://books.google.com/books?id=YNc9VRnnP_MC.

32. **"With Jack Carroll..."** Slide, p. 134.

33. **between $1,000 and $1,500** Slide, p. 134.

34. **Dressed in...** Huston, Reeve. "The Parties and 'The People': New York Anti-Rent Wars and the Contours of Jacksonian Politics." *Journal of the Early Republic* 20, no. 2, 2000, pp. 241–71, https://doi.org/10.2307/3124703.

35. **Anti-Rent War** Britannica, The Editors of Encyclopaedia. "Antirent War." *Encyclopaedia Britannica*, 1 Nov. 2013, https://www.britannica.com/event/Antirent-War.

36. **"an act to prevent persons appearing disguised and armed"**...

the act read as follows *Statutes at Large of the State of New York: Comprising the Revised Statutes, as They Existed on the 1st Day of July, 1862, and All the General Public Statutes Then in Force, with References to Judicial Decisions, and the Material Notes of the Revisers in Their Report to the Legislature, Volume IV,* ed. John Worth Edmonds. New York: Weare C. Little, 1863, p. 279. Digitized 21 May 2008, https://books.google.com/books?id=PhwbAAAAYAAJ&pg.

37. **In 1846...** Britannica, "Antirent War."

38. **used against the queer community...risked jail** Ryan, Hugh. "When Dressing in Drag Was Labeled a Crime." *History.com*, A+E Networks, 25 June 2019, https://www.history.com/news/stonewall-riots-lgbtq-drag-three-article-rule.

39. **"Obnoxious"** "The Masked Ball Law." *New York Times*, 7 Jan. 1876, p. 8, https://nyti.ms/3KBT5L2.

40. **Pussy Riot** Robbins, Christopher. "City Dodges Legal Challenge to 1845 Anti-Mask Law." *Gothamist*, 12 Dec. 2012, https://gothamist.com/news/city-dodges-legal-challenge-to-1845-anti-mask-law. Ryan, Hugh. "How Dressing in Drag Was Labeled a Crime in the 20th Century." *History.com*, A+E Networks, 25 June 2019.

41. **"Hooliganism"** Hollingsworth, Chauncey. "Scenes from the Pussy Riot Protests." *The Atlantic*, Atlantic Media, 18 Aug. 2012, https://www.theatlantic.com/national/archive/2012/08/scenes-from-the-pussy-riot-protests/261300/.

42. **repealed** "Attorney General James Applauds Repeal of Law Criminalizing Group Mask Use in Public." *New York State Attorney General*, 28 May 2020, https://ag.ny.gov/press-release/2020/attorney-general-james-applauds-repeal-law-criminalizing-group-mask-use-public.

43. **1872 "for the suppression..."** Anthony Comstock, O. B. Frothingham, J. M. Buckley. "The Suppression of Vice." *The North American Review* 135, no. 312, 1 Nov. 1882, pp. 484–501, http://www.jstor.org/stable/10.2307/25118217?refreqid=search-gateway:8cada8d9138 4ca1ef363c6b5ee9f9497.

44. **Sumner anti-gay crusade** Chauncey, George. *Gay New York: Gender, Urban Culture, and the Makings of the Gay Male World, 1890–1940.* New York: Basic Books, 1994, pp. 146–47.

45. **"Degenerate resorts"...sexual orientation** Chauncey, *Gay New York*, p. 33.

46. **Paresis Hall...syphilis** Biederman, Marcia. "Journey to an Overlooked Past." *New York Times*, 11 June 2000, https://www.nytimes.com/2000/06/11/nyregion/journey-to-an-overlooked-past.html.

47. **"The Wickedest Place in New York"** Pitillo, Angelo. "The History of Gay Bars." *New York Magazine*, 24 Jan. 2013, https://nymag. com/nightlife/features/gay-bar-history-2013-1/.

48. **"slide," "an establishment where..."** Chauncey, *Gay New York*, p. 68.

49. **"fairies" and their whereabouts** Chauncey, *Gay New York*, p. 34.

50. **"gay" or "straight"** Chauncey, *Gay New York*, p. 65.

51. Portions of section on Julian Eltinge reprinted with permission from Condé Nast, "Drag Herstory: This Drag Queen Was Once the Highest Paid Actor in the World," written by Elyssa Maxx Goodman and published in *Them* on 6 Apr. 2018, https://www.them.us/story/julian-eltinge-drag-queen-history.

52. **"a very pretty girl..."** "'Mr. Wix of Wickham.'" *The Tammany Times*, vol. XX, no. 22, 1 Oct. 1904, https://books.google.com/ books?id=35U6AQAAMAAJ&pg.

53. **shave and powder** Kasson, John F. "The Metamorphosis of Julian Eltinge." In *Houdini, Tarzan, and the Perfect Man: The White Male Body and the Challenge of Modernity in America*. New York: Hill and Wang, 2002.

54. **paramount to his reputation** Landis, Kevin. "Julian Eltinge's Manly Transformation." *The Gay & Lesbian Review*, 1 Sept. 2007, https:// glreview.org/article/article-26/.

55. **Eltinge Theatre** Gray, Christopher. "Streetscapes: The Eltinge/ Empire Theater; A Film Restores a Bit of 42d Street—in Faux Decay." *New York Times*, 28 Mar. 1993, https://www.nytimes. com/1993/03/28/realestate/streetscapes-eltinge-empire-theater-film-restores-bit-42d-street-faux-decay.html.

56. **Cohan and Harris Minstrels** Ullman, Sharon R. "'The Twentieth Century Way': Female Impersonation and Sexual Practice in Turn-of-the-Century America." *Journal of the History of Sexuality* 5, no. 4, 1995, pp. 573–600. *JSTOR*, https://www.jstor.org/stable/4617203.

57. **among the most popular** National Museum of African American History & Culture. "Blackface: The Birth of an American Stereotype." *Nmaahc.si.edu*, 30 Oct. 2017, https://nmaahc.si.edu/explore/ stories/blackface-birth-american-stereotype.

58. **stereotypes** Senelick, *The Changing Room*, pp. 297–98; Hill, Errol, and James V. Hatch. "American Minstrelsy in Black and White." In *A History of African American Theatre*, Cambridge: Cambridge University Press, 2003, p. 57.

59. **first Black minstrel troupe, 1855** Anderson, Lisa M. "From Black-face to 'Genuine Negroes': Nineteenth-Century Minstrelsy and the Icon of the 'Negro.'" *Theatre Research International*, vol. 21, no. 1, 1996, pp. 17–23, doi:10.1017/S0307883300012669.

60. **"wench", "yaller girl"** Senelick, *The Changing Room*, pp. 297–98.

61. **"mulatto"** "Mulatto." *Merriam-Webster.com Dictionary*, Merriam-Webster, https://www.merriam-webster.com/dictionary/mulatto.

62. **came from the minstrel world** Bean, Annemarie. "Black Minstrelsy and Double Inversion, Circa 1890." In *African-American Performance and Theater History: A Critical Reader*, ed. David Krasner and Harry J. Elam. New York: Oxford University Press, 2001, p. 179, https://books.google.com/books?id=PYBfz1l-6oIC&pg.

63. **born in Kentucky** Bean, p. 179.

64. **discovered by** Hill and Hatch, pp. 128–29.

65. **Pekin Theatre** Levitt, Aimee. "'An Evening at the Pekin Theatre' Re-Creates the Country's First Black-Owned Music Hall." *Chicago Reader*, 15 June 2017. https://www.chicagoreader.com/Bleader/archives/2017/06/15/an-evening-at-the-pekin-theatre-re-creates-the-countrys-first-black-owned-music-hall.

66. **wore a dress...tripped while wearing** Bean, p. 179

67. **Ophelia Snow** Bean, p. 179; Hill and Hatch, pp. 128–29.

68. **"a single-minded woman..."** Hill and Hatch, pp. 128–29.

69. *The Shoo-Fly Regiment* Ng Yong He, Gregory, et al. "The Shoo-Fly Regiment (1907)." *Black Work Broadway*. https://blackworkbroadway.com/The-Shoo-Fly-Regiment-1907.

70. *Ophelia Snow from Baltimo'* Hill and Hatch, pp. 128–29.

71. **"dean of Black entertainment critics"** Abbott, Lynn, and Doug Seroff. "Introduction." In *Ragged but Right: Black Traveling Shows, "Coon Songs," and the Dark Pathway to Blues and Jazz*. Jackson, MI: University Press of Mississippi, 2007, p. 5, https://books.google.com/books?id=u4rc-BKNCyoC&pg.

72. **"The greatest protean artist..."** Hill and Hatch, p. 129.

73. *The Darktown Revue* "Pioneers of African-American Cinema: The Darktown Revue." *Kino Now*, Kino Lorber, 2015, https://kinonow.com/film/pioneers-of-african-american-cinema-the-darktown-revue/5d654a685499035c7f2bd5a2; Bean, p. 179.

74. *The Creole Show* McAllister, Marvin Edward. "A Trip to Coontown." In *Whiting Up: Whiteface Minstrels & Stage Europeans in African American Performance*. Chapel Hill, NC: University of North Carolina Press, 2011, pp. 79–81, https://books.google.com/books?id=gBeFBAAAQBAJ&pg.

75. **cakewalk** McAllister, pp. 32–39

76. **ragtime…jazz** "History of Ragtime." *Library of Congress*, 2015, https://www.loc.gov/item/ihas.200035811/.

77. **racial backdrop** McAllister, p. 79.

78. **male impersonator Florence Hines** Ryan, Hugh. "This Black Drag King Was Once Known as the Greatest Male Impersonator of All Time." *Them*, 1 June 2018, https://www.them.us/story/themstory-florence-hines.

79. **"the greatest living female song and dance artist"** Abbott, Lynn, and Doug Seroff. "1891." In *Out of Sight: The Rise of African American Popular Music, 1889–1895*. Jackson, MI: University Press of Mississippi, 2009, p. 154.

80. **"dandy" attire** Ryan, "This Black Drag King."

81. **done for decades; don finery…both escape from and mock** Ryan, "This Black Drag King"; Casey, Kathleen. *Cross-Dressers and Race-Crossers: Intersections of Gender and Race in American Vaudeville, 1900–1930*, PhD diss., University of Rochester, 2010, pp. 195–99.

82. **not simply…a degradation** Ryan, "This Black Drag King."

83. **An essential part** Abbott and Seroff, pp. 154–56; Ryan, "This Black Drag King."

84. **"It is stated…which can be erected."** Committee of Fourteen (New York). *The Social Evil in New York City: A Study of Law Enforcement by the Committee of Fourteen*. New York: A.H. Kellogg Company, 1910, p. xv.

85. **regulate public spaces** Chauncey, *Gay New York*, p. 139.

86. **"Somewhere…zealots"** Ryan, *When Brooklyn*, p. 91.

87. **Masquerade balls…nineteenth century** Chauncey, *Gay New York*, p. 293.

88. **Thanksgiving, "ragamuffin parades"** Chauncey, *Gay New York*, p. 293.

89. **proper permits** Chauncey, *Gay New York*, p. 294.

90. **throwing attendees in jail** Chauncey, *Gay New York*, p. 295.

91. **wildly popular affairs** Miller, Neil. *Out of the Past: Gay and Lesbian History from 1869 to the Present.* New York: Alyson Books, 2006, p. 141.

92. **Grand United Order of Odd Fellows, Hamilton Lodge #710** "History." *Grand United Order of Odd Fellows in America and Jurisdiction*, https://guoof.org/household-of-ruth/history/.

93. **Masquerade and Civic Ball...Hamilton Lodge Ball** Chauncey, *Gay New York*, p. 257.

94. **"At an early hour...event of the season."** "Hamilton Lodge Ball." *New York Freeman*, 6 Mar. 1886. Republished on *Queer Music Heritage*, https://queermusicheritage.com/nov2014hamilton.html.

95. **Manhattan Casino, Rockland Palace** Chauncey, *Gay New York*, p. 270.

96. **"Casino"..."a building or place used for social amusements"** "Casino." *Merriam-Webster.com Dictionary*, Merriam-Webster, https://www.merriam-webster.com/dictionary/casino.

97. **Philip A. Payton, Jr., construction of Penn Station** Hassan, Adeel. "Philip Payton, the Real Estate Mogul Who Made Harlem a Black Mecca." *New York Times*, 31 Jan. 2019, https://www.nytimes.com/interactive/2019/obituaries/philip-a-payton-jr-overlooked.html.

98. **luxurious...elbow** Earl-Broady Studios. "Photograph of William Demont Evans and Lillyn Brown." Gelatin silver print, ca. 1930, *International Center of Photography*, https://www.icp.org/browse/archive/objects/william-demont-evans-and-lillyn-brown.

99. **Black and Iroquois, Queen City Minstrels, breeches** Dehn, Mura. Interview with Lillian [sic] Brown. *Mura Dehn Papers on Afro-American Social Dance, ca 1869–1987.* Jerome Robbins Dance Division, NYPL, p. 11; Casey, p. 162.

100. **"Youngest Interlocutor in the World"** *Black Women of the Harlem Renaissance Era*, ed. Lean'tin L. Bracks and Jessie Carney Smith. Rowman & Littlefield, 2014, p. 32.

101. **contralto** Casey, p. 154.

102. **Trousers...fingers** Dehn, interview with Lillian [sic] Brown, p. 11; Casey, p. 164.

103. **slyly calibrated presentation; subverted stereotypical characters; layered, satirical complexity; Al Jolson** Casey, pp. 204–5.

104. **Webster Hall...rendezvous** Miller, *Out of the Past*, p. 141.

105. **opening in 1886** Dowell, Chelsea. "What's in Webster Hall's Past—and Future?" *Village Preservation*, 8 Aug. 2017, https://www.village-preservation.org/2017/08/08/whats-in-webster-halls-past-and-future/.

106. **hotbed of...queer life** Miller, *Out of the Past*, p. 141.

107. **Ninth Ward and Fifteenth Ward** Strausbaugh, John. *The Village: 400 Years of Beats and Bohemians, Radicals and Rogues; a History of Greenwich Village*. New York: HarperCollins, 2013, p. 25.

108. **"Devil's Playground"** Strausbaugh, p. 132.

109. **"phenomenal men...young lady"** Chauncey, *Gay New York*, p. 236.

110. **twenty-one and thirty; eighteen and forty-five** "Mobilizing for War: The Selective Service Act in World War I." *National Archives Foundation*, https://www.archivesfoundation.org/documents/mobilizing-war-selective-service-act-world-war/.

111. **Pop culture had cast...; "disorderly conduct...perversion"** Chauncey, *Gay New York*, p. 141.

112. **Though it wasn't yet illegal...; "keeping a disorderly house"** Ryan, *When Brooklyn*, pp. 123–25.

113. **drag was still an important part of the war effort** Bérubé, Allan. *Coming Out Under Fire: The History of Gay Men and Women in World War Two*. New York: Plume, 1991, p. 75.

114. **"was bigger than Elvis"** Corliss, Richard. "That Old Christmas Feeling: Irving America." *Time*, 24 Dec. 2001, https://content.time.com/time/arts/article/0,8599,189846,00.html.

115. **"Army Takes Berlin!"** Corliss, "That Old Christmas."

116. **Camp Upton...musical revue...incredibly popular...Bert Savoy** Bérubé, p. 75.

117. **"immeasurable...inspired"** "'Yip! Yip! Yaphank!' Makes Rousing Hit." *New York Times*, 20 Aug. 1918, p. 7, https://nyti.ms/3KEse0J.

118. **"alleged females...than the female performers"** Canaday, Margot. *The Straight State: Sexuality and Citizenship in Twentieth-Century America*. Princeton: Princeton University Press, 2009, p. 61.

119. **Eighteenth Amendment** Drexler, Ken. "18th Amendment to the U.S. Constitution: Primary Documents in American History." *Library of Congress*, 14 Jan. 2020, https://guides.loc.gov/18th-amendment.

Chapter 2

1. **"You musssssst come over!"** "Savoy & Brennan, 'You Must Come Over,' Queer Humor." *YouTube*, https://www.youtube.com/watch?v=r0VYTKFM3-U.

2. **enormous feathers towering** Senelick, *The Changing Room*, pp. 317-18.

3. **drew them in** Senelick, *The Changing Room*, p. 312.

4. **"cooch dancer"** Slide, p. 456.

5. **streetcar** Slide, p. 456.

6. ***Passing Show of 1915*** Senelick, *The Changing Room*, p. 314.

7. **"waved her fat hands..."** Kingsley, Walter J. "Bert Savoy." *New York Times*, 1 July 1923, p. 115, https://timesmachine.nytimes.com/timesmachine/1923/07/01/issue.html.

8. **"You Must Come Over"** "Savoy & Brennan."

9. **catchphrases, "The Half of it Dearie Blues"** Senelick, *The Changing Room*, p. 316.

10. **Mae West...inspired by Savoy** Robertson, Pamela. "'The Kinda Comedy That Imitates Me': Mae West's Identification with the Feminist Camp." *Cinema Journal* 32, no. 2, 1993, pp. 57–72, https://doi.org/10.2307/1225605.

11. **"a greater comedian...bald, paunchy... After an hour...palm of his hand."** Anderson, John Murray, and Hugh Abercrombie Anderson. *Out Without My Rubbers: The Memoirs of John Murray Anderson.* Chicago: Pickle Partners Publishing, 2018.

12. **wasn't a threat** Senelick, *The Changing Room*, p. 317.

13. **"Mercy, ain't Miss God..."** de la Croix, St. Sukie. *Chicago Whispers: A History of LGBT Chicago Before Stonewall.* Madison: University of Wisconsin Press, 2012, p. 63.

14. **"incontestably one of the greatest"** Kingsley.

15. **"[N]o locale, not even Chicago,"** Strausbaugh, p. 155.

16. **32,000 speakeasies** Kugel, Seth. "Tell Them Seth Sent You." *New York Times*, 29 Apr. 2007, https://www.nytimes.com/2007/04/29/travel/29weekend.html.

17. **Organized crime...queer nightlife** Nianias, Helen. "How the Mafia Once Controlled New York Gay Scene." *Vice*, 30 July 2014,

https://www.vice.com/en/article/gqmym3/how-the-mafia-once-controlled-the-new-york-gay-scene-616.

18. **openly flouted** Strausbaugh, pp. 166–67.

19. **former composer, Volstead Act** Strausbaugh, pp. 166–67.

20. **"dating" as we know it today** "Dating Replaced Courtship During Prohibition." *The Mob Museum,* https://prohibition.themobmuseum.org/the-history/how-prohibition-changed-american-culture/dating-during-prohibition/.

21. **"The Parisian Fashion Plate"** "Vaudeville Reviews: Royal." *New York Clipper,* 9 Apr. 1919, p. 9, https://archive.org/details/Clipper67-1919-04/.

22. **"Shubert vaudeville boasts...ballroom floor."** "Why Broadway Beckons of an October Evening." *New York Tribune,* 16 Oct. 1921, p. 6, https://www.newspapers.com/image/100121216/?terms=%22 Francis%2BRenault%22.

23. **100-pound dress covered in "diamonds"** Murphy, William. "Renault, Good Impersonator, and Other Acts Win at Pantages." *The San Francisco Bulletin,* June 1924. Reprinted as part of an advertisement in *Variety,* June 1924. Republished on *Queer Music Heritage,* https://www.queermusicheritage.com/drag-SH-renault.html.

24. **"solid gold sequins"** "The Chat is the Most Complete Brooklyn Theatre Guide," *The Chat,* 24 Feb. 1924, p. 58, https://www.newspapers.com/newspage/576436653/.

25. **"Francis Renault, Stage Star, Is Clever Boxer."** *The Brooklyn Citizen,* 28 Dec. 1921, p. 4, https://www.newspapers.com/newspage/543798364/.

26. **"To see Renault's act...proper condition..."** *The Brooklyn Citizen,* 28 Dec. 1921, p. 4.

27. **billboard in Times Square** Senelick, *The Changing Room,* p. 378.

28. **"The Creole Fashion Plate"** Chauncey, *Gay New York,* p. 319.

29. **traveled with him** Cullen, Frank, et al. *Vaudeville, Old and New: An Encyclopedia of Variety Performers in America.* New York: Routledge, 2007, p. 833.

30. **broke a 1922 engagement** "How Many Mamas on the Honeymoon?" *The Ogden Standard-Examiner,* 27 Aug. 1922, p. 4. Republished on *Queer Music Heritage,* https://www.queermusicheritage.com/drag-SH-norman3.html.

31. **"The Queer Old Fashion Plate"** Marx, Harpo, and Rowland Barber. *Harpo Speaks!* New Jersey: Limelight Editions, 1985, p. 134, https://books.google.com/books?id=XCR14V7uMbsC&printsec.

32. **Soprano...baritone** Scholten, Alexandra. "Drag Performance in Minnesota, 1880–1950." *MNopedia*, Minnesota Historical Society, http://www.mnopedia.org/drag-performance-minnesota-1880-1950.

33. **switching from high to low** Rodger, Gillian. "Variety and Vaudeville." *GLBTQ Archives*, 2002, p. 4, http://www.glbtqarchive.com/arts/variety_vaudeville_A.pdf; **wrote his own song lyrics** "Nobody Lied." *Indianapolis Examiner*, 22 May 1922. Republished on *Queer Music Heritage*, https://www.queermusicheritage.com/drag-SH-norman2.html. References Norman's song "Nobody Lied When They Said That I Cried Over You."

34. **would start onstage** Willard, Avery. "Karyl Norman." *Female Impersonation*, 1971. Republished on *Queer Music Heritage*, https://queermusicheritage.com/fem-willard15.html.

35. **"reverse Kitty Doner"** Willard, "Karyl Norman."

36. *Lady Do*...**four roles.** Cullen, et al., p. 833; **designed the costumes** "Karyl Norman." *Broadway World*, https://www.broadwayworld.com/people/Karyl-Norman/.

37. **"the prime requisite...desired end."** Atkinson, Brooks. "'Lady Do' Has Merit as a Musical Play." *New York Times*, 19 Apr. 1927, p. 24, https://timesmachine.nytimes.com/timesmachine/1927/04/19/118641831.html?pageNumber=24.

38. **Eleanor Roosevelt..."she owed him one."** Slide, p. 375.

39. **six feet tall and 200 pounds** Bullock, Darryl W. "Pansy Craze: The Wild 1930s Drag Parties That Kickstarted Gay Nightlife." *The Guardian*, 14 Sept. 2017, https://www.theguardian.com/music/2017/sep/14/pansy-craze-the-wild-1930s-drag-parties-that-kickstarted-gay-nightlife.

40. **king of the "Pansy Craze"** Bullock.

41. **"Give them an inch..."** Skolsky, Sidney. "Tintypes." *Daily News*, 2 Apr. 1931, p. 202, https://www.newspapers.com/newspage/413933163/.

42. **"queerface"** Chauncey, *Gay New York*, p. 310.

43. **pitcher of hot water** Chauncey, *Gay New York*, p. 318.

44. **ruined his gown** Chauncey, *Gay New York*, p. 318.

45. **valuable space** Chauncey, *Gay New York*, p. 318.

46. **Rubaiyat closed** Chauncey, *Gay New York*, p. 314.

47. **"I'll lay you out in ten dozen shades of lavender!"** Skolsky, "Tintypes."

48. **"We have never watched..."** James, Rian. "Reverting to Type." *Brooklyn Daily Eagle.* 4 Feb. 1932, p. 21, https://www.newspapers.com/image/59863097/?terms=%22Jean%2BMalin%22; **"sophisticates"** Chauncey, *Gay New York*, pp. 327–28.

49. **inked with lavender** Chauncey, *Gay New York*, p. 319.

50. **"pansies on parade," "parade of the fairies"** Chauncey, *Gay New York*, p. 319.

51. **Schackno Bill, "attempting" solicitation** Ryan, *When Brooklyn*, p. 126.

52. **"depicting or dealing with..."** Sova, Dawn B. *Banned Plays: Censorship Histories of 125 Stage Dramas.* Infobase Publishing, 2004, p. 170.

53. **none other than Mae West** Shteir, Rachel. *Striptease: The Untold History of the Girlie Show.* Oxford: Oxford University Press, 2006, p. 106.

54. **April 26, 1926** "Sex—Broadway Play—Original." *Internet Broadway Database*, https://www.ibdb.com/broadway-production/sex-10051.

55. **posted bail** West, Mae. *Three Plays by Mae West*, ed. Lillian Schlissel. New York: Routledge, 1997, p. 14.

56. **sought out gay actors...had help from gay men** Chauncey, *Gay New York*, p. 312.

57. **handwritten ad** Schlissel, p. 12.

58. **"*The Drag* had no star..."** Schlissel, p. 12.

59. **"homosexual comedy-drama"** Hamilton, Marybeth. "Mae West Live: '*SEX, The Drag*, and 1920s Broadway.'" *TDR (1988–)* vol. 36, no. 4, 1992, pp. 82–100, https://doi.org/10.2307/1146217.

60. **mere scenery** Schlissel, p. 24.

61. **"just off Ocean Parkway..."** Manbeck, John. "Ask a Historian: What's the Story with Coney Island's Brothels of Yore?" *Brooklyn Daily Eagle*, https://brooklyneagle.com/articles/2019/06/07/coney-island-brothels/.

62. **"shanties or slum houses..."** Manbeck.

63. **"where song-pluggers included..."** Immerso, Michael. *Coney Island: The People's Playground.* Piscataway, NJ: Rutgers University Press, 2002, p. 116.

64. **In 1910, a seventeen-year-old musician** Laurie, Jr., Joe. "Thumbnose Sketch—Jimmy Durante." *Variety*, 5 June 1946, p. 33, https://ia800505.us.archive.org/34/items/variety162-1946-06/variety162-1946-06.pdf.

65. **"...the entertainers...nasty cracks."** Durante, Jimmy, and Jack Kofoed. *Night Clubs*. New York: A.A. Knopf, 1931, pp. 54–55; Ryan, *When Brooklyn*, p. 121.

66. **sympathetic** Chauncey, *Gay New York*, p. 312.

67. **all work on Broadway** Schlissel, p. 14.

68. **reflected the values** Chauncey, *Gay New York*, p. 301.

69. **"Essentially...underworld"** Shteir, p. 106.

70. **Broadway...row** Schlissel, p. 20.

71. **During one raid...** "MAYOR TAKES A HAND, SHOW AGAIN RAIDED." *New York Times*, 4 Oct. 1928, https://www.nytimes.com/1928/10/04/archives/mayor-takes-a-hand-show-again-raided-stay-set-aside-and-police-stop.html?searchResultPosition=20; Watts, Jill. *Mae West: An Icon in Black and White*. New York: Oxford University Press, 2001. p. 113.

72. **$60,000** Schlissel, p. 23.

73. **criticized** Schlissel, p. 25.

74. **"I love you, Miss West..."** Schlissel, p. 26.

75. **January 24, 1931, at approximately 5:50 a.m.** "Rothstein Aid Is Shot in Club." *Daily News*, 25 Jan. 1931, p. 4, https://www.newspapers.com/newspage/413585275/.

76. **"stampeding for their ermine wraps..."** "Rothstein Aid."

77. **1:00 a.m. on January 29, 1931** Cassidy, Tom. "Whoops, Dearie! Mean Old Police Raid Pansy Row." *Daily News*, 29 Jan. 1931, p. 3, https://www.newspapers.com/clip/50611440/daily-news/.

78. **seized a single bottle** Cassidy, p. 37.

79. **prohibited drag between 14th St and 72nd St** Chauncey, *Gay New York*, p. 333.

80. **"immaculate white...straight back"** Bentley, Gladys. "I'm a Woman Again." *Ebony*, Aug. 1952. Republished on *Queer Music Heritage*, https://www.queermusicheritage.com/bentley6.html.

81. **sexuality was different..."fix"** "Gladys Bentley: Gender-Bending Performer and Musician | Unladylike2020 | American

Masters | PBS." *YouTube*, 3 June 2020, https://www.youtube.com/
watch?v=7LeDbXK7H20.

82. **looking for a male pianist** "Gladys Bentley: Gender-Bending Performer and Musician | Unladylike2020 | American Masters | PBS."

83. **venue changed its name** Bentley, "I'm a Woman Again."

84. **"plays and sings until...over the place."** Skolsky, Sidney. "Behind News." *Daily News*, 29 Mar. 1930, p. 21, https://www.newspapers.com/newspage/412836049/.

85. **"an amazing exhibition...own rhythm."** Hughes, Langston. *The Big Sea*. New York: Hill and Wang, 1993, p. 226, https://books.google.com/books?id=louigOHnk0MC&source=gbs_navlinks_s.

86. **openly gay...a white woman** Senelick, *The Changing Room*, p. 339; Niven, Steven J. "Blues Singer Gladys Bentley Broke Ground with Marriage to a Woman in 1931." *The Root*, 11 Feb. 2015, https://www.theroot.com/blues-singer-gladys-bentley-broke-ground-with-marriage-1790858771.

87. **"You Bet Your Life"** "Gladys Bentley on 'You Bet Your Life.'" *YouTube*, 18 Dec. 2009, https://www.youtube.com/watch?v=j-LTJNasTMc.

88. **according to Dwandalyn Reece** "Gladys Bentley: Gender-Bending Performer and Musician | Unladylike2020 | American Masters | PBS."

89. **drag on the sidewalk** Chauncey, *Gay New York*, p. 249.

90. **possible violence..."The Jungle"** Chauncey, *Gay New York*, p. 249.

91. **the character was beloved** Wilson, James. *Bulldaggers, Pansies, and Chocolate Babies: Performance, Race, and Sexuality in the Harlem Renaissance*. Ann Arbor: University of Michigan Press, 2010, p. 89.

92. **Though the play...unheard of** Wilson, pp. 89–90.

93. **DuBois among its positive reviewers** Wilson, p. 104.

94. **white fascination** Wilson, p. 108.

95. **"slumming"** Heap, Chad C. *Slumming: Sexual and Racial Encounters in American Nightlife, 1885–1940*. Chicago: University of Chicago Press, 2008, p. 91.

96. **twenty-piece orchestra** Ki, Zay. "A Drag Ball in Harlem Was One of the Biggest Social Events in 1920s New York." *LGBTQ Nation*, 28 Feb. 2023, https://www.lgbtqnation.com/2023/02/a-drag-ball-in-harlem-was-one-of-the-biggest-social-events-in-1920s-new-york/.

97. **"From these boxes...on the chest."** Hughes, Langston. Excerpt from *The Big Sea* reprinted in Miller, Neil. *Out of the Past: Gay and Lesbian History from 1869 to the Present*, pp. 157–58.

98. **"the strangest and gaudiest..."** Hughes, Langston. Excerpt from *The Big Sea* reprinted in Miller, Neil. *Out of the Past*, pp. 157–58.

99. **later spawn voguing** Morgan, Thaddeus. "How 19th-Century Drag Balls Evolved into House Balls, Birthplace of Voguing." *History.com*, A+E Networks, 28 June 2021, https://www.history.com/news/drag-balls-house-ballroom-voguing.

100. **"Apparently, for a novitiate..."** Wilson, p. 80.

101. **8,000 attendees** Morgan, "How 19th-Century Drag."

102. **racial...Bonnie Clark** Chauncey, *Gay New York*, p. 261.

103. **"You may quote Bonnie Clark...girls to win."** "3,000 Attend Ball of Hamilton Lodge: Bonnie Clark, Last Year's Prize Winner, Disgruntled as another 'Sweet Young Thing' Is Chosen for First Place." *New York Amsterdam News (1922–1938)*, 1 Mar. 1933, p. 2. *ProQuest*, http://ezproxy.nypl.org/login?url=https://www.proquest.com/historical-newspapers/3-000-attend-ball-hamilton-lodge/docview/226264378/se-2; Chauncey, *Gay New York*, p. 263.

104. **one third of city dwellers** Toole, Pauline. "Unemployment in the Great Depression." *NYC Department of Records & Information Services*, 9 Oct. 2020, https://www.archives.nyc/blog/2020/10/9/9ovdpgn8lc5zxcild0ooltvzmfwx22.

105. **deemed a threat** Chauncey, George. "A Gay World, Vibrant and Forgotten." *New York Times*, 26 June 1994, https://www.nytimes.com/1994/06/26/opinion/a-gay-world-vibrant-and-forgotten.html.

106. **"the [nightclub] Chateau Madrid...future."** James, Rian. "Reverting to Type." *The Brooklyn Daily Eagle*, 14 Feb. 1931, p. 9, https://www.newspapers.com/image/57569558/?terms=%22Pansy%2BClub%22.

Chapter 3

1. **coiffed brows** Photograph of Jackie Maye, "Jackie Maye," ed. JD Doyle. Republished on *Queer Music Heritage*, https://queermusicheritage.com/f-maye-jackie.html.

2. **Metropolitan Opera...voice changed** *Female Impersonators on Parade*, 1960. *Digital Transgender Archive*, https://www.digitaltransgenderarchive.net/downloads/tx31qh73c.

3. **Trying to adapt** "Jackie Maye," *Female Impersonators on Parade.*

4. **"The main novelty…many a lass."** Skolsky, Sidney. "Behind News." *Daily News*, 20 Sept. 1930, p. 22, https://www.newspapers.com/newspage/413730096/.

5. **"I Must Have That Man"** Skolsky, "Behind News."

6. **"cabaret laws", "any room…or drink."** New York Supreme Court, Appellate Division—Second Department. "The People of the State of New York vs. Manasse Mouskajian." *Local Law* 8698, no. 12, 13 June 1928, p. 5, https://books.google.com/books?id=-PoA8-oPXjcC&pg=RA6-PP5#v=onepage&q&f=false.

7. **January 1, 1927** New York Supreme Court, p. 11.

8. **"an odd class of people"** Jeffreys, Joe E. 26 May 2022. An interview completed by Elyssa Maxx Goodman.

9. **to woo them** Chauncey, George. "The Forgotten History of Gay Entrapment." *The Atlantic*, 25 June 2019, https://www.theatlantic.com/ideas/archive/2019/06/before-stonewall-biggest-threat-was-entrapment/590536/.

10. **50,000 men** Chauncey, "The Forgotten History of Gay Entrapment."

11. **"the boys"…would help** Jeffreys, 26 May 2022 interview.

12. **get their cards en masse** Jeffreys, 26 May 2022 interview.

13. **December 5, 1933** "The Repeal of Prohibition." *The Mob Museum*, https://prohibition.themobmuseum.org/the-history/the-end-of-prohibition/repeal-of-prohibition/.

14. **"forbade the employment…offenses"** Chevigny, Paul. *Gigs: Jazz and the Cabaret Laws in New York City.* London and New York: Routledge, 2005, second ed., p. 59, https://books.google.com/books?id=KRgp68CKH88C&pg=PA59&lpg=PA59&dq#v=onepage&q&f=false.

15. **orderly conduct** Chauncey, *Gay New York*, pp. 336–37.

16. **Bars became strict…policy** Chauncey, *Gay New York*, pp. 336–37.

17. **searched…invariably closed** Chauncey, *Gay New York*, p. 339.

18. **1,200 acres** Taylor, Alan. "The 1939 New York World's Fair." *The Atlantic*, 1 Nov. 2013, https://www.theatlantic.com/photo/2013/11/the-1939-new-york-worlds-fair/100620/.

19. **April 30, 1939** Taylor, "The 1939 New York World's Fair."

20. **fifty-eight countries, thirty-three states, and more than 1,000 exhibitions** Weglein, Jessica, et al. *New York World's Fair 1939 and*

1940 Incorporated Records, 1935—1945. New York Public Library Manuscripts and Archives Division, June 2008, p. 4, https://www.nypl.org/sites/default/files/archivalcollections/pdf/nywf39fa.pdf.

21. **over $150 million** Taylor, "The 1939 New York World's Fair."

22. **over 44 million people, "The World of Tomorrow"** Taylor, "The 1939 New York World's Fair."

23. **"Campy behavior...carriage"** Chauncey, *Gay New York*, p. 344.

24. **A spate of crimes...panic** Chauncey, *Gay New York*, 359.

25. **performance card** *Phil and [Cora] Black, Female Impersonator.* https://collections.library.yale.edu/catalog/2006079.

26. **"host to...Cafe Society."** "New Revue 'a Sender' at Elks Rendezvous." *New York Age,* 18 Feb. 1939, p. 7, https://www.newspapers.com/newspage/40921104/.

27. **Thanksgiving night of 1947** Lang, Nico. "Celebrate Pride Month by Honoring These Black LGBTQ Trailblazers." *NBC News,* https://www.nbcnews.com/feature/nbc-out/celebrate-pride-month-honoring-these-black-lgbtq-trailblazers-n1232341.

28. **"packed to the rafters...prize"** Burley, Dan. "Dan Burley's Back Door Stuff." *New York Age,* 11 Dec. 1948, p. 8, https://www.newspapers.com/clip/119831627/the-new-york-age/.

29. **"weigh over...the bust."** *Jet,* 12 Nov. 1959. Section of article republished on *Queer Music Heritage,* https://www.queermusicheritage.com/f-black-phil.html.

30. **"too, too marvellous."** Limpwrist, Lucius. "'Les Girls' Had a Ball at Rockland, Honey!" *New York Age,* 7 Dec. 1957, p. 12, https://www.newspapers.com/newspage/40818816/.

31. **"best attended...city."** Limpwrist, "'Les Girls' Had a Ball at Rockland, Honey!"

32. **"When I say...democratic."** Limpwrist, "'Les Girls' Had a Ball at Rockland, Honey!"

33. **end before midnight** Limpwrist, "'Les Girls' Had a Ball at Rockland, Honey!"

34. **Committee for Racial Pride protested** "Photo Standalone 39." *New York Amsterdam News (1962–),* 7 Dec. 1963, p. 27. *ProQuest,* http://ezproxy.nypl.org/login?url=https://www.proquest.com/historical-newspapers/photo-standalone-39-no-title/docview/226671120/se-2.

35. **"Rear Admirals...local hoodlums"** Robinson, Major. "Phil Black

Loses Leg." *New Pittsburgh Courier (1959-1965)*, 16 Oct, 1965, p. 1. *ProQuest*.

36. **diabetes** Robinson, "Phil Black Loses Leg."

37. **"public life...negligees."** Nugent, Richard Bruce. "On 'Gloria Swanson' (Real Name: Mr. Winston)." In *Gay Rebel of the Harlem Renaissance*, ed. Thomas Wirth. Durham and London: Duke University Press, 2002, pp. 221–223.

38. **"And every...home", Austin claimed** Wilson, p. 194; Austin, Augustus. "Fletcher Henderson's Band Pleases at Opera House." *New York Age*, 1 Sept. 1934, https://www.newspapers.com/newspage/40885229/.

39. **"Lifting...limb"** Nugent, p. 222; Chauncey, *Gay New York*, p. 251.

40. **"masquerade"** Nugent, p. 223.

41. **Nugent posited...cardiac illness** Nugent, p. 223.

42. **"Regardless...consolation."** Dancer, Maurice. "'Gloria Swanson' Buried in Harlem." *Chicago Defender*, 3 May 1940. Republished on *Queer Music Heritage*, https://queermusicheritage.com/nov2014sepia.html; Wilson, p. 194.

43. **"folks who live...scorn"** Wilson, p. 194.

44. **"one of the world's...characters"** Dancer, "'Gloria Swanson' Buried in Harlem."

45. **"where the village begins and ends"** Walker, Danton, "Broadway." *Daily News*, 26 Jan. 1938, p. 284, https://www.newspapers.com/newspage/415995245/.

46. **1940 postcard** Davis, Lisa E. "Drag Kings of Village Nightlife: Before and Way before Stonewall." *Google Arts & Culture*, https://artsandculture.google.com/story/drag-kings-of-village-nightlife-before-and-way-before-stonewall/swUhRaa9JaRsbg.

47. **"Generally...society"** Davis, Lisa E. 13 Apr. 2020. An interview completed by Elyssa Maxx Goodman.

48. **"[male impersonator]...archives."** Davis, 13 Apr. 2020 interview.

49. **"The girls...weekend in tips."** Davis, 13 Apr. 2020 interview.

50. **"The girls...a lesbian."** Ryan, Hugh. "The Three Lives of Malvina Schwartz." *Hugh Ryan*, 18 Oct. 2016, https://www.hughryan.org/recent-work/2016/10/18/the-three-lives-of-malvina-scwartz. Originally published on *Hazlitt*, 11 Oct. 2016.

51. **"long been...celebrities."** "Outside Listening In." *The Brooklyn*

Times-Union, 20 June 1935, p. 18, https://www.newspapers.com/news-page/577794320/.

52. **"the entertainment was kind of rough."** "Jewels Lifted, Gypsy Rose Is So Cold Now." *Daily News*, 29 Nov. 1936, https://www.newspapers.com/newspage/421389140/.

53. **April 12, 1938** "Gunfight at Dawn." *Daily News*, 13 Apr. 1938, https://www.newspapers.com/newspage/421583056/.

54. **grinning under...dark hair** Davis, Lisa E. "1935–1950s Blackie Dennis." *Drag King History*, https://dragkinghistory.com/1934-1950s-blackie-dennis/.

55. **Italian family...East Harlem** Davis, "1935–1950s Blackie Dennis."

56. **Emcee..."Stardust."** Davis, "1935–1950s Blackie Dennis."

57. **"the Montmartre of New York"** "Jimmy Kelly's The Montmartre of New York." Menu, ca. 1939–1940, Collection of the Museum of the City of New York, https://collections.mcny.org/Collection/Jimmy-Kelly's-24UAKVNGA3EC.html.

58. **"Because...money"** Davis, Lisa E. "Back in Buddy's Day: Drag's Original Lesbians Reflect on Their Heyday." *Xtra*, 28 Feb. 2006, https://xtramagazine.com/power/back-in-buddys-day-22160.

59. **Why would they hire a lesbian?** Davis, "Back in Buddy's Day."

60. **"Greenwich...strange." "When Ernie...everything"** Ryan, "The Three Lives."

61. **"I was a hoofer...routines."** Davis, "Back in Buddy's Day."

62. **"Out of top hat...very flat."** Ryan, "The Three Lives."

63. **if same-sex partners were spotted** Chauncey, *Gay New York*, p. 337.

64. **Charles Gagliodotto** Smith, Sandy. "Power Struggle after the Death in the Family." *Life*, 28 Feb. 1969, pp. 51–57.

65. **"If anybody...same people."** Seligman, Michael, and Jessica Bendinger. "Chapter 1: Who Is Anna Genovese?" *Mob Queens*, season 1, episode 1, 19 Aug. 2019, https://podcasts.apple.com/us/podcast/chapter-1-who-is-anna-genovese/id1474675655?i=1000447208711; Kane, Michael. "How NYC's Gay Bars Thrived because of the Mob." *New York Post*, 3 May 2014, https://nypost.com/2014/05/03/why-nycs-gay-bars-thriyed-because-of-the-mob/.

66. **September 1939** History.com Editors. "Germany Invades Poland." *History.com*, A+E Networks, 22 Feb. 2019, https://www.history.com/this-day-in-history/germany-invades-poland.

67. **December 7, 1941** Citino, Rob. "Pearl Harbor Attack, December 7, 1941." *The National WWII Museum, New Orleans*, 11 Nov. 2021, https://www.nationalww2museum.org/war/topics/pearl-harbor-december-7-1941.

Chapter 4

1. **"'Ladies of the Chorus,' curtain."** *This Is the Army*. Directed by Michael Curtiz, 1943.

2. **Soon...shoes.** *This Is the Army*, Curtiz.

3. **September 1, 1939** History.com Editors, "Germany Invades Poland."

4. **December 7, 1941** Citino, "Pearl Harbor Attack, December 7, 1941."

5. **16 million men** "WWII Veteran Statistics." *The National WWII Museum*, New Orleans, 2019, https://www.nationalww2museum.org/war/wwii-veteran-statistics.

6. **Special Services Division** Bérubé, p. 68.

7. **July 4, 1942** The Broadway League. "This Is the Army—Broadway Musical" *IBDB.com*, 2023, https://www.ibdb.com/broadway-production/this-is-the-army-1208.

8. **$45,000** "'This Is the Army' a Rousing Hit." *New York Times*, 5 July 1942, https://www.nytimes.com/1942/07/05/archives/this-is-the-army-a-rousing-hit-throng-pays-45000-at-opening-soldier.html.

9. **$10 million** Bergreen, Laurence. "Irving Berlin: This Is the Army." *Prologue Magazine* 28, no. 2, Summer 1996. Reprinted online in the National Archives, https://www.archives.gov/publications/prologue/1996/summer/irving-berlin-1.

10. **July 28, 1943** "Overview: This Is the Army." *Turner Classic Movies*, https://www.tcm.com/tcmdb/title/92968/this-is-the-army/#overview.

11. **August 14, 1943** "Overview: This Is the Army."

12. **300 soldiers** "300 Soldiers in Musical; Begin Rehearsals Today for 'This Is the Army,' Due July 4." *New York Times*, 4 June 1942, https://timesmachine.nytimes.com/timesmachine/1942/06/04/104315206.html?pageNumber=22.

13. **"A Soldier's Dream", "Ladies of the Chorus"** *This Is the Army*, Curtiz.

14. **"What the Well-Dressed Man in Harlem Will Wear"** *This Is the Army*, Curtiz.

15. **"Stage Door Canteen"** *This Is the Army*, Curtiz.

16. **According to Barclift,** Chancellor, Alexander. "De-Lightful, De-Licious, De-Ceitful." *New York Times*, 29 Nov. 1998, https://www.nytimes.com/1998/11/29/books/delightful-delicious-deceitful.html; **inspired the classic** Pacheco, Patrick. "Cole Porter's Secret Life." *Los Angeles Times*, 15 Oct. 2000, https://www.latimes.com/archives/la-xpm-2000-oct-15-ca-36688-story.html.

17. **souvenir program calls back** The original 1942 *This Is the Army* souvenir program, found via online auction. https://www.ebay.com/itm/223974556068.

18. **"Morale is fuel...entertainment."** *This Is the Army* souvenir program.

19. **Pearl Harbor...91% of Americans** "How Did Public Opinion About Entering World War II Change between 1939 and 1941?" *USHMM.org*, 2018, https://exhibitions.ushmm.org/americans-and-the-holocaust/us-public-opinion-world-war-II-1939-1941.

20. **"wholesome, patriotic, and masculine."** Bérubé, p. 77. For more information, I recommend reading the entire Bérubé chapter "GI Drag: A Gay Refuge."

21. **Drag...queerness** Bérubé, p. 72.

22. **When drag was funny...relatable and comfortable** Bérubé, p. 71.

23. **South Pacific, "Honey Bun"** *South Pacific*. Directed by Joshua Logan, 1958. You can watch this clip on YouTube at https://www.youtube.com/watch?v=XjHFQDJbozk. Also referenced by Bérubé, p. 85, p. 88.

24. **"A hundred and one...tonight"** "Honey Bun-South Pacific." *YouTube*, https://www.youtube.com/watch?v=XjHFQDJbozk.

25. **The Andrews Sisters...Gypsy Rose Lee...Carmen Miranda** Bérubé, p. 85.

26. **her depiction trite** Bérubé, p. 89.

27. **"It's a great show...your country."** "Eisenhower Sees Show." *The Morning Post*: Camden, NJ, 3 Dec. 1945, https://www.newspapers.com/newspage/447689629/.

28. **Gay soldiers...armed services** Bérubé, p. 72.

29. **At each military examination** Bérubé, p. 20.

30. **Nurture those bonds** Miller, *Out of the Past*, p. 233, pp. 238–39.

31. **In 1952…mental illness** McHenry, Sara E. "'Gay Is Good': History of Homosexuality in the *DSM* and Modern Psychiatry." *American Journal of Psychiatry Residents' Journal*, vol. 18, no. 1, 8 Sept. 2022, pp. 4–5, https://doi.org/10.1176/appi.ajp-rj.2022.180103.

32. **"bring back the glories…art"** Paulson, Don, and Roger Simpson. *An Evening at the Garden of Allah: A Gay Cabaret in Seattle*. New York, Columbia University Press, 1996, p. 80.

33. **"Divorcing…audiences"** Dauphin, Mara. "'A Bit of Woman in Every Man': Creating Queer Community in Female Impersonation." *Valley Humanities Review*, Spring 2012, https://portal.lvc.edu/vhr/2012/Articles/dauphin.pdf.

34. **"We hope to reach…entertainment."** Paulson and Simpson, p. 80.

35. **Genovese family's monopoly** Jeffreys, 26 May 2022 interview.

36. **Federal-Aid Highway Act of 1944, nearly 40,000 miles** "Interstate Highway System—The Myths." *U.S. Department of Transportation, Federal Highway Administration*, https://www.fhwa.dot.gov/interstate/interstatemyths.cfm.

37. **"You were making…a novelty."** Paulson and Simpson, pp. 80–81.

38. **"We were very famous…a beautiful show."** Brandall, Bernie. 22 Apr. 2020. An interview completed by Elyssa Maxx Goodman.

39. **"Men's jackets were loose…wanted to believe."** *Stormé: The Lady of the Jewel Box*. Directed by Michelle Parkerson, 1987.

40. **"It was very easy… I was still a woman."** *Stormé: The Lady of the Jewel Box*, Parkerson.

41. **"Isn't just an excuse…as his forte."** Bourke, George. "Night Life." *The Miami Herald*, 5 Dec. 1951, p. 18A, https://www.newspapers.com/newspage/627127561/.

42. **Somebody told me…and they said "a girl."** *A Chorus Line*, 1975. Book by James Kirkwood, Jr., and Nicholas Dante. Music by Marvin Hamlisch, Lyrics by Edward Kleban. Reprinted in Coleman, Bud. "The Jewel Box Revue: America's Longest-Running, Touring Drag show." *Theatre History Studies* 17, 1997, p. 79. *ProQuest*, http://ezproxy.nypl.org/login?url=https://www.proquest.com/scholarly-journals/jewel-box-revue-americas-longest-running-touring/docview/2160549/se-2.

43. **"It was really tacky," "the asshole of show business,"** Coleman, p. 79.

44. **has been contested** Mann, Kurt. "The Kurt Mann Story." *Queer Music Heritage*, https://www.queermusicheritage.com/fem-mann1.html.

45. **it's noteworthy that** Coleman, p. 80.

46. **many ethnicities** Coleman, p. 89.

47. **he remembered Benner and Brown hiring** Mann, "The Kurt Mann Story."

48. **December 3, 1958** "Estimates for This Week." *Variety*, 3 Dec. 1958, p. 9, https://archive.org/details/variety213-1958-12/page/n9/mode/2up?q=jewel+box.

49. **sixteen hours...risk arrest** de la Croix, p. 239.

50. **took off lipstick and wore sunglasses** Mann, "The Kurt Mann Story."

51. **"Locals knew...next show"** Mann, "The Kurt Mann Story."

52. **"violent homophobic boycotts...community."** Parkerson, Michelle, quoted in Drorbaugh, Elizabeth. "Storme DeLarverie and The Jewel Box Revue." *Crossing the Stage: Controversies on Cross-Dressing*, ed. Lesley Ferris. London and New York: Routledge, 2005, p. 132.

53. **"During the 1960s..." "too strong to counter," new wave of liberalism** Coleman, p. 90.

54. **"You've got to figure...for a living."** Jeffreys, Joe E. "Who's No Lady? Excerpts from an Oral History of New York City's 82 Club." *New York Folklore*, vol. 19, no. 1, 1993, p. 185. *ProQuest*, http://ezproxy.nypl.org/login?url=https://www.proquest.com/scholarly-journals/whos-no-lady-excerpts-oral-history-new-york-citys/docview/1290832444/se-2.

55. **"When we walked in...kind of person here."** Jeffreys, "Who's No Lady?"

56. **850,000 New Yorkers** Roberts, Sam. "New York 1945; The War Was Ending. Times Square Exploded. Change Was Coming." *New York Times*, 30 July 1995, https://www.nytimes.com/1995/07/30/nyregion/new-york-1945-the-war-was-ending-times-square-exploded-change-was-coming.html.

57. **With no money down...$75–$125 a month** Moss, Brian. "Levittown and the Suburban Dream of Postwar New York." *New York Daily News*, https://www.nydailynews.com/new-york/levittown-suburban-dream-postwar-new-york-article-1.820845.

58. **whites only..."open housing"** Lambert, Bruce. "At 50, Levittown Contends with Its Legacy of Bias." *New York Times*, 28 Dec. 1997,

https://www.nytimes.com/1997/12/28/nyregion/at-50-levittown-contends-with-its-legacy-of-bias.html.

59. **With the home loan...less frequency.** Lambert, "At 50, Levittown."

60. **Between 1940 and 1950...suburbs.** Roberts, "New York 1945."

61. **white middle-and upper-class...grew deeper.** Heap, p. 277.

62. **suburban communities...among others.** Heap, p. 278.

63. **"Uptown...bohemian."** Strausbaugh, p. 275

64. **Located...lay underfoot.** Seligman, Michael, and Jessica Bendinger. "Chapter 5: Cheers, Queers!" *Mob Queens*, season 1, episode 5, 9 Sept. 2019, https://podcasts.apple.com/us/podcast/chapter-5-cheers-queers/id1474675655?i=1000449100971.

65. **"never a dull moment," and "It's Smart to be seen at Club 181."** Club 181 Advertisement. *New York Daily News*, 21 May 1946, p. 394, https://www.newspapers.com/newspage/444819927/.

66. **"Welcome to the 181...knows the difference."** "Which-Sex-Is-Which Club Loses License." *New York Daily News*, 28 Apr. 1951, p. 21. https://www.newspapers.com/newspage/451386101/.

67. **$500,000 annually** Seligman, Michael, and Jessica Bendinger. "Chapter 7: Blood in the Snow." *Mob Queens*, season 1, episode 7, 23 Sept. 2019, https://podcasts.apple.com/us/podcast/chapter-7-blood-in-the-snow/id1474675655?i=1000450839683

68. **"It was illegal...to see it."** Davis, 13 Apr. 2020 interview.

69. **Titanic...I'm Natalie Wood."** "A Case of Mistaken Identity." *Ladylike*, no. 38, 1999, p. 36.

70. **a wooden bar...a bandstand** *Moroccan Village, 23 W. 8th Street*. Postcard, https://www.cardcow.com/523685/greenwich-village-new-york-moroccan-23-8th-street/.

71. **"The Village's Gayest Nightspot"** Advertisement. *New York Daily News*, 18 Dec. 1947, p. 411, https://www.newspapers.com/newspage/445683320/.

72. **"Wall Street brokers, racketeers, the rich and famous"** Davis, Lisa E. "Map." *Under the Mink*, https://undertheminkonwix.wixsite.com/underthemink/resources.

73. **February 25, 1950** "Club Casualties." *New York Daily News*, 26 Feb. 1950, p. 87. https://www.newspapers.com/newspage/448785784/.

74. **But the robbers...on fingers.** "Club Casualties," p. 87.

75. **"In 1949...they said."** Davis, "Back in Buddy's Day."

76. **"branded a hangout...sexes"** "Which-Sex-is-Which Club Loses License," *New York Daily News*, 28 April 1951, pp. 21, https://www.newspapers.com/newspage/451386101/.

77. **"Male performers...their own sex."** "Which-Sex-is-Which Club Loses License," *New York Daily News*, 28 April 1951, pp. 21, https://www.newspapers.com/newspage/451386101/.

78. **10:30 p.m., 12:30 a.m., and 2:30 a.m.** Jeffreys, "Who's No Lady?"

79. **standing on...the time** Jeffreys, 26 May 2022 interview.

80. **Lines...avenue** Jeffreys, "Who's No Lady?"

81. **Drag became...fetishize.** Jeffreys, 26 May 2022 interview.

82. **"You name the age, they came,"** Jeffreys, "Who's No Lady?"

83. **"The audience...with us."** James Bidgood is interviewed in the film *In Search of Avery Willard*. Directed by Cary Kehayan, 2012, https://vimeo.com/76935485.

84. **"That crowd...not seen."** Jeffreys, 26 May 2022 interview.

85. **"I think eventually...82 Club."** Jeffreys, "Who's No Lady?"

86. **"Sexual perverts...actual communists."** D'Emilio, John. *Sexual Politics, Sexual Communities: The Making of a Homosexual Minority in the United States, 1940–1970*. Chicago: University of Chicago Press, 1983, p. 41.

87. **126 "perverts"** "126 Perverts Discharged; State Department Reports Total Ousted Since Jan. 1, 1951." *New York Times*, 26 Mar. 1952, https://timesmachine.nytimes.com/timesmachine/1952/03/26/84247094.html?pageNumber=25.

88. **"There is...security risks."** "126 Perverts Discharged."

89. **double to 381...nearly 300 more** Kaiser, Charles. *The Gay Metropolis: The Landmark History of Gay Life in America*. New York: Grove Press, 2007, pp. 78–81.

90. **an executive order..."sexual perversion."** D'Emilio, p. 44

91. **In 1953...the city** D'Emilio, p. 50.

92. **"High police officials...and perverts."** "23 More Undesirables Are Seized in Times Square as Round-Up Spreads; More Are Seized in City Round-Up." *New York Times*, 1 Aug. 1954, https://timesmachine.nytimes.com/timesmachine/1954/08/01/92831866.pdf.

93. **"Inspector...brought a wave...murder."** "23 More Undesirables Are Seized."

94. **Their message..."an oppressed minority...community."** D'Emilio, p. 58, p. 65.

95. **Marxism...community** D'Emilio, pp. 80–81.

96. **The conservative...politics** D'Emilio, p. 81.

97. **"pattern of behavior...state"** D'Emilio, p. 81.

98. **"not seeking...citizens"** D'Emilio, p. 84.

99. **"We hear...very pleasant."** Excerpts from "The Homosexual in Our Society" from the Pacifica Radio Archives appear and are transcribed. Brancaccio, Paul. "Seeing Themselves Queerly." *ArcGIS StoryMaps*, 26 Apr. 2020, https://storymaps.arcgis.com/stories/c8d52b1 2ad0542afaafe985500cfd670.

100. **"feel[s] like...to anything."** Brancaccio, "Seeing Themselves Queerly."

101. **September 11, 1961** *The Rejected*. Directed by Dick Christian, 1961. Bay Area Television Archive at San Francisco State University, https://diva.sfsu.edu/collections/sfbatv/bundles/225539.

102. **"We think the swish...rejected them..."** "The Rejected-Bay Area Television Archive." *The Bay Area Television Archive at San Francisco State University*, 2011, diva.sfsu.edu/collections/sfbatv/bundles/225539.

103. **"Back then...ne'er-do-wells."** As quoted by Strausbaugh, p. 230.

104. **cocktails, steak, and shrimp** Jeffreys, "Who's No Lady?"

105. **"The Bun"** Seligman and Bendinger, "Chapter 9: The Queen's Not Dead."

106. **Errol Flynn...penis** McLeod, Kembrew. "From the 82 Club to Club 82." *The Downtown Pop Underground*, 3 Sept. 2018, https://dsps.lib.uiowa.edu/downtownpopunderground/story/from-the-82-club-to-club-82/.

107. **"That was no lady!"** "Matchbook Covers." *Queer Music Heritage*, https://www.queermusicheritage.com/fem-mat.html.

108. **declaring him** "Another Julian Eltinge?" *Hit!*. September 1948. Republished on *Queer Music Heritage*, https://www.queermusicheritage.com/f-russell-kitt.html.

109. **"Offstage...youth"** "Another Julian Eltinge?"

110. **"high on the list of talented 'femme mimics'"** Winchell, Wal-

ter. "On Broadway." *Chillicothe Gazette*, 7 Apr. 1951, p. 6, https://www.newspapers.com/newspage/292156662/.

111. **"When Kit Russell...leopard license."** "Restaurateur Sees Spots Before Eyes and Calls Cops." *The Brooklyn Daily Eagle*, 21 June 1951, p. 7, https://www.newspapers.com/image/686546799/?terms=%22Kit%20Russell%22&match=1.

112. **She was seeking...queer herself; 750,000** Seligman and Bendinger, "Chapter 5: Cheers, Queers!"

113. **"If she's bisexual...easier."** Seligman and Bendinger, "Chapter 5: Cheers, Queers!"

114. **Anna and Duke** Seligman and Bendinger, "Chapter 9: The Queen's Not Dead."

115. **spend it all on alcohol** Seligman, Michael, and Jessica Bendinger. "Chapter 10: Off With His Head." *Mob Queens*, season 1, episode 10, 22 Oct. 2019, https://podcasts.apple.com/us/podcast/chapter-10-off-with-his-head/id1474675655?i=1000454304838.

116. **"model"** Jeffreys, "Who's No Lady?"

117. **never a formal law** Ryan, "When Dressing in Drag."

118. **check their underwear** Ryan, "How Dressing in Drag."

119. **"correct" attire, "three-piece" rule** Ryan, "How Dressing in Drag."

120. **she helped...gender affirmation surgery** *P.S. Burn This Letter Please*. Directed by Michael Seligman and Jennifer Tiexiera, 2020.

121. **attempted suicide...jail** Seligman and Bendinger, "Chapter 10: Off with His Head."

122. **found murdered...blue DeSoto sedan...ignition** "Village Nitery Boss Found Slain in Auto." *New York Daily News*, 20 June 1953, p. 118, https://www.newspapers.com/newspage/453461987/.

123. **East 37th Street and 3rd Avenue** "Body Found of Club Owner." *Poughkeepsie Journal*, 19 June 1953, p. 1, https://www.newspapers.com/clip/6282059/steve-franse-82-club-death/.

124. **"I won't kill you...kill yourself."** Seligman and Bendinger, "Chapter 9: The Queen's Not Dead."

125. **The Bijou Cinema** Richardson, Lance. "Cruising the Bijou, a Hidden Underground Cinema and Sex Den." *Bedford + Bowery*, 27 June 2014, https://bedfordandbowery.com/2014/06/discovering-the-bijou-a-hidden-underground-cinema-and-cruising-den/.

126. **"Pink Narcissus...pink."** Edgecomb, Sean Frederic. Interview with James Bidgood. "Camping out with James Bidgood: The Auteur of *Pink Narcissus* Tells All." *Bright Lights Film Journal*, 1 May 2006, https://brightlightsfilm.com/camping-james-bidgood-auteur-pink-narcissus-tells/#.ZDQX2ezMLBK.

127. **"the best Pearl Bailey imitation in town"** Club 82 Program, 1969, quoting *Variety*. Republished on *Queer Music Heritage*, https://www.queermusicheritage.com/FEMALE/Club%2082/1969%20 Program/club82-1969-19.jpg.

128. **"Cops Grab 44 in Dresses—And a Real Girl in Slacks"** Tyler, Robin. 13 Apr. 2020. An interview completed by Elyssa Maxx Goodman. Original article by Alfred T. Hendricks, *New York Post*, 28 Oct. 1962.

129. **"I thought...82 Club."** Tyler, 13 Apr. 2020 interview.

130. **Tyler...not a man** Tyler, 13 Apr. 2020 interview.

131. **"He said...the first!"** Tyler, 13 Apr. 2020 interview.

132. **first...Diller** Gianoulis, Tina. "Robin Tyler." *GLBTQ Archives*, 2015, http://www.glbtqarchive.com/ssh/tyler_r_ssh_S.pdf.

133. **Tyler...couples** Tyler, 13 Apr. 2020 interview; Gianoulis, "Robin Tyler."

134. **"Astonishingly skillful"**, **"sharp wit"** Chapman, John. "'New Faces of '56' Zippy, Cheery, Tuneful, Youthful and Intelligent." *New York Daily News*, 15 June 1956, p. 581, https://www.newspapers.com/ newspage/456058669/.

135. **"This would be...extraordinarily talented woman."** Sillman, Leonard. *Here Lies Leonard Sillman, Straightened Out at Last*. New York: Citadel, 1959, p. 90. Accessed on Archive.org, https://archive.org/de-tails/hereliesleonards00sill/page/n101/mode/2up.

136. **Connie Dickson** Osgood, Nancy. "Meet T.C. And His Mrs., Connie." *St. Petersburg Times*, 16 May 1962. Republished on *Queer Music Heritage*, https://www.queermusicheritage.com/DRAG/Jones%20TC/ b141-1962-TCJones-loose.jpg.

137. **nineteen Siamese cats** "Who's Who in the Cast." Playbill, 23 Sept. 1957, p. 29. Republished on *Queer Music Heritage*, https://queermusic-heritage.com/drag-jones.html#.

138. **"The rest of us...absolute burlesque."** Knight, Wes. "T.C. Jones: The Other Side of the Coin." *Mattachine Review*, vol. 1, no. 7, Christmas 1955. pp. 8–10.

139. **"He's the only...offensive."** Chapman, John. "Curtain Going Up!"

New York Daily News, 8 July 1956, p. 12, https://www.newspapers.com/newspage/455955340/.

140. **"Women smile...theatrical tradition."** Freedley, George. "History of Female Impersonation." *New York Times*, 16 Dec. 1956, p. 247, https://timesmachine.nytimes.com/timesmachine/1956/12/16/84939524.html?pageNumber=247.

141. **"Oh, the poor dear, she's bald."** "T.C. Jones' New Face Fools 'Em Every Time." *New York Daily News*, 22 June 1956, p. 334 https://www.newspapers.com/newspage/455223114/.

142. **"the road company Pearl"** "On the Town." *New York Daily News*, 13 Jan. 1971, p. 214, https://www.newspapers.com/newspage/463943872/.

143. **"the world's first television show for gay men and women"** O'Connor, John J. "TV: Cable Focuses on Homosexuals." *New York Times*, 2 June 1977, https://www.nytimes.com/1977/06/02/archives/tv-cable-focuses-on-homosexuals.html.

144. **"There's a great...just a woman."** "Emerald City Gay TV #46-Lynne Carter Part 2." *YouTube*, https://www.youtube.com/watch?t=289&v=wfPx094pjsc&feature=youtu.be.

145. **"I really wasn't harassed...where it's all at."** "Emerald City Gay TV #46."

146. **"Brooks Costumes was the biggest contributor to drag queenism in America"** *P.S. Burn This Letter Please*, Seligman and Tiexiera.

147. **Claudio...feathers** *P.S. Burn This Letter Please*, Seligman and Tiexiera.

148. **September 15, 1958** "17 of 33 Wigs Stolen at the Met Recovered." Camden, NJ: *The Courier Post*, 11 Dec. 1958, p. 21, https://www.newspapers.com/clip/18866465/met-wig-caper/.

149. **promptly stole...$3,000.** *P.S. Burn This Letter Please*, Seligman and Tiexiera. For more about this theft, please check out this fabulous documentary film.

150. **Josephine and Claudia...Rikers Island.** *P.S. Burn This Letter Please*, Seligman and Tiexiera.

151. **"Part ego...we got in."** *P.S. Burn This Letter Please*, Seligman and Tiexiera.

152. **109 East 12th Street, West 56th Street** Minette. Interview by Ms. Bob and Carol Kleinmayer, "Flashback: Part-Time Lady...Full Time Queen." *Ladylike* 36, 1999, pp. 32–36, https://queermusicheritage.

com/DRAG/Minette/1999%20Ladylike%20n37%20-p32-6%20Mi-nette%20interview%20pt2.pdf.

153. **"means many things...I've heard."** Minette. *Recollections of a Part-Time Lady*. New York: Flower-Beneath-the-Foot Press, 1979. Republished on *Queer Music Heritage*, https://www.queermusicheritage.com/drag-minette1.html.

154. **"The principal...female impersonator."** Minette, *Recollections*.

155. **"I felt so...gorgeous."** Minette, *Recollections*.

156. **"alcoholic haven...futility."** *Life* quoted by Carlson, Jen. "Sammy's Bowery Follies: Revisiting the Old 'Alcoholic Haven.'" *Gothamist*, 4 Jan. 2013, https://gothamist.com/food/sammys-bowery-follies-revisiting-the-old-alcoholic-haven.

157. **Rose Revere** Minette, *Recollections*.

158. **$10 a month...dented cans** Ms. Bob and Kleinmayer, "Flashback: Part-Time Lady."

159. **"stitch bitch"** Ms. Bob and Kleinmayer, "Flashback: Part-Time Lady."

160. **beaded black 1920s cocktail gown** Ms. Bob and Kleinmayer, "Flashback: Part-Time Lady."

161. **But...familiar bar.** Ms. Bob and Kleinmayer, "Flashback: Part-Time Lady."

162. **1958...two days** Ms. Bob and Kleinmayer, "Flashback: Part-Time Lady."

163. **"After a while...work for him."** Minette, *Recollections*.

164. **$32,500** Arbus, Diane. "Two Female Impersonators Backstage, N.Y.C." Gelatin silver print, ca. 1961, https://www.phillips.com/detail/diane-arbus/NY040319/55.

165. **"I really believe...photograph them."** Sayej, Nadja. "Unsung Portraits by Diane Arbus in Toronto." *Forbes*, 9 Sept. 2020, https://www.forbes.com/sites/nadjasayej/2020/09/09/unsung-portraits-by-diane-arbus-in-toronto/?sh=36017b5b6034.

166. **"He worked for...his dream."** amNY. "'Magic Time' at the Caffe Cino." *amNY*, 3 Dec. 2015, https://www.amny.com/news/magic-time-at-the-caffe-cino-2/.

167. **"This [the Caffé Cino] is the beginning!... They're lying."** Bottoms, Stephen J. *Playing Underground: A Critical History of the 1960s Off-Off-Broadway Movement*. Ann Arbor: University of Michigan Press, 2004, p. 7.

168. **red-and-yellow sign** Davis, Amanda, and Jay Shockley. "Caffe Cino." *NYC LGBT Historic Sites Project*, Mar. 2017, revised Nov. 2022, https://www.nyclgbtsites.org/site/caffe-cino/.

169. **the machine...the illusion.** Frost, Natasha. "The Gay Coffeehouse Where Off-Off Broadway Theater Was Born." *Atlas Obscura*, 9 Feb. 2018, https://www.atlasobscura.com/articles/caffe-cino-joe-cino-gay-off-off-broadway-theater.

170. **balloons, tinsel, and handmade mobiles** McElroy, Steven. "Portal to Off Off Broadway's Early Days." *New York Times*, 7 Dec. 2011, https://www.nytimes.com/2011/12/11/theater/donation-to-library-opens-new-portal-to-caffe-cino.html.

171. **art by friends and pictures of gorgeous celebrities** Strausbaugh, p. 360.

172. **"Cancer...was supreme"** amNY, "'Magic Time.'"

173. **Electricity...John Torrey.** Strausbaugh, p. 361.

174. **In full violation...the Mafia** Strausbaugh, p. 361.

175. **"It's Magic Time!"** McLeod, Kembrew. "Caffe Cino." *The Downtown Pop Underground*, 25 Aug. 2018, https://dsps.lib.uiowa.edu/downtownpopunderground/place/caffe-cino/.

176. **"Well, can we write a play about a screaming queen going crazy alone in her room one afternoon?"** Stone, Wendell Corbin. "Theatre at Caffe Cino: The Aesthetics and Politics of Revolt, 1958–1968." PhD diss., Louisiana State University, 2001, p. 318, https://digitalcommons.lsu.edu/gradschool_disstheses/318.

177. **"You. Are a faggot.... You know?"** Wilson, Lanford. *The Madness of Lady Bright.* 1964, p. 20, https://www.scribd.com/document/327642297/The-Madness-of-Lady-Bright.

178. **"the incredible freedom...like crazy"** Quoted in Frost, Natasha. "The Gay Coffeehouse."

Chapter 5

1. **100,000 people** Smith, David. "How This 1967 Vietnam War Protest Carried the Seeds of American Division." *The Guardian*, 21 Oct. 2017, https://www.theguardian.com/us-news/2017/oct/21/1967-vietnam-war-protest-american-division.

2. **"A drag queen is an amateur—a female impersonator is a professional"** Penny, Daniel. "The Last Queen of Greenwich Vil-

lage." *New Yorker*, 25 June 2017, https://www.newyorker.com/culture/persons-of-interest/the-last-queen-of-greenwich-village.

3. **"Up to the late...always draw it."** Charles Pierce quoted in Wallraff, John. *From Drags to Riches: The Untold Story of Charles Pierce.* New York: Routledge, 2003, p. 213.

4. **blond flip...dark liner** Photograph of Tish in Penny, Daniel, "The Last Queen."

5. **"No prudes will like it"** "Femmes Fatales: New York's Crazy Horse Cafe." *Female Mimics*, vol. 1, no. 5, 1965, pp. 44–51, https://archive.org/details/femalemimics15unse/page/44/mode/2up?view=theater.

6. **"Well, go soon and see for yourself!"** "Femmes Fatales."

7. **alcohol in brown paper bags** Jeffreys, Joe E. 16 June 2022. An interview completed by Elyssa Maxx Goodman.

8. **gay bar's backroom today** Jeffreys, 16 June 2022 interview.

9. **a fight broke out...the hospital** "Real Jumpin' Crazy Horse." *New York Daily News*, 27 Dec. 1965, p. 337, https://www.newspapers.com/newspage/463301698/.

10. **"Any woman...has talent"** "Femmes Fatales."

11. **His makeup...construction paper** Photograph in "Femmes Fatales."

12. **"I knew I could...better comically."** Roberts, Pudgy. "All About Your Editor: Mr. Pudgy Roberts." *The Great Female Mimics,* vol. 1, no. 1, Jan, 1973, pp. 24–29. Republished on *Queer Music Heritage*, https://www.queermusicheritage.com/f-roberts-pudgy.html.

13. **"And it was...in my life."** Ms. Bob and Kleinmayer, "Flashback: Part-Time Lady."

14. **"When I'm billed...an illusion of femininity."** Truman, Gil. "Girls Who Are and Can't: An Interview with Pudgy Roberts." *Female Mimics* vol. 1, no. 12, Spring 1968. Reprinted on Pagan Press Books, https://paganpressbooks.com/jpl/PUDGY.HTM.

15. **"a tragic farce."** Truman, "Girls Who Are."

16. **"more than pleased...our people."** Roberts, Pudgy. "Editorial." *Female Impersonators*, no. 1, Winter 1969, p. 3, https://www.digitaltransgenderarchive.net/downloads/ks65hc53c.

17. **"How to Dress as a Female Impersonator" and "Album of Impersonator Bests!"** *Female Impersonators*, Winter 1969 (cover).

18. **"Hard work...impersonation will be."** Roberts, Pudgy. *Female*

Impersonator's Handbook. Newark: Capri Publishers, 1967. Republished on *Queer Music Heritage,* https://www.queermusicheritage.com/fem-mags3.html.

19. **"the world's leading authority on cross-dressing."** Roberts, *The Great Female Mimics.*

20. **"The other sailors...beautiful, beautiful woman."** Seligman, Michael. 15 Mar. 2020. An interview completed by Elyssa Maxx Goodman.

21. **"[Drag] happened...at one time."** Seligman, 15 Mar. 2020 interview.

22. **"You are never going to be a lady if you weren't a gentleman first."** Strausbaugh, p. 459.

23. **"look queen"** Seligman, 15 Mar. 2020 interview.

24. **39,000-square-foot** Berke, Ned. "Salvation Army Has Officially Moved in to Former Cotillion Terrace Building on 18th Avenue." *Bklyner,* 15 May 2014, https://bklyner.com/salvation-army-officially-moved-former-cotillion-terrace-building-18th-avenue-bensonhurst/.

25. **1,600 tickets...sold out.** Seligman, 15 Mar. 2020 interview.

26. **"Anybody who was anybody in the drag world went"** *P.S. Burn This Letter Please,* Seligman and Tiexiera.

27. **"You walk up...they love it."** Bleyer, Jennifer. "Satin Frocks and Housing Law." *New York Times,* 24 June 2007, https://www.nytimes.com/2007/06/24/nyregion/thecity/24drag.html.

28. **"once-a-year funfest freak-out...a fantastic success."** "Best of the Bunch: Daisy Dee's Ball." *Female Mimics,* vol. 6, no. 2, Spring 1975, p. 4, https://archive.org/details/femalemimics62unse/page/4/mode/2up.

29. **"I loved going... It was very important."** Charles, Charity. 29 Mar. 2021. An interview completed by Elyssa Maxx Goodman.

30. **"You had gay people...if you will."** Seligman, 15 Mar. 2020 interview.

31. **closed down...red carpet** Seligman, 15 Mar. 2020 interview.

32. **Permits...event** Seligman, 15 Mar. 2020 interview.

33. **mafiosos' wives...rejudged** Seligman, 15 Mar. 2020 interview.

34. **getting an invite...high honor...to be among them.** Charles, 29 Mar. 2021 interview.

35. **Jaye Joyce was the group's leader** Jenkins, Dale Sharpe. "Pearl Box

Revue." *Queer Music Heritage*, June 2017, https://queermusicheritage. com/drag-pearl.html.

36. **"at a time when drag queens...disowned by family."** Jenkins.

37. *Call Me MISSter* The Pearl Box Revue. *Call Me MISSter.* Snake Eyes, 1972.

38. **quit the chic** Hunt, Richard P. "Mayor Quits Club over Bias Charge; He Notes Allegations That New York A.C. Bars Negroes and Jews Accused by 2 Groups Wagner Quits New York A.C. After Hearing Charge of Bias Rules on Entry Attorney General Quit." *New York Times*, 10 Feb. 1962, https://www.nytimes.com/1962/02/10/ archives/mayor-quits-club-over-bias-charge-he-notes-allegations- that-the-new.html.

39. **began a campaign...the city** Morgan, Thaddeus. "The Gay 'Sip-In' That Drew from the Civil Rights Movement to Fight Discrimination." *History.com*, A+E Networks, 18 June 2018, https://www. history.com/news/gay-rights-sip-in-julius-bar.

40. **$1 billion** Stinson, John. *New York World's Fair 1964–1965 Corporation Records, 1959–1971.* New York Public Library Humanities and Social Sciences Library Manuscripts and Archives Division, May 1986, p. iii, https://www.nypl.org/sites/default/files/archivalcollections/ pdf/nywf64.pdf.

41. **"He didn't feel...queer life."** Priborkin, Emily. "The Legacy of the Stonewall Riots." *American University*, 18 June 2019, https://www.amer- ican.edu/sis/news/20190618-the-legacy-of-the-stonewall-riots.cfm.

42. **Mattachines fought to end the practice by 1966**, Chauncey, "The Forgotten History."

43. **April 21, 1966** "The 'Sip-In' at Julius' Bar in 1966." *National Park Service*, https://www.nps.gov/articles/julius-bar-1966.htm.

44. **"Intimate encounters...in general.** Morgan, "The Gay 'Sip-In.'"

45. **It took five tries...denied.** Farber, Jim. "Before the Stonewall Uprising, There Was the 'Sip-In.'" *New York Times*, 20 Apr. 2016, https://www. nytimes.com/2016/04/21/nyregion/before-the-stonewall-riots-there- was-the-sip-in.html; Johnson, Thomas A. "3 Deviates Invite Exclusion by Bars; but They Visit Four Before Being Refused Service, in a Test of S.L.A. Rules." *New York Times*, 22 Apr. 1966, https://timesmachine.ny- times.com/timesmachine/1966/04/22/79298595.html?pageNumber=43.

46. **a way to entrap the government** Farber.

47. **But by then...Preservation.** "Julius' Bar, an LGBT Landmark."

Village Preservation, 5 Dec. 2017, https://www.villagepreservation. org/2017/12/05/julius-bar-an-lgbt-landmark/.

48. **"was to be outlandish...pass."** Arcade, Penny. 17 Nov. 2020. An interview completed by Elyssa Maxx Goodman.

49. **"The studio...photo shoots."** Siegel, Marc, et al. "Jack Smith Is an Ordinary Name." In "Jack Smith Report," *La Furia Umana*, 2016: https://www.gladstonegallery.com/sites/default/files/JS_ LaFuriaUmana_2016_1.pdf.

50. **"you can't get artistic results with 'Normals.'"** Verevis, Constantine. *Flaming Creatures*. New York: Columbia University Press, 2019, p. 19.

51. **Rivera immediately...purpose**. Siegel, Marc. "...FOR MM." *Criticism*, vol. 56, no. 2, 2014, pp. 361–74. *Project MUSE*, https://muse. jhu.edu/article/557255.

52. **devout Roman Catholic...his life** Martin, Douglas. "Mario Montez, a Warhol Glamour Avatar, Dies at 78." *New York Times*, 4 Oct. 2013, https://www.nytimes.com/2013/10/04/arts/mario-montez-a-warhol-glamour-avatar-dies-at-78.html.

53. **lovers and creative partners** Siegel, "... FOR MM."

54. **"there were lots...their costumes."** Hoberman, J. "Up on the Roof: On the Making of Jack Smith's *Flaming Creatures*." *Moving Image Source,* 5 Jan. 2012, http://www.movingimagesource.us/articles/up-on-the-roof-20120105.

55. **film...Camera Barn** Hoberman, "Up on the Roof."

56. **Tavel...earthquake** Hoberman, "Up on the Roof."

57. **"The Spanish Lady"** Siegel, Marc. "Marc Siegel on Mario Montez (1935–2013)." *Artforum*, https://www.artforum.com/passages/marc-siegel-on-mario-montez-1935-2013-43473.

58. **"I started making...the way through."** Smith, Jack. Interview by Sylvère Lotringer. "Uncle Fishook and the Sacred Baby Poo-Poo of Art." *Semiotext(e): Schizo Culture*, Vol. III, No. 2, 1978, p. 192, https://mono-skop.org/images/f/f9/Semiotexte_Vol_3_No_2_Schizo-Culture.pdf.

59. **April 29, 1963** "Jack Smith: *Flaming Creatures*, 1962–1963." *MoMA*, https://www.moma.org/learn/moma_learning/jack-smith-flaming-creatures-1962-1963/.

60. **A March 1964 screening...obscenity** "Avant-Garde Movie Seized as Obscene." *New York Times*, 4 Mar. 1964, https://www.nytimes. com/1964/03/04/archives/avantgarde-movie-seized-as-obscene.html.

61. **April 3, 1964...publication** Kreitner, Richard. "This Week in 'Nation' History: Susan Sontag on the Avant-Garde, Communism and the Left." *The Nation*, 22 June 2013, https://www.thenation.com/article/archive/week-nation-history-susan-sontag-avant-garde-communism-and-left/.

62. **"The only thing...shameful to apologize."** Sontag, Susan. "A Feast for Open Eyes." *The Nation*, 3 Apr. 1964, pp. 374–76, https://thenation.s3.amazonaws.com/pdf/feast1964.pdf.

63. **June 2, 1964** Frye, Brian L. "The Dialectic of Obscenity." *Hamline Law Review* 229–278, Hofstra Univ. Legal Studies Research Paper, Vol. 35, No. 11-10, 22 Mar. 2011. Available at SSRN.com, https://ssrn.com/abstract=1792810 or http://dx.doi.org/10.2139/ssrn.1792810.

64. **"moot because...obscene."** Frye, p. 250.

65. **four countries and twenty-two states** MoMA, "Jack Smith: *Flaming Creatures*, 1962–1963."

66. **"then *that writing*...in the auditorium."** Smith, interview by Lotringer, p. 192.

67. **"There is a...most passionate."** Smith, Jack. "The Perfect Filmic Appositeness of Maria Montez." In *Wait for Me at the Bottom of the Pool: The Writings of Jack Smith*, ed. J. Hoberman and Edward Leffingwell. New York: High Risk Books, 1997, p. 27, https://monoskop.org/images/4/49/Smith_Jack_Wait_for_Me_at_the_Bottom_of_The_Pool_The_Writings_of_Jack_Smith_1997.pdf.

68. **"he immediately enlists the sympathy of the audience."** Siegel, "...FOR MM."

69. **On screen...not bananas at all.** "Mario Banana." *YouTube*, https://www.youtube.com/watch?v=1Ku9sGT2Ugg.

70. **"one of the best...great comedy combinations"** Warhol, Andy, and Pat Hackett. *Popism: The Warhol '60s*. Boston: Mariner Books, 2006, p. 104.

71. **"If you saw him...this goddess muse..."** McLeod, Kembrew. "Mario Montez." *The Downtown Pop Underground*, 24 Aug. 2018, https://dsps.lib.uiowa.edu/downtownpopunderground/person/mario-montez/.

72. **"going into costume"** Martin, "Mario Montez."

73. **"scare queens...street queens."** Duberman, p. 232.

74. **"a show business transvestite" "socialsexual phenomenon."** Warhol and Hackett, p. 279.

75. **"As late as '67...depressing losers."** Warhol and Hackett, p. 279.

76. **Warhol goes on...even celebrated** Warhol and Hackett, p. 279.

77. Portions of this text on Theatre of the Ridiculous are reprinted with permission from Condé Nast, "How Theater of the Ridiculous Changed Drama, Performance, and Queer Visibility Forever," written by Elyssa Maxx Goodman and published in *Them* on 18 Apr. 2019, https://www.them.us/story/theater-of-the-ridiculous.

78. **"a willful incoherence...bawdy behavior."** Kaufman, David. *Ridiculous! The Theatrical Life and Times of Charles Ludlam.* New York: Applause Theatre & Cinema Books, 2005, p. 50.

79. **"simply to upturn propriety...where you stood."** Arcade, 17 Nov. 2020 interview.

80. **"John Vaccaro was dangerous...confrontational theater."** McNeil, Legs, and Gillian McCain. *Please Kill Me: The Uncensored Oral History of Punk.* New York: Grove Press, 2006, p. 88.

81. **"Drag came naturally to me...I am Norma."** Ludlam, Charles. *Ridiculous Theatre: Scourge of Human Folly—The Essays and Opinions of Charles Ludlam*, ed. Steven Samuels. New York: Theatre Communications Group, 1992, p. 13.

82. **"always supercharged...Ridiculous Theatrical Company."** Ludlam, p. 21.

83. **"I pioneered the idea...real acting in drag."** Kaufman, p. 187.

84. **John Holder, Jr...New York apartment.** Highberger, Craig B. *Superstar in a Housedress: The Life and Legend of Jackie Curtis.* New York: Chamberlain Bros, 2005. p. 6.

85. **This was all...East Village.** Bubbins, Harry. "Slugger Ann and Jackie Curtis—Part of the East Village Family." *Village Preservation*, 30 Apr. 2020, https://www.villagepreservation.org/2020/04/30/slugger-ann-and-jackie-curtis-part-of-the-east-village-family/.

86. **"I transformed myself...ward off evil spirits."** Highberger, p. 37.

87. **no ambitions of transitioning** Highberger, p. 39.

88. **Jackie was just Jackie.** Regelson, Rosalyn. "'Not a Boy, Not a Girl, Just Me, Jackie.'" *New York Times*, 2 Nov. 1969, https://www.nytimes.com/1969/11/02/archives/not-a-boy-not-a-girl-just-me-not-a-boy-not-a-girl-just-me-jackie.html?searchResultPosition=2.

89. **"Jackie ushered in...his own eroticism."** Highberger, p. 37.

90. **"Satin shorts...invitation."** Warhol and Hackett, pp. 280–81.

91. **"A skinny actress...have ever seen."** *New York Times* theater critic
     Dan Sullivan is quoted in McLeod, Kembrew. "Candy Darling Bends
     Gender and Warps Reality." *The Downtown Pop Underground*, 3 Sept.
     2018, https://dsps.lib.uiowa.edu/downtownpopunderground/story/
     candy-darling-bends-gender-and-warps-reality/.

92. **"I am not...qualified I am."** Diary excerpts are read in *Beautiful
     Darling*. Directed by James Rasin, 2009.

93. **"For the first time, I wasn't bored."** McLeod, "Candy Darling."

94. **"Grooving down St. Mark's...Off Off Broadway scene."** Re-
     gelson, "'Not a Boy.'"

95. **"Jackie was...a very great writer."** Highberger, p. 25.

96. **Then nineteen...some friends.** Ryan, Hugh. "Queen Sabrina,
     Flawless Mother." *Vice*, 7 Mar. 2015, https://www.vice.com/en/
     article/av4555/queen-sabrina-flawless-mother.

97. **"Bar Mitzvah mother"** *The Queen*. Directed by Frank Simon, 1968.

98. **"Mother," not competition** Ryan, "Queen Sabrina."

99. **hire 100 people.** Ryan, "Queen Sabrina."

100. **reportedly arrested over 100 times** Moore, Chadwick. "Why Drag
     Icon Mother Flawless Sabrina Is a Hero." *Out*, 13 Jan. 2015, https://
     www.out.com/entertainment/2015/01/13/why-drag-icon-mother-
     flawless-sabrina-hero.

101. **The Nationals Academy...enter and exit.** Moore, "Why Drag Icon."

102. **"Mind-Blow U.S.A."** Kaufman, p. 65.

103. **Andy Warhol...Hollywood producers.** Ryan, "Queen Sabrina."

104. **Linking it as a fundraiser...drag pageant.** Connolly, Holly. "The
     Film That Paved the Way for Paris Is Burning and RuPaul's Drag
     Race." *AnOther*, 16 Aug. 2019, https://www.anothermag.com/design-
     living/11865/the-drag-doc-that-preceded-paris-is-burning-and-ru-
     paul-s-drag-race.

105. **"Bobby Kennedy was...or whatever."** Ryan, "Queen Sabrina."

106. **Upon its release...Miss This or Miss That"** Adler, Renata.
     "Screen: 'Queen' of Drag Is Crowned: Documentary Depicts a Camp
     Beauty Contest Two Shorts Share Bill at Kips Bay Theater." *New
     York Times*, 18 June 1968, https://www.nytimes.com/1968/06/18/
     archives/screen-queen-of-drag-is-crowneddocumentary-depicts-a-
     camp-beauty.html.

107. **The 1968 Miss America pageant…around them.** Jeffreys, 26 May 2022 interview.

108. **"Usually it's naked women, but that year it was men in drag"** Grimes, William. "'The Queen' on the Runway Again." *New York Times*, 27 Mar. 1993, https://www.nytimes.com/1993/03/27/movies/the-queen-on-the-runway-again.html.

109. **5 East 73rd Street** Davis, Amanda. "Jack Doroshow (a.k.a. Flawless Sabrina) Residence." *NYC LGBT Historic Sites Project*, https://www.nyclgbtsites.org/site/jack-doroshow-a-k-a-flawless-sabrina-residence/.

110. **"If she didn't exist, we'd have to invent her"** Drucker, Zackary. From notes taken by Elyssa Maxx Goodman at "A Flawless Night: Long Live the Queen," 10 May 2018, Town Hall, 123 West 43rd St., New York, NY 10036.

111. **"She was constantly…young people."** Drucker, Zackary. 12 July 2018. An interview completed by Elyssa Maxx Goodman.

112. **"She demanded of all of us that we be flawlessly ourselves"** Tigger! From notes taken by Elyssa Maxx Goodman at "A Flawless Night: Long Live the Queen," 10 May 2018, Town Hall, 123 West 43rd St., New York, NY 10036.

113. **"Normal is…the universe"** "A Flawless Night: Long Live the Queen" notes, Elyssa Maxx Goodman.

114. **"If it doesn't…do it for you,"** "A Flawless Night: Long Live the Queen" notes, Elyssa Maxx Goodman

115. **"I recall…get home."** Harrity, Christopher. "Kim Christy's Lost World." *The Advocate*, 12 Feb. 2011, https://www.advocate.com/arts-entertainment/photography/2011/02/12/kim-christys-lost-world#article-content.

116. **"I was famous!…year or two."** Harrity, "Kim Christy's."

117. **"The street gave…high prices."** Harrity, "Kim Christy's."

118. Portions of this text on Crystal LaBeija are reprinted with permission from Condé Nast, "Drag Herstory: How Crystal LaBeija Reinvented Ball Culture," written by Elyssa Maxx Goodman and published in *Them* on March 23, 2018: https://www.them.us/story/how-crystal-labeija-reinvented-ball-culture

119. **"It created an entire scene…fixed for Harlow"** Freddie LaBeija, "A Flawless Night: Long Live the Queen" notes, Elyssa Maxx Goodman.

120. **"A butch makeup queen"** Kasino, Michael. "Pay It No Mind—the

Life and Times of Marsha P. Johnson." *YouTube*, 15 Oct. 2012, www.youtube.com/watch?v=rjN9W2KstqE.

121. **"I was no one…in the world."** "Marsha P. Johnson Memorial—Elizabeth Native and Transgender Activist for LGBTQ+ Rights: About Marsha P. Johnson." *Union County New Jersey*, 2022, https://ucnj.org/mpj/about-marsha-p-johnson/.

122. **"Hello, everybody! What a wonderful morning!"** Kasino, "Pay It No Mind."

123. **"All of us…patron saint."** Kasino, "Pay It No Mind."

124. **Stay off drugs…money first.** Machado, Agosto, to Strausbaugh, pp. 469–70.

125. **a little after 2 a.m.** "Marsha P. Johnson: Stonewall National Monument." *National Park Service*, 5 Oct. 2020, https://www.nps.gov/people/marsha-p-johnson.htm.

126. **Any raids were typically known in advance.** Duberman, p. 239.

127. **It was considered…appearance; people of color.** Strausbaugh, p. 470.

128. **selective about allowing drag queens.** Duberman, p. 236.

129. **"private bottle club"** Duberman, p. 231.

130. **21,000 fans** Waxman, Olivia B. "Some People Think Stonewall Was Triggered by Judy Garland's Funeral. Here's Why Many Experts Disagree." *Time*, 23 June 2019, https://time.com/5602528/judy-garland-funeral-stonewall/.

131. **"gay crimes"** Gan, Jessi. "'Still at the Back of the Bus': Sylvia Rivera's Struggle." *Centro Journal*, vol. XIX, no. 1, 2007, pp. 124–139, https://www.redalyc.org/articulo.oa?id=37719107.

132. **There was…against cops.** Duberman, pp. 241–42.

133. **As legend has it…attacked her.** Duberman, p. 242.

134. **"Nobody knows…she said she did"** Yardley, William. "Storme DeLarverie, Early Leader in the Gay Rights Movement, Dies at 93." *New York Times*, 29 May 2014, https://www.nytimes.com/2014/05/30/nyregion/storme-delarverie-early-leader-in-the-gay-rights-movement-dies-at-93.html.

135. **Whether this woman…retaliated.** Duberman, pp. 242–43.

136. **"…police found themselves…knees."** Duberman, p. 247.

Chapter 6

1. **"zaps"** Cohen, Sascha. "How Gay Activists Challenged the Politics of Civility." *Smithsonian Magazine*, 10 July 2018, https://www.smithsonianmag.com/history/how-gay-activists-challenged-politics-civility-180969579/.

2. **jobs at public agencies** "'Gay Is Good': Civil Rights for Gays and Lesbians 1969–2011." *Activist New York*, 2022, https://activistnewyork.mcny.org/exhibition/gender-equality/gay-rights; **sexual orientation** Cohen, "How Gay Activists Challenged."

3. **"homophobia"…George Weinberg** Grimes, William. "George Weinberg Dies at 87; Coined 'Homophobia' after Seeing Fear of Gays." *New York Times*, 22 Mar. 2017, https://www.nytimes.com/2017/03/22/us/george-weinberg-dead-coined-homophobia.html.

4. **"The Fourteenth Amendment"** "Fourteenth Amendment." *Cornell Law School Legal Information Institute*, https://www.law.cornell.edu/constitution/amendmentxiv.

5. **"Whereas it was once considered…drag ball"** "The Last of the Balls." *Drag Magazine*, vol. 6, no. 24, 1976, pp. 13–14.

6. **"Back in those days…a lot more showy…I broke that mold… for myself"** Herr, Barbra. 7 Apr. 2020. An interview completed by Elyssa Maxx Goodman.

7. **he threw fundraising drag balls.** Martin, Douglas. "Lee Brewster, 57, Style Guru for World's Cross-Dressers." *New York Times*, 24 May 2000, p. B11.

8. **"They were conservative… They didn't want to use…"** Saypen, Abby. "A Little Bit of Our History." *TV/TS Tapestry Journal*, no. 70, Winter 1995, pp. 56–57.

9. **"heterosexual transvestite."** "Drag Queens Demonstrate." *Drag Magazine*, vol. 1, no. 1, 1971, pp. 5–7.

10. **"their mission was…harassment."** Nichols, Jack. "Lee Brewster Dies at 57—Pioneering Transvestite Activist." *Gay Today*, 25 May 2000. http://www.gaytoday.com/garchive/events/052500ev.htm.

11. **3,000 people** Rosenberg, Zoe. "In Photos: 120 Years of the Meatpacking District's Evolving Landscape." *Curbed NY*, 17 Nov. 2015, https://ny.curbed.com/2015/11/17/9899614/in-photos-120-years-of-the-meatpacking-districts-evolving-landscape.

12. **"Make your boyself… Reasonable."** Advertisement. *Drag Magazine*, vol. 2, no. 5, 1972, p. 33.

13. **"It stinks... It's the closet bunch...represented."** The Pearl Box Revue.

14. **"screaming queens forming...tacky and cheap."** Duberman, p. 255.

15. **"Organizers...the back." "The parade...arrested."** Tucker, Neely. "Pride at 50: From Stonewall to Today | Library of Congress Blog." Blogs.loc.gov, 2 June 2020, https://blogs.loc.gov/loc/2020/06/pride-at-50-from-stonewall-to-today/.

16. **to that point...New York City** Fosburgh, Lacey. "Thousands of Homosexuals Hold a Protest Rally in Central Park." *New York Times*, 29 June 1970, https://www.nytimes.com/1970/06/29/archives/thousands-of-homosexuals-hold-a-protest-rally-in-central-park.html.

17. **"They wanted drag to be invisible."** Saypen, pp. 56–57.

18. **"The most satisfying thing... American citizens."** Brewster, Lee. "The Impossible Dream? No: Editorial." *Drag*, vol. 1, no. 1, 1971, pp. 6–7.

19. **"Marsha and I just...other kids."** Feinberg, Leslie. "Street Transvestite Action Revolutionaries: Lavender & Red, Part 73." *Workers World*, 24 Sept. 2006, https://www.workers.org/2006/us/lavender-red-73/.

20. **It was also...organization."** Rubin, Lena. "Revolutionaries on East Second Street: The STAR House." *Village Preservation*, 29 Oct. 2020, https://www.villagepreservation.org/2020/10/29/revolutionaries-on-east-second-street-the-star-house/.

21. **The first S.T.A.R. house...young people.** Duberman, p. 309.

22. **They weren't required...should they choose to.** Duberman, p. 309.

23. **Later...procure a building** Rubin, "Revolutionaries on East."

24. **213 Second Avenue** Feinberg, "Street Transvestite Action."

25. **a 1.5 billion deficit** McFadden, Robert D. "Abraham Beame Is Dead at 94; Mayor During 70's Fiscal Crisis." *New York Times*, 11 Feb. 2001, p. 1.

26. **The city...that particular month.** Roberts, Sam. "When the City's Bankruptcy Was Just a Few Words Away." *New York Times*, 31 Dec. 2006.

27. **a $200 million surplus** Getlin, Josh. "Abraham D. Beame; Former N.Y. Mayor." *Los Angeles Times*, 11 Feb. 2001, https://www.nytimes.com/2006/12/31/nyregion/when-the-citys-bankruptcy-was-just-a-few-words-away.html.

28. **Throughout the 1970s…insurance money.** McFadden, "Abraham Beame Is Dead."

29. **But failing…July 1971.** Rubin, "Revolutionaries on East."

30. **"I had to fight…"** Gan, "'Still at the Back of the Bus.'"

31. **"I will no longer…our rights"** Sylvia Rivera, "'Y'all Better Quiet Down' Original Authorized Video, 1973 Gay Pride Rally NYC." *You-Tube*, uploaded by LoveTapesCollective, 23 May 2019, https://www.youtube.com/watch?v=Jb-JIOWUw1o.

32. **"a man"…"When men impersonate women…profit."** "Jean O'Leary Speech at 1973 Gay Rally with Watermark." *YouTube*, uploaded by LoveTapesCollective, 6 June 2019, https://www.youtube.com/watch?v=USWWUVEFLUU.

33. **"you're celebrating…screw you!"** Clendinen, Dudley, and Adam Nagourney. *Out for Good: The Struggle to Build a Gay Rights Movement in America.* New York: Simon and Schuster, 2013, p. 172.

34. **"From my perspective…rest of the world."** Hansen, Thomas. 27 Oct. 2020. An interview completed by Elyssa Maxx Goodman.

35. **"Some looked down on… The premise was that…comedy."** Hansen, 27 Oct. 2020 interview.

36. **"The gay boys didn't…women's clothes."** Rims, Ruby. 29 Dec. 2020. An interview completed by Elyssa Maxx Goodman.

37. **"The gay drag is…our beginnings."** White, Edmund. "Stonewall 1979: The Politics of Drag." *The Village Voice*, 25 June 1979.

38. **"male actress"** Walraff, p. 216.

39. **"who by his own admission…mother's closets."** Barnes, Clive. "Stage: Women, Wittily." *New York Times*, 29 Jan. 1975, p. 22.

40. **"They wiped down the…actually sing."** Rims, 29 Dec. 2020 interview.

41. **"In my own version… I'm still wielding."** Kelly, John. 28 July 2020. An interview completed by Elyssa Maxx Goodman.

42. **May 26, 1971** Taubin, Amy. "Amy Taubin on Superstar in a Housedress: The Life and Legend of Jackie Curtis." *Artforum*, May 2004, https://www.artforum.com/print/200405/superstar-in-a-housedress-the-life-and-legend-of-jackie-curtis-6708.

43. **"unabashed trash"** Gussow, Mel. "Stage: 'Vain Victory,' Campy Transvestite Musical Spectacle." *New York Times*, 25 Aug. 1971, p. 46.

44. **"awful, abominable, execrable, beyond description and beyond belief."** Novick, Julius. "'Vain Victory'... Shall Not Have Dyed in Vain." *The Village Voice*, 19 Aug. 1971. Republished on Warhol Stars, https://warholstars.org/vain-victory-2.html.

45. **"the best play I've ever seen."** Highberger, p. 152.

46. **"living testimony...want to be."** "Andy Warhol (1928-1987): Ladies and Gentlemen." *Christie's,* 2020, https://www.christies.com/en/lot/lot-5701742.

47. **"I never thought...pill in the other."** Woodlawn, Holly, and Jeffrey Copeland. *A Low Life in High Heels: The Holly Woodlawn Story.* New York: Harper Perennial, 1992. p. 3.

48. **"Holly was a delight...memorial."** Musto, Michael. 21 Apr. 2022. An interview completed by Elyssa Maxx Goodman.

49. **Penny Arcade remembered..."look fabulous?"** Arcade, Penny. "Penny Arcade Remembers Holly Woodlawn." *Out,* 10 Dec. 2015, https://www.out.com/entertainment/2015/12/10/penny-arcade-remembers-holly-woodlawn.

50. **originally intended...gender nonconforming stars.** Rems, Emily. "Behind the Scenes on Andy Warhol's 'Women in Revolt.'" *Salon,* 19 Nov. 2019, https://www.salon.com/2019/11/19/the-secret-history-of-andy-warhols-women-in-revolt/.

51. **"madcap soap opera..."** Canby, Vincent. "Warhol's 'Women in Revolt,' Madcap Soap Opera." *New York Times,* 17 Feb. 1972, p. 30, https://timesmachine.nytimes.com/timesmachine/1972/02/17/79421731.html?pageNumber=30.

52. **It didn't help...demanded money.** *Beautiful Darling,* Rasin.

53. **"Don't get involved with drag queens"** *Beautiful Darling,* Rasin.

54. **"They were all immortalized...'Walk on the Wild Side.'"** Reed, Lou. "Walk on the Wild Side." *Transformer,* RCA Records, 1972. *Spotify,* https://open.spotify.com/track/5p3JunprHCxClJjOmcLV8G?si=b40d973daf354c54.

55. **"They gave her a...on the door"** Johnson, Richard. "New Details about Candy Darling's Difficult, Short Life." *Page Six,* 10 June 2018. https://pagesix.com/2018/06/10/new-details-about-candy-darlings-difficult-short-life/.

56. **In 1974...*Ladies and Gentlemen.*** "Ladies and Gentlemen." *Tate,* https://www.tate.org.uk/art/artists/andy-warhol-2121/ladies-and-gentlemen.

57. **Warhol asked...their time.** "Ladies and Gentlemen: New York City's Drag Community Through Andy's Lens." *Hedges Projects,* http://hedges-projects.com/exhibition-test-7.

58. **"Andy Warhol silkscreens...outside, broke."** Watson, Steve. "Stonewall 1979: The Drag of Politics." *The Village Voice,* 15 June 1979, https://www.villagevoice.com/2019/06/04/stonewall-1979-the-drag-of-politics/.

59. **"to learn...gender-bending performance."** "School of Drag Workshop Series Questions." *The Andy Warhol Museum,* https://www.warhol.org/teens/school-of-drag-workshop-series-questions/.

60. **"a landmark in the history of new, liberated theater."** Cruickshank, Douglas. "The Cockettes: Rise and Fall of the Acid Queens." *Salon,* 23 Aug. 2000, https://www.salon.com/2000/08/23/weissman/.

61. **"a Cockette wedding..."** Guthmann, Edward. "Glitter, Acid and Bearded Queens—Sweet Pam Details Her Cockette Days in All Their Far-Out Glory." *SFGate,* 3 Dec. 2004, https://www.sfgate.com/books/article/Glitter-acid-and-bearded-queens-Sweet-Pam-2667319.php.

62. **"to go...in Jersey."** Kelly, 28 July 2020 interview.

63. **top billing** Blondie (@BlondieOfficial). "On this day, Oct. 31, back in 1974, BLONDIE & The Ramones performed w/ the Savage Voodoo Nuns at CBGB. Here's an ad." *Twitter,* 31 Oct. 2014, https://twitter.com/BlondieOfficial/status/528178880482648064.

64. **"Post-Stonewall liberation crawled...1972."** Camicia, Jimmy. *My Dear, Sweet Self: A Hot Peach Life.* Silverton: Fast Books, 2013, p. 48, p. 51.

65. **They rehearsed...especially in drag.** Camicia, p. 53.

66. **"When we showed up...end of that."** Camicia, p. 111.

67. **"David Johansen borrowed...rock and roll."** McNeil and McCain, pp. 116–17.

68. **Johansen...onstage.** McLeod, Kembrew. "Pam Tent Meets David Johansen." *The Downtown Pop Underground,* 3 Sept. 2018, https://dsps.lib.uiowa.edu/downtownpopunderground/story/pam-tent-meets-david-johansen/.

69. **"We weren't trying to...constituency."** Spitznagel, Eric. "Sex, Drugs, and Drag." *Vanity Fair,* 3 Mar. 2011, https://www.vanityfair.com/hollywood/2011/03/new-york-dolls.

70. **"I wanted to...pop star."** Bernadicou, August. "Sink Your Teeth into Jayne County." *QueerCore Podcast,* episode 7, 17 Sept. 2020,

https://player.captivate.fm/episode/ff03da19–44fa–4a93–a0a5–
5f9b0fe88652.

71.   **"It was real...clicked with me."** County, Jayne, and Rupert Smith.
      Man Enough to Be a Woman. London: Serpent's Tail, 1995, p. 50.

72.   **At that point...era.** McNeil and McCain, p. 95.

73.   **"After us, David started...more freaky."** McNeil and McCain, p. 95.

74.   **In 1972...degrading to women.** County and Smith, p. 88.

75.   **"In her memoir...asshole."** County and Smith, p. 89.

76.   **"drag rock Lenny Bruce...with a pitchfork..."** County and
      Smith, p. 91.

77.   **"Gene Simmons...tongue thing"** County, Jayne. "Jayne County,
      the Trans Rock'n'Roll Star Who Influenced David Bowie, in Her
      Own Words." *Interview Magazine*, 19 April 2018, https://www.
      interviewmagazine.com/culture/jayne-county-trans-rocknroll-star-
      influenced-david-bowie-words.

78.   **"U.S. Ballet Soars..."** *TIME*, 1 May 1978, https://content.time.
      com/time/covers/0,16641,19780501,00.html.

79.   **"The credo of Larry...hilarity"** Kelly, 28 July 2020 interview.

80.   **"The parody company...success"** Croce, Arlene. "The Two
      Trockaderos." In *Writing in the Dark, Dancing in New Yorker*. New
      York: Farrar, Straus and Giroux, 30 Apr. 2003, https://books.google.
      com/books?id=Unl-kVxVs3sC&pg.

81.   **"The pointe work really...something with it."** **"Splinter City"**
      Anastos, Peter. 6 May 2020. An interview completed by Elyssa Maxx
      Goodman.

82.   **"His legacy was that...cutting edge."** Souza, Gabriella. "John
      Waters and Pat Moran Discuss Divine's Legacy." *Baltimore Maga-
      zine*, 9 Oct. 2015, https://www.baltimoremagazine.com/section/
      artsentertainment/we-talk-to-john-waters-and-pat-moran-about-
      divines-70th-birthday/.

83.   **"I'm a character actor...female roles"** "Celebrating 30 Years Of
      'Fresh Air': Character Actor Divine." *Fresh Air*, NPR, 1 Sept. 2017,
      https://freshairarchive.org/segments/celebrating-30-years-fresh-air-
      character-actor-divine.

84.   **the latter of whom..."house drag queen."** Colacello, Bob. "Me
      and Andy...and Ronald Reagan," *Tate Etc.*, 1 Sept. 2009, https://

www.tate.org.uk/tate-etc/issue-17-autumn-2009/me-and-andy-and-ronald-reagan.

85. **"Every queen… I mean."** Reynolds, Jim. "Potassa: The Great Pretender." *Interview Magazine*, Apr. 1977, pp. 32–33. Also referenced by Carmack, Kara. "'I'm a person who loves beautiful things': Potassa de Lafayette as Model and Muse." *Journal of Visual Culture*, vol. 19, no. 2, 24 Aug. 2020, http://www.cylemetzger. com/uploads/1/1/5/6/115687553/full_version_-_jvc_new_work_ in_transgender_art_and_visual_culture_studies.pdf.

86. **"I am not a man…beautiful things."** McEvoy, Marian. "Eye View: Potassa—an Epitome." *Women's Wear Daily*, vol. 129, no. 46, 1974, pp. 14. Also referenced by Carmack.

87. **However, there were…"drag queen."** Carmack, p. 253.

88. **"She joyfully weaponized…couture catwalks."** Carmack, p.252

89. **"Gorgeous still, and *bones*, cheekbones."** Warhol, Andy, and André Leon Talley. "New Again: Grace Jones." *Interview Magazine*, Oct. 1984, reprinted 16 July 2014, https://www.interviewmagazine. com/music/new-again-grace-jones.

90. **flashing her genitals** Carmack, p. 254.

91. **In an article entitled…help them.** Sterne, Michael. "In Last Decade, Leaders Day, Harlem's Dreams Have Died." *New York Times*, 1 Mar. 1978, p. 1, p. 13.

92. **Participants could complete…High Fashion Eveningwear, and more.** *Paris Is Burning.* Directed by Jennie Livingston, 1990.

93. **"It was our goal…women."** Cunningham, Michael. "The Slap of Love." *Open City* 6, 13 Oct. 2000, https://opencity.org/archive/ issue-6/the-slap-of-love.

Chapter 7

1. **"Under the headline…Homosexuals."** Altman, Lawrence K. "Rare Cancer Seen in 41 Homosexuals." *New York Times*, 3 July 1981, p. 20, https://www.nytimes.com/1981/07/03/us/rare-cancer-seen-in-41-homosexuals.html.

2. **"AIDS victims have been…dread"** Daly, Michael. "AIDS Anxiety." *New York Magazine*, 20 June 1983, https://nymag.com/news/ features/47175/.

3. **"I didn't do theater… follow you around?"** Lucas, Craig.

"Peggy Shaw." *Bomb*, 1 Oct. 1999, https://bombmagazine.org/articles/peggy-shaw/.

4. **"Hot Peaches taught me... a drag group."** McCabe, Allyson. "Sound & Vision: Lois Weaver and Peggy Shaw." *The Rumpus*, 26 Oct. 2017, https://therumpus.net/2017/10/26/sound-vision-lois-weaver-and-peggy-shaw/.

5. **"Nothing that we saw in... the old."** Myers, Victoria. "An Interview with Split Britches: Peggy Shaw and Lois Weaver." *The Interval*, 8 Jan. 2018, https://www.theintervalny.com/interviews/2018/01/an-interview-with-split-britches-peggy-shaw-and-lois-weaver/.

6. **"When you perform with...audience."** WOW Documentary Project. From "Theater of Desire: The WOW Aesthetic." 2 May 2017, https://www.facebook.com/wowdocumentary/videos/372322033164237/.

7. **"A paradise of playwriting..."** Johns, Merryn. "A World of Women: Celebrating the WOW Café." *Stamps School of Art & Design*, https://stamps.umich.edu/news/world-of-women.

8. **"a desire for women...portrayals."** Davy, Kate. *Lady Dicks and Lesbian Brothers: Staging the Unimaginable at the WOW Café Theatre.* Ann Arbor: University of Michigan Press, 2011, p. 160.

9. **Scholar and performance artist...** Davy, p. 160.

10. **"If I hadn't found..."** Hughes, Holly. "Interview with Holly Hughes." *What is Performance Studies?* uploaded 2007, https://scalar.usc.edu/nehvectors/wips/holly-hughes-what-is-performance-studies-2007-.

11. **"Inspired more by a lot of..."** Hughes, "Interview."

12. **"Drag was a style..."** WOW Documentary Project. Holly Hughes and Peggy Shaw describe WOW's roots in drag theater. From "Theater of Desire: The WOW Aesthetic." 2 May 2017, https://www.facebook.com/wowdocumentary/videos/372322033164237/.

13. **The roles that did...** Davy, p. 160.

14. **Many roles at WOW...** Davy, Katy. "Fe/Male Impersonation: The Discourse of Camp." In *The Politics and Poetics of Camp*, ed. Moe Meyer. New York: Routledge, 1994, pp. 130–48.

15. **"Looking for girls and..."** Román, David, and Carmelita Tropicana. "Carmelita Tropicana Unplugged: An Interview with David Román." *TDR (1988–)*, vol. 39, no. 3, 1995, pp. 83–93, https://doi.org/10.2307/1146466.

16. **She developed…lesbian twist.** Román and Tropicana, p. 87.

17. **"Socrates of [Havana's] M15…"** Davy, *Lady Dicks*, p. 158.

18. **"drag king"** Drag King History. "DK Timeline." *Drag King History*, https://dragkinghistory.com/dk-timeline/.

19. **"I had such a…"** Torr, Diane. "Remembered." *Transgender Tapestry*, no. 114, 2008, p. 20.

20. **"I was encouraged…"** Sprinkle, Annie. "Remembered." *Transgender Tapestry*, no. 114, 2008, pp. 20-21.

21. **"I always say it…"** Busch, Charles. 22 Apr. 2020. An interview completed by Elyssa Maxx Goodman.

22. **"counterculture hotbed… A mix of artists…"** Glueck, Grace. "Gallery View; A Gallery Scene that Pioneers in New Territories." *New York Times*, 26 June 1983, p. 27.

23. **"The East Village sensibility… But it was done…"** Simpson, Linda. 28 Mar. 2018. An interview completed by Elyssa Maxx Goodman.

24. **Living in New York…make art.** *Arias with a Twist*. Directed by Bobby Sheehan, 2010.

25. **"They didn't like that…" "None of this Marlene…"** Espejo-Saavedra, Eduardo Gion. "For Alexis Del Lago Life Is So Much More Than Just Cabaret." *GPS Radar*, 14 Nov. 2018, https://www.gpsradar.com/blog/industry/for-alexis-del-lago-life-much-than-just-cabaret/.

26. **"My mother used to tell me…"** "He Made Herself a Star." *Vimeo*, uploaded 2011, https://vimeo.com/26639862.

27. **"I never made a… I wanted to make…"** Espejo-Saavedra, "For Alexis."

28. **"She'd also refer to…"** "He Made Herself A Star."

29. **"In the 80s I…"** Espejo-Saavedra, "For Alexis."

30. **"Once I met Alexis…" "Alexis came to see Holly…"** Wittman, Scott. 17 May 2020. An interview completed by Elyssa Maxx Goodman.

31. **"A glitter, Las Vegas…"** Hager, Steven. *Art After Midnight: The East Village Scene*. New York: St. Martin's Press, 1986, p. 80.

32. **Ann Magnuson… "Hot Stuff"** Club 57 by Ann Magnuson. Photo and Text. *Facebook*, 16 May 2011, https://www.facebook.com/214932585193130/photos/214934295192959/; **matador burlesque** Lawrence, Tim. *Life and Death on New York Dance Floor, 1980–*

1983. Durham: Duke University Press, 2016, p. 33. Also features Magnuson.

33. **"I didn't like it…"** Arias, Joey. 1 June 2021. An interview completed by Elyssa Maxx Goodman.

34. **"Beloved as the…"** Bateman, Kristen. "Oral History: Remembering New York's Fiorucci Store." *New York Times Style Magazine*, 19 Sept. 2017.

35. **"It was social commentary" "It was wearing"** Keeps, David A. "Pop View; How RuPaul Ups the Ante for Drag." *New York Times*, 11 July 1993, https://www.nytimes.com/1993/07/11/archives/pop-view-how-rupaul-ups-the-ante-for-drag.html.

36. **Old Polish men…vodka.** Romano, Tricia. "Nightclubbing: New York City's Pyramid Club." *Red Bull Music Academy*, 4 Mar. 2014, https://daily.redbullmusicacademy.com/2014/03/nightclubbing-pyramid/.

37. **"They [told] me…" "And they're like…"** Butterick, Brian, aka Hattie Hathaway. 1 May 2018. An interview completed by Elyssa Maxx Goodman.

38. **"She sang her own…"** Butterick, 1 May 2018 interview.

39. **wormed** Dunning, Jennifer. "'Tempest's' Villain, Ethyl Eichelberger, Is a Real Fire-Breather Supposed to Teach." *New York Times*, 21 Aug. 1987, https://www.nytimes.com/1987/08/21/theater/tempest-s-villain-ethyl-eichelberger-is-a-real-fire-breather-supposed-to-teach.html.

40. **"Serious tragedian, club and…"** Dunning, "'Tempest's' Villain."

41. **"The conceptual construct…"** Finley, Karen. 24 July 2018. An interview completed by Elyssa Maxx Goodman.

42. **"Wearing an upside-down…"** Romano, "Nightclubbing."

43. **"[Saint Sebastian is] considered…"** Romano, "Nightclubbing."

44. **"It was character driven…" "There was this weird gender…"** Kelly, 28 July 2020 interview.

45. **"Which is great for…"** Butterick, 1 May 2018 interview.

46. **"Really, the thing we…"** *Secrets of the Great Pyramid: The Pyramid Cocktail Lounge as Cultural Laboratory*, curator Brian Butterick, aka Hattie Hathaway. Exhibition catalog, Howl! Happening: An Arturo Vega Project, Oct. 17–Nov. 7, 2015.

47. **"They loaded their feminine…"** Eubanks, Tom. *Ghosts of St. Vincent's*. New York: TOMUS NYC, 2017, p. 52.

48. **Commenting on being** Colucci, Emily. "From Nefertiti to Kly-temnestra: The Ethyl Eichelberger Video Lounge." *Filthy Dreams*, 21 Nov. 2014, https://filthydreams.org/2014/11/21/from-nefertiti-to-klytemnestra-the-ethyl-eichelberger-video-lounge/.

49. **"I try to tell…"** Dunning, "'Tempest's' Villain."

50. **"He is an original…"** Gussow, Mel. "Stage: 2 Eichelberger 'Classics.'" *New York Times*, 18 Aug. 1987, p. 13.

51. **"Why did I want…"** Epperson, John. 23 Apr. 2020. An interview completed by Elyssa Maxx Goodman.

52. **"I thought to myself…"** Epperson, 23 Apr. 2020 interview.

53. **"The greatest chanteuse who…"** Brantley, Ben. "The Wasp Goddess, Imperious, Vulnerable and (Gasp) Unmasked." *New York Times*, 13 Nov. 2014, https://www.nytimes.com/2014/11/14/theater/john-epperson-returns-in-lypsinka-the-trilogy.html.

54. **"I think the performance…"** Musto, 21 Apr. 2022 interview.

55. **"A 7-foot-tall drag queen…"** Mallett, Whitney. "A Maybe Exaggerated, Definitely Foggy, Look Back at The World—the Most Iconic Nightclub You've Never Heard Of." *Interview Magazine*, 6 Sept. 2018, https://www.interviewmagazine.com/culture/a-maybe-exaggerated-definitely-foggy-look-back-at-the-world-the-most-iconic-nightclub-youve-never-heard-of.

56. **"Immediately whisked him in…" "He had long…"** Buckley, Cara. "Disquieting Death Stills the Night Life." *New York Times*, 14 Oct. 2007, https://www.nytimes.com/2007/10/14/fashion/14dean.html.

57. **"Live bands • drag queens • hot go-go trash…"** Flyer. Colucci, Emily. "Role Models: Dean Johnson." *Filthy Dreams*, 6 July 2013, https://filthydreams.org/2013/07/06/role-models-dean-johnson/.

58. **"Everyone here is just…" "It's really fun…"** "Dean Johnson Interviewed for MTV." *YouTube*, uploaded by 5NinthAvenueProject, 27 Mar. 2009, https://www.youtube.com/watch?v=dIEvSaJh-ec.

59. **"They signed me based…" "Homeless people pulled…"** "Dean Johnson—Death of a Legendary Legend." *MotherboardsNYC*, 29 Sept. 2007, https://motherboardsnyc.hoop.la/topic/dean-johnson—death-of-a-legendary-legend.

60. **"Hairdressers, display queens, theatre folk…" "The Complete Suburban Gay Experience"** "Whispers Tribute: Hosted by Hapi Phace" *Howl!* 24 Oct. 2015, https://www.howlarts.org/event/whispers-hosted-by-hapi-phace/.

61. **"Whoever has the Subaru, your lights are on!"** Yarritu, David, and Svetlana Kitto. "Onboard at the Pyramid: 1984–1988." *Danspace Project*, 8 Nov. 2016, https://danspaceproject.org/2016/11/08/onboard-at-the-pyramid-1984-1988/.

62. **"[It was] everybody on our..." "This created a need..."** Giddio, Tobie. 15 Mar. 2020. An interview completed by Elyssa Maxx Goodman.

63. **"escape laughter" "survival laughter"** Giddio, 15 Mar. 2020 interview.

64. **"It was a guaranteed..." "We were losing..."** Musto, 21 Apr. 2022 interview.

65. **September 17, 1985** Bennington-Castro, Joseph. "How AIDS Remained an Unspoken—But Deadly—Epidemic for Years." *History.com*, A+E Networks, 1 June 2020, https://www.history.com/news/aids-epidemic-ronald-reagan.

66. **"to ensure that we..."** Reagan, Ronald. *Public Papers of the Presidents, Book 1.* Washington, DC: United States Government Printing Office, 1989, p. 463.

67. **"deliberate, disgusting, revolting conduct"** Seelye, Katharine Q. "Helms Puts the Brakes to a Bill Financing AIDS Treatment." *New York Times*, 5 July 1995, https://www.nytimes.com/1995/07/05/us/helms-puts-the-brakes-to-a-bill-financing-aids-treatment.html.

68. **"being used to provide..."** *U.S. Constitution.* Amend. 963 to H.R. 3058.

69. **a portion of which...AIDS.** *Health Omnibus Extension of 1988.* S.2889. 4 Nov. 1988; **to create programs for...AIDS.** Molotsky, Irvin. "Congress Passes Compromise AIDS Bill." *New York Times*, 14 Oct. 1988, https://www.nytimes.com/1988/10/14/us/congress-passes-compromise-aids-bill.html.

70. **January 12, 1982** "AIDS in New York: A Biography." *New York Magazine*, 26 May 2006, https://nymag.com/news/features/17158/.

71. **$50,000** "AIDS in New York."

72. **3,799 people** New York City AIDS Memorial. "HIV/AIDS Timeline." *New York City AIDS Memorial*, https://www.nycaidsmemorial.org/timeline.

73. **12,529 total** "HIV/AIDS Timeline."

74. **one third of all AIDS cases** "HIV/AIDS Timeline."

75. **memorably at an event...West 51st Street.** Cohen, "How Gay Activists Challenged."

76. **"ACT UP provided not..."** Schulman, Sarah. "Interview 133— Hunter Reynolds." *Act Up Oral History Project*, 2 June 2012, https://static1.squarespace.com/static/6075fe20d281ea3f320a7be9/t/610334 47b196bb203e5477b2/1627599943846/133+Hunter+Reynolds.pdf.

77. **A group focused on...art world.** Schulman, "Interview 133."

78. **third gender** Reynolds, Hunter. Interview by Theodore Kerr. "Oral History Interview with Hunter Reynolds, 2016 August 10–September 7." *Archives of American Art*, https://www.aaa.si.edu/collections/interviews/oral-history-interview-hunter-reynolds-17412.

79. **"I want to express, reflect..."** Schulman, "Interview 133."

80. **"I wasn't prepared for..." "I did six weeks..."** Miss Rosen. "Hunter Reynolds, the Artist Who Uses Drag to Fight Homophobia in the Arts." *AnOtherMan*, 28 Nov. 2019, https://www.anothermanmag.com/life-culture/11039/hunter-reynolds-patina-du-prey-drag-to-dervish-1980s-new-york-drag.

81. **The first time...she had arrived.** Schulman, Michael. "Lady Bunny Is Still the Shadiest Queen Around." *New York Times*, 29 Sept. 2018, https://www.nytimes.com/2018/09/29/style/lady-bunny-drag-queen.html.

82. **"I thought, 'What can...' "I can..."** Schulman, "Lady Bunny."

83. **"I can do a..." "Honey I used..."** RuPaul. "Episode 165: Lady Bunny." *RuPaul: What's the Tee? with Michelle Visage*, episode 165, 14 Aug. 2018, https://soundcloud.com/rupaul/episode-165-lady-bunny.

84. **"[Warhol's] mentality and his..."** Miller, Gregory E. "RuPaul Talks His Wild and Crazy '80s Club Kid Days." *New York Post*, 28 Feb. 2015, https://nypost.com/2015/02/28/rupaul-talks-his-wild-and-crazy-80s-club-kid-days/.

85. **"black bustier bikini thing..."** RuPaul. *Lettin' It All Hang Out: An Autobiography.* New York: Hyperion, 1996, p. 55.

86. **"Seemingly overnight, Restaurant Florent..."** Miller, Bryan. "Diner's Journal." *New York Times*, 21 Feb. 1986, p. 22.

87. **"Young and convivial crowd"** Miller, "RuPaul Talks."

88. **"Florent at night was just..." "All the performers..."** Mitchell, John Cameron. 28 April 2020. An interview completed by Elyssa Maxx Goodman.

89. **"In *Cheers* everybody knew..."** Amsden, David. "The 25th Hour of Florent Morellet." *New York Magazine*, 23 May 2008, https://nymag.com/restaurants/features/47227/.

90. **"I got a little bit..." "I was so wowed..."** RuPaul, "Episode 165: Lady Bunny."

91. **August 18, 1985** "Guide to the Nelson Sullivan Video Collection, 1976–1989." *Fales Library & Special Collections*, https://dlib.nyu.edu/findingaids/html/fales/mss_357/dscaspace_ref10.html.

92. **In Sullivan's video...quizzically. She wears...and shake.** "Wigstock: Getting Bigger Every Year, 1985–1987." *Youtube*, uploaded by 5NinthAvenueProject, 9 Mar. 2015, https://www.youtube.com/watch?v=4vMuG7c3mW8&t=54s.

93. **"Hello, everybody! Welcome to..."** "Wigstock: Getting Bigger Every Year, 1985–1987."

94. **"The Pyramid and I..."** "Wigstock: Getting Bigger Every Year, 1985–1987."

95. **"We, a wayward band..."** "Memories." *Wigstock*, https://web.archive.org/web/20190429070739/https://wigstock.squarespace.com/memories/.

96. **"I can also remember..."** "Memories."

97. **6,458 AIDS deaths** "AIDS in New York."

98. **"We raised money back..." "As the years..."** Shapiro, Eileen. "The Imperial Court of New York: Night of a Thousand Gowns." *Get Out! Magazine*, 30 Mar. 2015, https://getoutmag.com/the-imperial-court-of-new-york-night-of-a-thousand-gowns/.

99. **"It's not all about..."** Hansen, 27 Oct. 2020 interview.

100. **"The theater department wasn't..." "I was too light..."** Busch, Charles. "Charles Busch on the First Time He Performed in Drag." *New York Times*, 20 Dec. 2016, https://www.nytimes.com/2016/12/20/theater/charles-busch-drag.html.

101. **"Being exposed to the work..." "Seeing Ludlam..."** Busch, 22 Apr. 2020 interview.

102. **"We sent out a flyer..." "We just had..."** Busch, 22 Apr. 2020 interview.

103. **"The camp comedy began..."** Pacheco, Patrick. "Theater; When the Lady In Question Is a Man." *New York Times*, 23 July 1989, p. 5.

104. **"I was in awe..." "So it was always..."** Mitchell, 28 Apr. 2020 interview.

105. **"What will people think?" "That's a question..."** Busch, "Charles Busch on the First Time."

106. **"dragophobic" "I was completely subjugated..." "Without him..."** Siff, Ira. 1 May 2020. An interview completed by Elyssa Maxx Goodman.

107. **"The audience went berserk..." "But I had no idea..."** Serinus, Jason Victor. "Interview: Ira Siff of La Gran Scena Opera Company." *Home Theater and Audio Review*, Aug. 2004, https://hometheaterhifi. com/volume_11_3/feature-interview-ira-siff-8-2004.html.

108. **"La Gran Scena Opera..."** Holland, Bernard. "Opera: Falsettos in Gowns." *New York Times*, 24 Nov. 1981, p. 7.

109. **"You know, with paper..." "...guilty pleasure." "When people from the Met..."** Siff, 1 May 2020 interview.

110. **"La Gran Scena is..."** Serinus, "Interview: Ira Siff."

111. **"older and straighter..."** Siff, 1 May 2020 interview.

112. **"Have you *seen* men's...anything in them."** Shewey, Don. "Harvey Fierstein: Fanfares, Fandangos and Flatbush Flap-Draggin.'" *The Advocate*, 14 June 1978, http://www.donshewey.com/theater_articles/ harvey_fierstein_1978.html.

113. **The play upended both...comic relief.** Shewey, "Harvey Fierstein."

114. **Indeed, drag is one...a family.** Portwood, Jerry. "Harvey Fierstein and Moisés Kaufman on the Eternal Message of 'Torch Song.'" *Rolling Stone*, 9 Dec. 2018, https://www.rollingstone.com/culture/culture-features/harvey-fierstein-torch-song-broadway-michael-urie-758676/.

115. **"People would say..."** Reif, Robin. "How Harvey Fierstein's *Torch Song* Became the *Trilogy*." *Playbill*, 10 June 2017, https://playbill.com/ article/how-harvey-fiersteins-torch-song-became-the-trilogy.

116. **"Three plays that give..."** Gussow, Mel. "Theatre: Fierstein's 'Torch Song.'" *New York Times*, 1 Nov. 1981, p. 81.

117. **"middle-class"** Wetzsteon, Ross. "'La Cage Aux Folles' Comes to Broadway." *New York Magazine*, 22 Aug. 1983. p. 35.

118. **After all...arrested himself.** Wetzsteon, "'La Cage Aux Folles.'"

119. **"The greatest young actress..."** Fierstein, Harvey. *I Was Better Last Night: A Memoir*. New York: Knopf, 2022, pp. 154–55.

120. **But director Arthur Laurents...appeared.** Senelick, *The Changing Room*, p. 502.

121. **Eventually he called up...mistake.** Fierstein, p. 156.

122. **"The glitz, showmanship, good..."** Rich, Frank. "Stage: The Musical 'Cage Aux Folles.'" *New York Times*, 22 Aug. 1983, p. 13.

123. **But these...showgirls.** Wetzsteon, "'La Cage Aux Folles.'"

124. **"Gay men, [McGregor] said..."** Kleinfield, N. R. "On the Street of Dreams." *New York Times*, 22 Nov. 1992, p. 8.

125. **"At the time the... It was the lowest... Weird little dive..."** Glamamore, David. 14 July 2021. An interview completed by Elyssa Maxx Goodman.

126. **"Every week the BoyBar..."** Dynell, Johnny. 18 Apr. 2018. An interview completed by Elyssa Maxx Goodman.

127. **"The reputation that drag...slick, professional...we were professional..."** Fleming, Connie. 31 July 2020. An interview completed by Elyssa Maxx Goodman.

128. **"One of the holdouts... We started to perform..."** H.R.H. Princess Diandra. 15 July 2021. An interview completed by Elyssa Maxx Goodman.

129. **"Kastenisms" ...too much black.** "BoyBar." *MotherboardsNYC*, 27 Aug. 2001, https://motherboardsnyc.hoop.la/topic/boybar.

130. **"Pat Field wanted anyone..."** Musto, Michael. "'Valley of the Dolls' Was Our Bible': Talking to Drag Legend Perfidia." *Paper* magazine, 16 June 2016, https://web.archive.org/web/20160719065127/https://www.papermag.com/perfidia-pyramid-bar-boy-bar-1860456360.html.

131. **"Because they were visually..."** Scelfo, Julie. *The Women Who Made New York*. New York: Seal Press, 2016, p. 170.

132. **"We would stop in..."** Schulman, Michael. "Patricia Field Hangs Up Her Retail Wig." *New York Times*, 26 Dec. 2015, https://www.nytimes.com/2015/12/27/fashion/patricia-field-hangs-up-her-retail-wig.html.

133. **Glamamore remembers...their way through.** Glamamore, 14 July 2021 interview.

134. **"She literally was the..."** Harrity, "Kim Christy's."

135. **"For many trans women..."** King, Jordan. 30 May 2021. An interview completed by Elyssa Maxx Goodman.

136. **"She came up in..."** Fleming, 21 Apr. 2021 interview.

137. **Chemotherapy...sing. "Somehow dragged herself across... performed brilliantly..."** Camicia, pp. 164–65.

138. **Transgender model...loved her. It was through...possible.** Bollen, Christopher. "A Guide to Living By One Who Has," originally published in *Dossier Journal*. Republished on *Christopher Bollen*, https://static1.squarespace.com/static/61b8d67c3758ba5d4057dbc4/t/61c3b0103444286b83230428/1640214546448/joey_gabriel.pdf.

139. **Upon... "standout."** Canby, Vincent. "Review/Film; Nick Nolte as a Corrupt Detective." *New York Times*, 27 Apr. 1990, p. 20.

140. **"one of the great...humble and generous."** Madden, Steve. *The Cobbler: How I Disrupted an Industry, Fell from Grace, and Came Back Stronger Than Ever.* New York: Radius Book Group, 2020, https://books.google.com/books?id=hdWuDwAAQBAJ&pg=.

141. **"I was cold because..."** Ortiz, Luna Luis. 30 June 2021. An interview completed by Elyssa Maxx Goodman.

142. **"Avis had these really... We just thought... We were so..."** Ortiz, 30 June 2021 interview.

143. **"We had to go... A lot of them..."** Ortiz, 30 June 2021 interview.

144. **"Leather... Muscular"** Silver, Jocelyn. "Back in Vogue: Revisiting Paris Is Burning in 2017." *Dazed*, 6 Sept. 2017, https://www.dazeddigital.com/life-culture/article/37223/1/voguing-on-new-yorks-streets-revisiting-paris-is-burning.

145. **Drag...Milan.** Rodriguez, Felix, aka Felix Milan. 9 June 2021. An interview completed by Elyssa Maxx Goodman.

146. **"[Butch queens] only wanted... In the '90s... Now I think..."** Rodriguez, 9 June 2021 interview.

147. **"In a ballroom you... You're not really..."** Brathwaite, Les Fabian. "Striking a 'Pose': A Brief History of Ball Culture." *Rolling Stone*, 6 June 2018, https://www.rollingstone.com/culture/culture-features/striking-a-pose-a-brief-history-of-ball-culture-629280/.

148. **"One of the missions... Ballroom when it started..."** Rodriguez, Felix, aka Felix Milan. Speech recorded by Elyssa Maxx Goodman at "BAAD! Presents Its Second Annual Mini Kiki Ball," 12 June 2021.

149. **"Your category says number... I've been asleep..."** Sunbeam, Harmonica. 4 June 2021. An interview completed by Elyssa Maxx Goodman.

150. **"The trans women who performed... They would always..."** Herr, 7 Apr. 2020 interview.

151. **"Now people live there... New York used to..."** Ortiz, 30 June 2021 interview.

152. **"This is where the... Someone made... I still to this day... I credit everything..."** Sunbeam, 4 June 2021 interview.

153. **The expression...1976.** Boston, Nicholas. "What Gymnast Nadia Comăneci's Perfect 10 Meant to Me." *Vogue*, 29 July 2021, https://www.vogue.com/article/nadia-comaneci-vogueing.

154. **In Comăneci...greatness.** Boston, "What Gymnast Nadia."

155. **"We remember or pay... That means..."** Boston, "What Gymnast Nadia."

156. **"pop, dip, and spin"** Morgan, "How 19th-Century Drag."

157. **According to legendary DJ...voguing."** Lawrence, Tim. "'Listen, and You Will Hear all the Houses that Walked There Before': A History of Drag Balls, Houses and the Culture of Voguing." *Tim Lawrence*, 2 July 2013, https://www.timlawrence.info/articles2/2013/7/16/listen-and-you-will-hear-all-the-houses-that-walked-there-before-a-history-of-drag-balls-houses-and-the-culture-of-voguing.

158. **There were also...Christopher.** *Love Is in the Legend*. Directed by Myra Lewis, 2020.

159. **With the support of... Field.** *Love Is in the Legend*, Lewis.

160. **"It was an article..."** Masters, Troy. "Donald Suggs Recalled Fondly from All Walks of Life." *Gay City News*, 24 Oct. 2012, https://gaycitynews.com/donald-suggs-recalled-fondly-from-all-walks-of-life/.

161. **over 19,000 lives** "HIV/AIDS Timeline."

162. **"So many of my..."** Musto, Michael. "The 10 Most Fabulous Moments in Susanne Bartsch Party History." *Paper* magazine. 30 Mar. 2016, https://web.archive.org/web/20211205205746/https://www.papermag.com/susanne-bartsch-nightlife-party-history-1697669538.html.

163. **Because the scene...had died.** Ortiz, 30 June 2021 interview.

164. **"The epidemic had just... So it was..."** Picardi, Phillip. "Chapter Three: How ACT UP and the Downtown Fashion Scene Came to the Rescue." *Vogue*, 16 Dec. 2020, https://www.vogue.com/article/aids-epidemic-oral-history-chapter-three.

165. **"The evening had all..."** Hochswender, Woody. "Vogueing Against AIDS: A Quest of 'Overness.'" *New York Times*, 12 May 1989, p. 5.

418   ELYSSA MAXX GOODMAN

Chapter 8

1. **"Some 50,000 New York..."** Murphy, Tim. "7 New Yorkers Remember the Early Days of the AIDS Epidemic." *New York Magazine*, 29 May 2014, https://nymag.com/intelligencer/2014/05/memories-aids-new-york.html.

2. **over 75,000 people** "HIV/AIDS Timeline."

3. **"A desire by urban..." The problem was...** Vitale, Alex S. *City of Disorder: How the Quality of Life Campaign Transformed New York Politics.* New York: NYU Press, 2008, p. 30.

4. **"Every microphone I got... Because if..."** Formika, Mistress. 28 Sept. 2018. An interview completed by Elyssa Maxx Goodman.

5. **"Rudy Gives Disney Blow Jobs..."** *The REALIST* no. 138, Spring 1998, p. 12, https://www.ep.tc/realist/pdf/TheRealist138.pdf.

6. **"Behind the announcement..."** Onishi, Norimitsu. "Police Announce Crackdown on Quality-of-Life Offenses." *New York Times*, 13 Mar. 1994, https://www.nytimes.com/1994/03/13/nyregion/police-announce-crackdown-on-quality-of-life-offenses.html.

7. **"Obtaining one is costly..."** Correal, Annie. "After 91 Years, New York Will Let Its People Boogie." *New York Times*, 20 Oct. 2017, https://www.nytimes.com/2017/10/30/nyregion/new-york-cabaret-law-repeal.html.

8. **"Led by New York..."** "Multi-Agency Response to Community Hotspots (M.A.R.C.H.) Operations Q1–Q2 2020 Report." Mayor's Office of Media and Entertainment, New York City, 1 Sept. 2020, https://www.nyc.gov/assets/mome/pdf/q1-q2_2020_march_report_090120.pdf.

9. **"While Giuliani's mayoralty led..."** Francis, David R. "What Reduced Crime in New York City." *National Bureau of Economic Research: The Digest*, no. 1, Jan. 2003, https://www.nber.org/digest/jan03/what-reduced-crime-new-york-city.

10. **"Nightlife Under Siege...anything goes?"** *New York Magazine,* 5 May 1997; **"Club Crisis!...to party?"** *Time Out New York*, 8-15 May 1997.

11. **With clubs and bars...dominated.** Musto, Michael. "How Mayor Giuliani Decimated New York City Nightlife." *Vice*, 6 Mar. 2017, https://www.vice.com/en/article/bjjdzq/how-mayor-giuliani-decimated-new-york-city-nightlife.

12. **"If anyone hadn't heard... Eighties clubs..."** Musto, "How Mayor Giuliani."

13. **"In her sporty combination... You can probably... All the drug..."** Kolker, Robert. "Tootsie Cop." *New York Magazine*, 28 June 1999, https://nymag.com/nymetro/news/crimelaw/features/1084/. Also on @Queer_Happened_Here by Marc Zinaman, *Instagram*, 23 Apr. 2022, https://www.instagram.com/p/CcsQzAIrrai/.

14. **"Some drag performers loved..."** Fleisher, Julian. *The Drag Queens of New York: An Illustrated Field Guide*. New York: Riverhead, 1996, pp. 23–24.

15. **"The drag became stronger... Drag to me..."** Arias, 1 June 2021 interview.

16. **"She dragged me off..."** Herr, 7 Apr. 2020 interview.

17. **"I wasn't used to dealing... If you were talented..."** Herr, 7 Apr. 2020 interview.

18. **"Everybody wants to make..."** "Dorian Corey: Self." *IMDB*, https://www.imdb.com/title/tt0100332/characters/nm0179776.

19. **"Ran an article called..."** Green, Jesse. "Paris Has Burned." *New York Times*, 18 Apr. 1993, https://www.nytimes.com/1993/04/18/style/paris-has-burned.html.

20. **"I love the movie... But I feel... But then the film..."** Green, "Paris Has Burned."

21. **"I wasn't as bold... It's funny because..."** Sunbeam, 4 June 2021 interview.

22. **"On a college-circuit..."** Kasindorf, Jeanie Russell. "The Drag Queen Had a Mummy in Her Closet." *New York Magazine*, 2 May 1994, pp. 50–56, quote on p. 54.

23. **"I'll tell you who... Once you do something... The truth is I..."** Green, p. 1.

24. **"Her final performance..."** Kasindorf, "The Drag Queen Had."

25. **"*New York Magazine* ran..."** Kasindorf, "The Drag Queen Had."

26. **"I literally went to see... Many people in ballroom... A film-maker himself..."** Rodriguez, 9 June 2021 interview.

27. **"Before *Paris is Burning*..." "They were at..."** Rodriguez, 9 June 2021 interview.

28. **"Part of the glory... Rodriguez remembers... They lost me..."** Rodriguez, 9 June 2021 interview.

29. **"Between '89 and '94..."** Ortiz, 30 June 2021 interview.

30. **"Offers year-round programs..."** "Youth & Young Adults." *GMHC*, https://www.gmhc.org/communities/youth-young-adults/.

31. **"About dance, self-expression..."** "Chosen Families: Luna Luis Ortiz on Youth and Project Vogue." *GMHC*, https://www.gmhc. org/project-vogue/.

32. **"I had this bodysuit..."** Aviance, Kevin. 3 June 2021. An interview completed by Elyssa Maxx Goodman.

33. **"Aviance does not work..."** Muñoz, José Esteban. "4. Gesture, Ephemera, and Queer Feeling: Approaching Kevin Aviance." *Cruising Utopia, 10th Anniversary Edition: The Then and There of Queer Futurity*, New York: New York University Press, 2019, pp. 65–82, https://doi. org/10.18574/nyu/9781479868780.003.0009.

34. **"I have one little..."** Aviance, 3 June 2021 interview.

35. **"Where's the bitch..."** Renee, Moi. "Miss Honey." *Project X Records*, 1 Jan. 1992. *Genius*, https://genius.com/Moi-renee-miss-honey-lyrics.

36. **"The ballroom bitch bombshell..."** "Official Jade Elektra/DJ Relentless Facebook Group!" *Facebook*, https://m.facebook.com/groups/ RelentlessEntertainment/.

37. **"I told him that..."** "Relentlessly Cunty." *Last.fm.* https://www. last.fm/music/Relentlessly+Cunty/+wiki.

38. **"I have no desire..."** Jones, Anderson. "Freaks and Beats," *The Advocate*. 11 Apr. 2000, pp. 59–60.

39. **"I was [told] by..."** Aviance, 3 June 2021 interview.

40. **"It was the dive..."** Herr, 7 April 2020 interview.

41. **"Blanquitos..."** Moss, Jeremiah. "Club Escuelita." *Jeremiah's Vanishing New York*, 26 Feb. 2016, http://vanishingnewyork.blogspot. com/2016/02/club-escuelita.html.

42. **"A rundown little place... When I did..."** Dumont, Laritza. 3 Dec. 2021. An interview completed by Elyssa Maxx Goodman.

43. **"All of the drag queens..."** Guzmán, Manuel. "Pa' La Escuelita Con Mucho Cuida'o y por La Orillita." In *Puerto Rican Jam: Rethinking Colonialism and Nationalism*, ed. Frances Negrón-Muntaner and Ramón Grosfoguel. Minneapolis: University of Minnesota Press, 2008; also referenced in Moss, "Club Escuelita."

44. **"Things were changing... And the music..."** Tate, Nathan. 20 July 2022. An interview completed by Elyssa Maxx Goodman.

45. **"If you've ever seen..."** Sunbeam, Harmonica. 13 July 2022. An interview completed by Elyssa Maxx Goodman.

46. **"I'm glad I started..."** "On Point With: Harmonica Sunbeam." *Thotyssey!* https://thotyssey.tumblr.com/post/149505857652/on-point-with-harmonica-sunbeam.

47. **"She'd do 'My Way'..."** Musto, Michael. "A Rosie by Any Other Name..." *Out*, 15 Oct. 2007, https://www.out.com/entertainment/2007/10/15/rosie-any-other-name.

48. **"She was one that... She would perform..."** Dumont, 3 Dec. 2021 interview.

49. **Lady Catiria...only nineteen.** Suggs, Donald. "Queen of Hearts." *Poz*, 1 June 1999.

50. **"I didn't want everyone..."** Suggs, "Queen of Hearts."

51. **When passing her crown...status.** Ortiz-Fonseca, Louie. "Remembering NYC's Queen of Nightlife: Lady Catiria, HIV-Positive Transgender Performer." *The Body*, 5 Dec. 2019, https://www.thebody.com/article/lady-catiria-reyes-legendary-hiv-positive-trans-performer.

52. **"If in my mind's..."** RuPaul. *Lettin' It All Hang Out*, p. 61.

53. **"Larry Tee called me..."** Snetiker, Marc. "RuPaul: America's First Lady of Drag Covers EW's LGBTQ Issue." *Entertainment Weekly*, 15 June 2017, https://ew.com/tv/2017/06/15/rupaul-first-lady-of-drag-lgbtq-issue/.

54. **"If that's what the..."** RuPaul. *Lettin' It All Hang Out*, p. 108.

55. **Ru noticed...photo shoot.** RuPaul, pp. 119–20.

56. **"It was very New York..."** RuPaul, p. 159.

57. **"The only way..."** Snetiker, "RuPaul: America's."

58. **Bx13 bus... "I didn't want to..."** Alexander, J. *Follow the Model: Miss J's Guide to Unleashing Presence, Poise, and Power.* New York: Gallery Books, 2010, pp. 66–67.

59. **"Me being on Mugler's..."** Dijon, Honey. "Connie Girl and Honey Dijon on Being at the Wrong Place at the Right Time." *Interview Magazine*, 3 Sept. 2020, https://www.interviewmagazine.com/culture/connie-girl-honey-dijon-compare-notes-star-14th-street-nyc.

60. **"It was the... The pendulum had swung..."** Fleming, 31 July 2020 interview.

61. **"Everybody saw it..."** Beyond, Billy. 24 Mar. 2020. An interview completed by Elyssa Maxx Goodman.

62. **"When you're doing a..."** Oldham, Todd. 22 Sept. 2022. An interview completed by Elyssa Maxx Goodman.

63. **"the drag model..."** Beyond, 24 Mar. 2020 interview.

64. **"alien fashion drag... I couldn't grow facial hair... I'm American..."** Zaldy. 22 June 2021. An interview completed by Elyssa Maxx Goodman.

65. **"Cut for men since 1850"** "Levi's 501 Commercial Taxi 1995 Zaldy." *YouTube*, https://www.youtube.com/watch?v=Xli40zF84yQ.

66. **"There was a stigma..."** Zaldy, 22 June 2021 interview.

67. Portions of section on Joan Jett Blakk reprinted with permission from Condé Nast, "Drag Herstory: The Drag Queen Who Ran For President in 1992," written by Elyssa Maxx Goodman and published in *Them* on 20 Apr. 2018.

68. **"Chicago drag queen Joan..."** Felshman, Jeffrey. "Lick Bush in '92!" *Chicago Reader*, 23 Jan. 1992, https://chicagoreader.com/news-politics/lick-bush-in-92/.

69. **"political energy... I noticed how the..."** Belverio, Glenn. 18 June 2021. An interview completed by Elyssa Maxx Goodman.

70. **"Gay, Lesbian, and Drag Queen..."** Belverio, Glenn. "A History of Drag: The Glenn Belverio Archive Is Now Available from Video Data Bank." *ASVOF*, 22 Jan. 2020, https://ashadedviewonfashion.com/2020/01/22/a-history-of-drag-the-glenn-belverio-archive-is-now-available-from-video-data-bank/.

71. **"What would you do..."** Belverio, Glenn. "On the Campaign Trail with Joan Jett Blakk." *VDB*, 1992, https://www.vdb.org/titles/campaign-trail-joan-jett-blakk.

72. **"Make the Supreme Court..."** Baim, Tracy. *Out and Proud in Chicago: An Overview of the City's Gay Community.* Evanston: Agate Surrey, 2008, p. 183.

73. **"You can watch the..."** Belverio, "On the Campaign Trail."

74. **"ACT UP was regularly..."** Kaiser, p. 330.

75. **In his book...magazine in 1992.** Kaiser, p. 339/

76. **"Before Bill Clinton's election... In *Out*, that... But what many saw..."** Kaiser, p. 339.

77. **The Stonewall 25th...parade.** Dommu, Rose. "Hundreds of Drag Queens Fill the NYC Streets Every Year for This 'Drag March.'" *HuffPost*, 25 June 2018, https://www.huffpost.com/entry/nyc-drag-march_n_5b2fb345e4b0040e274410a0.

78. **But the committee...scaring them off.** Lynch, Scott. "Photos: Drag March Kicks off Pride Weekend 2022 with Rage and Defiance." *Gothamist*, 25 June 2022, https://gothamist.com/news/photos-drag-march-kicks-off-pride-weekend-2022-with-rage-and-defiance.

79. **"They want to normalize..."** Dommu, "Hundreds of Drag Queens."

80. **"Some 10,000 people gathered..."** Dommu, "Hundreds of Drag Queens."

81. **Griffin, a long time...flag** Dommu, "Hundreds of Drag Queens."

82. **"In 1993, there were..."** H.R.H. Princess Diandra, 15 July 2021 interview.

83. **"Back in 1993, I couldn't..."** Sunbeam, 4 June 2021 interview.

84. **"My inspiration... Drag is a part of..."** Frutkin, Alan. "*To Wong Foo*'s Gay Crew." *The Advocate*, 5 Sept, 1995, p. 50.

85. **"We're hoping Americans who..."** Frutkin, "*To Wong Foo*'s."

86. **"People keep telling me..."** Daly, Steve. "'To Wong Foo' Takes Off." *Entertainment Weekly*, 22 Sept. 1995, https://ew.com/article/1995/09/22/wong-foo-takes/.

87. **"It really felt like..."** Musto, 21 Apr. 2022 interview.

88. **"Manhattan, at this moment..."** Busch, Charles. "Every Man a Queen." *New York Magazine*, 17 July 1995, p. 27.

89. **"She was like...tits and makeup... People were coming up... I didn't say..."** Arias, 1 June 2021 interview.

90. **"He said: Hey you..."** Kim, Alexey. "Bar d'O: The 27 Year History of Downtown Manhattan's Best-Kept-Secret Drag Cabaret." *Sibewalkkilla*, 18 Dec. 2020, https://sidewalkkilla.medium.com/bar-do-the-27-year-history-of-downtown-manhattan-s-best-kept-secret-drag-cabaret-81910baf1044.

91. **"Nowhere is cabaret fever..."** Gavin, James. "Come to the Cabaret! Cabaret's Twenty-Five Greatest Hits." *Town & Country*, March 1992, p. 90.

92. **"I'm a māhū…"** Raven O. 19 Nov. 2021. An interview completed by Elyssa Maxx Goodman.

93. **"Drag queens usually that… I wasn't impersonating anybody…"** Leupp, Clinton. 19 Oct. 2018. An interview completed by Elyssa Maxx Goodman.

94. **"We were serving drag…"** Moss, Jeremiah. "Stingy Lulu's." *Jeremiah's Vanishing New York*, 19 Nov. 2008, http://vanishingnewyork. blogspot.com/2008/11/stingy-lulus.html.

95. **"Midnight drag shows that…"** Burzynski, Martha. "Drink Up: A New Lulu." *Gothamist*, 7 Mar. 2008, https://gothamist.com/food/ drink-up-a-new-lulu.

96. **"did a dozen push-ups…"** Richman, Alan. "Food Noir." *GQ*, 6 Feb. 2006, https://www.gq.com/story/manhattan-food-early-morning-1-am.

97. **"You got $20 extra… I was a…"** World Famous ★BOB★. 3 Dec. 2021. An interview completed by Elyssa Maxx Goodman.

98. **"It was the East Village…"** Rollenhagen, Luisa. "Tim Murphy, Author of Christadora, On the East Village Then and Now." *Bedford + Bowery*, 24 Aug. 2016, https://bedfordandbowery.com/2016/08/tim-murphy-author-of-christadora-on-the-east-village-then-and-now/.

99. **"There was a close…"** Horbelt, Stephan. "7 Queens Look Back at Lucky Cheng's, the NYC Drag Dinner Show Celebrating 25 Years in Business." *Hornet*, 19 Oct. 2018, https://hornet.com/stories/lucky-chengs-nyc-stories/.

100. **"We had just given…"** Kravitz Hoeffner, Melissa. "Four Stages, One Drag Restaurant: The Evolution of Lucky Cheng's in NYC." *Thrillist*, 17 Aug. 2016, https://www.thrillist.com/eat/new-york/ lucky-chengs-nyc-drag-restaurant.

101. **"The idea was to…"** Span, Paula. "The Tender Loin Cafe; this Restaurant's a Hit. Right on the Behind." *Washington Post*, 30 July 1997, https://www.washingtonpost.com/archive/lifestyle/1997/07/30/the-tender-loin-cafe/2cf31525-93f4-418f-9696-33d4d70305a2/.

102. **It would be a drag take on…quiet pride."** Span, "The Tender Loin Cafe."

103. **"[we] were making money…"** H.R.H. Princess Diandra, 15 July 2021 interview.

104. **"For me, she was…"** Bradford, Lina. 1 Dec. 2021. An interview completed by Elyssa Maxx Goodman.

105. **"I wanted to be..."** Musto, Michael. "Ex-Drag Queen Nashom Wooden, aka Mona Foot, on Hanging up the Heels." *Paper* magazine, 15 June 2020, https://www.papermag.com/mona-foot-nashom-wooden-conversation-2480025020.html.

106. **"To say that Mona Foot..."** Fleisher, p. 121.

107. **"My family embraced me... Crowbar was really where..."** Bradford, 1 Dec. 2021 interview.

108. **"also had a dance studio... Triple pirouettes in four-inch..."** Bernstein, Jacob. "Candis Cayne, from Chelsea Drag Queen to Caitlyn Jenner's Sidekick." *New York Times*, 21 Aug. 2015, https://www.nytimes.com/2015/08/23/fashion/caitlyn-jenner-candis-cayne-i-am-cait.html.

109. **"The front door opened..."** Pontarelli, Bob. "Memory Lane: Crowbar" *Next Magazine*, 23 May. 2013, https://feature802.rssing.com/chan-12758970/all_p1.html.

110. **"When we met..."** Bradford, 1 Dec. 2021 interview.

111. **"In the gay community..."** Musto, Michael. "Candis Cayne on Caitlyn's Politics, Dating & Returning to Barracuda!" *Out*, 7 Sept. 2015, https://www.out.com/michael-musto/2015/9/07/candis-cayne-caitlyns-politics-dating-returning-barracuda.

112. **"A hot muscled guy..."** Pontarelli, Bob. 13 June 2021. An interview completed by Elyssa Maxx Goodman.

113. **"A big part of...the brunt..."** Musto, 21 Apr. 2022 interview.

114. **"Barracuda was the first..."** Coleman, David. "Dives No Longer, New Gay Bars Let in the Light." *New York Times*, 1 Feb. 1998, p. 1.

115. **"*New York Magazine* wrote in 2003..."** "Best Gay Bar: Barracuda." *New York Magazine*, 12 May 2003, http://images.nymag.com/urban/guides/bestofny/nightlife/03/gaybar.htm.

116. **"We wanted people..."** Pontarelli, 13 June 2021 interview.

117. **"A three-foot moat... It changed... You just book... Women loved us... Women doing drag..."** Blackmer, Tracy, aka Buster Hymen. 13 Aug. 2021. An interview completed by Elyssa Maxx Goodman.

118. **"I was like, wow..."** Hasten, LW. "Mildred Gerestant." *Gender Pretenders: A Drag King Ethnography*, Feb. 1999, http://lwhasten.com/genderpretenders.html#mildred.

119. **"Dred blurred and blended..."** Dick, Mo B. "1995–2012 Dred." *Drag King History*, 2023, https://dragkinghistory.com/1995-2012-dred/.

120. **"I went, 'Oh shit'..."** Dick, Mo. B. 26 Mar. 2020. An interview completed by Elyssa Maxx Goodman.

121. **"When I first started..."** Hasten, LW. "Maureen Fischer," *Gender Pretenders: A Drag King Ethnography*, Feb. 1999, http://lwhasten.com/genderpretenders.html#maureen.

122. **"The hardest working... When I got to..."** Musto, Michael. "Michael Musto's Icons: Murray Hill." *The Advocate*, 5 May 2016, https://www.advocate.com/current-issue/2016/5/05/michael-musto-lobs-7-questions-murray-hill.

123. **to "pass"** Lopate, Leonard. "So You Want to Do Drag?" *The Leonard Lopate Show*, WNYC, 25 Apr. 2014, https://www.wnyc.org/story/please-explain-so-you-want-do-drag/.

124. **"Mayor Ghouliani is trying..."** Carr, C. "Run, Murray, Run." *The Village Voice*, 28 Oct. 1997, p. 61.

125. **"The reigning patriarch of..."** Calhoun, Ada. "Meet Downtown's New 'It' Boy." *New York Times*, 9 Jan. 2005, https://www.nytimes.com/2005/01/09/theater/newsandfeatures/meet-downtowns-new-it-boy.html.

126. **"I don't want to be..."** Cronberg, Anya Aronowsky. "A Conversation with Murray Hill, Drag King and Comedian." *Vestoj*, https://vestoj.com/a-conversation-with-murray-hill/.

127. **"It was like this..."** Simpson, Linda. 28 Mar. 2018. An interview completed by Elyssa Maxx Goodman.

128. **"It was like a..."** Simpson, 28 Mar. 2018 interview.

129. **"Big titted, honky soul..."** "Sweetie-Know Your gAy-B-Cs (Master Class Part 1)." *YouTube*, uploaded by Sherry Vine, 13 Feb. 2017, https://www.youtube.com/watch?v=EmKfuatCg6U&t=319s.

130. **"It was the later... This massive...beautiful and tragic..."** Cavadias, Michael. 18 July 2022. An interview completed by Elyssa Maxx Goodman.

131. **"Gory retellings of Jack..."** Romano, Tricia. "Blacklips Performance Cult: The Gothic Drag Theater Troupe Where Anohni Got Her Start." *Red Bull Music Academy*, 16 May 2016, https://daily.redbullmusicacademy.com/2016/05/the-story-of-blacklips.

132. **"It was mayhem..."** Anohni. "A Blacklips Remembrance: Brian Butterick A.K.A. Hattie Hathaway, The Blond in the Black Helmet." *Facebook*, 9 Feb. 2019, https://www.facebook.com/126703733551/photos/a.129953318551/10157145318573552.

133. **"General standard of decency…"** Finley v. National Endowment for the Arts, 100 F.3d 671 (9th Cir. 1996). United States Court of Appeals for the Ninth Circuit. No. 92-56028, No. 92-56387, No. 92-55089.

134. **"Our flyers said…"** Wilkerson, Marti. "RSVP: Singer Anohni Talks Her Monday Service at the Pyramid Club." *V Magazine*, 4 Aug. 2019, https://vmagazine.com/article/singer-anohni-talks-her-monday-service-in-the-club/.

135. **"SqueezeBox! is a gay club…"** Formika, 28 Sept. 2018 interview.

136. **"We wanted a rock party…"** Guy, Miss. 10 Apr. 2020. An email interview completed by Elyssa Maxx Goodman.

137. **"I heard that SqueezeBox!…"** Bond, Justin Vivian. 4 May 2020. An interview completed by Elyssa Maxx Goodman.

138. **"That was really how…"** Bond, 4 May 2020 interview.

139. **"I was such a rock…"** Mitchell, 28 Apr. 2020 interview.

140. **"Don't you know me, baby?"** *Whether You like It or Not: The Story of Hedwig.* Directed by Laura Nix, 2001.

141. **"I ripped my drag…"** Mitchell, 28 Apr. 2020 interview.

142. **"We invited a bunch…"** *Whether You like It or Not*, Nix.

143. **corpse had to be…** *Whether You like It or Not*, Nix.

144. **"[M]agnetically impersonated by the…"** Marks, Peter. "Theater Review; How to Be Captivating Without a Sense of Self." *New York Times*, 16 Feb. 1998, p. 1.

145. **"The people who cared…"** Wood, Jennifer. "Gender Bender: An Oral History of 'Hedwig and the Angry Inch.'" *Rolling Stone*, 7 May 2014, https://www.rollingstone.com/movies/movie-news/gender-bender-an-oral-history-of-hedwig-and-the-angry-inch-185066/.

146. **"Jackie 60… The Management"** "Jackie 60 'The Trailer.'" *YouTube*, uploaded by AllNight60, https://www.youtube.com/watch?v=VI2tfogW5qo.

147. **"a combination of…"** Roth, Rob. "Night Paving: The Aural History of Jackie 60 and Mother." *Mixcloud*, 2020, https://www.mixcloud.com/robroth/night-paving-the-aural-history-of-jackie-60-and-mother/.

148. **"They did the whole…"** Musto, Michael. "From the Vaults: A Tribute to Iconic '90s Gay Club Jackie 60." *Out*, 9 Aug. 2017, https://

www.out.com/vaults/2017/8/09/vaults-tribute-iconic-90s-gay-club-jackie-60.

149. **"Rose was extremely..."** Speegle, Trey. "#RIP: NYC Drag Legend, Rose Royale Dies of Coronavirus - the WOW Report." Worldofwonder.net, 10 Apr. 2020, https://worldofwonder.net/rip-nyc-drag-legend-rose-royale-dies-of-coronavirus/.

150. **"Approved are leather, rubber..."** "Jackie 60: The Dress Code." *Jackie 60*, http://www.mothernyc.com/jackie/60archive/classic.html. Reprinted with permission from Chi Chi Valenti of The Jackie Factory.

151. **"There were supermodel..."** Dynell, 18 Apr. 2018 interview.

152. **"We introduced drag queens... Incredibly strict..."** Roth, Rob. 7 June 2021. An interview completed by Elyssa Maxx Goodman.

153. **"Bladerunner, Sci-Fi..."** Van Meter, William. "Remembering Web 1.0's Click + Drag Subculture." *The Cut*, 24 Apr. 2015, https://www.thecut.com/2015/04/remembering-web-10s-click-drag-subculture.html.

154. **"Drag in the title..."** Roth, 7 June 2021 interview.

Chapter 9

1. **"I went to the top... The bars were closed..."** Aviance, 3 June 2021 interview.

2. **"Within a week..."** Bond, 4 May 2020 interview.

3. **"The whole city stopped."** World Famous *BOB*, 3 Dec. 2021 interview.

4. **"'Oh we're all going...'"** Matronic, 16 Dec. 2021 interview.

5. **"Either you are with..."** Bush, George W. "Address to a Joint Session of Congress and the American People." *The White House Archives: President George W. Bush*, Sept. 2001, https://georgewbush-whitehouse.archives.gov/news/releases/2001/09/20010920-8.html.

6. **"Gallup polls revealed..."** Smith, Caroline, and James M. Lindsay. "Rally 'Round the Flag: Opinion in the United States Before and After the Iraq War." *Brookings*, 1 June 2003, https://www.brookings.edu/articles/rally-round-the-flag-opinion-in-the-united-states-before-and-after-the-iraq-war/.

7. **"To give activism..."** Dazzle, 11 Feb. 2022 interview.

8. **"GLAMericans are a non-partisan..."** "Dissent Is Hot." *Bloggy*, 15 Feb. 2003, http://bloggy.com/2003/02/dissent_is_hot.html.

9. **"The original Dazzle Dancers..."** Dazzle, 11 Feb. 2022 interview.

10. **"What protesters would recall..."** "Signs of the Times." *WNYC News*, 17 Feb. 2003, https://www.wnyc.org/story/85435-signs-of-the-times/.

11. **"Would allow protest march..."** Powell, Michael. "In New York, Thousands Protest a War Against Iraq." *Washington Post*, 16 Feb. 2003, https://www.washingtonpost.com/archive/politics/2003/02/16/in-new-york-thousands-protest-a-war-against-iraq/ba206965-e456-46a6-b393-73223acd6676/.

12. **"Draped in campy boas..."** Chvasta, Marcyrose. "Anger, Irony, and Protest: Confronting the Issue of Efficacy, Again." *Text and Performance Quarterly*, vol. 26, no. 1, Jan. 2006, pp. 5–16.

13. **"Corporate drag"** Shepard, Benjamin. *Play, Creativity, and Social Movements: If I Can't Dance, It's Not My Revolution*. New York: Routledge, 2013, p. 236.

14. **"More Blood for Oil"** United States District Court Southern District of New York. Kunstler v. City of New York, 04 Civ. 1145 (RWS), https://ccrjustice.org/sites/default/files/assets/A7%201st%20Amended%20Complaint.pdf.

15. **"A cowboy hat"** Kunstler v. City of New York.

16. **"Almost enough nudity..."** "Live Patriot Acts: Patriots Gone Wild!" *Performance Space New York*, https://performancespacenewyork.org/archived_event/live-patriot-acts-patriots-gone-wild/.

17. **"Began developing judy's own..."** Edgecomb, Sean F. "The Ridiculous Performance of Taylor Mac." *Theatre Journal*, vol. 64, no. 4, 2012, pp. 549–63. *JSTOR*, http://www.jstor.org/stable/41819889.

18. **"A modern-day East Village..."** Galtney, Smith. "Boîte; Bar Meets History." *New York Times*, 9 Mar. 2003, https://www.nytimes.com/2003/03/09/style/boite-bar-meets-history.html.

19. **"Spent part of the blackout..."** Edgecomb, pp. 549–63.

20. **"Naked in a station..."** "It was the NYC power blackout..." *JackieBigelow.com* (blog), 2 April 2016, https://jackiebiggs.tumblr.com/post/142137645355/it-was-the-nyc-power-blackout-aug-22-2003-we.

21. **"Raucous night of bacchanalia..."** Romano, Tricia. "Dancing (Naked) in the Dark." *The Village Voice*, Aug. 2003, p. 16.

22. **"Arguably the first theatre…"** Romano, p. 16.

23. **"It wasn't her imperfectly-painted…"** Mac, Taylor. "The Queens: Mother Flawless Sabrina." *Taylor Mac Holiday Sauce*, https://www. taylormacholidaysauce.com/the-queens.

24. **"The rubric of Weimar…"** Stewart, Chris. "Weimar New York." *Gayletter*, 15 July 2015, https://gayletter.com/weimar-new-york/.

25. **"The other fun thing…"** Crosland, Matt. 7 Jan. 2022. An interview completed by Elyssa Maxx Goodman.

26. **"I hated, *hated* being… This confused most…"** World Famous *BOB*, 3 Dec. 2021 interview.

27. **"I just saw everything… There was just this…"** World Famous *BOB*, 3 Dec. 2021 interview.

28. **"I basically created this… Which in the mid…"** Bond, 4 May 2020 interview.

29. **"The party was insane…"** Simpson, Linda (@LindaSimpson). *Instagram*, 30 Dec. 2021, https://www.instagram.com/p/CYHb6M-cOW8G/.

30. **"Everything was so different…"** Sequinette. 21 July 2021. An interview completed by Elyssa Maxx Goodman.

31. **"I said to Mario… And then eventually…"** Bond, 4 May 2020 interview.

32. **"I thought it was…"** Bond, 4 May 2020 interview.

33. **"She had a daisy…"** Aviance, 3 June 2021 interview.

34. **"She was one of…"** Aviance, 3 June 2021 interview.

35. **"It's been kinda hard…"** "Kevin Aviance Gives Ignorance a Present." *YouTube*, uploaded by Francis Legge, 17 June 2006, https://www. youtube.com/watch?v=L-edsGuHyaA&t=90s.

36. **"Finally my friends have… Elements of Bowie… The more queer you…"** Matronic, 16 Dec. 2021 interview.

37. **"That sort of DIY… 100% a love letter…"** Matronic, 16 Dec. 2021 interview.

38. **"All I can really…"** Shears, Jake. 18 Nov. 2021. An interview completed by Elyssa Maxx Goodman.

39. **"It was kind of…"** Epiphany. 9 Dec. 2021. An interview completed by Elyssa Maxx Goodman.

40. **"Gender fuckery and..."** Marras, Charmy. "The Alchemy of Drag: Gender Fluidity and the Coniunctio." Master's thesis, Pacifica Graduate Institute, 2021.

41. **"Interested in creating... I'm interested in..."** "10: Krystal Something Something & Indica." *DragCast*, 22 Sept. 2015, https://dragcast.net/10-krystal-something-something-indica/.

42. **"We didn't understand..."** "10: Krystal Something Something & Indica."

43. **"They would actually..."** Hanson, Harry James. 6 Dec. 2021. An interview completed by Elyssa Maxx Goodman.

44. **"The northern parts..."** Walker, Ruth. "Growing up Fast in Hell's Kitchen." *W42ST.nyc*, 25 July 2020, https://w42st.com/post/kimani-ashley-growing-up-fast-in-hell-s-kitchen-new-york-52nd-street-project/.

45. **"Gentrified by New Yorkers... 'Go to Hell's Kitchen...'"** Shaftel, David. "Under the Rainbow." *New York Times*, 25 Mar. 2007, https://www.nytimes.com/2007/03/25/nyregion/thecity/25gay.html.

46. **"I remember living..."** Shequida. 10 Aug. 2022. An interview completed by Elyssa Maxx Goodman.

47. **"In the aughts..."** Musto, 21 Apr. 2022 interview.

48. **"I was like... It was a great... The performing drag..."** Shequida, 10 Aug. 2022 interview.

49. **"This was a time..."** Cuby, Michael. "After 'RuPaul's Drag Race,' Peppermint Couldn't Be Doing Better." *Paper* magazine, 15 Sept. 2017, https://www.papermag.com/after-drag-race-peppermint-couldnt-be-doing-better-2485748538.html.

50. **"I've always believed..."** Mock, Janet. "*Drag Race* Finalist Peppermint Reveals How Drag Enabled Her to Experiment as a Trans Woman." *Allure*, 26 July 2017, https://www.allure.com/story/peppermint-interview-how-drag-created-safe-space-trans-woman.

51. **"Wearing full drag..."** Allen, Timothy. "Bob The Drag Queen Recollects the Time She Was Thrown in Jail in Full Drag." *Queerty*, 18 Apr. 2016, https://www.queerty.com/bob-the-drag-queen-recollects-the-time-she-was-thrown-in-jail-in-full-drag-20160418.

52. **"The queens chanting..."** "Drag Queens March to Gov Cuomo's Office," *Youtube*, uploaded by Steven Thrasher, 4 Apr. 2011, https://www.youtube.com/watch?v=gFBCixvpSzU.

53. **"Chanting, 'Our streets!'... A line of drag..."** Robbins, Chris-

topher. "Video: Last Night's Gay Marriage Celebration Outside Stonewall." *Gothamist*, 25 June 2011, https://gothamist.com/news/video-last-nights-gay-marriage-celebration-outside-stonewall.

54. **"Prohibiting federal contractors…"** Hudson, David. "President Obama Signs a New Executive Order to Protect LGBT Workers." *The White House Archives: President Barack Obama*, 21 July 2014, https://obamawhitehouse.archives.gov/realitycheck/blog/2014/07/21/president-obama-signs-new-executive-order-protect-lgbt-workers-0.

55. **"A Hedda Lettuce ornament…"** Anthony, Brett. "Drag Ornament Sparks 'Controversy' on Obama's Tree." *GoPride*, 24 Dec. 2009, https://chicago.gopride.com/news/article.cfm/articleid/9066016.

56. **"I would hear… So now when…"** Cummings, Marti Gould, and Mathew Rodriguez. "Marti Gould Cummings Has Come Out Many Times. They Have Some Advice." *Them*, 9 Oct. 2020, https://www.them.us/story/coming-out-day-2020-marti-gould-cummings.

57. **"I thought oh… The act of doing… I wanted to make… Everybody was like…"** Gould Cummings, Marti. 27 Jan. 2022. An interview completed by Elyssa Maxx Goodman.

58. **"Education is power…"** Gould Cummings, 27 Jan. 2022 interview.

59. **"Issue formal recommendations…"** Manskar, Noah. "NYC Names First-Ever Nightlife Advisory Board." *Patch*, 12 July 2018, https://patch.com/new-york/new-york-city/nyc-names-first-ever-nightlife-advisory-board.

60. **"I was really proud…"** Gould Cummings, 27 Jan. 2022 interview.

61. **"Housing justice for…"** Spector, Emma. "Marti Gould Cummings Wants Your Vote. But More Than That, They Want a Revolution." *Vogue*, 1 Oct. 2020, https://www.vogue.com/article/marti-gould-cummings-city-council.

62. **"A nonpartisan, nonprofit…"** "Media Kit," *Drag Out the Vote*, https://dragoutthe.vote/media-kit.

63. **"Requiring the federal government…"** Radde, Kaitlyn. "What Does the Respect for Marriage Act Do? The Answer Will Vary by State." *NPR*, 8 Dec. 2022, https://www.npr.org/2022/12/08/1140808263/what-does-the-respect-for-marriage-act-do-the-answer-will-vary-by-state.

64. **"Abuse of power…"** History.com Editors. "President Donald Trump Impeached." *History.com*, A+E Networks, 5 Feb. 2021, https://www.history.com/this-day-in-history/president-trump-impeached-house-of-representatives.

65. **"By the time..."** Lang, Nico. "Meet the Drag Queen Who Stole Trump's Impeachment Hearings." *Out*, 14 Nov. 2019, https://www.out.com/drag/2019/11/14/meet-drag-queen-who-stole-trumps-impeachment-hearings.

66. **"He didn't want..."** Fernandez, Maria Elena. "Behind the Rise of *RuPaul's Drag Race*." *Vulture*, 22 Aug. 2017, https://www.vulture.com/2017/08/behind-the-rise-of-rupauls-drag-race.html.

67. **"The Obama movement..."** Fernandez, "Behind the Rise."

68. **"440,000 viewers every week..."** Fernandez, "Behind the Rise."

69. **"High tide raises..."** Macias, Ernesto. "Lady Bunny and Linda Simpson Contemplate the Future of Drag." *Interview Magazine*, 1 Feb. 2021, https://www.interviewmagazine.com/culture/lady-bunny-and-linda-simpson-contemplate-the-future-of-drag.

70. **"Running around in..."** Callahan, Maureen. *Poker Face: The Rise and Rise of Lady Gaga*. New York: Hachette Book Group, 2010.

71. **"It was the shittiest... It was an amazing..."** Shequida, 10 Aug. 2022 interview.

72. **"If you look... And then once... To look at my..."** Shequida, 10 Aug. 2022 interview.

73. **"How can we..."** Geller, Theresa L. "Trans/Affect: Monstrous Masculinities and the Sublime Art of Lady Gaga," *Lady Gaga and Popular Music: Performing Gender, Fashion, and Culture*, ed. Iddon, Martin and Melanie L. Marshall. London and New York: Routledge, 2014, p. 211.

74. **"I want her..."** "Jo Calderone (Lady Gaga) You and I Live—VMAs 2011." *Youtube*, uploaded by RoberCamachoVEVO, 24 Oct. 2011, https://www.youtube.com/watch?v=SkWoA25V4tQ.

75. **"I have always..."** "Lady Gaga Brings Eureka O'Hara to Tears, RuPaul's Drag Race Season 9." *Youtube*, uploaded by RuPaul's Drag Race, 20 Mar. 2017, https://www.youtube.com/watch?v=AZ2_JsobKvM.

76. **"Hip-hop has always..."** Ganz, Caryn. "The Curious Case of Nicki Minaj." *Out*, 12 Sept. 2010, https://www.out.com/entertainment/music/2010/09/12/curious-case-nicki-minaj.

77. **"New Queen..."** Hiatt, Brian. "Nicki Minaj: The New Queen of Hip-Hop." *Rolling Stone*, 9 Dec. 2010, https://www.rollingstone.com/music/music-news/nicki-minaj-the-new-queen-of-hip-hop-103304/.

78. **"She leaves it all..."** Evans, Shalwah. "Nicki Minaj Has Always Been a Hair and Makeup MVP and a 'Drag Race' Inspiration." *Es-*

sence, 6 Dec. 2020, https://www.essence.com/beauty/nicki-minaj-rupauls-drag-race/.

79. **"It was across the... The important part... People just had..."** Hanson, 6 Dec. 2021 interview.

80. **"Bathsalts will be..."** Farrell, Greg. "R.I.P. BathSalts." *Posture*, 29 June 2015, http://posturemag.com/online/r-i-p-bathsalts/.

81. **"Nondescript sweaty room..."** Moen, Matt. "New York Nightlife Haven 'The Spectrum' Forced to Relocate Again." *Paper* magazine, 18 January 2019, https://www.papermag.com/spectrum-relocation-gofundme-2626335928.html.

82. Portions of this section reprinted with permission from *Vice*, originally published as "How the Brooklyn Drag Renaissance Was Born" by Elyssa Maxx Goodman, 12 Oct. 2017.

83. **"Selena-meets-Morrissey..."** Bizet, Ballerina. "The Lovechild of Selena and Morrissey: Say Hello to Horrorchata." *Posture*, 4 Sept. 2013, https://posturemag.com/online/the-lovechild-of-selena-and-morrissey-say-hello-to-horrorchata/.

84. **"Manhattan audiences don't..."** "On Point With: Ruby Roo." *Thotyssey!* 10 Oct. 2016, https://thotyssey.com/2016/10/10/on-point-with-ruby-roo/.

85. **"Sasha Velour's 2017 win..."** Shorey, Eric. "What Is This Whole Brooklyn Drag Renaissance, Anyway?" *Brokelyn*, 2 Aug. 2017, https://brokelyn.com/brooklyn-drag-renaissance/.

86. **"I just want to..."** Nett, Dani. "'RuPaul's Drag Race' Winner Sasha Velour Cut from A Different Fabric." *NPR*, 25 June 2017, https://www.npr.org/2017/06/25/534313492/rupauls-drag-race-winner-sasha-velour-cut-from-a-different-fabric.

87. **"Initially a drag..."** "Chez Deep, Chez Deep." *Colin Self*, http://colin-self.com/chez-deep.

88. **"Chez Deep was..."** "Chez Deep, Chez Deep."

89. **"A modest donation..."** Incarnate, Charlene (@CharleneIncarnate). *Instagram*, 2 Jan. 2016, https://www.instagram.com/p/BABpVdBQvx0/.

90. **"Charlene I feel..."** Self, Colin. 10 Mar. 2022. An interview completed by Elyssa Maxx Goodman.

91. **"I'm not square... I'd never really seen... I realized how... When Charlene performed..."** Black, Remy. 21 Mar. 2022. An interview completed by Elyssa Maxx Goodman.

92. **"Stepped out of the..."** Black, 21 Mar. 2022 interview.

93. **"You can identify..."** Aitkenhead, Decca. "RuPaul: 'Drag Is a Big F-You to Male-Dominated Culture." *The Guardian*, 2 Mar. 2018, https://www.theguardian.com/tv-and-radio/2018/mar/03/rupaul-drag-race-big-f-you-to-male-dominated-culture.

94. **"By drawing a distinction..."** Incarnate, Charlene. "RuPaul's Version of LGBT History Erases Decades Of Trans Drag Queens." *BuzzFeed*, 8 Mar. 2018, https://www.buzzfeed.com/charleneincarnate/rupauls-drag-race-trans-women-drag-queens.

95. **"We're engaging in hyperqueer..."** Dommu, Rose. "How Charlene Incarnate Inherited the Legacy of NYC's Drag Scene." *Out*, 21 Nov. 2019, https://www.out.com/print/2019/11/21/how-charlene-incarnate-inherited-legacy-nycs-drag-scene.

96. **"Casa Diva was our queer..."** Self, Colin. "Casa Diva Was Our Queer Family..." *Facebook*, 1 Jan. 2009, https://www.facebook.com/506275142755603/posts/casa-diva-was-our-queer-family-household-home-for-the-majority-of-the-time-i-liv/1976850389031397/.

97. **"They knew drag..."** Hanson, 6 Dec. 2021 interview.

98. **"There's a ton of full-time..."** Oliver, Isaac. "Is This the Golden Age of Drag? Yes. And No." *New York Times*, 17 Jan. 2018, https://www.nytimes.com/2018/01/17/arts/drag-queens-rupaul-drag-race.html.

99. **"If you want... The clubs know..."** Musto, 21 Apr. 2022 interview.

100. **"It's almost like..."** Garan, Gina. 12 Dec. 2021. An interview completed by Elyssa Maxx Goodman.

101. **"They do a lot... We just threw..."** Butterick, 1 May 2018 interview.

102. **"The younger generation..."** Shequida, 10 Aug. 2022 interview.

103. **"These [*Drag Race*] girls..."** Garan, 12 Dec. 2021 interview.

104. **"I do think things..."** Bob the Drag Queen. 4 June 2021. An interview completed by Elyssa Maxx Goodman.

105. **"I want people..."** Gould Cummings, 27 Jan. 2022 interview.

106. **"That song takes us... The more songs..."** Cooper, T. 27 Oct. 2021. An interview completed by Elyssa Maxx Goodman.

107. **"The king scene..."** Newton, Wang. 29 Mar. 2022. An email interview completed by Elyssa Maxx Goodman.

108. **"1970s-Vegas-style..."** Goodman, Elyssa. "Miss Manhattan Hangs

Out…with Dr. Wang Newton." *Miss Manhattan*, 8 Aug. 2018, http://
miss-manhattan-nyc.blogspot.com/2018/08/miss-manhattan-hangs-
outwith-dr-wang.html.

109. **"When chatting with… Would you believe…"** Newton, 29
Mar. 2022 interview.

110. **"In 2009 kings… I held up…a sparkly pink…"** Peacock, Goldie. 13
Mar. 2020. An email interview completed by Elyssa Maxx Goodman.

111. **"As a trans guy…"** Nicholas, James Michael. "Queer New
World: Meet Brooklyn's K.James And Pussy Diet." *Huffington Post*,
28 Dec. 2013, https://www.huffpost.com/entry/brooklyn-drag-
kings_n_4499490.

112. **"Dealing with the…"** K.James. 30 June 2015. An interview completed by Elyssa Maxx Goodman.

113. **"They saw a niche…"** Reprinted with permission from *Insider*,
"Drag queens have dominated the scene for years. This alternative
competition showcases what drag can look like when everyone is included," 24 Sept. 2021.

114. **"I don't think…"** Reprinted with permission from *Insider*, Sept. 2021.

115. **"Art collective that…"** "About." *Papi Juice*, https://www.papijuice.
com/about.

116. **"Our collective's work…"** Hosking, Taylor. "Art Collective Papi
Juice Reminds Us That Nightlife Can Be a Revolution." *Vice*, 26
June 2019, https://www.vice.com/en/article/8xz7d4/art-collective-
papi-juice-reminds-us-that-nightlife-can-be-a-revolution.

117. **"A Pan-Asian Drag Revue… For a stunning display…"** "A+
The Pan-Asian Drag Revue." *Do NYC*, 18 May 2019, https://donyc.
com/events/2019/5/18/a-the-pan-asian-drag-revue.

118. **"Nobody wants to *hear*…"** Mintt, Junior. 25 Jan. 2022. An interview completed by Elyssa Maxx Goodman.

119. **"Highly melanated & genderfully…"** @inlivingcolorbk. *Instagram*, https://www.instagram.com/inlivingcolorbk/.

120. **"Drag is about…"** Mintt, 25 Jan. 2022 interview.

121. **"Mona was the shit…"** Bradford, 1 Dec. 2021 interview.

122. **"Drag performers are pillars…"** Mintt, 25 Jan. 2022 interview.

123. **"This time has…"** Cherry, Merrie (@merrie_cherry). *Instagram*, 6 June
2020, https://www.instagram.com/p/CBDOX8jpbou/?img_index=1.

124. **"I will be there..."** @merrie_cherry.

125. **"*Time Out New York* reported..."** Sutter, Collier. "Bushwig Drag Festival Is Hosting a Giant Bike Party on Friday to Aid Black Lives Matter." *Time Out New York*, 25 June 2020, https://www.timeout.com/newyork/news/bushwig-drag-festival-is-hosting-a-giant-bike-party-on-friday-to-aid-black-lives-matter-062520.

126. **"West Dakota's idea blossomed..."** Patil, Anushka. "How a March for Black Trans Lives Became a Huge Event." *New York Times*, 15 June 2020, https://www.nytimes.com/2020/06/15/nyregion/brooklyn-black-trans-parade.html.

127. **"I hope this..."** Guerrero, Desiree. "How West Dakota's Idea Became the Largest Trans March in History." *Out*, 20 Nov. 2020, https://www.out.com/print/2020/11/20/how-west-dakotas-idea-became-largest-trans-march-history.

128. **"[Helping] children develop empathy..."** "FAQs," *Drag Story Hour NYC*, https://www.dshnyc.org/faqs.

129. **"Today, I witnessed..."** Bottcher, Erik (@ebottcher). "Today I witnessed pure hatred and bigotry outside Drag Queen Story Hour at a public library in Chelsea. Inside, I witnessed a loving and peaceful reading of children's books to kids. Warning: this video contains foul language and hate speech." *Twitter*, 17 Dec. 2022, https://twitter.com/ebottcher/status/1604184960167878657?lang=en.

130. **"Seeking to pass legislation..."** Kindy, Kimberly. "GOP Targets Drag Shows with New Bills in at Least 14 States." *Washington Post*, 14 Feb. 2023, https://www.washingtonpost.com/politics/2023/02/14/drag-shows-republican-bills-bans/.

131. **"We can't let outdated..."** Yakes, Ben. "NYC Moves to Finally Fully Legalize Dancing by Fixing Zoning Laws." *Gothamist*, 1 Sept. 2021, https://gothamist.com/arts-entertainment/nyc-cabaret-law-legislation.

Epilogue

1. **She had...her attention** Information about Bobbie's backstory is featured in Cerezo III, Fernando. "Spotlight on Bobbie Hondo: Trans Femme Dancer & HIV/AIDS Advocate (Part One)." *AIDS Drug Assistance Program*, 28 Jan. 2021, https://adapadvocacyassociation.blogspot.com/2021/01/spotlight-on-bobbie-hondo-trans-femme.html.

2. **"That's where I... LGBTQ+ people."** Cerezo III, "Spotlight on Bobbie."

3. **"To be honest...strong suit is."** "John Epperson and Bobbie Hondo

Reflect on Drag Careers Decades Apart." *NowThis News*, 12 July 2019, https://nowthisnews.com/videos/news/john-epperson-and-bobbie-hondo-reflect-on-drag-careers-decades-apart.

4. **"Then I heard...wait, what?"** "John Epperson and Bobbie Hondo Reflect."

5. **She was driven...she had procured.** Walschlager, Megan. "Coolest Person in the Room: Bobbie Hondo." *Paper* magazine, 28 Jan. 2020, https://www.papermag.com/coolest-person-in-the-room-2644898890.html.

6. **"I think people...unique path also."** Simpson, 4 Aug. 2022 interview.

7. **"I think Bobbie...as involved with."** Simpson, 4 Aug. 2022 interview.

8. **"You know, she had a checklist...impression on people."** Simpson, 4 Aug. 2022 interview.

9. **As chronicled...Formika herself.** *Wig*. Directed by Chris Moukarbel, 2019.

10. **"I would want...too quickly."** Simpson, 4 Aug. 2022 interview.

11. **"I came here as a little kid...co-conspirators and friends."** Walschlager, "Coolest Person."

12. **"Unfortunately there was...help from them."** Walschlager, "Coolest Person."

13. **"Well, you just be yourself!...that they had"** Mintt, 25 Jan. 2022 interview.

14. **"Taking the face off...be a woman."** Mintt, 25 Jan. 2022 interview.

15. **"I have found new ways...everything that we do."** Mintt, Junior. 2 June 2022. Speech recorded by Elyssa Maxx Goodman at Thirteen Lune's Drag Dinner Celebrating Pride, Hotel Chantelle Rooftop, 92 Ludlow St., New York, NY 10002.

16. **Participants walk in categories...those who don't will learn.** Milan, Felix. "BAAD! Presents Its Second Annual Mini Kiki Ball." Flyer, 12 June 2021.

INDEX